TOWARDS UNDERSTANDING THE MESSAGE OF THE QURAN

SURAH 1-20

SERENA HUSAIN YATES

Copyright © 2025 by *Serena Yates*

All rights reserved. No part of this publication may be reproduced, stored in any form of retrieval system or transmitted in any form or by any means without prior permission in writing from the publishers except for the use of brief quotations in a book review.

ISBNs:

Hardback: 978-1-80227-156-0

eBook: 978-1-80227-157-7

Paperback: 978-1-80623-911-5

Table of Contents

DEDICATION 1

INTRODUCTION 2

MY LEGACY 17

CHAPTER 1 TOWARDS UNDERSTANDING SURAH FATIHAH 19

CHAPTER 2 TOWARDS UNDERSTANDING SURAH BAQARAH 23

CHAPTER 3 UNDERSTANDING SURAH IMRAN 66

CHAPTER 4 SURAH AN-NISA (THE WOMEN) 101

CHAPTER 5 UNDERSTANDING S MAIDA 118

CHAPTER 6 TOWARDS UNDERSTANDING SURAH AL- ANAAM 154

CHAPTER 7 TOWARDS UNDERSTANDING SURAH AL ARAF 180

CHAPTER 8 UNDERSTANDING SURAH ANFAL 200

CHAPTER 9 TOWARDS UNDERSTANDING SURAH TAWBAH 221

CHAPTER 10 TOWARDS UNDERSTANDING THE MESSAGE OF SURAH YUNUS 237

CHAPTER 11 TOWARDS UNDERSTANDING SURAH HUD 250

CHAPTER 12 QUR'AN TOWARDS UNDERSTANDING THE STORY OF 273

CHAPTER 13 TOWARDS UNDERSTANDING SURAH AL'ARAD 283

CHAPTER 14 TOWARDS UNDERSTANDING THE MESSAGE OF SURAH IBRAHIM 298

CHAPTER 15 UNDERSTANDING THE MESSAGE OF SURAH HIJR 308

CHAPTER 16 TOWARDS UNDERSTANDING SURAH NAHL 323

CHAPTER 17 TOWARDS UNDERSTANDING SURAH AL-ISRAA 343

CHAPTER 18 TOWARDS UNDERSTANDING SURAH KALF 374

CHAPTER 19 TOWARDS UNDERSTANDING SURAH MARYAM (MARY) 394

CHAPTER 20 TOWARDS UNDERSTANDING SURAH TAHA 422

ABOUT THE AUTHOR 438

Dedication

TO OUR PARENTS

MOHAMMED HUBDAR HUSAIN OUR CHILDREN

AND OUR FUTURE GENERATION

Introduction

At some point in my life, I will ask myself the following questions:

1. Where did I come from?
2. What is my purpose here on earth?
3. What is my place in the Universe and was the Universe made for us?
4. What happens after I die?
5. Are human beings created by a series of chaotic incidences and random circumstances?

Let us look at question 5 by examining how complex and intriguing the human body is.

The human body contains complex systems and organs that together allow it to function involuntarily; our hearts beat continuously, non-stop, pumping blood throughout our circulatory system. Our brain and nervous systems are more powerful and complex than any computer. And what about the eye? It is one of the most amazing organs in the human body.

Let us look at the reproductive system.

Despite all our complexities, every human being and animal began as a series of ever-dividing cells, relatively simple in nature, yet eventually culminating into an incredibly complex being.

When examining the nature of the human body one can begin to see its design. Our creation is far too complex to have happened by mere accident.

Let's us look at William Paley's watch argument. After examining the watch, with its intricate parts, that work together in a most precise coordination to maintain the time, one must conclude that someone made it; it did not just develop by itself.

Now let us look at the Universe.

The universe possesses innumerable creations with balance order, meeting all conditions to sustain life. Such a creation must have a creator; it is impossible for the universe to have created itself or to have been created by nothing.

So, what about the question of where we came from?

Let us answer this question by accepting that the universe and all living things on Earth, are creations of a higher being. This higher being is referred to as God in English, Elohim in

Hebrew, the language of the Jewish scriptures, Alaha in the Bible – the Bible was revealed in the Aramaic language, and Allah in the Arabic language. So let us group these three words together that means God in English:

- **Judaism... Alohim**
- **Christianity... Alaha**
- **Arabic... Allah**

Sounds similar, don't they.

Islam tells us that the souls were created before their bodies at the same time Prophet Adam was created. So, the beginning of our journey started in the world of the souls, continuing that journey through our mothers' wombs, then childhood, youth, agedness, graveyard, purgatory (waiting place between Hell and Heaven), and finally ending in Hell or Heaven.

Prophet Muhammed (pbuh) said:

"Souls are like crowds which gather together. The ones who met before gets on well. The ones, who did not meet before, cannot get on very well and separate." (Bukhari, Anbiya, 2; Muslim, Birr, 159; Abu Dawud, Adab, 19).

Allah then made an agreement with the children of Adam:

Chapter 7, Al-Araf, verse 172

And recall (O Prophet) when your Lord brought forth descendants from the loins of the sons of Adam, and made them witnesses against their ownselves. asking them:

'Am I not your Lord?'

They replied: 'Assuredly you are Our Lord.' Then Allah told them: 'I call upon the sky and the earth and father, Adam, to be witness against you lest you should say on the Day of Judgement that you were ignorant of this. Know well that no one other than Me deserves to be worshipped and no one other than Me is your Lord. So do not ascribe any partner to Me. I shall send to you My Messengers who will remind you of this covenant which you made with Me. I shall send down to you My Books.' In reply all said: 'We witness that You are Our Lord and our Deity. We have no lord or deity other than You.' (Ahmad b. Hanbal, Musnad, vol. 5, p. 135 - Ed.)

What is the soul?

Some people asked the Prophet (Pbuh) about soul. He did not answer, waiting for revelation. The revelation which was sent down was quite clear.

They ask you about the spirit.

Say: *"The spirit is among the affairs of my Lord, you have been given little knowledge of it"*. — Surat al-Isra' 17:85

Then, He fashioned him and blew into him the spirit. He made for you hearing, seeing, and hearts, yet little are you grateful. — Surat al-Sajdah 32:8

So, from the above verses we know that the existence of the soul (spirit) is confirmed, yet its essence is not explained because it is impossible for us to comprehend it. The human mind is incapable of comprehending a being from the spiritual world.

Imaam Al-Ghazali writes:

Everyone has the natural capacity to activate and cultivate the spirit, their higher level of consciousness in relation to Allah. Like a mirror, a pure heart reflects divine light from the spirit into the world. In order to achieve such a pure heart, one must follow the influence of the spirit upon the heart, as opposed to the whims of the lower self.

OUR INNER-SELF

Our inner self is made up of four parts:

The heart (*qalb*),

the soul (*ruh*),

the self or ego,

the mind (*'aql*).

Let us look at the heart.

We have a spiritual heart and a physical heart.

Our physical heart is the organ within the chest that pumps blood throughout the body.

Our prophet describes our physical heart as:

"There lies within the body a piece of flesh. If it is sound, the whole body is sound; and if it is corrupted, the whole body is corrupted. Verily this piece is the heart." Allah said:

"A Day in which wealth and children will not benefit, except one who comes to Allah with a pure heart." — Surat al-Shu'ara 26:88-89

Both the physical and the spiritual hearts are essential for the health of the human being. If the physical heart is damaged or malfunctioning, it can quickly lead to sudden death. If the spiritual heart is corrupted by spiritual diseases, it will lead to a type of spiritual death resulting in damnation in the Hereafter.

Hence, the matters of the heart are among the most important branches of knowledge in the religion of Islam. Purifying the heart of internal sins like arrogance, malice, and envy is paramount to our success in this life and the next.

Henceforth, we do not want to reach the end of life with a corrupt heart. So now let us look at the corrupt heart:

The Corrupt Heart

The heart is corrupted by committing acts of sins or disbelief. The Prophet said: "When a person commits an evil deed, a black spot is appears on his heart".

There are some sins that we unwittingly commit that are leaving those spots on our hearts, and these are the ones which we should be most mindful of.

A common example is backbiting. It has become so common everywhere that not criticizing someone behind their back might label you as being too conservative

Another common practice is "showing-off", and it is actually a kind of hidden *shirk*. Let us see how Allah can seal a corrupt heart.

(Allah has set a seal on their hearts),

"A stamp. It occurs when sin resides in the heart and surrounds it from all sides, and this submersion of the heart in sin constitutes a stamp, meaning a seal." Ibn Jurayj also said that the seal is placed on the heart and the hearing. In addition, Ibn Jurayj said, that `Abdullah ibn Kathir narrated that Mujahid said, "The stain is not as bad as the stamp, the stamp is not as bad as the lock which is the worst type." Al- A`mash said, "Mujahid demonstrated with his hand while saying, `They used to say that the heart is just like this - meaning the open palm. When the servant commits a sin, a part of the heart will be rolled up - and he rolled up his index finger. When the servant commits another sin, a part of the heart will be rolled up' - and he rolled up another finger, until he rolled up all of his fingers. Then he said, `Then, the heart will be sealed.' Mujahid also said that this is the description of the Ran (refer to in Al Muttafifin 83:14)."

Allah has described Himself with sealing and closing the hearts of the disbelievers, as a punishment for their disbelief.

Allah said in An Anisa 4:155

"Nay, Allah has set a seal upon their hearts because of their disbelief".

Let us expand on the sealing of the heart.

Let us compare the sealing of hearts to sealed bottles. These seals carry labels describing the contents of the containers. It also provides details such as nutrition facts and expiry dates.

A 'seal' is basically a 'stamp' used to authenticate the value or worth of an object.

Thus does Allah stamp the hearts of those who understand not. Ar-Rum 30: 59

In two other verses, God uses the same word "taba'a" (meaning, to stamp) to mention how He 'seals' the hearts of the disbelievers *(Al araf 7: 101)* and those who transgress (Yunus 10: 74).

A sealed heart is one that has been 'labelled' by God; which has been 'tagged' as belonging to a non-believer or transgressor. This stamp serves as a serious warning for those who continue to disobey God.

Purifying the corrupt heart

How do we cure the heart?

1. *Tazkiyah* (Purification)

"Successful indeed are those who purify themselves".(Al-Ala 87.14)

For curing the heart, it needs to be purged from all kinds of impurities like envy, hypocrisy, arrogance, gluttony and other diseases. The first step towards purification is istighfar.(Asking forgiveness from God).

2. Another form of tazkiyah is charity. The words zakah and tazkiyah come from the same root word, meaning purification. Both zakah and sadaqah are purifying. The Prophet said:

Charity extinguishes sin as fire extinguish water (Trimidhi)

3. Reading and reflecting on the Qur'an

O humankind! There has come to you an instruction from your Lord, and a cure for what (of sickness or doubt) is in the breasts, and guidance and mercy for the believers. (Yunus 10.57).

Allah calls the Qur'an shifa, i.e. medicine for hearts. Reciting the Qur'an itself is purifying even if we do not understand the meaning, because it is as if Allah is speaking to us.

4. Patience in the face of trials

The Prophet said:

In all cases, trials can be good for the true believer. If he is tested with prosperity, he should remain grateful and he will receive a reward. If he is tested with hardship, he should remain patient and he will also receive a reward, perhaps even greater.

Suhaib reported: The Messenger of Allah, peace and blessings be upon him, said:

Wondrous is the affair of the believer for there is good for him in every matter and this is not the case with anyone except the believer. If he is happy, then he thanks Allah and thus there is good for him. If he is harmed, then he shows patience and thus there is good for him.

Source: Sahih Muslim 2999, Grade: Sahih

Trials can be a sign that Allah intends good for us, because through trials our sins are expiated.

Duas

There are many *duas* which we can make and the best *dua* is that of which comes from the heart.

So let us go to Question 3.

What is my purpose here on earth? Why are we here? What are we doing here.

So far we have established that we are created beings living in a universe created by God, precisely to sustain life.

Allah tells us that there are THREE categories of human beings. Surah Baqarah, in its early verses, outlines those as follows:

1. Believers in Allah as the only one worthy of being worshipped
2. Unbelievers who worship other than Allah
3. Hypocrites, who give the impression that they believe but truly they do not.

One of these classifications can be found in Suraah Al Baqarah (ayaahs 3-20). That classification is for those who have intimately interacted with the Qur'an (and ponder on the meanings of its aayah's) and Islam and believe that the Qur'an is the truth sent down by The Lord of the heavens and the earth (as a blessing for all mankind). These are referred to as the Believers.

The second group consists of those who have no belief in a creator.

The third and last group is the trickiest of them all. In Arabic, these people are called al munafiqoon, the hypocrites. While the first two groups were described briefly by Allah in two or three aayahs (verses), the hypocrites are described by a staggering twelve aayahs. They are the ones that say that they believe in Allah and His Messenger, while they actually don't. They are those who "think" that they are doing goodness on this earth, but the truth is, they are actually doing nothing but destruction (corruption, pollution, exploitation, and all kinds of mischief). When they are told to believe (to follow certain aspects of the Qur'an and Hadeeth), they undermine it and say that they will not follow what the foolish people have followed. They are the ones that after testifying belief in front of people who believe, will go back to their "gods" and false deities (their jobs, their career, their wealth, etc.) and say that they are only mocking the true believers (by testifying belief). These people will eventually become the losers, similar to the second group (the disbelievers), and that they will wonder in their confusion and darkness because of their heedlessness.

Regarding the last type of people, the hypocrites, we find them everywhere, including in predominantly Muslim populated countries. Many people say that they are Muslims, but they are so far away from the guidance of the Qur'an and Hadeeth, and do not do anything to seek guidance, and if they are guided, they don't take it seriously. They put their belief in Allah at the very bottom of their priority, while they seek to fulfil their pleasure and their false sense of "achievement".

Now is perhaps a good time to stop reading and examine which category I fall in. Re-addressing the question, "Why did Allah create us?"

Muslims are very clear of the purpose of their creation. For Allah says:

"I created the jinn and humankind only that they might worship Me". (Al Dhariyat 51 verse 56)

So let us look at the concept of worship in Islam.

The word worship encompasses a much broader view, it is not just limited to prayer, fasting, hajj, zakat, reciting Qur'an and zikr etc.

It includes all other explicit and implicit actions that Allah loves, for example: taking care and maintaining one's own family, being patient, being charitable, maintaining honesty, fulfilling trusts, being dutiful to parents, maintaining ties of relationship, promoting goodness, making tawbah (repentance), encouraging others to do good deeds and discouraging evil. In addition to all of the foregoing, comes: loving Allah and His messengers, fearing and being thankful to Allah for His infinite blessings, accepting His decree, depending on Him, aspiring for His mercy and fearing His punishment. Most importantly, being conscious that we all are in fact returning to Allah and believing in the day of resurrection. All of these are examples for acts of worship to Allah.

Thus leading a life abiding by the rules permissible by our lord; trying to please him and abstaining from forbidden activities places us in a state of constant worship of Allah (which is the ultimate purpose of our creation and existence).

Allah says, *"Say, 'My prayer and my sacrifice and my life and my death are all for Allah, the Lord of the worlds;"* {Qur'an Al-Anam: Ayat 162}

This way Islam bestows the quality of "worship" on any action that seeks the satisfaction of Allah and which are not forbidden. Hence the farmer, the manufacturer, the trader, the doctor, the engineer, the teacher and the student are all in a state of worship if their actions are directed towards the benefit of mankind, aiming for self-sufficiency and gaining proper sustenance for one's family etc.

Righteousness is not that you turn your faces toward the east or the west, but true righteous is one who believes in Allah, the Last Day, the angels, the Book, and the prophets and gives wealth, in spite of love for it, to relatives, orphans, the needy, the traveller, those who ask for help, and for freeing slaves; who establishes prayer and gives zakah; fulfill their promise when they promise; and who are patient in poverty and hardship and during battle. Those are the ones who have been true, and it is those who are the righteous. {Surah Al-Baqarah: Ayat 177}

This ayat establishes that, prayer/zikr/zakah alone are not sufficient enough to achieve righteous in Islam, as we have an obligation towards mankind at large.

The other two categories of people may feel that the objective of their lives is to accumulate wealth, obtain high positions in their jobs or society or pursue pleasure to the greatest extent possible. But none of that will benefit them in the long run.

True happiness for a Muslim does not come from material things. The Prophet Muhammad said:

Wealth is not in having vast riches, it is in contentment. (**Bukhari, Muslim**)

What is contentment?

Money can't buy it, and poverty doesn't give it. Contentment comes from being satisfied and thankful for who you are and where you find yourself in life. Believing that inner peace is more valuable than all the world's riches is a good start.

Now to answer the final question. Is death really the end of Life?

The life of a Muslim includes trials and test by means of which his final destiny is determined. For him, death is the return of the soul to its Creator, God, and the inevitability of death and the Hereafter is never far from his consciousness. This serves to keep all his life and deeds in perspective as he tries to live in readiness for what is to come. For Muslims, the concept of death and the afterlife in Islam is derived from the holy Qur'an, the final revealed message from God.

We learn that death is synonymous with sleep; complete with dreams (6:60, 40:46). The period between death and resurrection passes like one night of sleep (the holy *Qur'an*: 2:259; 6:60; 10:45; 16:21; 18:11, 19, 25; 30:55). At the moment of death, everyone knows his or her destiny; heaven or hell. For the disbelievers, death is a horrible event; the angels beat them on the faces and rear ends as they snatch away their souls (the holy *Qur'an*:8:50, 47:27, 79:1).

The Holy *Qur'an*, contains various death themes that add significantly to our insight into the meaning of death, the concept is left undefined and always portrayed in close relationship with the concepts of life, creation, and resurrection.

All that is on earth will perish. (The Holy Qur'an 55:26)

Allah says in the Qur'an: "Everyone shall taste death. And only on the day of resurrection shall you be paid your wages in full. And whoever is removed away from the fire and admitted to paradise, this person is indeed successful. The life of this world is only the enjoyment of deception." (The Holy Qur'an: 3:185)

In other words, the holy Qur'an says that every person, which comprises of his body and soul, must taste death.

Death is the termination of that complex being, which was capable of believing or disbelieving.

In the same way that a person does not cease to exist in sleep, he does not cease to exist in death. And in the same way that a person comes back to life when emerging from sleep, he will be resurrected at the great awakening, the Day of Judgement. Hence, Islam views death merely as a stage in human existence. Physical death should not be feared but one should, however, worry about the agonies of spiritual death caused by living a life of immmorality.

The mystery of life and death is resolved in the holy Qur'an by linking it to the working of human conscience and its ability to maintain a healthy status of human spiritual-moral existence with faith in God. Human efforts should be concerned with the revival of human conscience, leading to a meaningful life.

Muslims, when they die have to be buried, never cremated. It is a religious requirement that the body be ritually washed and draped before burial, which should be shortly after death. The dying person is encouraged to recite and declare his or her faith. When a Muslim is buried his or her face is turned right facing towards the Ka'aba in Makkah (127 South-east from United Kingdom). The arms and legs should be straightened, and the mouth and eyes closed; and the body covered with a sheet.

Death is divinely willed and when it arrives it should be readily accepted. There should, therefore, be no reasoning by the bereaved as to why they have lost their loved one. Islamic scholars such as the twelfth century theologian, Al Ghazali stress that death is unpredictable and can happen at any time and as such Muslims should always be prepared for the inevitable and for what is about to occur. It is but a gateway from this short but mortal existence to a life of immortality in the afterlife.

The belief of Prophets and Messengers in Islam

Believing in God's Prophets and Messengers is a fundamental part of Islam. Muslims believe God sent Prophets and Messengers to convey his Message to humanity. The Holy Qur'an states:

"And We certainly sent into every nation a messenger, [saying], 'Worship Allah and avoid Ta'ghut (false deities).' And among them were those whom Allah guided, and among them were those upon whom error was [deservedly] decreed. So, proceed through the earth and observe how was the end of the deniers" (Qur'an 16:36)

To every people and to every nation was sent one or many Prophets, and they were sent with the tongue of their people. Muslims believe that Prophet Muhammad SAW, is the only universal Prophet meant for the whole Globe. All other Prophets and Messengers including Prophet Moses and Prophet Jesus peace be upon them were only sent for a particular group of people/tribe who lived before us. Islam states all Prophets came with the same general Message to Worship Only One God and Follow His Commandments. Whereas some finer details differed from one nation or Book to another, the concept of God, one God, never changed.

Due to God's Mercy and Love for humanity, God continued to send Prophets and Messengers to give good news and warning to their people. The general Message was whoever worships the One God and follows His commandments will go to Paradise for eternity. And whoever worships other than Allah and goes against His Commandments will enter the Hell Fire. The Prophets also came to teach their people how to purify themselves. Every Messenger was given Inspiration from God, some of which resulted in what we know as scriptures.

The Prophet & Messengers that God sent to humanity to convey His Message could not make mistakes for speaking on behalf of God. Humanity could not attain true knowledge of morality and ethics without guidance from their Creator to reveal what is truly good and truly evil. Muslims believe that God communicates His guidance through human Prophets. These Prophets were sent to their people, not only by preaching people to worship the One God and follow His commandment but by live by example with their actions.

A *Messenger (Rasool in Arabic)* has a higher rank than a Prophet *(Nabi in Arabic)*. A Messenger is sent to a tribe or people that did not believe in the Message and generally sent with a new Revelation (Divine Laws). A Prophet (Nabi in Arabic) is someone that was sent to a people or a tribe that have already received the Message. He is sent to remind them. Every Messenger is a Prophet, but not every Prophet is a Messenger by definition. The Islamic Tradition states there were about 124,000 Prophets that were sent to people and nations. There are 25 Prophets mentioned by name in the Holy Qur'an.

1. Prophet Adam
2. Prophet Enoch (Idris in Arabic)
3. Prophet Nuh (Noah)
4. Prophet Eber or Heber (Hud in Arabic)
5. Prophet Methuselah (Saleh in Arabic)
6. Prophet Abraham (Ibrahim)
7. Prophet Lot (Lut in Arabic)
8. Prophet Ishmael (Ismail in Arabic)
9. Prophet Isaac (Ishaq in Arabic)
10. Prophet Jacob (Yaqoob in Arabic)
11. Prophet Joseph (Yusuf in Arabic)

12. Prophet Job (Ayoub in Arabic)
13. Prophet Jethro (Shuaib in Arabic)
14. Prophet Moses (Musa in Arabic)
15. Prophet Aaron (Harun in Arabic)
16. Prophet Ezekiel (Dhul-Kifl in Arabic)
17. Prophet David (Daud in Arabic)
18. Prophet Solomon (Suleiman in Arabic)
19. Prophet Elijah (Ilyas in Arabic)
20. Prophet Elisha (Al-Yasa in Arabic)
21. Prophet Jonah (Younus in Arabic)
22. Prophet Zachariah (Zakariya in Arabic)
23. Prophet John (the Baptist), (Yahya in Arabic)
24. Prophet Jesus (Isa in Arabic)
25. Prophet Muhammad

Peace be upon them all.

Prophet Muhammad, SAW, was chosen by God to deliver His Message of Peace, namely Islam. He was born in 570 C.E. (Common Era) in Makkah, Arabia. He was entrusted with the Message of Islam when he was at the age of forty. The revelation that he received, over a period of about 22 years, is called the Qur'an, while the message is called Islam.

Muhammad is the very last Prophet of God to mankind. He is the final Messenger of God. His message was and is still for all mankind, including Jews and Christians. It was sent to confirm and clarify what was sent before in the scrolls of Abraham, the Torah, The Pslams, and the Gospel.

Prophet Muhammad SAW is the summation and the culmination of all the prophets and messengers that came before him. He purified the previous messages from adulteration and completed the Message of God for all humanity. He was entrusted with the power of explaining, interpreting, and living the teachings of the Qur'an.

Source of Islam

The legal sources of Islam are the Qur'an and the sunnah of Muhammad on whom be peace. The Qur'an is the exact words of God; its authenticity, originality and totality are intact. The sunnah is the report of the sayings, deeds and approvals of the Prophet Muhammad. The Seerah is the writings of followers of Muhammad about the life of the Prophet. Hence, it is the life history of the Prophet Muhammad which provides examples of daily living for Muslims.

The Qur'an

The Noble Qur'an was sent to both the Arabs and to Mankind. There are Verses in the Noble Qur'an where Allah Almighty explicitly talks to the Arabs and for the Arabs, and there are Noble Verses in the Noble Qur'an where Allah Almighty talks to Mankind and for Mankind.

The Prophets and Messengers that were sent to mankind were given miracles from Allah, in order to strengthen their dawah (preaching).

Unlike the miracles of the other prophets which is only experienced by a group of people, the miracle that is given to the Prophet Muhammed is experienced by the whole humanity until the end of time. It is the Holy Qur'an, the direct unchanged words of Allah.

Those perfect words of Allah were sent down to guide humankind out of the darkness and into the light; they are guidance and a mercy. (Surah Maida, verse 16).

On the night known as the 'Night of Decree', in the Islamic month of Ramadan, Laila-tul-qadr, the Qur'an descended, from the Preserved Tablet to the Lowest Heaven.

It was then revealed to Prophet Muhammed in stages, and Allah gave us the reason for this:

"And those who disbelieve say: Why is not the Qur'an revealed to him all at once? Thus (it is sent down in parts), that We may strengthen your heart thereby. And We have revealed it to you gradually, in stages." (Surah Al Furqan verse 32).

The Qur'an reveals many matters of the unseen and made several prophecies that were all fulfilled exactly as they were foretold. For example, the Persians defeated the Byzantines in one of their battles and the Qur'an recorded this defeat foretelling that the Byzantines would defeat the Persians within three to nine years and that was exactly what happened.

(The Byzantines have been defeated In the nearest land. But they, after their defeat, will overcome. Within three to nine years.) [Qur'an Al-Ghafir: 2-4]

The Qur'an includes many miraculous scientific facts that were only discovered fourteen centuries later. For example, the Qur'an told us about a barrier separating the salty water from the fresh water not to mix with each other.

(He Released the two seas, meeting [side by side]; Between them is a barrier [so] neither of them transgresses.) [Qur'an Ar Rahman:19,20] After about fourteen centuries, modern science confirmed this scientific fact.

There are many more predictions and scientific facts to be found in the Qur'an. Reading and listening to the Qur'an sends one into a state of peace and tranquility unlike the human speeches or writings. Allah, The Exalted, Says:

"Those who have believed and whose hearts are assured by the remembrance of Allah; pay heed. Unquestionably, by the remembrance of Allah hearts are assured." [Qur'an Ar-rad:28]

The Qur'an is also a cure and it expels the devils when it is recited. Allah, The

Almighty, Says (what means):

(And We send down of the Qur'an that which is healing and mercy for the believers...) [Qur'an Al-Isra:82]

This is the Qur'an, the Speech of Allah that has been challenging humankind and proving its inability to produce something to its effect as to its eloquence, wise judgments, and authentic news. The challenge is still valid, and the inability of mankind to face that challenge remains. Thus, the Qur'an will remain the everlasting Argument of Allah, The Almighty, against all opponents and disbelievers.

Protection of Qur'an

Allah has taken an oath to protect the Qur'an from change and error that has happened to the earlier holy texts, the Gospel and the Torah.

Allah says:

Verily We: It is We Who have sent down the Dhikr (i.e. the Qur'an) and surely, We will guard it (from corruption). (Surah Hijr, verse 9)

The copies of the Qu'ran we have in our homes contains the exact words that were revealed to Prophet Muhammad (Pbuh) 1400 years ago.

Arrangement of the Qur'an

Lo! upon Us (resteth) the putting together thereof and the reading thereof. (Surah Al Qiyamah, v 17)

It is the consensus of the scholars of Islam that the Qur'an is not complied in the order it was revealed. It is in the order as it is written in the Mother of Books, AL Lau AL Mahfuz. If we look at the end of most suras, they flow into the suras following them. Archangel Gabriel (alaihi salaam) not only brought revelation to the Prophet but also made him memorise in this same format as we see it compiled because of Divine Order from Allah.

The 1st Chapter of the Qur'an called Surah Al Fatiha (The Opening). Even though, this Surah was revealed much later that other suras, yet it is placed in the opening of the Qur'an because "Fatiha" means "To Open". In other words "Fatiha" also means the "Entrance". When one enters a place, it is only through the entrance. If Surah Fatiha was to be placed somewhere within the Qur'an, not beginning, then it would not have made sense to place the entrance somewhere else other than where it belongs. In surah Fatiha, which is essentially a dua, contains the verse to seek guidance from Allah, "Guide us onto that straight path….". The surah that follows it, Baqarah, "That book, in which there is no doubt, is a guide to those who believe".

Similarly, we also learn divine wisdom when reading beginning verse of the 2nd chapter called Surah Al Baqara (The Cow). Before the reader commences his or her journey through the Qur'an the first thing they are informed is that purpose of Qur'an is to give you guidance, it's not a book of history, science or any other subject that may occur to your mind: "*This is the Scripture in which there is no doubt, containing guidance for those who are mindful of God.*"[2] (There are however, scientific facts in the Qur'an that are being confirmed by scholars of various desclipines. Allah says that it is to teach us our origins). Thus, it perfectly makes sense why this verse has been placed in its absolute beginning even though the Surah it belongs to was revealed 10 years after Prophet's declaration of prophethood. Then the verses following that mention the basic principles of Islam and Imaan (Faith). They are: giving charity/zakah, performing salaah (5 times prayers), belief in the unseen (Hell, Paradise, Angels, previous revelations, etc.) and with certainty, in the hereafter: "*who believe in the unseen, keep up the prayer (salaah), and give out of what We have provided for them (charity/zakah); those who believe in the revelation sent down to you [Muhammad], and in what was sent before you (previous prophets/books), those who have firm faith in the Hereafter (meeting with Allah, angels, Judgment day).*" Those basics listed at the beginning, make absolute sense, since every believer must understand what is required of him from the beginning of his journey on the path of Islam.

The name of the Surah is called "Baqara" meaning "Cow", because of an incident occurring during the time of the Children of Israel mentioned in verse 67–73 when they made their case difficult due to unnecessary questioning of Prophet Musa (Moses) (alaihi salaam). The story is about trying to find a murderer of a Jew. They asked Moses to inquire of Allah who was the guilty person and Allah revealed to Moses to tell them to slaughter a cow. They sought so many clarifications that the cow ended up being very expensive, a mound of gold.

MY LEGACY

My children,

My grandchildren,

I leave this book as a legacy to you. In this journey of life Allah has chosen me to be your guardian, your protector. Allah has entrusted me, gifted me with the best of treasures, my beautiful family.

Live your life in the submission and affirmation to the one God.

All that exists belongs to Him as He is the Originator of all. He, subhanahu, alone is worthy of worship and all other deities are to be shunned.

Everything happens by the Qader (will) of subhanahu. What was never meant for you will never reach you and what is meant for you, you will never have missed.

Live your life with kindness, gratitude. Live everyday as the last day of your life. Seek refuge in Allah from the accursed Shaitan who lies waiting to trap you.

Fulfil your duties to one another. You might be four different families but live your life as one. There is nothing greater than kinship.

Remember that happiness comes with a pure heart free from jealousy, hatred, arrogance. Establish your prayers regularly and with humility. Nothing in your life is more important than your Salaat. Prayer is your connection to Allah.

Feel the hunger and thirst of others. Thank Allah in all conditions. He may know a thing that's good for and that what is bad.

Learn the lessons from the Prophets. Put your trust in Allah and avoid those who aim to cause mischief. Speak well of others and avoid slander and backbiting.

Live your life with contentment and avoid excess. Have pleasure in giving than receiving.

Be charitable to your neighbours and love for yourself what you love for your brother. Live your life with tolerance and be accepting of others, even if their beliefs differ from you. Ask forgiveness from those you harm and repent to Allah.

I pray that Allah protect and guide each and everyone one of you and we meet again and live as one family in Jannatul Firdous.

AMEEN

Mummy, Nani Serena.

Chapter 1

Towards Understanding Surah Fatihah

Prophet Muhammad (Pbuh) said Surah Al-Fatihah is considered 'The Greatest Surah' of the Qur'an

"And certainly, We have given you seven of the oft-repeated (verses) and the grand Qur'an". (Surah Hijr 15:87).

This Surah is called the seven oft repeated verse because it is recited in every rakah (unit) of Salah (formal prayer). No Salah is valid without the recitation of Surah Al- Fatihah.

Al-Fatiha itself means The Opening because it opens The Holy Qur'an. Some of the scholars have said that it is as if the rest of the Qur'an is a commentary of Surah Fatiha, acting as an introduction to the book of Allah.

Also, if you can imagine being surrounded by problems and there comes an opening, Surah Fatiha introducing the Qur'an to take you from the darkness that surrounds you into light.

("With it Allah guides those who follow His pleasure to the pathways of peace, and brings them out, by His will, from the depths of darkness into the light, and guides them to a straight path". Surah Maida, verse 16)

Surah Al-Fatiha is also referred to by other names:

Umm al-Qur'an means the Mother of the Qur'an, and **Umm al-Kitab**, Mother of the Book. Ibn Jarir at-Tabari said that it was so named because the meaning of the entire Qur'an is summarised therein. In other words, it is the gist of the Qur'an.

'Ubadah ibn al-Samat reported: The Messenger of Allah, peace and blessings be upon him, said,

"There is no prayer for one who does not recite the opening of the Book, Surat al-Fatihah."

Source: Sahih al-Bukhari 723, Sahih Muslim 394

Sab'ul-Mathani means The Seven Oft-Repeated Verses.

As-Salah means The Prayer. The reason why it is named The Prayer is that its recitation is a condition for the validity of the prayer.

Ash-Shifa, means The Cure.

Asas al-Qur'an that is the Foundation of the Qur'an. Ash-Sha'bi recorded on the authority of Ibn Abbas that he named it, and that he said, "The Foundation of Al- Fatiha is,

"Bismillahirrahmanirrahim" which means In the Name of Allah, the All- Merciful, the Most Merciful.

Surah Fatiha includes some of the most essential elements constructing the core beliefs of Islam which are Monotheism, Prophethood and belief in the hereafter. It is recited as a cure for spiritual and physical illness and is considered a direct loving link between the servant and his creator.

The most profound verse is surah is verse 5:

Iyyaaka na'budu wa Iyyaaka nasta'een – Thee do we worship, and Thine aid we seek.

It is mentioned in this verse that human progress depends upon two factors: actions of the body and actions of the heart. It is necessary to reform both the actions of the body and the heart. However, this reformation cannot come to be without the guidance of Allah. Hence the words used are, 'Thee alone do we worship and Thee alone do we implore for help'.

The reason why the Qur'an is called **Umm al-Qur'an** and **Umm al-Kitab** is because the most powerful names of Allah are mentioned in this one surah - Allah, Ar Rab, and Rahaman. Surah fatiha also mentions two other names – Malik and Raheem but those three names are the primary names of our creator and all other names comes under these names.

Surah Fatiha talks about the social conditions of mankind.

Verses

1. *Alhamdu lillaahi Rabbil 'aalameen* – We praise Allah because he is worthy of being praise. We praise the one we love – indicating the love for our creator.

2. *Ar-Rahmaanir-Raheem* – Allah is Merciful. We have hope in his mercy.

3. *Maaliki Yawmid-Deen* – He is the Master of Judgement day. We are terrified of Judgement Day.

Lets us look at Tawheed. Muslims not only belief in One God, it goes further than that. Islam teaches us that God is also the One through whose command and orders the universe continues to function. It is for this reason that His help and succour is of immense benefit to man. This is inferred by the words bismillāh in which every surah begins with.

Verse

4. Ihdinas-Siraatal-Mustaqeem

5. Siraatal-lazeena an'amta 'alaihim ghayril-maghdoobi 'alaihim wa lad-daaalleen

The three categories of mankind:

- Those who have knowledge and acts upon it. (Believers)
- Those who have knowledge and don't act upon it. (Hypocrites)
- Those who have knowledge and are trying to act without knowledge. (Non-believers)

These categories are referenced in detail in Surah Baqarah.

The three pillars of worshipping Allah are indicated in this Surah- Love, Hope and Fear.

In conclusion, the beauty and message of Surah al-Fatiḥa is the comprehensive summary of the message of the Qur'an. Each and every time we recite this surah, whether in or out of the prayer, it should be a reminder of these three core principles of Islam, Love, fear and hope.

Chapter 2

Towards Understanding Surah Baqarah

Surah Baqarah is the longest surah in the Qur'an, containing 286 verses. Baqarah means cow. Verses 67 to 73 discusses a story of a cow.

In Surah Baqarah, Allah Almighty introduces us to the Qur'an and tells us about three different types of people populating the world:

Those who will benefit from the guidance of the Qur'an, the believers. Those who will not, the disbelievers.

Those who are only pretending to be people of the Qur'an. The Hypocrites

The surah describes that the most successful attributes of the believers are their faith and belief in the unseen.

And the most obvious characteristic of unsuccessful people is their absolute materialism. This reference is made to the hypocrites and the unbelievers.

Success. What does success really mean to you?

Ponder on the following statement:

Success is the achievement of acquiring, wealth respect and fame. But these materialistic gains are temporary, and sometimes can become more of a detriment.

Islam teaches us that the life of this world is short and fleeting, and that the purpose of our existence is not to lust after beauty, fame and wealth, but rather to worship Allah correctly and live by His rules.

Please revisit the introduction chapter to remind ourselves of what worship in Islam means.

Islam view success as being one who is contented and happy. Let's look at how Muslims strive to attain success:

Avoiding Riba (interest, usury)

In the Qur'an, there is a theme of success (falaah in Arabic) connected to the avoidance of Riba (Interest). Let's look at Surah Imran verse 130:

O you who have believe, do not consume usury, doubled and multiplied, but fear Allah that you may be successful. — Saheeh Internationa

Let us now expand on Riba:

Riba is an Arabic noun derived from the verb Raba, meaning 'to increase', 'to grow', and 'to exceed'. It includes interest which is paid by banks or on loans such as car loans, home loans or credit card debt.

Why is Riba Haram?

The first and foremost reason riba is haram is because Allah declared it so. It is based on Allah's infinite wisdom that He deems an action to be obligatory or prohibited, prescribing matters in man's best interests, in this life and in the Hereafter, as He is the All-Wise, All-Knowing. The scholars of Islam have suggested the following reasons as to why riba is haram:

- Riba conflicts with the spirit of brotherhood and sympathy, and is based on greed, selfishness and hard heartedness.
- Riba is one of the major contributors towards inflation.
- Riba causes trauma and depression due to mounting debts.
- Riba is a sure gain without any possibility of loss, hence all the risk is taken by the borrower, rather than sharing the risk and the profits with both parties.
- Riba creates a monopoly in society, where the rich are rewarded for being wealthy, while those who are not are forced to pay extra!

When examining this issue of riba, we should remember that true success lies with the help of Allah alone. If we abide by that which is lawful, and avoid that which is haram, our wealth will be blessed and beneficial in this world and the Hereafter.

What good is extra money earned through riba if there is no blessing in it, and it is cursed - a source of misery?

On the Day of Resurrection, people will rise from their graves quickly, except those who engaged in riba. They will stand up and then fall down like epileptics because:

"Those who consume riba cannot stand on the Day of Resurrection, except as one stands who is beaten by Satan in insanity. This is because they say trade is just like riba. But Allah has permitted trade and forbidden riba (Surah Baqarah, verse 275)

Tyranny, crime, lying and conning others

In the pursuit of wealth, respect, or fame, some may attempt vile shortcuts with oppression, crime, or lying or deceiving others. The Qur'an is clear that, yes, perhaps in the short term it may seem like they are winning, but ultimately those who take this path will never ultimately succeed.

(Qur'an Surah Yunus/Verse 17)

So, who is more unjust than the one who forges a lie against Allah or gives the lie to His signs? Indeed (such) guilty people shall not achieve success. — Mufti Taqi Usmani

Purifying one's heart and soul

What a beautiful understanding of success that Islam teaches us. That success isn't when one accumulates wealth, power, or fame. Genuine success and Paradise is when one purifies their heart and soul! Subhan Allah. (Qur'an As-Shams/ 9 and Al - Hashr/9)

Keeping Allah present in your life (Taqwa)

Allah's Messenger, sal Allahu alayhi wa sallam, said, "Worship Allah as if you see Him. If you cannot see Him, then indeed Allah sees you."

It is this life of Taqwa, of keeping Allah ever present in your conscious, that leads to success.

O you who have believed! Be patient in adversity, and vie in patience with one another, and be ever ready [to do what is right], and remain conscious of Allah (Taqwa), so that you might attain success! Qur'an Surah Imran/200

Salah (Prayer)

In the call to prayer: Hayy 'ala alFalaah — Come to success

On the authority of Abu Hurayrah (may Allah be pleased with him) from the Prophet (Pbuh), who said:

Allah (mighty and sublime be He) says: The first of his actions for which a servant of Allah will be held accountable on the Day of Resurrection will be his prayers. If they are in order, then he will have prospered and succeeded: and if they are wanting, then he will have failed and lost.

Benefits of Surah Baqarah

There are many benefits of Surah Baqarah some of them are mentioned below:

- In the house where Surah Baqarah is recited Shaytan will not enter. Abu Hurayrah (RA) said that the Prophet Muhammad (Pbuh) said: "Do not turn your houses into graves. Verily, Shaytan does not enter the house where Surah Al-Baqarah is recited" (Tirmidhi)

- Surah al Baqarah helps to protect the person who recites it against the evil eye, witchcraft, evil whispers, and it also brings immense barakah into one's time and overall peace in life.

- Surah Baqarah brings greater reward on The Day of Judgment and adds blessings in this worldly life. In a hadith Prophet Muhammad (Pbuh) said: "Recite the Qur'an, for on the Day of Resurrection it will come as an intercessor for those who recite it. Recite the two bright ones, al-Baqarah, and Surah Al 'Imran, for on the Day of Resurrection they will come as two clouds or two shades, or two flocks of birds in ranks, pleading for those who recite them. Recite Surah al-Baqarah, to take recourse to it is a blessing and to give it up is a cause of grief, and the magicians cannot confront it." (Muslim)

- The last two verses of Surah al-Baqarah are the most memorised verses of Qur'an among Muslims and it is for a good reason. In hadith Prophet Muhammad (Pbuh) said: "Whoever recites the last two verses of Surah al- Baqarah by night that will suffice him" (Bukhari)

- Holy Prophet Muhammad (Pbuh) said: "Indeed Allah wrote in a book two thousand years before He created the heavens and the earth, and He sent down two Ayahs (verses) from it to end Surah al Baqarah with. If they are recited for three nights in a home, no Shaitan (devil) shall come near it." (Tirmidhi)

THE SURAH IS DIVIDED INTO 9 SECTIONS

- Part 1: Allah describes the characteristics of believers, disbelievers and hypocrites. The key is the belief in the unseen and the quest for guidance.

- Part 2: The story of Adam. This story is about human greed. Allah is Merciful and He accepts repentance.

- Part 3: The story of the Children of Israel. They were supposed to be a role model for humanity. However, they changed part of their book. They expected that the last prophet would be a Jew, so they refused to accept Prophet Muhammad (peace be upon him) as he was Arab.

- Part 4: The story of Prophet Ibrahim (peace be upon him). He was tried several times and obeyed Allah perfectly. In building the Ka'bah, he asks Allah to protect Makkah from fear and hunger. This section highlights the shared lineage between the Jews and the Arabs.

- Part 5: This section discusses the handing over to the Muslims the responsibility of being the role model for humanity.

- Part 6: The Muslim nation will be tested with fear and hunger. Will the Muslims make the same mistakes that the Children of Israel made?

- Part 7: This section highlights the laws given to the Muslims to reform society.

- Part 8: Protect yourself from greed by spending on charity. The opposite of charity is getting involved in Riba (Interest). Doing business is permissible but Riba is not.

- Part 9: The last two ayah is a prayer to strengthen the believers so that they hear and they obey the call of the Prophet (peace be upon him).

Let's us look at the primary and secondary addressees of this Surah. The Primary is the Pagan Arabs and the Jews living in Medina. The secondary audience is the entire world, as unlike the other scriptures which were revealed only to a particular group of people.

To understand the verses referencing the Jews in the Surah we have to examine their presence in Medina.

Why and what they were doing there?

In A.D. 70, the Roman general, Titus, captured Jerusalem and put an end to the Jewish rule of Palestine. Following the Roman conquest, many of the Jews left their homeland and wandered into other countries. Some Jewish tribes crossed the Syrian desert and entered the Arabian peninsula where they settled in Hijaz. In course of time they built up numerous colonies in Medina and between Medina and Syria. They are also said to have converted many Arabs to Judaism. Among other reasons for these Jews choosing to settle in Medina is that their scriptures foretold the coming of another prophet, their prophet. Some of the Jews accepted Prophet Muhammed as the prophet. However, other Jews rejected him as he was from the Lineage of Ishmael and not Isaacs. They also qualified to the title of being the "Hypocrites" referred to in the Surah.

Surah Baqarah references them in many verses.

Verses 1 – 7

The surah begins with alif, lam and meem. We have no knowledge of the meanings of combination of letters.

The second verse is:

Thalika alkitabu la rayba feehi hudan lilmuttaqeena

"That is the book, in it is guidance sure, without doubt, to those who are muttaqi (truly conscious, pious)"

Here it is made clear in a single powerful statement, that this book has no doubt in it. In one bold statement we are told how we should approach and regard this revelation, this guidance which has come down to us.

In the opening chapter, Surah Fatiha, Allah taught us how to ask for guidance and in this second chapter he presenting us with a book of guidance. There is no doubt about its origin. From the beginning Allah stresses the fact that it is only those with God consciousness (taqwa) that will ask for and accept guidance.

Only a certain category of people will benefit from this book which is the direct speech of Allah. This category are those who have taqwa, believe in the unseen, establish the prayer, give charity from what Allah has provided, believe in this revelation and the previous revelations, and believe in the Hereafter. These people will prosper. So Allah is describing one of the three categories of people populating the world – the believers.

Then we are introduced to the second category – the disbelievers. This group of people will take no heed to the message of the Prophet.

Allah tells us that the beneficent has covered their ears, eyes and hearts as a direct result of their arrogance and persistent sinfulness. Indeed, we are told that a great punishment is awaiting them.

Verses 8 – 20 The hypocrites

Prior to the migration of the Muslims from Madina, the people in Yatrib (Medina) fell into two categories. The believers and the non believers. However, after the migration there is a new category of people. These are the hypocrites.

Now who are these hypocrites. Many of the Jews occupying Medina at that era falls into this category. The Qur'an describes them in many surahs, including Surah Baqarah.

They are known as those who say they believe, but secretly they are not among the believers. They only mock.

They are being described like those who are in darkness. The darkness of their own desires, the darkness of evil. They are aware of the situation. They want a way out and seek to find the right path. They are given that path of light, but they ignore it, and because of this Allah calls them:

Summum bukmun 'umyun fahum laa yarji'oon

(Deaf, dumb and blind, and so they do not think and understand).

Allah has blocked their guidance and they will not benefit from the Qur'an. Hypocrisy is a serious sickness and a great crime. We have hypocrites in every period and every society.

Hypocrisy means making an outward display of Islam whilst inwardly concealing kufr. Hypocrisy is more dangerous than kufr (disbelief) and the punishment for it is more severe, because it is kufr mixed with Islam and its harmful effects are greater. Hence Allah will put the hypocrites in the lowest level of Hell, as He says (interpretation of the meaning):

"Verily, the hypocrites will be in the lowest depth (grade) of the Fire; no helper will you find for them [al-Nisaa' 4:145]

The hypocrites are always confused, always planning deceit and plots. Although outwardly they appear to be with the believers, inwardly they are with the kaafireen (unbelievers). So sometimes they are inclined towards the believers and sometimes they are inclined towards the kaafireen.

Time for Reflection: Which category of People do you fall in?

Verses 21 – 29 Worship God Alone

These verses are making us aware of the being that created us, and to be conscious of him.

The miracle of our creation is also addressed

Verse 21 commence with:

O Mankind worship your Lord who created you and those before you!

So what is worship in Islam?

Worship in Islam has so many aspects that it is difficult to describe them all in words. The most general meaning of worship in Islam is inclusive of everything which is pleasing to Allah, whether they deal with issues of belief, or deeds of the body. It may include everything a person perceives, thinks, intends, feels, says and does. It also refers to everything that Allah requires, external, internal or interactive. This includes rituals as well as beliefs, work, social activities, and personal behaviour, as human being is a whole, such that every part affects every other.

Now one may ask oneself:

"Why worship Allah when he is free of All needs?

The purpose of worshipping our creator is to elevate ourselves for goodness. It is the highest training and ethics in the school of Islam because:

a) The worship of Allah creates a sense of thankfulness, respect and honour.

b) The worship of Allah elevates the soul of man. It gives you peace, contentment, and happiness. In Islam we recognise that these qualities cannot be achieved by monetary gain but by the connection to the one who created us.

Verse 23:

And if ye are in doubt as to what We have revealed from time to time to Our servant, then produce a Sura like thereunto; and call your witnesses or helpers (If there are any) besides Allah, if your (doubts) are true.

This challenge has been offered to demonstrate the miracle of the Qur'an, to show that it is a Book sent down by Allah, there is no doubt in it; that it has been revealed as an everlasting miracle that will remain alive till the end of the world. This challenge has repeatedly been given in the Qur'an:

The Qur'an is the word of Allah. When Qur'an was in its revelation phase, many of the polytheists in Makkah used to call the Qur'an as a written scripture from Prophet Muhammad Peace be Upon Him. They also accused him of being a liar, deluded godman & mad, although they knew Prophet Muhammad was illiterate.

The Qur'an is a miracle from Allah. Some of things that we have figured out is that it is a literary masterpiece, as told by the people of literature of all times since it is revealed, especially 1400 years ago. It is one of the only scriptures, which has accurate historical facts mentioned (talking about 5000+ years ancient), some of them being reinforced by the actual historical discoveries done in current times. In terms of scientific processes, it states of many modern theories & scientific facts which only came to light few decades ago.

So, the challenge is to produce a book with such literary style, historical facts and scientific facts that has never come to light but will do in times to come.

Hence, the verse is counter to every person doubting the Qur'an as the word of Allah. It says, bring out a Surah (Chapter) of your own like what there is in the Qur'an. Which to this date has never been accomplished and will remain the same till the day of Judgement.

Then Allah gives us a contrasting description of heaven and hell. Our creator is telling the unbelievers to fear the hellfire whose fuel is humankind and stones, and for the believers there are gardens where rivers flow. Among the food for the residents of heaven will be fruits, although resembling what they have on earth will not be the same. The occupants of heaven will have everlasting life with their spouses.

Allah presents us with examples and similitudes; the believers know they are with the truth. The disbelievers ask what the examples mean. Allah causes the rebels to go even further astray. The ones who break their covenants or spread corruption are the losers. Why would you deny God? He gave you life and will cause you to die before bringing you to life again. You will return to Him.

Verses 30 — 39 The story of Adam

Stories are mentioned multiple times in the Qur'an. However, anytime there is a repetition there is always a different point to the story. The story of Adam (AS) is mentioned in many places in the Qur'an.

In these verses Allah is telling us about the creation of Adam (AS).

The story of Prophet Adam (AS) in Surah Baqarah comes up because Adam AS is where revelation began in the first place. He was the first human and the first prophet and the first human to receive communication from Allah.

The incident of Prophet Adam (AS) inculcates within it the narrative of the whole human race. The first verse in this lesson discusses the way Adam received knowledge from Allah. In the next verse we learn about the angels saying, they do not possess any knowledge except that which is taught to them by Allah.

"I know what you don't know." "He taught Adam all the names." The angels said "we have no knowledge except that which you taught us." Allah says to the angels "didn't I tell you I know the unseen of the heavens and the earth…" So in the story of Adam, what's mentioned over and over is a knowledge from Allah.

When Allah told the angels He was putting humankind on earth, they asked why He would put those who cause bloodshed and damage there. They pointed out that they (the angels) only celebrate His praises and glorify His name. Allah answered that He knew things that they did not know.

Adam (AS) was taught the names of all things but when Allah showed the angels they could not tell Him the names of anything.

Allah then asked the angels to bow down before Adam (AS). They all bowed respectfully except for the disobedient Iblis (Satan) who was arrogant.

Adam was told to live in Paradise with his wife. They could eat freely and abundantly but ordered not to approach, or eat, from a certain tree. Satan tempted them to disobey, and they were expelled from Paradise. Allah said He would send them all down to earth where they would live for a certain amount of time and some would be enemies to the other. He then spoke with Adam and taught him how to repent. Allah accepted his repentance and told Adam (AS) that although they were expelled, guidance would come, and those that accepted the guidance would have no reason to fear or grieve. But those who continued to disbelieve even after the messengers had come would abide eternally in the Fire.

Lessons to be learnt from the Story of Adam (AS)

1. We are in war with the Satan. He is our enemy!

2. Satan works by making tricks on us. Just look at the choice of words he used to deceive Adam and Hawwa. He wouldn't say directly to disobey Allah. He used the name of Allah to swear, he promised that the tree is of eternity and immortality (human's

weakness). Satan knows our weakness, what more after thousands of years of experience and he will work around it.

3. Satan makes bad things look good and good things look bad.

4. We must quickly ask for forgiveness (repent) when we have sinned for Allah loves that and Allah is Al Ghafur and Arrahim. Allah is merciful. We must never forget to repent.

5. The difference between Prophet Adam. a.s. and Satan being asked to leave heaven is that Prophet Adam (AS) was sincerely sorry for what he had done and asked for forgiveness whereas Satan was still arrogant and in fact blamed Allah for him being astray.

6. Let us be the one who always ask for Allah's forgiveness and not that like Satan who refuse and remain arrogant.

Verses 40 – 52 Remember God's favours

These verses are speaking directly to the Jews in Medina who rejected the Prophet, and in our times to the Jews everywhere.

It is so evident here that Prophet Muhammed SAW is the true prophet. How else can an unlettered prophet knows the Tawrah if it wasn't sent down direct from Allah?

Allah *subhanahu wa ta'ala* is reminding the Children of Israel (the Jews) that He did favour them, but they were ungrateful. From among the favours that Allah (Exalted be He) has bestowed upon the children of Israel are the following:

1. The selection of messengers from among them.

2. The revelation of the holy books.

3. Saving them from the agonies of Firun and his people.

4. Enabling them to gain power on earth.

5. Causing springs of water to gush forth out of stone.

6. Feeding them with Al-Manna and quails.

So Allah Almighty ordered the children of Israel to remember what He has bestowed upon their grand fathers and not to forget His favours.

"And fear Me and Me alone" means,

"Fear the torment that I might exert on you, just as I did with your fathers, like the mutation, etc." This Ayah contains encouragement, followed by warning. Allah first called the Children of Israel, using encouragement, then He warned them, so that they might return to the Truth, follow the Messenger peace be upon him, heed the Qur'an's prohibitions and commands and believe in its content. Surely, Allah guides whom He wills to the straight path.

Allah said next,

"And believe in what I have sent down, confirming that which is with you (the Tawrah and the Injil)" meaning, the Qur'an that Allah sent down to Muhammad peace be upon him, the unlettered Arab Prophet, as bringer of glad tidings, a warner and a light. The Qur'an contains the Truth from Allah and affirms what was revealed beforehand in the Tawrah and the Injil (the Gospel).

Allah is telling the Jews to believe in the Qur'an as it confirms their own scriptures, the Tawrah. They are further advised to establish prayers, pay the prescribed alms and bow down with others that bow down.

Verses 53 – 62 Prophet Musa on the other side of the Red Sea

Here again the Unbelieving Jews in Medina and all times are addressed.

In these verses Prophet Muhammed SAW is told to tell the story of the Bani Israel to the Jews. The Jews had altered the authentic revelations given to Prophet Musa (AS). Only a true prophet will have details of the Tawrah in its original form as its from divine revelation.

This is the summary of the verses:

When the Bani Israel reached the other side of the Red Sea, it was scorching hot. Allah bestowed them with many favours.

Allah sent clouds for shades.

Prophet Musa also prayed to Allah to send food for them as everyone was hungry. Allah answered his prayers and sent special food called mannaa and quails from the sky. Indeed, Allah is great and merciful and can do all things.

Even so the Bani Israel were not happy and kept complaining to Prophet Musa. They wanted onion and lentils like they had in Egypt. The prophet scolded them and told that they should be thanking Allah rather than complaining.

They were then commanded to help the oppressed people in Palestine. They refused. They felt that they had just come out of oppression and were not willing to enter another place of oppression.

So, their punishment came from Allah.

The Bani Israel's Days of Wandering began.

Everyday was the same. They were walking aimlessly, with no destination in mind. Eventually they reached Mount Sinai.

There, Allah commanded Prophet Musa to fast for 30 days. At the end of the 30 days he had to fast an extra ten days.

After the fast was completed, Prophet Musa was ready to once again communicate with Allah.

So now forty days had passed since Prophet Musa left the Bani Israel. The Israelites were becoming restless. Among them was an evil man name Samiri. He began to lead the people astray. He told them that the prophet will not return, and they need another God. He asked everyone to give him all their gold jewelry they brought from Egypt. He dug a hole in the ground and built a big fire, threw all the gold ornaments in, and then like a magician scattered some sand over it. He fashioned a golden calf from the melted gold. It was a hollow calf and made sounds when the wind passes through it.

Prophet Haroon was helpless as he watched the Bani Israel practicing idolatry. The true believers distant themselves from this idol worshipping.

Whilst on the top of the mountains Allah gave Prophet Musa the ten Commandments in two tablets. These are the rules that the Bani Israel must follow.

When the prophet retuned to the people, he was furious, and his heart was filled with shame. The Idol worshippers were singing and dancing around their "living God", the golden cow Samiri made.

He tugged his brother, Prophet Haroon's beard, and questioned why he let this happened. But the prophet understood that his brother was helpless as they would have killed him if he had intervened.

Prophet Musa punished Samiri by sending him into exile to live the rest of his life. The Prophet took 70 elders from the Bani Israel to Mount Sinai to repent to Allah.

They stood back whilst Prophet Musa went up to speak to Allah. When he returned to the elders, instead of finding them in repentance they demanded to see Allah and only then they will follow him.

Allah showed his might and power and caused the ground to shake and the Bani Israel were struck by a bolt of lightning that killed all of them.

Prophet Musa became very scared because these seventy elders were the best of people and now, they were all dead. He was fearful of facing the Bani Israel with such news.

Prophet Musa prayed to Allah and they were all brought back to life.

They returned to the people and Prophet Musa informed them about the Ten Commandments that he had received from Allah.

Verses 62 — 74 Broken covenants including the sacrifice of the cow

After Allah described the condition - and punishment - of those who defy His commands, fall into His prohibitions and transgress set limits by committing prohibited acts, He stated that the earlier nations who were righteous and obedient received the rewards for their good deeds. This shall be the case, until the Day of Judgment. Therefore, whoever follows the unlettered Messenger and Prophet shall acquire eternal happiness and shall neither fear from what will happen in the future nor become sad for what has been lost in the past.

Verses 65 and 66

65. And indeed you knew those amongst you who transgressed in the matter of the Sabbath (i.e. Saturday). We said to them: "Be you monkeys, despised and rejected."

66. So We made this punishment an example for those in front of it and those behind it, and a lesson for Al-Muttaqin (the pious).

The Bani Israel were being very deceitful by failing to avoid honouring the Sabbath day. They were not allowed to work on this day. So they tried to be smart by placing nets, ropes and artificial pools of water for the purpose of fishing before the Sabbath. When the fish came in abundance on Saturday as usual, they were caught in the ropes and nets for the rest of Saturday. During the night, the Jews collected the fish after the Sabbath ended. When they did that, Allah changed them from humans into monkeys. (M.A.S. Abdel Haleem says in his notes in his Oxford University Press translation (2004) that this is a figure of speech). This story is explained in detail in Surat Al-A`raf, (7:163)

The Story of the Cow

From verses 67 to 74, we have the story of the cow. Here again, this story is told to the Jews to point out the arrogance of their forefathers. They have to complicate a simple request. So, here the story goes.

A very wealthy childless man was murdered. His nephew who stood to inherit his uncle's wealth accused a poor man of the crime, who of course denied it. So they took the matter to Prophet Musa (AS).

Prophet Musa (AS) prayed to Allah swt. seeking his help in this matter.

Allah inspired the prophet to tell them to slaughter a cow, and this will lead them to the killer.

The Bani Israel couldn't believe that it would be as simple as that, so they started posing ridiculous questions at Prophet Musa (AS):

"Are you making fun of us"?

"Are you taking us in mockery and jest"?

"What possible connection can there be between a man who was killed and sacrificing a cow"?

They thought that the decision of Allah swt did not correspond with their concern. Prophet Musa responded:

"Allah swt forbid that I should be among the foolish!" They wanted Allah swt to be more specific

The Prophet clarified,

"It should be a handsome yellow cow."

They once again asked Prophet Musa for more information. "Because all cows look the same to them".

"Call on your Lord for us," they said, "that He might inform us what kind she should be."

"Neither old nor young says God, but of age in between," answered Moses. "So do as you are bid."

"Call on your Lord," they said, "to tell us the colour of the cow."

"God says," answered Moses, "a fawn coloured cow, rich yellow, well pleasing to the eye."

"Call on your Lord," they said, "to name its variety, as cows are all alike to us. If God wills we shall be guided aright."

And Moses said: "He says it's a cow unyoked, nor worn out by ploughing or watering the fields, one in good shape with no mark or blemish."

"Now have you brought us the truth," they said; **[2:67-71]**

So the Bani Israel set out to find such a cow.

They came to a field and there was a young man with a cow which seemed to match the prophet's description.

So they approach the young boy. He had just lost his father and the cow was his only inheritance. He lived a humble life with his poor mum. He was a very dutiful son.

"Will you sell your cow to us"? they asked him.

The youth told them that he will have to consult with his mother. They all accompanied him to his house.

"We will offer you three gold coins for your cow", one of them proposed.

"Oh, no, no, no. My cow is worth a lot more than three gold coins", she replied. They went on increasing their offer and the mother kept on refusing. Finally, they urged the son to speak to his mother to be reasonable. He told them:

"I will not sell the cow without my mother's approval, even if you offered me its skin filled with gold!"

On hearing this, his mother smiled and said: "Let that be the price: its skin filled with gold."

They realised that no other cow would do; they had to have it at any price. They agreed to buy the cow and paid the price.

They brought the cow to the prophet.

They slaughter the cow and took a chunk of the animal and touched the dead man with it.

Then a miracle happened!!! The corpse came back to life.

Despite this sign, Allah tells us that the heart of the Bani Israel became harder than rocks. The following verse went on to say there are some rocks from which rivers burst forth, others that split open with water, and there are some that fall from fear of Allah.

Verses 75 – 93 Revelation rejected

Some of the habitants of Medina had recently embraced Islam. They had acquired knowledge about Prophethood, Heavenly Scriptures, Angels, the After-life, Divine Law and so on from their Jewish neighbours as they had prophets before. They had also heard that another Prophet was about to appear, and that his followers would prevail over the rest of the world.

It would have been expected now that this prophet has come, they would readily accept the religion of Islam.

So Allah revealed the following verse:

75. *Can ye (o ye men of Faith) entertain the hope that they will believe in you?- Seeing that a party of them heard the Word of Allah, and perverted it knowingly after they understood it.*

Allah *subhanahu wa ta'ala is* asking the believers if they expect that the Jews will accept Islam, when they are the ones who modified their own Book.

76. *Behold! when they meet the men of Faith, they say: "We believe": But when they meet each other in private, they say: "Shall you tell them what Allah hath revealed to you, that they may engage you in argument about it before your Lord?"- Do ye not understand (their aim)?*

The above verse gives us their classification as "Hypocrites".

And when those Jews met other Jews, they said: Our pretence to believe in him (Prophet Muhammed) has removed his harm from us, and our **apparent** belief has helped us to remain secure from him and his companions as they are certain that we are on their side.

After learning their secrets, we inform their enemies so that they may attack at an opportune time when they are defenceless.

Thus, Allah informed His Prophet about their wrong beliefs and bad character: These people deny that you are Muhammad in front despite seeing your miracles and hearing your clear arguments.

79. Woe, then, to those who write out the Scriptures with their own hands and then, in order to make a trifling gain, claim: "This is from Allah." Woe to them for what their hands have written and woe to them for what they thus earn.

This verse relates to the rabbis about what they did to the Torah, and Allah swt is making it clear to the prophet by revealing this verse.

They are not only misinterpreting their own scriptures, they are also interjecting stories from their national history, superstitious ideas, philosophical doctrines and legal rules. The result was that the Divine and the human became inextricably mixed. They claimed, nevertheless, that the entire thing was divine!

These people in their arrogance believe that the Fire will not touch them except for a few days. Allah reprimand them by saying that they have no evidence of such matter.

Then Allah described the end for both the believers and the unbelievers, and gave the description of the people who will reside in the hell and heaven:

Whoever earns evil and is surrounded by his sin will abide in the Fire, forever.

On the other hand, those who believe and do good deeds will be in Paradise, forever.

Allah commanded the Children of Israel to worship none but He (Allah), and to be good to parents and family, and to orphans and the destitute; to speak mildly and kindly, and to establish the prayer, and pay the obligatory charity. All but a few turned away and broke the covenant.

And there was yet another covenant, to not shed blood amongst one another or to drive one another from their homes. They acknowledged it at the time but now their progenies are engaging in persecution and aggression, breaking the covenants made with God.

Then the question is asked:

Do they believe in some parts of the revelation but not all parts? What punishment do they deserve, disgrace in this world and severe punishment on the Day of Judgement? They trade this life for the Hereafter, so their punishment will not be lightened.

We gave Moses the Tawrah and then sent Jesus with clear signs and supported him with Jibraeel, the Holy Spirit. Allah asks the Jews, why did you call some of the prophets imposters and kill others? Their hearts are sealed. Allah has cursed them for their disbelief. A Book (Qur'an) has come confirming the revelations before it, but they reject it. They sell their souls for a small price. A humiliating torment awaits them.

When they are told to believe in Allah's revelations, they say we believe in what was revealed to us but not in what came after it, even though it confirms their own scriptures. If they truly believed in their own scriptures, why did they kill their prophets? They are then reminded of their forefathers worshipping of the calf.

Verses 94 — 110 Faithlessness

The Messenger of Allah is commanded to tell the Jews that if Heaven is exclusively theirs, they must strive for death in order to get rid of their disasters and miseries of this world. It is only in this situation that they would attain eternal happiness which they falsely think belongs to them alone. However, these are people who live for the life in this world with their greed and will never long for death. Such longing is coming from their heart and not their tongue.

The Jews not only reviled the Prophet (peace be on him) and his followers but also Allah's chosen angel, Gabriel (Jibrael) because he had brought the Qur'an from Allah, and the Qur'an on the whole confirms the Torah and highlights their innovations.

The Jew consider Jibrael (Gabriel) as an enemy and the angel of punishment, annoyance, displeasure, indignation, and execution; while Mikaeel (Michael) was not, and if Michael would have been the one who came down to the Prophet, then they would believe in him. *So, Allah (s.w.t.) sent down this verse:*

97. Say: Whoever is an enemy to Gabriel-for he brings down the (revelation) to thy heart by Allah's will, a confirmation of what went before, and guidance and glad tidings for those who believe,-

Thus, the Qur'an attests to the rightfulness of all the heavenly Books such as the Torah, the Injil, Psalms of David, the scrolls of Abraham, and what *Allah* had sent to other prophets (as).

Let's look at verses 102 and 103

This verse is used in Rukayah to expel the shaitan and also for protection.

Before the revelation of the Qur'an, the devils used to ascend to heaven and eavesdrop on the conversations of the angels about what will occur on the earth regarding death, other incidents, or unseen matters.

They would convey this news to the soothsayers, and the soothsayers would in turn convey the news to the people. The people would believe what the soothsayers told them as being true. When the soothsayers trusted the devils, the devils started to lie to them and added other words to the true news that they heard, to the extent of adding seventy false words to each true word. The people recorded these words in some books. Soon after, the Children of Israel said that the Jinns know matters of the Unseen.

When Suleiman (Solomon) *'alayhi salaam* was sent as a prophet, he collected these books in a box and buried it under his throne; any devil that dared getting near the box was burned. Suleiman *'alayhi salaam* said, **"I will not hear of anyone who says that the devils know the Unseen, but I will cut off his head."** When Suleiman *'alayhi salaam* died and the scholars who knew the truth about him perished, there came another generation. To them, the devil materialized in the shape of a human and said to some of the Children of Israel, "Should I lead you to a treasure that you will never be able to use up?" They said, "Yes!" He said, "Dig under this throne," and he went with them and showed them Prophet Suleiman's throne. They said to him, "Come closer." He said, "No. I will wait for you here, and if you do not find the treasure then kill me." They dug and found the buried books, and Satan said to them, "Suleiman only controlled the humans, devils and birds with this magic." Thereafter, the news that Suleiman *'alayhi salaam* was a sorcerer spread among the people, and the Children of Israel adopted these books. When Muhammad *salAllahu 'alayhi wa sallam* came, they disputed with him relying on these books, hence Allah *subhanahu wa ta'ala* defended Suleiman in his grave by saying:

"It was not Suleiman (Solomon) who disbelieved, but the devils disbelieved."

The Story of Harut and Marut — the Two Angels sent as a Trial

There was a time when black magic had grown popular in the world, particularly in Babylon. Seeing its astonishing efficacy, ignorant people began to confuse its effects with the miracles of the prophets, and to suppose that the two were identical in nature. Some even looked upon magicians as being holy men, and worthy of being obeyed; still others actually started learning and practicing black magic as if it were a good deed bearing a divine sanction.

Harut and Marut are two angels who came down to Babylon. They explained the basic principles of magic, its different forms and the specific formulas, and then dissuaded the people from involving in these activities or with the magicians.

All sorts of people started coming to the angels seeking information about the nature and the specific formulas magic in case their ignorance should lead them into error. In order to provide the correct teaching on this subject and to protect the people from error, the angels were scrupulous enough to make it a point to warn them of possible dangers in giving them the information. They insisted on making it quite clear that in allowing them to provide this kind of information to the people, Allah *subhanahu wa ta'ala* intended to put His servants through a trial. He would see who uses this knowledge for protecting his *emaan* (faith) by recognizing evil and avoiding it, and who falls into misguidance by adopting evil that he has come to recognize as evil – a choice which can easily lead one to *Kufr* (disbelief).

The angels repeatedly advised to seek this dangerous information only with a good intent and to remain steadfast in this good intent, and not to misuse the knowledge to earn perpetual damnation.

Lets now look at verses 109 to 110

109. Quite a number of the People of the Book wish they could Turn you (people) back to infidelity after ye have believed, from selfish envy, after the Truth hath become Manifest unto them: But forgive and overlook, Till Allah accomplish His purpose; for Allah Hath power over all things.

110. And be steadfast in prayer and regular in charity: And whatever good ye send forth for your souls before you, ye shall find it with Allah. for Allah sees Well all that ye do.

These verses are exposing the Jews again as being hypocrites. They pretended to be well-wishers of the Muslim. But their intentions were evil.

Allah reveals these *ayahs to* warn the Muslims against their intentions, which are motivated, not by sincerity and friendship, but by envy. The *ayahs* also asks the Muslims not to give way to their justifiable anger at such misconduct, but to forgive the Jews and wait till Allah *subhanahu wa ta'ala* sends a new commandment with regard to such matters. For the time being, the Muslims were encouraged to perform their prayers perfectly, pay their Zakah [obligatory charity], and preserve the practice of these righteous deeds.

SO WHAT LESSONS CAN WE LEARN FROM THIS

We learn that we should not blindly follow people or be influenced by what they say. We should be judicious and ascertain the truth on our own.

We should ask Allah *subhanahu wa ta'ala* **for courage to follow the right path.**

We also learn the reason that why people stop others from doing something. "…out of envy from their own selves," they are jealous.

Allah *subhanahu wa ta'ala* responded, **"But forgive and overlook, till Allah brings His command."**

Verses 111 – 121 Religious prejudices

111. And they say: "None shall enter Paradise unless he be a Jew or a Christian." Those are their (vain) desires. Say: "Produce your proof if ye are truthful."

112. Nay,-whoever submits His whole self to Allah and is a doer of good,- He will get his reward with his Lord; on such shall be no fear, nor shall they grieve.

113. The Jews say: "The Christians have naught (to stand) upon; and the Christians say: "The Jews have naught (To stand) upon." Yet they (Profess to) study the (same) Book. Like unto their word is what those say who know not; but Allah will judge between them in their quarrel on the Day of Judgment.

114. And who is more unjust than he who forbids that in places for the worship of Allah, Allah's name should be celebrated?-whose zeal is (in fact) to ruin them? It was not fitting that such should themselves enter them except in fear. For them there is nothing but disgrace in this world, and in the world to come, an exceeding torment.

115. To Allah belong the east and the West: Whithersoever ye turn, there is the presence of Allah. For Allah is all-Pervading, all-Knowing.

116. They say: "(Allah) hath begotten a son" :Glory be to Him.-Nay, to Him belongs all that is in the heavens and on earth: everything renders worship to Him.

117. To Him is due the primal origin of the heavens and the earth: When He decreeth a matter, He saith to it: "Be," and it is.

118. Say those without knowledge: "Why speaketh not Allah unto us? or why cometh not unto us a Sign?" So said the people before them words of similar import. Their hearts are alike. We have indeed made clear the Signs unto any people who hold firmly to Faith (in their hearts).

119. Verily We have sent thee in truth as a bearer of glad tidings and a warner: But of thee no question shall be asked of the Companions of the Blazing Fire.

120. Never will the Jews or the Christians be satisfied with thee unless thou follow their form of religion. Say: "The Guidance of Allah,-that is the (only) Guidance." Wert thou to follow their desires after the knowledge which hath reached thee, then wouldst thou find neither Protector nor helper against Allah.

121. Those to whom We have sent the Book study it as it should be studied: They are the ones that believe therein: Those who reject faith therein,- the loss is their own.

The Jews and the Christians were hostile not only to the Muslims, but also to each other. Each of the two groups claimed that it had the exclusive right to go to the Paradise. The Jews read the Tawrah, while the Christians read the Injeel (Gospel). In their blindness and arrogance, they fail to see that the two books confirm each other. Each group assert that the other religion was baseless. This gave an excuse to the *mushrikeen* (polytheists) who, despite their ignorance, began to say the same of both the religions.

The Qur'an dismisses these pretensions and ask them to produce their proof.

The Jews had previously made similar claims which were refuted by Allah *subhanahu wa ta'ala*.

For example, they said: **"We are the children of Allah and His loved ones."** (Al- Ma'idah 5:18)

Previously they had claimed that the Fire would not touch them for more than a few days, after which they would be put in Paradise. Allah *subhanahu wa ta'ala* rebuked this claim, and He said about this being baseless.

Allah *subhanahu wa ta'ala* instructs the Prophet *salAllahu 'alayhi wa sallam* to ask them evidence. But of course they cannot produce any evidence.

LESSONS:

We learn the requirement of proof or evidence for basing our opinions. We cannot say anything (especially when it pertains to religion) unless it is supported by a valid proof such as an ayah from the Qur'an, a Prophetic tradition or a saying of the Companions radhi Allahu 'anhum.

There are two kinds of followers of religion: those who follow it on the basis of knowledge and those who follow it in veneration. The latter group might have no knowledge of the religion and their only association is reverence for the Prophet salAllahu 'alayhi wa sallam and his Companions. Following Deen without knowledge is dangerous, as there is a fear of falling into innovations and Shirk [associating partners with Allah].

Ayah **112** lays down the general principle in this respect. The essence of religion whether it be Islam, Christianity or Judaism lies in two things: (1) obedience to Allah *subhanahu wa ta'ala* in one's belief as well as in one's actions and (2) submission to the Divine commands in all sincerity.

It should be noted that it is not enough to have a sincere intention to obey Allah *subhanahu wa ta'ala* and then to invent aspects of worship. We cannot invent our ways of worship.

We learn there are two conditions for a deed to be accepted: one, it must be performed for the sake of Allah *subhanahu wa ta'ala* alone (if one does a good deed to gather praises from the people, then his deed will be rejected), and two, it must conform to the Shar'iah. When the deed is sincere, but does not conform to the Shar'iah, then it will not be accepted.

Allah *subhanahu wa ta'ala* says whoever submits to Him sincerely and does good deeds then he will find his reward with his Lord. Such a person has guaranteed rewards and safety from what they fear and grieve about what they abandoned in the past. They will have no fear on the Day of Judgment or grief about their imminent death. It has been recorded in the Qur'an and *ahadeeth* that when a righteous person dies (and he is a believers), the angels that descend at the time of death are kind and merciful to him and give him the glad tidings of Paradise. May Allah *subhanahu wa ta'ala* make us of those who will receive good tidings, ameen.

The Arguments between the Jews and Christians

In *ayah* 113, Allah *subhanahu wa ta'ala* says, **"The Jews said that the Christians follow nothing (i.e. are not on the right religion); and the Christians said that the Jews follow nothing (i.e. are not on the right religion); though they both recite the Scripture."**

Muhammad bin Ishaq reported that Ibn 'Abbas *radhiAllahu 'anhu* said, "When a delegation of Christians from Najran came to the Messenger of Allah *salAllahu 'alayhi wa sallam*, the Jewish rabbis came and began arguing with them before the Messenger of Allah. Rafi' bin Huraymilah said, 'You do not follow anything,' and he reiterated his disbelief in Jesus and the Injeel (Gospel). Then a Christian man from Najran's delegation said to the Jews, 'Rather, you do not follow anything,' and he reiterated his rejection of Musa's [Moses] prophethood and his disbelief in the Torah. So, Allah *subhanahu wa ta'ala* revealed this *ayah*:

113. The Jews say: "The Christians have naught (to stand) upon; and the Christians say: "The Jews have naught (To stand) upon." Yet they (Profess to) study the (same) Book. Like unto their word is what those say who know not; but Allah will judge between them in their quarrel on the Day of Judgment.

Ibn Katheer writes that Allah *subhanahu wa ta'ala* made it clear that each party read the affirmation of what they claimed to reject in their Book. Consequently, the Jews disbelieve in Jesus, even though they have the Tawrah in which Allah *subhanahu wa ta'ala* took their Covenant by the tongue of Moses to believe in Jesus. Also, the Gospel contains Jesus' assertion that Moses' prophethood and the Tawrah came from Allah *subhanahu wa ta'ala*. Yet, each party disbelieved in what the other party had.

Allah *subhanahu wa ta'ala* says that He will decide on the Day of Judgment who is on the right religion and who has gone astray.

These *verses* provide a warning to the Muslims as well. Merely, being born in a Muslim family or embracing Islam does not mean you have got your confirmed ticket to the Paradise. Sincere belief in and submission to Allah *subhanahu wa ta'ala,* and righteous deeds that conform to the teachings of the Prophet Muhammad *salAllahu 'alayhi wa sallam* are mandatory.

The Unjust Ones

The most unjust are those who prevent the mention of God's name and try to destroy the mosques. They will have disgrace in this world and punishment in the Hereafter. Both the east and the west belong to God so no matter where you turn you will find His Face. They say that God has a son! Exalted is He above all they falsely attribute to Him. Everything belongs to Him, He only has to say "Be," and it is. They ask why God does not speak to them, but there are clear signs for those who have faith. Prophet Muhammad was sent with the truth to convey the message, and he is not responsible for the inhabitants of the Fire.

The Jews and Christians will never be satisfied until you follow them, but if you turn from the truth you will lose. Those who disbelieve are losers, but some who follow the previous scriptures recognize the truth.

On the day of Treaty of Hudaybiyyah the polytheists of Mecca did not allow the

Allah of Messenger the into enter to city of Makkah. Allah then revealed verse 114 of Surah Baqarah:

114. And who is more unjust than he who forbids that in places for the worship of Allah, Allah's name should be celebrated?-whose zeal is (in fact) to ruin them? It was not fitting that such should themselves enter them except in fear. For them there is nothing but disgrace in this world, and in the world to come, an exceeding torment.

No one before has ever prevented people from entering the House of Allah. One would even see the killer of his father and brother, but would not prevent him (from entering the House of Allah).)

The treaty of Ḥudaybiyyah was very important and is one of the most significant events to take place in Islamic history.

The Muslims yearned to see the Ka'bah and perform ṭawāf around it. They would say: "When will Allāh swt will give us that day when we will see the blessed place of the remembrance of Allāh that our father Prophet Ibrahim has built?

Seeing this longing of his Companions, the prophet set off with 1,400 Muslims towards Makkah.

The prophet knew that the Quraysh would not let the Muslims perform 'umrah and would block their path; he therefore decided to take the road less travelled by people and reached a place called Ḥudaybiyyah. Ḥudaybiyyah is about one day's journey on foot from Makkah.

The Muslims set up camp there and the Quraysh were ready to fight, however, the Muslims were in the state of iḥrām, when one cannot even kill a fly. Considering the situation, the Messenger of Allāh swt decided that it would be best to reach an agreement with the Quraysh rather than fight them. He therefore sent Sayyidunā 'Uthmān al-Ghanī I to Makkah to propose a peace treaty.

The Quraysh did not listen to what Sayyidunā 'Uthmān al-Ghanī had to say. However, because he was honoured and respected greatly by the Quraysh, they told him that they would allow him to perform both the ṭawāf of the Ka'bah but they will not allow the messenger of Allah to enter. Of course, Sayyidunā 'Uthmān al-Ghanī was repulsed by this suggestion and declined that offer.

The conversation between Sayyidunā 'Uthmān al-Ghanī and the Quraysh became heated, and he was prevented from leaving Makkah for awhile.

In the meantime, a rumour spread in Ḥudaybiyyah that 'Uthmān al-Ghanī was killed.

Upon hearing about this, the Messenger of Allāh swt announced that if this was the case, it would be necessary for the Muslims to avenge the martyrdom of Sayyidunā 'Uthmān al-Ghanī I. The Prophet SAW then sat under an acacia tree and addressed his Companions:

"O my Companions, promise me that you will be supportive and loyal to me until your last breaths."

All of the Companions gave their allegiance.

This pledge is known as Bay'at al-Riḍwān, which has been mentioned in the Qur'ān: Indeed Allāh swt was pleased with the believers when they were swearing allegiance to you under the tree. After this pledge, news reached the Muslims that Sayyidunā 'Uthmān al-Ghanī I was alive and well. However, the Quraysh became worried and afraid upon hearing that the companions had sworn an oath at the hands of the Messenger of Allāh SWT. They therefore sent Suhayl ibn ʿAmr as an ambassador to reach an agreement with the Messenger of Allāh SWT.

It was then the Treaty of Ḥudaybiyyah was drafted.

FACING THE QIBLAH (DIRECTION OF THE PRAYER)

This ruling brought comfort to the Messenger of Allah and his Companions, who were driven out of Makkah and had to depart from the area of Al-Masjid Al-Haram. In Makkah, the Messenger of Allah used to pray in the direction of Bayt Al-Maqdis, while the Ka`bah was between him and the Qiblah. When the Messenger migrated to Al-Madinah, he faced Bayt Al-Maqdis for sixteen or seventeen months, and then Allah directed him to face Al-Ka`bah in prayer. This is why Allah said,

(And to Allah belong the east and the west, so wherever you turn (yourselves or your faces) there is the Face of Allah (and He is High above, over His Throne).

REFUTING THE CLAIM THAT ALLAH HAS BEGOTTEN A SON

ALLAH states here that He is the Supreme Master Whom there is no equal or rival, everything and everyone was created by Him, so how can he have a son from among them.

The Jews claimed that Prophet Uzayr [Ezra] *ʿalayhi salaam* was the son of God. They called themselves the Children of God. The Christians took Prophet ʿEesa [Jesus] *ʿalayhi salaam* as the son of God and God himself [see At-Tawbah 9: 30]. The polytheists of Makkah considered the angels to be the daughters of God [see An- Nahl 16: 57].

Allah *subhanahu wa ta'ala* is not like the humans that He will be in need of a son or children. He is above all such needs.

Clear Signs for People who Believe

The disbelievers used to deny the prophethood of Muhammad *salAllahu ʿalayhi wa sallam*;

Allah swt reveals the following two verses:

118. Say those without knowledge: "Why speaketh not Allah unto us? or why cometh not unto us a Sign?" So said the people before them words of similar import. Their hearts are alike. We have indeed made clear the Signs unto any people who hold firmly to Faith (in their hearts).

119. Verily We have sent thee in truth as a bearer of glad tidings and a warner: But of thee no question shall be asked of the Companions of the Blazing Fire.

They insisted that Allah *subhanahu wa ta'ala* Himself should speak to them, either directly as He speaks to the angels, or through the angels as He speaks to the prophets. And that He should Himself proclaim his commands to them to make the intervention of a new prophet unnecessary. If not that then He should at least announce that He sent Muhammad *salAllahu 'alayhi wa sallam* as a prophet, thus, making it easy for them to have faith in him and to follow his guidance. Should Allah *subhanahu wa ta'ala* choose not to accept this demand, they were ready with an alternative demand. They said then Allah *subhanahu wa ta'ala* should send them a sign or proof in confirmation of Muhammad's *salAllahu 'alayhi wa sallam* prophethood.

Verses 122 – 132 Ibrahim the leader

122. O Children of Israel! call to mind the special favour which I bestowed upon you, and that I preferred you to all others (for My Message).

123. Then guard yourselves against a-Day when one soul shall not avail another, nor shall compensation be accepted from her nor shall intercession profit her nor shall anyone be helped (from outside).

124. And remember that Abraham was tried by his Lord with certain commands, which he fulfilled: He said: "I will make thee an Imam to the Nations." He pleaded: "And also (Imams) from my offspring!" He answered: "But My Promise is not within the reach of evil-doers."

125. Remember We made the House a place of assembly for men and a place of safety; and take ye the station of Abraham as a place of prayer; and We covenanted with Abraham and Isma'il, that they should sanctify My House for those who compass it round, or use it as a retreat, or bow, or prostrate themselves (therein in prayer).

126. And remember Abraham said: "My Lord, make this a City of Peace, and feed its people with fruits,- such of them as believe in Allah and the Last Day." He said: "(Yea), and such as reject Faith,-for a while will I grant them their pleasure, but will soon drive them to the torment of Fire,- an evil destination (indeed)!"

127. And remember Abraham and Isma'il raised the foundations of the House (With this prayer): "Our Lord! Accept (this service) from us: For Thou art the All-Hearing, the All- knowing.

128. "Our Lord! make of us Muslims, bowing to Thy (Will), and of our progeny a people Muslim, bowing to Thy (will); and show us our place for the celebration of (due) rites; and turn unto us (in Mercy); for Thou art the Oft-Returning, Most Merciful.

129. "Our Lord! send amongst them an Messenger of their own, who shall rehearse Thy Signs to them and instruct them in scripture and wisdom, and sanctify them: For Thou art the Exalted in Might, the Wise."

130. And who turns away from the religion of Abraham but such as debase their souls with folly? Him We chose and rendered pure in this world: And he will be in the Hereafter in the ranks of the Righteous.

131. Behold! his Lord said to him: "Bow (thy will to Me):" He said: "I bow (my will) to the Lord and Cherisher of the Universe."

132. And this was the legacy that Abraham left to his sons, and so did Jacob; "Oh my sons! Allah hath chosen the Faith for you; then die not except in the Faith of Islam."

The true mission of Ibrahim (AS) was to invite people to obey Allah and hence practice a monotheistic religion. He was himself obedient to Allah and followed the teaching received from Him, and constantly strove to spread it and make all human beings live in obedience to it. It was because of this that he was appointed the religious leader and guide of the whole world. After his death, the task of guiding the world was entrusted to the branch which had issued from Isaac and Jacob, and which came to be known as the Children of Israel. It is in this branch that many Prophets were born. It was also this branch which was given the knowledge of the Straight Way, and was designated to lead all the nations of the world along that Way. It is of this favour that Allah again and again reminds these people.

At various places the Qur'an enumerates the severe tests through which Ibrahim

(AS) passed. It was only after these had been completed successfully that he was able to establish his worthiness to serve as the religious guide and leader of all mankind. From the moment when the truth was revealed to him till the moment he died, his life was a continuous tale of sacrifice and suffering for his cause. There is no conceivable object of man's love and attachment in the world which Ibrahim (AS) did not sacrifice for the sake of the truth.

Together, Ibrahim and Ismail continued to call people to worship Allah but there was no place solely for praying to Him. Ibrahim wished that there was a special place for people to find peace and focus completely on the praise of Allah. Soon after, <u>Allah ordered Ibrahim to build the Sacred House, or the Kaaba.</u>

Ibrahim and his son worked together to build the Kaaba. They chose a hillock, elevated from the surrounding land and began laying foundations. Ismail found the stones, while his father placed them to build high walls. When the construction was finished, the Angel Jibreel came down from heaven to teach Ibrahim the rituals of Hajj.

Using a large stone as a platform, Ibrahim addressed his people, urging them to obey Allah. This large stone can still be seen near the Kaaba. It is known as 'Makam Ibrahim'.

They asked Allah to make them and their descendants Muslims. Allah chose Ibrahim (AS) to be a Muslim and he left this legacy to his sons. And Jacob commanded his sons to devote themselves to Allah, warning them not to die unless they are Muslims.

Verses 133 — 145 The religion of Ibrahim (AS)

The Jews were not there when Jacob was dying. He asked his sons what they intended to worship after he was gone. The sons answered that they would worship his God and the God of Abraham, Isaac and Ishmael. That community passed away and they will be answerable for their own deeds. When they ask you to be Jews or Christians, answer that you follow the religion of Abraham. The believers should answer that they believe in Allah and what was sent down to all the prophets without making a distinction between them. Believers should say Allah ordained our religion.

Prophet Muhammad (Pbuh) is told to tell the disbelievers not dispute about Allah and that all will be held accountable to Him. Are you saying that Abraham and his descendants were Jews or Christians? Who would know better, you or God? Who could be more wicked than the person who hides the truth from the previous scriptures attesting to the nature of God's religion and the coming of Prophet Muhammad SAW. This nation has passed on and only they will be questioned about their deeds.

Verses 146 — 154 A new direction

Those who received the scriptures before you conceal their knowledge. The truth is from Allah, do not doubt it. Each religious community has its own direction (to face), so compete with each other to do good deeds, and Allah will bring you all together on the Day of Judgment. When you pray, turn towards the Holy Kabah in Mecca. Prophet Muhammad SAW recites the Qur'an and teaches you wisdom. Remember Me (God), be grateful and do not deny Me, and I will remember you. Seek help through patience and prayer because God is with the patient. Do not say that those who die in God's cause are dead; they are alive, but you are unable to perceive it.

Verses 155 - 167 Punishment for disbelief

Here Allah swt is telling us that we will be tested with fear, famine and losses, but we must bear it patiently to find blessings from Allah. The hills in the sacred mosque in Mecca, Safa and Marwah, are two of Allah's signs, so perform the major and minor pilgrimage rites – Haj and Umrah. Allah tells us to walk between the hills without fear.

Allah goes on to tell us about Monotheism – that there is only one God and there is no deity worthy of worship except Him.

Allah draws our attention to the creation of the universe with all its wonders is a sign for people who think. However, some still worship other than God. Allah tells us what will happen to these people on the day of judgement.

That is the day when the disbelievers will ask for one last chance, but Allah will show them the fruits of their actions and they will feel bitter regret.

Verses 168 — 177 Righteousness explained

Allah is addressing us, humankind and we are told to eat from what is lawful and good, and not to follow our enemy Satan.

Those who follow Satan will only lead to evil and immorality. When asked to follow the religion of Islam they refuse saying that they will follow what their forefathers did. This makes no sense. Calling to disbelievers is like calling to the deaf, dumb and blind. They are incapable of understanding. Eat from the good and lawful things provided and give thanks to Allah. Do not eat dead meat, blood, pig meat, or meat that has been slaughtered in the name of something other than Allah. If you are compelled to do so out of necessity it is not a sin.

Before the advent of the holy Prophet of Islam (p.b.u.h.), the Jewish scholars used to tell their people about that happy advent and described the signs of that promised Prophet for them from the Torah. But as soon as the Prophet of Islam (p.b.u.h.) was divinely appointed and announced his Call, they did not confess the prophethood of Muhammad (p.b.u.h.) for they thought they would lose their position, wealth, etc. It was why they neglected everything and concealed the Truth. Such people, by concealing the fact, might remain in their position receiving some presents and gifts for a length of time but this is a little price comparing to that great sin of theirs.

" Surely those who conceal any part of the Book which Allah has sent down (to them), and sell it for a small price-..." What they take and eat in this bargain is naught, indeed, but Fire.

This meaning is similar to the content of the verse where eating the wealth of orphans is likened to Fire, too, as if they ate Fire in their bellies.

(1) So, it says:

"...they shall eat naught but Fire into their bellies,..."

Turning your faces one way or the other is not righteousness. True righteousness is to believe in Allah, the Day of Judgment, the angels, the scriptures and the prophets. The righteous person gives in charity, despite the fact that they love their wealth and riches. And they give to relatives, orphans, the needy, the travellers, to the destitute, and to free those in bondage. They establish the prayer, pay the obligatory charity, keep their promises and are steadfast in misfortune. They are truthful and pious.

Verses 178 — 195 Rules for the believers

O you who believe. Fair retribution is prescribed in cases of murder; the murderer will be put to death and no one else in his place. If the culprit is pardoned be fair and pay what is due. This process is a mercy from Allah. Exceeding the limits will result in a painful punishment. When death approaches a bequest for parents and near relatives is incumbent upon you. If a bequest is changed it is a sin on the one who changes it, but there is no blame on one who suspects an error and brings about a settlement.

The Qur'an was revealed in Ramadan, a book to guide all of mankind. Fast in this month, but if you are ill or on a journey, then you should make up the lost days later. Allah does not want you to undergo hardship but He does want you to glorify Him and show gratefulness. Allah is near and responds to those who call Him. Therefore be obedient and put your trust in God.

It is permissible to have sexual relations with your lawful partners the night before fasting. You are like clothing for each other. Allah knows it was difficult for you to abstain so He made this easy for you. Eat and drink until the white thread of dawn becomes distinct from the black thread of night, then fast until nightfall. Do not have sexual relations during your retreat in the mosques in the last ten days of Ramadan.

Do not overstep the set limits.

Do not consume one another's wealth unjustly or in bribery. When they ask about the crescent moons say that they are to determine periods of time and the time of the pilgrimage. Do not enter houses from the back doors; enter through the proper doors and fear God.

190. "And fight in the cause of Allah (against) those who fight you, but be not aggressive, for surely Allah loves not the aggressors."

Occasion of Revelation

It is narrated by Ibn -'Abbas that this verse was revealed about the 'Peace of Hudaibiyah Treaty'. The incident was in this manner that the holy Prophet (S) started on a journey to go to Mecca for 'Umrah accompanied by 1400 people out of his companions.

When they arrived Hudaibiyah, (a land near Mecca), pagans hindered them from entering into Mecca and doing the sacred rites of the 'Umrah.

After a lot of debates and discussions, they agreed with the Prophet (S) that Muslims would go to Mecca the following year when the pagans would empty the City for them to circumambulate the Sacred House for three days.

The next year, when they set out towards Mecca, they were scared that the pagans might not be loyal to their promise and prohibit them, hence, consequently, a battle could come forth and the Prophet was not willing to fight in the forbidden month. So, this verse was sent down and permitted them to defend and fight against the enemies if they initiated fighting.

Verses 196 -203 The pilgrimage

Complete the pilgrimages, taking care to follow the rules set out by Allah. The major pilgrimage Hajj is in the well-known months and those who undertake it must refrain from sexual relations, obscene language, and fighting or bickering. Take provisions but piety is the best provision. There is no harm in doing business. When you return from Arafah stop at Muzdalifah and then depart from the place where all the people depart. And after fulfilling your duties remember Allah more passionately than how you used to remember your forefathers before Islam.

Those who only pray for good in this world will have no share in the Hereafter, but those who ask for good in this world and the next, and seek protection from the Fire will achieve what they have worked for. Remember Allah on the days after the sacrifice. You can leave after two days or stay on.

Verses 204 — 212 Embrace Islam and reject Satan

Among the people there are some hypocrites who impress you with their views and call upon Allah to witness what is in their hearts, but when away from you they cause mischief and destruction, and do not take heed when told to fear Allah. Hell will be their abode. On the other hand, there are some who give their lives to seek God's pleasure. Allah is affectionate to his devotees. O believers embrace Islam completely and do not follow in the footsteps of Satan, your avowed enemy. If you deviate after clear proofs have come to you, then know that no one can escape His punishment or defeat Him. Are they expecting God to come down? All matters will be presented to Him.

Ask the Jews about the clear cut signs they were given. Anyone who changes Allah's revelations should understand that Allah's retribution will be severe. The life of this world is charming to the disbelievers but those who fear God will rank above them on the Day of Judgement. Allah gives provision to whom He wills without limit.

Verses 213 – 242 Instructions for life

Humankind was one nation with one religion but soon people invented their own religions. Thus Allah sent prophets and messengers with good news, warnings, and guidance with which to settle disputes. They started more disputes because of rivalry. Allah guided those who believed; He guides whoever He wants.

Do you think you will enter Paradise without trials, even though you have seen what happened in the past? They were afflicted with poverty and hardship until even their messengers cried out to Allah. Allah's help is close at hand.

When they ask what they should spend in charity tell them to spend on their parents and relatives, and orphans, the needy and the traveller. Allah knows the good you do. Fighting is obligatory even though you might dislike it. Perhaps you dislike things that are good for you and love things that are bad for you. God knows, you do not.

Fighting in the sacred month and creating mischief in the sacred mosque are offences greater than killing. When they ask about charity tell them to spend whatever they can. Allah makes His revelations clear so that you may reflect. Deal justly with orphans. Do not marry a polytheistic person until they believe. A believing slave is better than a polytheist free person. The polytheists invite you to the Hellfire while God invites you to Paradise and forgiveness.

Do not have sexual intercourse when your wife is menstruating; wait until she becomes pure. Allah loves those who are clean. Have sexual intercourse in any way that is pleasing to you but do not contravene God's commandments. Take care of your future. Do not use God's name in oaths or as an excuse. You are not blamed for what is unintentional.

Those who renounce sexual relations with their wives have a limitation of four months. After that is reconciliation or divorce. Divorced women must wait three menstrual periods before remarrying and must not conceal a pregnancy. In that period they can reconcile. Wives have rights similar to their obligations but husbands have a degree of responsibility above them. There are only two revocable divorces. The third is irrevocable. Do not take back any gifts unless you make a mutual arrangement. After the third divorce a couple cannot marry unless the wife marries and is divorced by another man. During the divorce act with dignity and honour and do not cause trouble; Allah sees everything.

Breastfeeding is for two years if it is desirable; maintenance is the responsibility of the father. No person should suffer on account of their child. Treat wet nurses in an honourable manner. A widow must wait four months and ten days before she remarries. It is permissible to propose marriage during the waiting period, however, do not confirm the marriage until after. A divorce is acceptable before consummation or the dowry is settled but pay them something; and if the dowry is settled then pay half, unless the woman waives it, full is more honourable. Guard your regular prayers especially the middle one. If you fear danger, pray while walking or riding. Maintain widows for one year and do not expel them from their homes. Treat divorced women in a fair manner.

Verses 243 – 260 Stories

Reflect upon the people who fled their homes fearing death. God caused them to die and then return to life.

The above story is referencing the Bani Israel who were living in Palestine. It was a time when a plague attacked the village. People started getting sick and were dying.

Islam tells us that where there is a plague one must not leave that area and travelled to another. However, there was some disobedient people who did exactly that.

They travelled for many days and settled on top of a mountain. It was there that the angel of death appeared to them all and took all their lives.

They all died at once.

After a very long time a prophet called Prophet Hizqeel was passing and saw the skeletal remains of all these dead people.

He stood wondering over them, twisting his jaws and fingers. Allah then spoke to him and asked if he wanted Allah to show him how he can bring all these people back to life.

And of course he wanted to see this miracle.

A voice said to him:

"Call: 'O you bones, Allah commands you to gather up.'"

The bones began to fly one to the other until they became skeletons. Then Allah revealed to him to say;

"Call: 'O you bones, Allah commands you to put on flesh and blood and the clothes in which they had died.'"

And a voice said: "Allah commands you to call the bodies to rise."

And they rose. When they returned to life they said: "Blessed are You, O Lord, and all praises is Yours."

As the years went by the Israelites started committing a lot of sins and even became idolaters. The ruler of the land was an evil king who mistreated them and shed their blood. They fought many battles. They will take their Ark of the Covenant to these wars because they believe it brought them luck.

The Ark of the Covenant was a chest containing relics from the time of the people of Prophet Musa.

They won every war they went to.

But there came a time when they lost the war against the Philistines and their Ark was snatched from them.

When the king heard what happened he had a heart attack and died instantly.

The Israelites now were without a king and were like sheep without a shepherd. There was no one to rule the country.

It was then that Allah sent Prophet Shammil (Sammuel) to guide the people of Israel.

As time goes by, they requested that the prophet appoint a leader. They wanted to go into battle with the Philistines and win back their Ark.

One day Prophet Shammil prayed to Allah to help him choose a king. His prayers were answered, and Allah gave him signs of the chosen person.

There was a young boy name Talut (Saul), who lived far away with his father in a farm.

One day Talut and his servant were out looking for their missing donkeys. They spent several days looking without any luck. Eventually, Talut decided they must return home as his father will be worried about them and had no help in his farm.

However, his servant informed him that as Prophet Shammil lived in this land, they should pay him a visit and asked whether he can shed any light about the missing donkeys.

As they were walking they met a group of women who directed them to the prophet's house.

When they arrived, they saw a large gathering in front of the prophet's house. People had assembled there with the hope that they will be the chosen one for the leadership of Israel.

Talut greeted the prophet with much respect and asked about his missing donkeys. He was assured that all his donkeys were on their way home. Talut was relieved.

Prophet Shammil immediately recognised him as the chosen one. The prophet told Talut there and then.

He is going to be the King of Israel.

The crowds protested at the Prophet's choice. They objected because they felt that Talut was a descendant of Benyameen and was very lowly without much wealth.

But the Prophet had made his choice informing everyone that it was by the will of Allah.

Talut's role will be to unite the Bani Israel and protect them from their enemies.

He was worried about taking on such a big responsibility and felt he knew nothing about leadership and was just a poor shepherd.

But when Prophet Shammil told him that it was the will of Allah, he accepted the role.

King Talut started his duties.

An army was organised to fight the Philistines to win back their Ark of Covenant. He only chose those who were free from responsibilities. He did not accept anyone who was building homes, recently got married, and who was engaged in business affairs.

He prepared his army for battle by putting them through strenuous training. When he felt that they were ready he started putting his plan in action.

They travelled for many days and nights until they came to a stream. King Talut decided to test his army and commanded them only to drink amounts of water to quench their thirst.

Not all of them follow his instructions. Some were gulping down like there was no tomorrow. The king was very disappointed and dismissed the greedy ones from his army.

He needed his army to be sincere.

During the journey he put his army through many tests and by the time they reached the land of the Philistines, there were only 30 soldiers. But Talut was not scared.

He preferred an army of small believers rather than a large army of unreliable men", replied Nani Serena.

The Phillistines army was a large one. The soldiers were well equipped with their weapons. Their leader was a giantlike soldier name Jalut.

When faced with such a large army some of the Israelite soldiers ran away.

Rather than the whole army fighting, it was their custom to send one soldier from each side to fight with each other.

Hence, Talut asked his army who will volunteer for this position. No one did. They were all scared. He even offered his daughter's hand in marriage to the one who will fight Jalut. Yet no one volunteered.

Talut was very disappointed with his army.

But then a young boy from his army came forward and volunteered.

When the soldiers from the Philistines saw him, they roared with laughter. They thought it was a done deal that they will win the battle.

His name was Dawood (David) and was from Bethlehem. His brothers were all soldiers and he was the youngest. He came to the battlefield to update his family of the news on the warfront. His father told him that he must not take part in any fighting.

Talut admired young Dawood's courage but felt that he was no match for the strong giantlike Jalut.

Indeed, Dawood was a very courageous young man and related that he had killed a lion and a tiger all by himself.

Talut was impressed and asked the soldiers to dress young Dawood in battle clothes and to give him a sword.

Dawood refused because he had a plan, a very good plan. He collected pebbles and put it in his pouch and took his slingshot out.

By now Talut was getting very worried and wondered how a few pebbles and a slingshot can help their victory against this huge army.

As he approached Jalut the roar of laughter from the opponent army grew louder and louder.

With a sword in his hand, Jalut was ready to cut off Dawood's head.

Dawood said to him:

"I face you in the name of Allah whose laws you have mocked, l am not scared of you. I believe in Allah".

With that he took a pebble, put it in his slingshot and hit Talut's head with extreme force. Blood was gushing out from his forehead. Talut fell dead to the ground.

The shocked army upon seeing the death of their leader ran away.

THE ISRALITIES HAD WON THE WAR

Their sufferings from the Philistines had finally come to an end. Victory were theirs.

Dawood was a hero and the soldiers fetched him on their shoulders back to the palace.

King Talut kept his word and Dawood and his daughter were married. Despite becoming the most famous man in Israel he remained humble.

He went to the desert to glorify Allah. Dawood was chosen to be a prophet of Allah. And revealed the Zabour (Psalms) to him.

Allah also blessed Prophet Dawood to understand the language of the birds and animals.

Prophet Sulayman was his son.

THE STORY OF PROPHET UZAIRS (Ezra)

The miracle of this prophet is that Allah made him sleep for one hundred years.

One day prophet Uzair went for a walk with his donkey and took some food. After several hours of walking he came to a deserted place. It was a scorching hot day. He dismounted his donkey and sat under the shade of the Khaiba tree and ate his food.

He got up and saw the ruins of a city and the skeletal remains of people.

Upon looking at the bones, Prophet Uzairs wondered out of curiosity how would Allah bring these bones back to life.

Allah then sent the angel of death to take the prophet's life. And he lay dead for one hundred years.

And of course his donkey also died during this period.

Allah then brought the prophet and his donkey back to life. He now understood how Allah revives death when he realised, he himself had died for one hundred years.

He then travel back to his Home.

When he arrived, everything was so different. He didn't know anyone. He rode his donkey to his house and still didn't recognise anyone. A hundred years is a very long time. Some people would have been dead, others a hundred years older and many more people were born.

He keeps introducing himself as Uzairs but everyone shook their head and said they didn't know him.

He then saw an old crippled blind woman sitting in front of his house. When he enquired whether the house was his, the old woman agreed. Prophet Uzairs came to realise that this old woman was his maid,

He introduced himself and told her how he had died for a hundred years and Allah brought him back to life. Although she recognised his voice she couldn't be sure.

She told him to cure her blindness and immobility, as the Prophet Uzairs used to supplicate to Allah to perform miracles.

This the prophet did. And she could see and walk again.

She was overjoyed and told everyone that the stranger was indeed Prophet Uzairs. She took the prophet to meet his son who was 118 years old. There he saw many of his children and grandchildren. It was unbelievable what the maid was saying to them.

How could this young man be their father? They were very doubtful.

His son decided to settle the matter to see whether the stranger had a black mark between his shoulders. His father had one.

When the prophet showed him the mark, the entire family was overjoyed.

They told him that whilst he was away the evil king destroyed all the copies of the

Torah, their holy book given to prophet Musa.

The prophet remembered that he had buried a copy and went to retrieve it. Unfortunately, it was damaged and could not be read.

The prophet, surrounded by all of his children sat under a tree and because he had memorised the Torah, he began to write a new copy.

Prophet Uzairs died after 40 years.

The Importance of Qur'an Surah al-Baqarah Verses 285-286

The Messenger has believed in what has been revealed to him from his Lord, and the believers as well. All have believed in Allah, and His angels and His Books, and His Messengers. "We make no division between any of His Messengers," and they have said: "We have listened, and obeyed. Our Lord, Your pardon! And to You is the return."

Allah does not obligate anyone beyond his capacity. For him is what he has earned, and on him what he has incurred.

"Our Lord, do not hold us accountable, if we forget or make a mistake and, Our Lord, do not place on us a burden such as You have placed on those before us.

And our Lord, do not make us bear that for which we have no strength. And pardon us. And grant us forgiveness. And have mercy on us. You are our Lord. Help us, then, against the disbelieving people."

Commentary -

These are the last two verses of Surah al-Baqarah. Great merits have been attributed to these two verses in authentic ahadith. The Holy Prophet Sallallahu

'Alayhi Wasallam: Peace be upon him has said that one who recites these two verses during the night, they will be sufficient for him.

As narrated by Sayyidna Ibn 'Abbas Radhi-Allahu Anh: Allah be pleased with him, the Holy Prophet Sallallahu 'Alayhi Wasallam: Peace be upon him said that Allah Almighty has sent forth these two verses out of the treasures of Paradise and the 'Rahman had already written them by His own hand two thousand years earlier than the creation of all things and beings.

These verses were given directly to the prophet in his accession to heaven.

Chapter 3

Understanding Surah Imran

Surah Imran was revealed after the second Hijrah of Prophet Muhammad (PBUH) from Mecca to Medina.

So let us look at Medina (Yatrib) at the time of the Prophet's and his followers migration.

When the prophet and his followers (Muhajirun) migrated from Mecca to Medina, they co-existed with other groups of people in Medina. Among them were the Ansars and the Jewish tribes of Medina.

Who were the Ansars?

In The twelfth year of the Prophet Mission a delegation of 12 men came to Mecca during the Hajj season from Medina. They approached the Prophet at Al-Aqabah and reverted to Islam. The prophet then sent Musab Ibn Umayr with them to Yatrib (Medina) to teach the people there the religion of Islam. There, many reverted to Islam.

The Prophet created a religious co-existence between the different groups.

The first thing the Prophet did upon arriving in Medina was to construct a mosque that served as the first community centre for Muslims. It also served as the headquarters of leadership and a social centre. He afterwards established the bond of brotherhood between the Muhajirun [immigrants from Mecca] and Ansar [the helpers from Medina].

The next challenge that the Prophet (peace and blessings be upon him) faced was economic. Nearly half of the Muslim population back then was originally from Mecca. They had abandoned their wealth, trade, homes and property to escape the torture and oppression of the Quraysh in Mecca. It required great wisdom from the Prophet (peace and blessings be upon him) to address this issue. He decided to establish the bond of brotherhood between the Muhajirun and Ansar. The Ansar shared their trade and wealth with the Muhajirun. Ibn Is-haq narrated that when the Prophet (peace and blessings be upon him) established the bond of brotherhood among his Companions, the Muhajirun and Ansar he told them: "Be brothers for the sake of God."

The Covenant of Medina

The Prophet (peace and blessings be upon him) had to deal with a new reality in Medina. The city consisted of the tribes of Al-Aws and Al-Khazraj in addition to the Muslims, Jews,

Christians, disbelievers, as well as a group of hypocrites. The Muslims themselves were divided into the Muhajirun and Ansar. Despite this diversity, the Prophet (peace and blessings be upon him) sought to establish a strong state on the basis of peace, solidarity, and harmony.

Thus the historic Covenant of Medina came into being. It is rightly considered the first constitution in the world and outlined the characteristics of the new state. It established the first constitutional principles on basis of equality without regard to religion, race or gender. The covenant stipulated that all citizens are duty-bound to protect the city, share the common responsibility of caring for and aiding one another, and enjoin what is good for the nation and ward off whatever may threaten it. The covenant stressed that securing the borders of the city was a common responsibility shared by all citizens of the city and laid strict emphasis on the values of equality, mutual care and peaceful coexistence.

Who were the Primary Addressees of Surah Imran

Surah Baqakah addresses the Jews and Christians and this surah is an extension/continuation of this message. We have learnt from the previous surah how the Jews have tampered with their own scriptures, the Torah and the Gospel. They have been told here that Muhammad (Allah's peace be, upon him) taught the same right way of life that had been preached by their own Prophets; that it alone was the Right Way, the way of Allah; hence any deviation from it will be wrong even according to their own Scriptures.

Surah Imran is also addressed to the Muslims, the community which has been entrusted with the responsibility of reforming the world by spreading Islam.

The Muslims have also been warned to learn a lesson from the People of the Book and to refrain from treading into their footsteps.

Above all, they have been warned to guard against those weaknesses which had come to the surface in the Battle Uhud.

Let us briefly look at the Battle of Uhud.

THE BATTLE OF UHUD

The Battle of Uhud is seen in Islam as evidence that victory is never guaranteed, disobedience and greed cause defeat, and neither defeat nor victory are permanent. The Makkans were a society described as being rife with vices and oppression, perversion, and ignorance. Another lesson Muslims take from the Battle of Uhud is obedience to Prophet

Muhammad, for without it, as the archers in this battle experienced, there are negative consequences.

In A.D. 625, the Muslims of Madinah learned a difficult lesson during the Battle of Uhud. When attacked by an invading army from Makkah, it initially looked like the small group of defenders would win the battle. But at a key moment, some fighters disobeyed orders and left their posts out of greed and pride, ultimately causing the Muslim army a crushing defeat.

The Muslims Are Outnumbered

After the Muslims' migration from Makkah, the powerful Makkan tribes assumed that the small group of Muslims would be without protection or strength. Two years after the Hijrah (the migration of Prophet Muhammad and his followers from Makkah to Yathrib), the Makkan army attempted to eliminate the Muslims in the Battle of Badr. The Muslims showed that they could fight against the odds and defend Madinah from invasion. After that humiliating defeat, the Makkan army chose to come back in full force to wipe out the Muslims for good.

They set out from Makkah with an army of 3,000 fighters, led by Abu Sufyan. The Muslims gathered to defend Madinah from invasion with a small band of 700 fighters, led by Prophet Muhammad himself. The Makkan cavalry outnumbered the Muslim cavalry with a 50-to-1 ratio. The two mismatched armies met at the slopes of Mount Uhud, just outside the city of Madinah.

Defensive Position Taken at Mount Uhud

Using Madinah's natural geography as a tool, the Muslim defenders took up positions along the slopes of Mount Uhud. The mountain itself prevented the attacking army from penetrating from that direction. The Prophet Muhammad assigned about 50 archers to take up post on a nearby rocky hill to prevent the vulnerable Muslim army from attack at the rear. This strategic decision was meant to protect the Muslim army from being surrounded or encircled by the opposing cavalry.

The archers were under orders to never leave their positions under any circumstances unless ordered to do so.

The Shifting Battle

After a series of individual duels, the two armies engaged. The confidence of the Makkan army quickly began to dissolve as Muslim fighters worked their way through their lines. The Makkan army was pushed back, and all attempts to attack the flanks were thwarted by the Muslim archers on the hillside. Soon, Muslim victory appeared certain.

At that critical moment, many of the archers disobeyed orders and ran down the hill to claim the spoils of war. This left the Muslim army vulnerable and shifted the outcome of the battle.

The Retreat

As the Muslim archers abandoned their posts out of greed, the Makkan cavalry found their opening. They attacked the Muslims from the rear and cut off groups from one another. Some engaged in hand-to-hand combat, while others tried to retreat to Madinah. Rumors of the Prophet Muhammad's death caused confusion. The Muslims were overrun, and many were injured and killed.

The remaining Muslims retreated to the hills of Mount Uhud, which the Makkan cavalry could not ascend. The battle ended, and the Makkan army withdrew.

The Aftermath and Lessons Learned

Nearly 70 prominent early Muslims were killed in the Battle of Uhud, including Hamza bin Abdul-Mutallib and Musab ibn Umayr. They were buried on the battlefield, which is now marked as the graveyard of Uhud. The Prophet Muhammad was also injured in the fighting.

The Battle of Uhud taught the Muslims important lessons about greed, military discipline, and humility. After their previous success at the Battle of Badr, many had thought that victory was guaranteed and a sign of Allah's favor. A verse of the Qur'an was revealed soon after the battle that chastised the Muslims' disobedience and greed as the reason for defeat. Allah describes the battle as both a punishment and a test of their steadfastness.

"Allah did indeed fulfill His promise to you when you, with His permission, were about to annihilate your enemy, until you flinched and fell to disputing about the order, and disobeyed it after He brought you in sight [of the booty] which you covet. Among you are some that hanker after this world and some that desire the Hereafter. Then did He divert you from your foes in order to test you. But He forgave you, For Allah is full of grace to those who believe." (Qur'an 3:152)

However, the Makkan victory was not complete. They were not able to achieve their ultimate aim, which was to destroy the Muslims once and for all. Rather than feeling demoralized, the Muslims found inspiration in the Qur'an and reinforced their commitment. The two armies would meet again at the Battle of the Trench two years later.

Verses 1- 6 Qur'an confirms previous revelations

Like Surah Baqarah this surah also opens with the same combination of letters - Alif, Lam, Meem.

In verses 3 to 4 Allah tells us that:

It is He Who has sent down the Book (the Qur'an) to you with truth, confirming what came before it. And he sent down the Taurat and the Injil. Aforetime, as a guidance to mankind, And He sent down the criterion (of judgement between right and wrong -

[Ali Imran 3:3-4]

We learn here that just like the Qur'an is sent for a guidance for us, so were the Taurat (Torah) and the Injill (The gospel).

However, because the other two scriptures had been tampered with, Allah s.w.t. has sent down THE criterion - The Qur'an. The Qur'an is now the Book of Guidance calling people back to Allah s.w.t. Surah Al Imran addresses the people of the book (Taurat and Injil) - particularly the Christians.

The Primary audience of Surah Baqarah were the Jews.

Verses 7 — 13 — The Way People Reacted to the Qur'an

1. The hypocrites

So as for those in whose hearts there is a deviation, they follow that which is not entirely clear thereof, seeking Al-Fitnah (polytheism and trials), and seeking for its hidden meanings, but none knows its hidden meanings save Allah... [Al Imran 3:7]

How did the hypocrites react to the Revelation? These people, who have crookedness in their hearts, ignore the authority of the Qur'an but they focus on the ambiguous ayat and interpreted them wildly in numerous ways. They tried to manipulate the ayat with wrong interpretations to fit and conform with their lowly desires and to cause corruptions. If a person has this hypocrisy disease in his heart, he will continue to spin things out of control leading himself and others astray.

2. The believers

And those who are firmly grounded in knowledge say: "We believe in it; the whole of it (clear and unclear ayat) are from our Rabb." And none receive admonition except men of understanding. [Ali Imran 3:7]

The believers who are people of knowledge, on the other hand, say that they believe in the whole Qur'an - that all of the ayat are from their Rabb, so they do not reject a single ayah, nor try to look for loopholes to escape from any ruling or commandment of Allah.

Let us re-visit the last verse of Al-Baqarah describing the characteristics of the believers:

The Messenger believes in what has been sent down to him from his Rabb, and (so do) the believers. Each one believes in Allah, His Angels, His Books, and His Messengers.

(They say), "We make no distinction between one another of His Messengers" and they say, "We hear, and we obey. (We seek) Your Forgiveness, our Rabb, and to You is the return (of all)." [Al-Baqarah 2:286]

Verses 14 -20 An invitation

14. Fair in the eyes of men is the love of things they covet: Women and sons; Heaped-up hoards of gold and silver; horses branded (for blood and excellence); and (wealth of) cattle and well-tilled land. Such are the possessions of this world's life; but in nearness to Allah is the best of the goals (To return to).

Allah subhanahu wa ta'ala has beautified some things to test mankind. Shaytan beautifies our deeds, which is why many people fall in self-obsession as well as sins. Man keeps committing sins and Shaytan keeps assuring us that these are good.

The love for this temporary life is the source of all errors. Allah subhanahu wa ta'ala names some of the most desired things that have been made to look attractive so that people go after them enticed by their glamour having no concern for the life yet to come. The things named here are the centre of attraction for human beings, out of which, women (men in the case of women) come first and then the children. For whatever man goes about procuring is because of the needs of his family – wife and children. Then come other forms of wealth and possessions – gold, silver, cattle and tillage – means for earning a living and competing with others.

Why has man been made in a way that he is temperamentally attracted to these things? The answer is that Allah subhanahu wa ta'ala has done so in His ultimate wisdom. Let us consider: If man was not naturally inclined to and even enamoured with these things, where would the test be? No one would go to work, get married and have a family. People would be living in isolation having no concern with one another. But that is not how communities live and grow. Therefore, Allah subhanahu wa ta'ala placed the love of the delights of this world in our heart and in them lies our test. A person who has understood the reality of this life recognizes that these delights are only a test and a mean to fulfil one's needs lawfully. One works to sustain himself. He gets married and has children because it is natural to have a family and loved ones. His work and family do not make him negligent of the Hereafter; his eyes are set on the "real life" of the Hereafter. If man was free from trials and temptations, then Paradise would become meaningless for him.

Love for Wealth

The desire of wealth sometimes results out of arrogance, and the desire to dominate the weak and control the poor, and this conduct is prohibited. Sometimes, the "want" for more money is for the purpose of spending it on acts of worship, being kind to the family, the relatives, and spending on various acts of righteousness and obedience; this behavior is praised and encouraged in the religion. Love for Horses The desire to have horses can be one of three types. Sometimes, owners of horses collect them to be used in the cause of Allah subhanahu wa ta'ala, and when warranted, they use their horses in battle. This type of owner shall be rewarded for this good action. Another type collects horses to boast, and out of enmity to the people of Islam, and this type earns a burden for his behaviour. Another type collects horses to fulfill their needs and to collect their offspring, and they do not forget Allah's right due on their horses. This is why in this case, these horses provide a shield of sufficiency for their owner. Today, people do not commonly ride on horses but we have cars which are used for the same purpose. One can thank Allah subhanahu wa ta'ala and use his car to attend a Qur'an class or go to places to do da'wah work. The owner of this car will be rewarded because he is using his resource for a good cause. The second kind is where a person buys a new model and shows off to people. The car has no other purpose than to compete with one another and boast one's standing. This is a despicable act. If Allah subhanahu wa ta'ala has given you a blessing then thank Him do not brag about it or hurt the deprived. The third kind is where the person mainly uses his car for personal needs such as going to work, shopping, taking and collecting children from school, visiting relatives, etc. The car is a need for him due to long distances. He does not use it put others down.

Lessons:

We learn that having blessings and material wealth from Allah subhanahu wa ta'ala is not abhorrent, rather it is the use that makes it a Fitnah. If one thanks Allah subhanahu wa ta'ala and uses the blessings for his needs without neglecting his religious duties or putting others down then there is no issue. But when one becomes negligent of his obligation to the religion or uses the blessings to compete with others then it is wrong. He is committing a sin both by neglecting his duties and hurting others. Therefore, when we are blessed we should ask Allah subhanahu wa ta'ala to allow us to use our resources in ways that please Him. We should ask Him to let us indulge in the world so much that we forget the Hereafter. We should also not forget to thank Him lest the blessings are taken away. We seek Allah's protection from being negligent toward our religious duties, from looking down on other people and expending our energies in futile matters, ameen.

The follow on verses is telling the prophet to tells us:

The things mentioned above are good and according to human instincts, but there is better than it all. Say to those who love the world and to anyone, "Shall I tell you something better than this?" For those who guard (against evil), there will be with their Lord gardens beneath which rivers flow, wherein they will have no trouble watering them.

Verse 20

20. "So if they dispute with you, say: 'I have submitted myself (totally) to Allah, and whoever follows me'. And say to those who have been given the Book and the unlettered ones: 'Do you (also) submit yourselves?' So if they submit then indeed they are rightly guided, and if they turn back, then upon you is only the delivery of the message, and Allah is well-aware of the servants."

The Lord, addressing the Prophet (Pbuh), has commanded him that if the Jews and the Christians disputed with him upon the religion, he would tell them that he had surrendered his self wholly to *Allah,* the One, and had taken no partner for Him with himself and had not worshipped another god with Him.

If they refrain and do not accept Islam, there will be no harm on you, O' Muhammad! You are the Messenger of *Allah* and your duty is only to convey the Message and to attract their attention to the way of right and guidance.

Verses 21-30 Fear retribution

21. As to those who deny the Signs of Allah and in defiance of right, slay the prophets, and slay those who teach just dealing with mankind, announce to them a grievous penalty

Background of this Ayat

In Ruh al-Ma'ani, Iraqi Islamic scholar, Mahmoud Al-Alusi writes:

The Children of Israel slew 43 prophets in one go because they used to call the people to what differed from the desires and opinions of the Jewish leaders. Later, when 170 pious people stood up from among them to condemn these unjust killings, they were slain as well.

So Ayah 21 chastises the People of the Book for their transgression. Allah also talks about the punishment that awaits them.

There will be a painful punishment for those who deny the revelations, kill the Prophets without justification, and kill those who order justice; they will be beyond help. Those who were given one of the earlier revelations refuse to settle their disputes according to God's commandments; they think the fires will not burn them. They deceive themselves and will come to know the torment of the fire. Praise God, the One who has power and control over all things. He is the one who causes the night to change into the day and separates the living from the dead and gives provision to whomever He pleases.

Verse 28

28. Let not the believers Take for friends or helpers Unbelievers rather than believers: if any do that, in nothing will there be help from Allah. except by way of precaution, that ye may Guard yourselves from them. But Allah cautions you (To remember) Himself; for the final goal is to Allah.

The above verse taken out of context can be mis-understood.

Below is the explanation of the verse.

During the time the Qur'an was revealed Muslims were surrounded by polytheists and Jews who waged wars against Muslims. Their aim was to destroy the Muslims and to bring an end to Islam.

At this critical time, there were relatives and friends of the Muslims who were on the non-Muslims side. This verse is ordering them not to take disbelievers as their allies to prevent them from leaking information.

Here is the explanation of this from the Qur'an itself:

O you who have believed, take not those who have taken your religion in ridicule and amusement among the ones who were given the Scripture before you nor the disbelievers as allies. And fear Allah, if you should [truly] be believers. 5:57

O you who have believed, do not take My enemies and your enemies as allies, extending to them affection while they have disbelieved in what came to you of the truth, having driven out the Prophet and yourselves [only] because you believe in Allah, your Lord. 60:1

Allah does not forbid you from those who do not fight you because of religion and do not expel you from your homes - from being righteous toward them and acting justly toward them. Indeed, Allah loves those who act justly.

Verses 31 — 53 The people of Najran, The story of Maryam and Prophet Esa (PBUH). The story of Mary and Jesus

THE PEOPLE OF NAJRAN

From the previous verses we learnt that Prophet Muhammad (PBUH) had become the head of state of Medina. He drafted the Peace Treaty so everyone can exist and support each other. His next mission now was to call people to the religion of Islam.

Prophet Muhammed wrote to the heads of different countries to call people to the religion of Islam.

Among these was a letter **to Abu Harith, the Bishop of Najran.**

The text of the said letter runs as under:

In the name the Lord of Ibrahim, Ishaq and Ya'qub.

This is a letter from Muhammad, the Prophet and Messenger of Allah to the Bishop of Najran. I praise and glorify the Lord of Ibrahim, Ishaq and Ya'qub, and invite you all to worship Allah instead of worshipping His creatures, so that you may come out of the guardianship of the creatures of Allah and take place under the guardianship of Allah Himself.

And in case you do not accept my invitation you must (at least) pay Jizyah (tribute) to the Islamic Government (in lieu of which it will undertake the protection of your lives and property), failing which you are hereby warned of dangerous consequences

They visited the prophet in response to this invitation to find out more about the religion of Islam. The population then was under the rulership of three Christian chiefs.

The first of these, 'aqib, was the head of the community.

The second, **sayyid,** looked after the collective and political affairs of the people. The third, **usquf (bishop),** was their religious leader.

Usquf the religious leader was consulted, and he said that there could be a possibility that this religion could be true as their scriptures the Gospel advised the coming of another prophet from the lineage of Bani Ishmael.

When they entered the Masjid al-Nabawi, the Prophet Mohammad (S) looked at the precious stones, gold and silk clothes that they were wearing and turned away his face and did not pay any attention to them. After a while when no one noticed their pomp and show, they left the mosque and met Uthman b. 'Affan and 'Abd-ur- Rahman b. 'Awf outside and asked them as to why they were invited by the Muslims and then treated in this manner.

Uthman suggested that they consult Imam Ali (AS). When the delegation came to Imam Ali (AS) he told them that they were wearing dresses of silk and ornaments of gold which depicted their pride and that they should take them off and dress simply. Only then would the Prophet (S) allow them to visit him and entertain them. When they followed the instructions of Imam Ali (AS), they were allowed to visit the Prophet Mohammad (S) after the prayers of 'Asr and have discussions with him.

THE MEETING WITH THE PROPHET

The visit of the Christians of Narjan to the city of Medina in 631CE is perhaps the most important noted interfaith interaction between Christians and Prophet Muhammad.

The prophet spoke to them in his friendly manner. During the course of their meeting the Christians evening prayers were due.

Muhammad allowed them to pray in Nabawi mosque where the Muslims also prayed. This invitation was not only the first example of Christian-Muslim dialogue, but it was the first time that Christians prayed in a mosque. While Prophet Muhammad and the Najrans were not able to reach common ground on all theological issues, he nonetheless gave them a place to stay near his home, and even ordered Muslims to pitch their tent.

Muhammad opened the doors of his mosque to give Christians a safe space to pray is an unprecedented example of engaging with religious diversity.

The Christians asked the prophet:

"What do you say about Jesus? Since we are Christians, we would love to know your opinion so that we may be able to tell our people."

The Prophet said,

"I have nothing to say about him today. You have to stay until I can tell you what will be said to me about Jesus, peace be upon him."

Next morning, the Prophet received fresh Qur'anic revelations which stated:

'Jesus, in God's view, is the same as Adam, whom He had created from dust and said to him:

'Be', and he was there. This is the truth from your Lord. Be not, therefore, one of the doubters. Should anyone argue with you about him after what has been given to you of true knowledge, say to them: let us call in our children and your children, our women and your women, and ourselves and yourselves. Let us then all pray God and ask that God's curse overwhelm the liars." (3: 59-61)

When the Prophet told the Najran delegation the following day what information he had received about Jesus, they refused to accept it. The Prophet then offered them the challenge which was outlined in the Qur'anic verses quoted above. It was a serious challenge. It meant for the Najran people that they risked being cursed by a Prophet and a Messenger of God. Such a prospect was not to be trifled with.

The Event or Eid al-Mubahalah

In the Name of Allah, the Most Compassionate, the Most Merciful.

O Allah! Send your blessings to the chief of Your Messengers and the Last of Your Prophets, Muhammad (S), and his pure and cleansed progeny.

Should anyone argue with you concerning him, after the knowledge that has come to you, then say: 'Come! Let us call our sons and your sons, our women and your women, our souls and your souls, then let us pray earnestly and call down Allah's curse upon the liars'. (Qur'an 3:61)

When they finished, they came to the Prophet (S) and said: "To what do you call"? He (S) said: "To bear witness that there is no God but Allah and that I am the Messenger of Allah and that 'Isa (Jesus) (a.s) is created a slave (of Allah), and he used to eat, drink and relieve himself".

They said: "Then who was his father"?

The revelation was then revealed to the Messenger of Allah (S) saying:

"Say to them - what do you say about Adam, was he a created slave (of Allah), who would eat, drink, relieve himself and cohabit"? So the Prophet (S) asked them and they replied:

"Yes". He (S) asked them: "Then who was his father"? They could not answer, so Allah revealed:

Verily, the similitude of Jesus with Allah is as the similitude of Adam; Allah created him out of dust, then said to him, 'Be', and he became (3:59) till the verse:

And should anyone argue with you concerning him, after the knowledge that has come to you.... and call down Allah's curse upon the liars. (3:61)

The Messenger of Allah (S) said:

"So challenge me: if I am telling the truth the curse falls on you, and if I am a liar the curse falls on me". They said: "You have been just".

They agreed on a date for 'mubahala' (mutual imprecation). [The term 'Mubahala' is derived from its Arabic root 'bahlah' meaning 'curse'. Thus the act of al-Mubahala means that each of the two parties invokes the curse of Allah on the other if the latter is untruthful].

When they returned to the places they were staying in, their leaders al-Sayyid, al-'Aqib and al-Ahtam said:

"If he challenges us with his people, we accept the challenge for he is not a Prophet; but if he challenges us with his family in particular we don't challenge him, for he is not going to put forward his family unless he is truthful".

In the morning, they came to the Messenger of Allah (S), and there with him were the Commander of the Faithful (Ali a.s), Fatimah, al-Hasan and al-Husayn (a.s), so the Christians said:

"Who are those"? The people replied: "This is his cousin and successor and son-in-law, and this is his daughter Fatimah, and these are his grandsons, al-Hasan and al-Husayn".

When the Christian delegation saw a woman, two children and only one man with the Prophet (S), they were frightened and worried and said to the Messenger of Allah (S): "We will pay you whatever pleases you so excuse us from the 'mubahala'". Then the Messenger of Allah (S) made a settlement with them for them to pay the Jizya and they left.'

A Treaty Signed

The following morning the Prophet met with them as Shurahbil offered to accept the Prophet's judgment without question, giving him 24 hours to make it known to them, what meant that they wanted a peace treaty with the Prophet, and left it to him to specify the terms of that treaty, promising to accept those terms whatever they were. They relied on what they knew of his absolute fairness.

The following day they went to the prophet as he caused the terms of the peace agreement to for them. The agreed provisions were as follows:

"In the name of God, the Merciful, the Beneficent. This is what Muhammad, the Prophet and God's Messenger, has written down for the people of Najran when he has the authority over all their fruits, gold, silver, crops and slaves. He has benevolently left them all that in return for 2,000 hullas every year, 1,000 to be given in the month of Rajab and 1,000 in the month of Safar. Each hulla is equal to one ounce [a measure equal to 4 dirhams]. The Najran are also required to provide accommodation and expenses for my messengers, for up to 20 days. None of my messengers shall be kept in Najran more than one month. They are also required to give, as a loan, 30 shields, 30 horses and 30 camels, in case of any disorder and treachery in Yemen. If anything is lost of the shields, horses or camels they loan to my messenger, it will remain owing by my messenger until it is given back. Najran has the protection of God and the pledges of Muhammad, the Prophet, to protect their lives, faith, land, property, those who are absent and those who are present, and their clan and allies.

They need not change anything of their past customs. No right of theirs or their religion shall be altered. No bishop, monk or church guard shall be removed from his position.

Whatever they have is theirs, no matter how big or small. They are not held in suspicion and they shall suffer no vengeance killing. They are not required to be mobilized and no army shall trespass on their land. If any of them requests that any right of his should be given to him, justice shall be administered among them. He who takes usury on past loans is not under my protection. No person in Najran is answerable for an injustice committed by another."

When this was done, the Najran delegation returned home. And when so they left with an agreement with Prophet Muhammad that will protect their life, liberty, and pursuit of happiness.

A Prophet, By God!

On their way back they met with their Bishop and the notables of Najran who had travelled for one night in order to meet them. The Bishop was handed the written peace treaty. As he was reading it, with Abu 'Alqamah on his she camel alongside him, the camel slipped. In his anger, Bishr said: "Confound that man", meaning the Prophet.

The Bishop said to him:

"You have indeed confounded a Prophet sent by God." Bishr replied:

"Indeed! By God, I shall not get my camel to relax until I have gone to him."

He directed his she-camel towards Madinah and proceeded to go. He went straight to the prophet and declared his acceptance of Islam. He stayed in Madinah until he died as a martyr in one of the battles, fighting for the cause of Islam.

The delegation then went to the city of Najran, where they were received by the rest of the people. A short while later they visited a monk called Ibn Abi Shammar al- Zubaydi. He was at the top of his monastery. They gave him an account of the contacts between Najran and the Prophet, since the Prophet first wrote to the Bishop.

The monk was excited and wanted to get down. He carried a present and went to the Prophet. His present included a garment which continued to be worn by caliphs long after the Prophet had passed away. The monk stayed in Madinah for some time, listening to the Qur'anic revelations, learning about Islamic practices, obligations and punishments for crimes and sins.

However, he did not declare his acceptance of Islam. He sought the prophet's permission to go back home and said: "I have some business to do, and I shall come back, God willing." However, he did not go back to Madinah during the lifetime of the Prophet.

It is useful to mention here that should a follower of an earlier religion state that Muhammad is a Prophet or a Messenger of God, his statement does not bring him into the fold of Islam. This statement is not sufficient to make him a Muslim. What it signifies is that the man knows that Muhammad is a messenger of God, but to be a Muslim is much more than mere knowledge, even when it is expressed in words and statements. To be a Muslim is to believe in God's oneness and in the message of Muhammad and to accept that in practice, making obedience to God and to the prophet, in public and in private, one's way of life.

Later On …

The story of the Najran people is not complete unless a later episode is mentioned; when the Prophet sent his military commander, Khalid ibn al-Walid, to the tribe of Al-Harith ibn Ka'b, in Najran. The Prophet ordered Khalid to call on those people to accept Islam and to give them a period of three days to make up their minds.

When Khalid arrived there, he sent his emissaries all over the place, calling on the people to accept Islam. They did so without much hesitation.

Khalid stayed there for some time to teach the people how to live according to Islam. He wrote to the Prophet about the results of his mission, and the Prophet wrote back asking him to return to Madinah bringing a delegation from that tribe. When they arrived in Madinah and spoke to the Prophet, he asked them: "How did you achieve your victories in pre-Islamic days?"

They said: "We used to stick together and allow nothing to divide us into groups. We also never started any injustice."

The Prophet said: "You are telling the truth"

God in the Qur'an says, 'This nation of yours is one nation, and I am your God, so worship Me'. (Qur'an 21:92)

The Story of Maryam

"When a woman of 'Imran said, My Lord! Surely I vow to Thee what is in my womb, to be devoted (to thy service); accept therefore from me, surely Thou art the Hearing, the knowing." (3:35)

'Imran's wife Hanna was the maternal grandmother of 'Isa, may peace and blessings of Allah be upon him. Zakariyya's wife, Elizabeth and Hanna were sisters.

Yahya and Maryam were cousins.

Hanna was from the descendant of Prophet Dawood.

Hanna and her husband prayed to Allah for a child and one day their wish was granted. Hannah was pregnant.

She was overjoyed and promised to dedicate her child for the service of Allah. Just before the birth, tragedy struck. Hannah's husband Imran died.

When Maryam was born her mother was very surprised because she was expecting a son. She was now facing a difficult situation. She had vowed that her child will serve Allah but women were not allowed in the mosque without a guardian and her father had died.

Regarding Hanna, the mother of Maryam it is said,

"So when she brought forth, she said, My Lord! Surely I have brought forth a female- and Allah knows best what she brought forth- and the male is not like the female, and I have named it Maryam, and I command her and her offspring into Thy protection from the accused Satan." (3:36)

Imam Ja'far as-Sadiq said, female is not like male as (when female comes in menstrual period, she cannot stay in mosque. She must leave the place and go away) and the keeper of mosque should not go out.

The Qur'an says,

"So her Lord accepted her with a good acceptance and made her grow up a good growing." (3:36)

It is said that she was growing day by day in wisdom with others. When she completed nine years she became perfect in prayers and in fasting. She became more perfect than others in worship.

In continuation of Ayat 36, Allah gave Zakariyya the responsibility of taking care of her.

O Maryam! keep to obedience to your Lord and humble yourself, and bow down with those who bow. "This is of the announcements relating to the unseen which we reveal to you; and you were not with them, when they cast their pens (to decide) which of them should have Maryam in his charge and you were not with them when they contented one with another." (3:43-44)

To find out the right person they decided to cast their pens in flowing water. They all were twenty-nine. The pens were very heavy, made up of iron and were used for writing the verses of Torah. They cast their pens in flowing water one by one, Zakariyya also cast his pen. All the pens sank. Only the pen of Zakariyya floated. The Qur'an further states,

"Whenever Zakariyya entered the sanctuary to (see) her, he found with her food. He said, O Maryam! Whence comes this to you? She said, It is from Allah. Surely Allah gives to whom He pleases without measure." (3:37)

Whenever Zakariyya went to see Maryam he found fruits of different seasons with her, when he inquired about the fruits of summer in winter and winter fruits in summer Maryam replied, "It is from Allah. Surely Allah gives to whom he pleases without measures."

Inspired by this Zakariyya prayed to Allah to grant him a virtuous offspring.

Prophet Yahya

Allah in His infinite mercy removed the defect of Zakariya wife's barrenness so that she might become mother. She gave birth to Prophet Yahya. (peace be upon him) who was destined to be honourable, chaste, and a prophet from among the righteous. The Prophet Zakariya (peace be upon him) felt satisfied as his son grew up and became a symbol of piety. He was graced with wisdom, obedience and self- discipline. The Prophet Zakariya (peace be upon him) continued preaching the religion of Allah even in old age.

Prophet John or Yahya is also honoured as a prophet in Islam as Yaḥyā ibn Zakarīyā (Arabic), or "John, son of Zechariah". John was one of the prophets whom Prophet Muhammad (PBUH) met on the night of the Mi'raj, his ascension through the Seven Heavens. It is said that he met John and Jesus in the second heaven, where the prophet greeted his two 'brothers' before ascending with archangel Gabriel to the third heaven. John's story was also told to the Abyssinian king during the Muslim refugees' Migration to Abyssinia in the first Hijrah. According to the Qur'an, John was one on whom Allah sent peace on the day that he was born and the day that he died.

John is also honoured highly in Sufism as well as Islamic mysticism, primarily because of the Qur'an's description of John's chastity and kindness. Sufis have frequently applied commentaries on the passages on John in the Qur'an, primarily concerning the God-given gift of "Wisdom" which he acquired in youth as well as his parallels with Jesus. Although several phrases used to describe John and Jesus are virtually identical in the Qur'an, the manner in which they are expressed is different. The Prophet Yahya (peace be upon him) was the precursor of Prophet Isa (Jesus Christ). He was his cousin and contemporary as well. His fidelity to his mission as a preacher soon deprived him of his liberty and subsequently his life.

THE BIRTH OF PROPHET ISA (JESUS AS,)

The birth of Prophet Isa (AS) was no ordinary birth, it was a miracle! When Maryam (AS) found out that she was expecting a child, she was very confused:

"She said, 'My Lord, how will I have a child when no man has touched me?' [The angel] said, 'Such is Allah; He creates what He wills. When He decrees a matter, He only says to it, "Be," and it is.'" **(Surah Al-Imran:47)**

Thereafter, Maryam (AS) submitted to the will of Allah (SWT) and secluded herself from society and gave birth to Isa (AS) under a date palm tree, which served as her source of of nourishment during labour. When she returned to her people with a son in hand, she was denounced and condemned for supposedly falling in sin but that did not deter Maryam as her faith in Allah (SWT) was supreme and unrelenting. Allah (SWT) did not leave Maryam (AS) alone, He had granted several miracles to the child, Isa (AS), who was a miracle himself. As the people were doubting Maryam (AS), Isa (AS) spoke from his cradle, thereby astonishing the people and confirming Maryam's (AS) story.

Apart from talking since infancy Prophet Isa (AS) had other gifts from Allah (SWT);

"And [make him] a messenger to the Children of Israel, [who will say], 'Indeed I have come to you with a sign from your Lord in that I design for you from clay [that which is] like the form of a bird, then I breathe into it and it becomes a bird by permission of Allah. And I cure the blind and the leper, and I give life to the dead - by permission of Allah. And I inform you of what you eat and what you store in your houses. Indeed in that is a sign for you, if you are believers." **(Surah Al-Imran:49)**

Isa (AS) was a miracle from Allah (SWT) for the people of Israel.

VERSES 54 -69

Christians believe that Jesus died on the cross to take away the sins of the world. However, in the eyes of a Muslim, how could Jesus the prophet of God be defeated in such a humiliating way?

Muslims believe Jesus was, indeed, a prophet of God. Herein lies the dilemma. How could He then lose to men by dying the death of a criminal? Was God not able to protect His prophet?

The question that troubles Muslims is, why would God have allowed His prophet Jesus to die on the cross?

Of course, God did protect his prophet and Allah tells us about this in Surah Imran verses 54 to 69

Verses 54 to 69

PROPHET ISA (PBUH). The Jews did not acknowledge Jesus as the messenger of God.

The Jews do not regard Prophet (PBUH) as a messenger from God. They had tampered with the Torah for their own selfish greed, they have put verses in and took some out to satisfy their own situations.

Surah Imran and Surah Maryam tells that Prophet Isa informed the people of what they did. They live off the money of the oppressed. Most of the followers of Jesus as with Prophet Musa and Prophet Mohammed (peace be upon them all) were the poor people of society.,

RIBBA- Jesus expose the Jewish Rabbis in their Riba dealing.

Has anyone studied Shakespeare's the Merchant of Venice and the character Shylar in the Pound of flesh?

Shylar is the money Lender and Shakespeare took him to task. In the hadith of the prophet salli alyahi asalm Ribba is like the sucking of blood, in Shakespeare "it's the pound of flesh".

Hmmm!!! How many Shylar do we have today dressed in black suits sitting in a

Bank dishing out RIBA. I want you to further explore this.

And what does Jesus, son of Mary thinks about the money banker??

Let's look at what happened when he went into the temple:

He walked in and found the Jews engaging in the Ribba, but it not money lending but it was ripping off people. This is also RIBA, and he cursed them. He turned over their tables and he chased them out.

When Jesus restored the masjid into a place of worship without any ill doing the

Rabbis and the king of Rome decided he must die.

Allah prohibited Ribba in the Torah. The Jews changed the Torah. They re- wrote it. The Torah now says that you can lend money, but not to the Jews but to others. Basically don't rip your brother off others off.

Present day Torah state that it is:

IT IS HARAM FOR A JEW TO LEND MONEY WITH INTEREST TO ANOTHER JEW.

DOUBLE STANDARDS

Plotting to kill Jesus

Verses 54 and 55

54. And (the unbelievers) plotted and planned, and Allah too planned, and the best of planners is Allah.

55. Behold! Allah said: "O Jesus! I will take thee and raise thee to Myself and clear thee (of the falsehoods) of those who blaspheme; I will make those who follow thee superior to those who reject faith, to the Day of Resurrection: Then shall ye all return unto me, and I will judge between you of the matters wherein ye dispute.

They are now plotting with the Roman King to kill Jesus by crucifixion. They decided that Jesus should die on the cross.

Why did they choose this method because the Torah state that whosoever died by hanging/crucifixion, is a cursed one. The rational for them would be that if Jesus died on the cross then he would be the cursed on and couldn't be the messenger of God. Of course we all know that they are still waiting for the Messiah.

So when they thought it was Jesus that died on the cross they rejoiced because they are now convinced that he couldnot have been the Messiah. They see him now as the imposter who has the curse of the Lord upon him because he did not die on the cross.

He is dead and never rule the world from Jerusalem.

Jesus did not die on the cross Qur'an contends that Jesus did not die by crucifixion. Instead, it states in Surah 4:157 that 'they neither killed him nor crucified him, but so it was made to appear to them'.

Islam maintains that the Jews intended to crucify Jesus, and a historical crucifixion indeed happened, but Allah controverted the Jews by placing Jesus' visage on another person who, subsequently, took his place on the cross.

The Story

Prophet Isa was sitting in his house with his twelve disciples. He addressed them and said that one among them had betrayed him.

It was Judas who was the betrayer. He consulted with the head priest and asked what reward will be given to him if he delivered the Prophet to him.

He was promised thirty pieces of shekels. This was a lot of money in those days. When this question was asked, he was so ashamed that he left the room.

Prophet Isa asked for one of his disciples to take his place as the soldiers were coming to arrest him. He said that person will be his companion in paradise. He asked that question three times and the same young man volunteered.

Allah changed his appearance to look like Prophet Isa.

Allah then raised Prophet Isa from a window from the corner of his house and raised him to heaven.

The soldier arrived and took that young man instead and crucified him.

The disbelievers rejoiced. They believed that they had killed Prophet Isa, son of Maryam.

But the Prophet is very much alive today and living in the second heaven. Prophet Isa will return to earth before the Day of Judgement.

(From the Tasfeer of Ibn Kathir)

How Christians came to believe in the Holy Trinity

1.Baptism in the early Church, as discussed by Paul in his letters, was done only in the name of Jesus; and

2) The "Great Commission" was found in the first gospel written, that of Mark, bears no mention of Father, Son and/or Holy Ghost – see Mark 16:15.

The only other reference in the Bible to a Trinity can be found in the Epistle of 1 John 5:7. Biblical scholars of today, however, have admitted that the phrase:

"...there are three that bear record in heaven, the Father, the Word, and the Holy Ghost: and these three are one"

…is definitely a "later addition" to Biblical text, and it is not found in any of today's versions of the Bible.

It can, therefore, be seen that the concept of a Trinity of divine beings was not an idea put forth by Jesus or any other prophet of God. This doctrine, now subscribed to by Christians all over the world, is entirely man-made in origin.

While Paul of Tarsus, the man who could rightfully be considered the true founder of Christianity, did formulate many of its doctrines, that of the Trinity was not among them. He did, however, lay the groundwork for such when he put forth the idea of Jesus being a "divine Son". After all, a Son does need a Father, and what about a vehicle for God's revelations to man? In essence, Paul named the principal players, but it was the later Church people who put the matter together.

Muslims and the Holy Trinity

Muslims believe in one and only God which was worshiped by All prophets including Adam, Moses, Abraham, Noah Jesus, Muhammad (peace be upon them all). Islam is the continuation of the message by earlier prophet and prophet Muhammad (pbuh) was the last and final messenger in the chain of prophets.

All prophets preached nothing but pure monotheism. Muslims believe that **The Holy Trinity** is man made and this doctrine was accepted 325 year after prophet Jesus left the earth in the Council of Nicea.

The word Trinity does not exist in the bible but in Qur'an Almighty God says: "Surely, disbelievers are those who said: 'Allah is the third of the three (in a Trinity).' But there is no Ilaah (god) (none who has the right to be worshipped) but One Ilaah (God -Allah). And if they cease not from what they say, verily, a painful torment will befall on the disbelievers among them" [al-Maa'idah 5:73].

"The Messiah 'Esa (Jesus), son of Maryam (Mary), was (no more than) a Messenger of Allah and His Word, ("Be!" - and he was) which He bestowed on Maryam (Mary) and a spirit (Rooh) [] created by Him; so believe in Allah and His Messengers. Say not: 'Three (trinity)!' Cease! (it is) better for you. For Allah is (the only) One Ilaah (God), glory be to Him (Far Exalted is He) above having a son. To Him belongs all that is in the heavens and all that is in the earth. And Allah is All-Sufficient as a Disposer of affairs" [an-Nisa' 4:171].

Verses 70 — 80 Who is trustworthy?

(3:70) O People of the Book! Why do you reject the signs of Allah even though you yourselves witness them?

The People of the Book (Jews and Christians) know in their hearts that Muhammad was the very Prophet whose coming had been announced by the preceding Prophets.

(3:72) A party of the People of the Book said: 'Believe in the morning what has been revealed to those who believe, and then deny it in the evening that they may thus retract (from their faith).

This was one of the ploys adopted by some of the rabbis. They will send their people to embrace Islam publicly, only to renounce later. They will then announce that it was because of the faults they had found in Islam. They will then encourage the true believers to leave the religion of Islam.

Some amongst the People of the Book are trustworthy; others are not, because they do not think it is a sin to cheat someone not of their faith. Those who have the correct faith, fear God, and keep their promises, are loved by God. There are some who will sell out the truth for a small price, an agonising punishment awaits them. Others twist God's words into a lie. No Prophet would ever say "Worship me, instead of God". He would never suggest that angels or prophets be lords (gods) and he would never ask anyone to turn away from belief.

Verses 81 — 92 A reminder

[81-82] Remember, Allah made this Covenant with His Messengers: "Now that We have given you the Book and Wisdom, you are hereby bound to believe in and help a Messenger, who comes to you afterwards, confirming the teachings you already possess." After this, He asked, "Do you confirm this and take up the heavy responsibility of your Covenant with Me?" They said, "Yes, we confirm." Then Allah said, "Very well, bear witness to this and I also bear witness with you. Now whosoever breaks the Covenant after this, he shall be a transgressor."

Allah is addressing the people of the Book, reminding them that they are bound by the Covenant of their own Prophets to believe in and help Muhammad (Allah's peace be upon him) as his message confirm their own message.

The above implies that the people of the Book were breaking their covenant with Allah by rejecting Prophet Muhammad (God's peace be upon him) and opposing his mission; they were disregarding that covenant which their Prophets had made with Allah. Hence, they were perverted transgressors who had gone beyond the limits imposed by Allah.

[83-85]

83. Do they seek for other than the Religion of Allah. -while all creatures in the heavens and on earth have, willing or unwilling, bowed to His Will (Accepted Islam), and to Him shall they all be brought back.

84. Say: "We believe in Allah, and in what has been revealed to us and what was revealed to Abraham, Isma'il, Isaac, Jacob, and the Tribes, and in (the Books) given to Moses, Jesus, and the prophets, from their Lord: We make no distinction between one and another among them, and to Allah do we bow our will (in Islam)."

Allah is saying that we do not have different ways of treatment his Prophets: we accept each and everyone of them as all prophets come bearing the truth with the same message.

[86-87] How can it be that Allah would guide the people who adopted disbelief after they had acknowledged the Faith and after they themselves had borne witness that he was a true Prophet and after clear Signs had come to them?[73] For Allah does not guide the unjust people. The fitting recompense for their iniquity is that they are under the curse of Allah and of the angels and of all mankind.

Here, it has been reiterated here that the Jewish scholars, who lived in Arabia at the time of the Holy Prophet, had understood clearly and borne witness to it that Prophet Muhammad (Pbuh) was a true Prophet of God and that his teachings were the same as those of the former Prophets. Their opposition is based solely because he was not from the Bani Israel, but from Bani Ishmael.

The rest of the verses goes on to tell us that a religion other than Islam will not be accepted and will lead to the Hellfire. God will not guide those who reject belief after it has come to them. There will be no respite except if they repent and correct themselves. Those who disbelieved and died in that state will not be able to buy their way out of punishment even with enough gold to fill the whole earth. No one will gain the greatest reward until he gives charity from what he cherishes, and God knows what is given.

Verses 93- 101 God knows everything

[93-95] All these articles of food (which are lawful in the Muhammadan Law), were also lawful to the children of Israel except those which Israel had forbidden for himself before the Torah had been sent down. Say to them, "Bring the Torah and read out any passage from it (in support of your objection), if what you say be true. "-If even after this, some people persist in attributing to Allah false things of their own fabrication, they are, indeed, unjust people. Say, "What Allah has said is the very Truth; so follow exclusively the way of Abraham, and Abraham was not of those who associated other gods with Allah."

Verse 93 answers an objection. When the Jews could not find fault with the basic teachings of the Qur'an and of the Holy Prophet (Allah's peace be upon him), for there was absolutely no difference between these and the teachings of the previous Prophets, they began to raise legal objections. One of their objections was that the Holy Prophet had made lawful certain things which had been unlawful during the time of the previous Prophets.

If Israel refers to the children of Israel, then it would mean that before the revelation of the Torah, they themselves had made certain things unlawful because these had been unlawful by custom. But if it refers to Jacob (and that is more probable), then it means that he did not eat certain things because he did not like them or abstained from them on account of some illness, but his children began to believe these to be unlawful. The subsequent verse shows that the law in the Bible which declared the camel and the hare etc., to be unlawful was not in the Torah, but was later on inserted in it by the Jewish scholars.

In the follow on verses, the Jews are warned against making up lies about God and told to follow the religion of Abraham. Then they are reminded that the first House of God was at Mecca, The Kaaba. It is a blessed place and a sanctuary. Pilgrimage to the House of God is a duty for all those who are able to find their way there. God however does not need their pilgrimage; He is all Sufficient. The People of the Book are asked why they deny the revelations from God and try to stop others from following the correct path. God knows everything that they do. He (God) reminds the believers that many People of the Book are trying to turn them from belief back to disbelief. Think! God's revelations are being recited and the Messenger (Muhammad) lives amongst you, He says. Whoever clings to God will be shown the right path.

Verses 102 – 109 The best community

[102-103] *O Believers, fear Allah as He should be feared and see that you do not die save as true Muslims - Hold fast together to Allah's cord and let nothing divide you. Remember the favour of Allah upon you, when you were enemies to one another, then He united your hearts, and by His grace, you became like brothers, and you were on the brink of the abyss of Fire and He rescued you from it. Thus does Allah make His signs clear to you so that you may find the right path to true success by these.*

"Hold fast together to Allah's cord" implies that the Muslims should give the greatest importance to Allah's Way, and should make it the centre of all their interests, and exert their utmost to establish it and co-operate with one another for its service. When and if they let loose this cord and deviate from its basic principles, they would inevitably suffer from disunity and would be divided into sections and sub-sections, like the communities of the former Prophets. As a consequence of this, they would mat with disgrace both in this world and in the Next.

This refers to that horrible state of the Arabs from which they were rescued by Islam. Before Islam, the clans of the Arabs were divided into hostile waring camps. Human life had little value and people were killed without any pangs of conscience. The fire of enmity would have burnt to ashes all the Arabs, if blessed Islam had not rescued them from it.

And here in Medina there was a similar situation between the clans of Aus and Khazraj- who had been enemies for years. After embracing Islam they became brethren.

Verses 110 – 120 Misbehaviour

(3:110) You are now the best people brought forth for (the guidance and reform of) mankind.[88] You enjoin what is right and forbid what is wrong and believe in Allah. Had the People of the Book[89] believed it were better for them. Some of them are believers but most of them are transgressors.

It is interesting that the reason of being the best of nations for Muslims is the fulfilment of 'enjoining the right and forbidding the wrong' and' belief in Allah'. This shows that the improvement of human society, without belief in *Allah* and not being accompanied with invitation to the Truth and struggling against corruption, is impossible.

Then it points out that the benefits of a religion (Islam) which is so clear. Therefore, if the People of the Book (the Jews and the Christians) do believe, it is for their own benefit.

But, unfortunately, only a minority of them do whilst the majority of the People of the Book have disobeyed the command of *Allah*.

Verse 111- brings glad tidings for the Muslims. It is assuring them that under the shade of belief and unity they are insured. Therefore, they would not be afraid of the threats of the enemy, because the enemy is insignificant, and the victory is for the Muslims.

Verses 121 – 129 Victory is in the hands of God

These verses talk about the lessons from the early Muslims' battles at Badr and Uhud.

Details of the Battle of Uhud can be found in the beginning of this Surah.

Our beloved Prophet Muhammad (Pbuh) is reminded of how Allah intervened in the Battle of Uhud by strengthening the hearts of those who were wavering and how at the Battle of Badr He granted them victory over a large opposing force.

There are lessons to be learnt from these battles.

Victory is only from God. He forgives or He punishes according to His will.

Allah's help will come if we have faith, obedience, discipline, unity, and the spirit of acting in righteousness and justice. His Plan may be to bring sinners to repentance, and to teach us righteousness and wisdom through those who seem in our eyes to be rebellious or even defiant. There may be good in them that He sees and we do not – a humbling thought that must lead to our own self-examination and self-improvement.

Verses 130 – 145- Usury

130. "O' you who have Faith! Do not devour usury, doubling it over and over again, and be in awe of Allah; that you may be prosperous."

The verses on the prohibition of usury have been revealed gradually and in several stages. The first step of the prohibition of usury was a critical attack against the usury of the Jews.

This verse is for the prohibition of the usury doubling it over and over again, but, later, Islam gradually prohibited devouring even a penny of usury and introduced it as a fighting against *Allah*.

131. "And be in awe of the Fire which has been prepared for the disbelievers."

In this holy verse the ordinance of piety and purity is emphasised again.

From the word /Kafirin/ (disbelievers) mentioned in the verse, it is understood that, principally, usury does not fit with the nature of Faith. Therefore, the usurers have a share from the Fire which is prepared for the disbelievers.

132. "And obey Allah and the Messenger, that you may be shown Mercy."

The cause of the failure of Muslims in the Battle of 'Uhud was their disobedience from the command of the Prophet (Pbuh). He had told them not to leave the defensive region located between the vales of 'Uhud Mount, but the guardian group left that site and, in spite of the order, went to gather the spoils of war. Therefore, the enemy attacked the Muslims from the same site and defeated them.

133. "And hasten towards forgiveness from your Lord, and a Garden whose width is (as) the heavens and the earth, prepared for the pious ones."

Following to the former verses, which threatened the wrong doers to the punishment of Fire and encouraged the good doers to ask for forgiveness and receive eternal blessings in Heaven.

Summary of the other verses

Prophet Muhammad, may the mercy and blessings of God be upon him, was a Messenger and others like him passed through this world before him. God asks the believers if Prophet Muhammad were to die would they reject his message. Doing so would not harm God. No one dies without God's permission and he dies at a predetermined time. Those who work for the sake of this life only, will get what God decides for them and they will not have a share in the Hereafter. And those who work for the sake of the Hereafter, God will give them a share in the Hereafter, along with what He decides for them in this life.

Let us look at verse 145

And no person can ever die except by Allah's Leave and at an appointed term. And whoever desires a reward in (this) world, We shall give him of it; and whoever desires a reward in the Hereafter, We shall give him thereof. And We shall reward the grateful

There is a slight touch of irony in this. As applied to the archers at Uhud, who deserted their post for the sake of plunder, they might have got some plunder, but they put themselves and the whole of their army into jeopardy. For a little worldly gain, they nearly lost their souls. On the other hand, those who took the long view and fought with staunchness and discipline, their reward was swift and sure. If they died, they got the crown of martyrdom. If they lived, they were heroes honoured in this life and the next.

Verses 146 — 152 Remain steadfast

146. *"And how many a prophet there has been with whom were many Godly men fought; so they did not falter despite what afflicted them in the way of Allah, nor did they weaken, nor did they yield, and Allah loves the patient, (the steadfast)."*

Following the adventures of 'Uhud, this verse refers to the bravery, faith and perseverance of the strivers and followers of the former prophets. It encourages the Muslims to bravery, self-sacrifice and constancy while it scorns those who escaped from the battle of 'Uhud.

147. *"And their statement was nothing but that they said: ' Our Lord! Forgive us our sins and our prodigality in our affair and make our feet firm and help us against the disbelieving folk '."*

When facing with the enemy they entangled with difficulties as a result of some mistakes, or shortcomings they had. So, instead of leaving the battlefield, or yielding to the enemy, or arising the thought of apostasy or returning to infidelity in their mind, they turned to the glory of *Allah*.

148. *"So Allah gave them the reward of the world and the goodness of the reward of the Hereafter; and Allah loves the doers of good."*

With that kind of thought and practice, they would get their reward from *Allah* soon. Thus, *Allah,* too, gave them both the reward of this world, which was their victory and overcoming against the enemy, and the good reward of the Hereafter.

149. *"O' you who have Faith! If you obey those who disbelieve, they will turn you back to your (faithless) ancestors, so you will turn back losers."*

After the end of the Battle of 'Uhud the enemies of Islam, in the form of advice and sympathy, scattered the seed of discord among the Muslims, and made them distrustful unto Islam.

This verse warns the Muslims and awares them that they must avoid following the enemies, because, after paving the honourable spiritual development along the path of Islam, they will bring Muslims back to corruption and disbelief.

150. *"Nay! Allah is your Guardian and He is the best of the helpers."*

In this verse, the Qur'an emphasizes that *Allah* is the helper who will never be defeated. No power can match His Power. But other helpers may be involved with failure and be destroyed.

151. *"We shall cast terror into the hearts of those who disbelieve, for that they have associated with Allah for which He has sent down no authority, and their abode in the Fire; and how bad is the abode of the unjust!"*

In this verse, it points to the marvellous security of Muslims after the Battle of 'Uhud. It says:

"We shall cast terror into the hearts of those who disbelieve..."

That is, We do the same as you saw the example of it at the end of the Battle of 'Uhud. In the second sentence of the verse, the reason of casting fear into the hearts of the disbelievers is stated such:

"....for that they have associated with Allah for which He has sent down no authority,.."

Finally, at the end of the verse, it has pointed out to the end of these people. It indicates that such people have done injustice to themselves and to their society; that is why:

"…. and their abode is the Fire; and how bad is the abode of the unjust!"

Verses 160 – 168

Here we see that the topic of the Battle of Uhud is continuing. Below is the summary of the verses.

If God aids you none can overcome you, but if He forsakes you none can aid you. Therefore, the believers should put all of their trust in God. It is inconceivable that any Prophet would withhold the spoils of war from the faithful. Whoever deceives others will be accountable to God on the Day of Judgement.

A person seeking the pleasure of God does not behave like a person who has incurred the wrath of God. In the eyes of God, they are on two completely different levels. It was a great favour from God when Prophet Muhammad was made a Messenger to his people. He is among them reciting the Qur'an, purifying them and teaching them how to behave even though before this they were clearly astray.

What happened on the day of the battle (Uhud) was a test from God to see who the true believers were and who the hypocrites were. On that day the hypocrites were closer to disbelief when they spoke with their mouths what was not in their hearts. God knows what is concealed.

Verses 169 – 179

169) Think not of those slain in the way of Allah as dead.[120] Indeed they are living, and with their Lord they have their sustenance.

170) rejoicing in what Allah has bestowed upon them out of His bounty, jubilant that neither fear nor grief shall come upon the believers left behind in the world who have not yet joined them.

There is a Tradition from the Prophet (Pbuh) that he who leaves the world after having lived righteously is greeted with a life so felicitous that he never wishes to return to the world. The only exception to this is martyrs who wish to be sent back to the world so that they may once again attain martyrdom and thereby enjoy that unique joy, bliss and ecstasy which one experiences at the time of laying down one's life for God. (Ahmad b. Hanbal, Musnad, vol. III)

172) There were those who responded to the call of Allah and the Messenger after injury had smitten them for all those who do good and fear Allah there is a mighty reward.

The above verse is referencing events that took place after the battle of Uhud. One must understand that the Muslims neither won nor lose this battle.

On their return to Mecca, the polytheists were reflecting on their mistakes of having missed the opportunity to crush the power of our noble prophet (Pbuh). At one point they were even contemplating to launch another attack. They quickly dismissed the idea and continued their journey to Mecca.

The Prophet also realised that possibility and gathered the Muslims the day after the battle to pursue the unbelievers.

The Prophet, for his part, also realized that they might attack once again. On the second day of Uhud, therefore, he gathered the Muslims and urged them to pursue the unbelievers. Even though this was a highly critical moment, the true men of faith girded their loins and were prepared to lay down their lives at the behest of the Prophet. They accompanied him to Hamra' al-Asad, eight miles from Medina. The present verse refers to these dedicated men.

173) When people said to them: 'Behold, a host has gathered around you and you should fear them', it only increased their faith and they answered: 'Allah is Sufficient for us; and what an excellent Guardian He is!

175) It was Satan who suggested to you the fear of his allies. Do not fear them; fear Me, if you truly believe

These verses are refencing the ploy of Abu Sufyan. He sent an agent to Medina to inform Muslims that they are preparing for another war at Badr, and that their army would be a large and powerful one.

He wanted to discourage the Muslims from advancing towards Mecca, so that when the confrontation did not take place it would be blamed on the timidity of the Muslims.

When the Prophet (peace be on him) urged the Muslims to accompany him to Badr their initial response was not encouraging. The Prophet publicly announced that if no one would accompany him, he would go alone. In response, fifteen hundred soldiers accompanied him to Badr.

Abu Sufyan did have a large army, two thousand men. He changed his mind after travelling for two days and re treated.

However, The Prophet and his Companions stayed at Badr for eight days awaiting the threatened encounter. Of course, there was no battle. But the Muslims used their time to conduct business with a trade caravan which yielded them considerable profit. The Prophet and his army returned to Medina, having the assurance that the enemies were no where in sight.

176) Let not those who run towards disbelief grieve you; they shall not hurt Allah in the least. Allah will not provide for them any share in the Next Life. A mighty punishment awaits them.

177) Indeed those who have purchased unbelief in exchange for faith shall not hurt Allah in the least. Theirs shall be a painful chastisement.

178) Do not let the, unbelievers imagine that the respite We give them is good for them. We give them respite so that they may grow in wickedness. A humiliating chastisement lies in store for them.

179) Allah will not let the believers stay in the state they are:^{125} He will set the wicked apart from the good. Allah is not going to disclose to you what is hidden in the realm beyond the reach of perception,^{126} but He chooses from among His Messengers whom He wills (to intimate such knowledge). Believe, then, in Allah and in His Messengers; and if you believe and become God-fearing, yours will be a great reward.

SUMMARY OF THE ABOVE VERSES

Allah is telling the Prophet Muhammad not to grieve over those who turn back to disbelief. They will cause Allah no harm at all and they will find a terrible torment awaiting them in the Hereafter. Those who barter faith for disbelief will also face a fierce punishment. Some disbelievers are given more time on this earth but it is not a reward it is just a way to increase their burden of sins. Allah will separate the believers from the hypocrites but not by revealing the unseen. If you want to know about the unseen, know this, Allah chooses whomever he wants to be a Messenger, so believe in Allah and His Messenger and guard yourselves from evil.

Verses 196 -200

These verses are talking about the description of the believers. They are described as people who reflect on the creation of Allah, believe in the hereafter and also in his severe punishment. They are the ones who are successful.

In contrast there are those who have all worldly gains living the life of the world without taking heed of the hereafter. Allah describes their enjoyment as being brief, and indeed they are the losers.

Chapter 4

Surah An-Nisa
(The Women)

Surah Nisa is so named so because it mainly discusses issues and laws regarding women, marriage, inheritance, and Rights of women.

In order, to understand the surah we have to look at what was happening in Madina at the time this surah was revealed. Surah Nisa was revealed in Madina a few years after Surah Imran, which we did last week.

Now what was happening then.

Madina had become a state. Last week we talked about the Peace Treaty of Allegiance. By the way, this has been discussed in detail in my book Understanding Surah Baqarah. Surah Baqarah gives us information about all the laws and regulations and Peace treaties.

The themes of the Surah.

The underlying theme of Surah is the family life. Laws have been given for marriage and the status of women.

Orphans also have a central theme of this Surah as because of battles this issue was becoming intense as more and more families were becoming victims. Thus, laws and regulations have been laid down for the proper care of orphans and their inheritance.

The opening verse of Surah Nisa.

O humanity! Be mindful of your Lord Who created you from a single soul, and from it He created its mate,[1] and through both He spread countless men and women. And be mindful of Allah—in Whose Name you appeal to one another—and ˹honour˺ family ties. Surely Allah is ever Watchful over you.

So this verse sets the tone for the entire Surah.

The Qur'an advocates equality between all and says that the only good deeds may raise the status of one human over another.

No other religion is so explicit in this matter

Its telling us that we are literally one global family. We go back to the same couple. We are all Brothers and sisters in humanity. We are all from the same flesh and blood. In terms of humanness, all humanity is equal. Allah tells us we are all equal.

This is also re-forced in Chapter 49, Verse 13, in Qur'an

It reads, "O mankind we have created you from one male and female and made you into nations and the tribes that you may know one another. Surely the most honourable among you with Allah is the one who is the most righteous. Verily Allah is all-knowing all aware."

Prophet Muhammad (PBUH) stated in his farewell sermon,

"O people. Your Lord is one and your father is one. (Adam) An Arab has no superiority over non-Arab, nor a non-Arab has any superiority over Arab, also white has no superiority over black nor does black have any superiority over white, except by piety and righteousness. All humans are from Adam and Adam is from dust."

THE RIGHTS OF WOMEN

Basically, under the tribal law, in the times of jahaliyah, women had no rights, no legal status. They were not allowed to inherit. Only the males can. Women are considered property to be inherited or seized in tribal conflicts.

There were also homicidal abuse of women and girls, including instances of killing female infants if they were considered a liability. Daughters used to be buried alive.

So Surah Nisa was revealed to introduce new moral, cultural, social, economic and political laws and practices to replace the old ones of the pre-Islamic period.

I want us to look at Verse 34. This verse has certainly caused a lot of controversy because of the misunderstanding of its context. This mis understanding give rise to the notion that Islam condones domestic violence.

But before we come to this verse I want us to look at what Islam says about Domestic violence with special note on how this is reflected in the practices of our Prophet's life.

The Qur'an says the relationship is based on tranquillity, unconditional love, tenderness, protection, encouragement, peace, kindness, comfort, justice and mercy.

Prophet, Muhammad (PBUH), set direct examples of these ideals of a marital relationship in his personal life. When asked about a husband's responsibility towards his wife, the response was:

Give her food when you take food, clothe her when you clothe yourself, do not revile her face, and do not beat her.

The prophet further stressed the importance of kindness toward women in his farewell pilgrimage. He equated the violation of their marital rights to a breach of the couple's covenant with God.

Abusive behaviour towards a woman is also forbidden because it contradicts the objectives of Islamic jurisprudence – specifically the preservation of life and reason, and the Qur'anic injunctions of righteousness and kind treatment.

Domestic violence is addressed under the concept of harm in Islamic law.

Islam allows an abused wife to claim compensation under *ta'zir* (discretionary corporal punishment). The 19th-century Syrian jurist Ib Abidin said *ta'zir* is mandatory for a:

… man who beats his wife excessively and "breaks bone", "burns skin", or

"blackens" or "bruises her skin".

What about Verse 4:34?

But if Islam condemns all forms of violence against women, what about Verse 4:34 of the Qur'an?

Scholars say that this verse is relating to those women who are arrogant, and even physically violent to their husbands, and if a man strikes a woman is to use something like a miswak or a feather so there is no hurt experienced by the women.

THE RIGHTS OF THE ORPHANS

DEVOURING THE PROPERTIES OF ORPHANS

The above is considered to be one of the major sins in Islam. The Qur'an says,

"(As for) those who swallow the property of the orphans unjustly, surely they only swallow fire into their bellies and they shall enter burning fire." (Surah an-Nisā' 4:10)

It is mentioned in Tafsir al-Kabir that one who cheats an orphan of his property will be raised on the Day of Judgement in such a condition that the flames of fire will be protruding from his mouth, nose and ears. By looking at him people will recognize that he is the one who in his lifetime had usurped the property of the orphans. The last phrase, "They shall enter burning fire" indicates that one who deprives an orphan of his rightful property will be liable to be burnt in Hell-fire, even if he has not committed any other sin.

The Almighty Allah (S.w.T.) says,

"And give to the orphans their property, and do not substitute worthless (things) for (their) good (ones) and do not devour their property (as an addition) to your own property; this is surely a great sin." (Surah an-Nisā' 4:2)

The above verse gives clearcut instructions to those who are guardians and caretakers of the orphans, on how to fulfill their responsibility. They should spend the property in their trust in a correct manner for the benefit of the orphan and without stinginess. A caretaker should be very careful not to spend any of the orphan's money on himself. This is a very serious offence that will cause his entire Halāl wealth to become Harām. Under no circumstances should an orphan's valuable possessions be substituted with anything inferior. Finally, when the child reaches maturity, all his property should be returned to him with complete honesty.

In the same chapter of Surah an-Nisā', Allah (S.w.T.) says in verse number nine:

"And let them fear who, should they leave behind them weakly offsprings, would fear on their account, so let them be careful of (their duty to) Allah, and let them speak right words." (Surah an-Nisā' 4:9)

It is mentioned in Tafsir-al-Mizan that whoever betrays the trust of orphans and oppresses them, their children will suffer a similar fate. This is an amazing reality that is revealed by the Holy Qur'an. Similarly in other numerous verses, the Qur'an informs us that the returns of our deeds will be evident if not in this world but in the world of the hereafter as well.

It is our confirmed duty to wish for others as we wish for ourselves. A good or bad action directed towards others therefore implies that we wish the same for ourselves. So, by carrying out these actions, we, in effect have prayed for it for ourselves.

The marvellous functioning of our body is the result of the co-ordination between the various composite parts and organs. We as individuals are also composite members of a large body, which is our community. Just as the malfunction of one organ in the body, causes distress in the other organs, so also whatever hurt or misery that we may inflict on another is bound to take us also in its grip. So be careful not to do injustice to someone's else child.

So it is, that the injustice we do to another's child will cause our own children to suffer the repercussions of our actions. It is of course another matter that the Almighty in his Infinite Mercy allows some of our good deeds to compensate for the bad actions.

Two conditions have been laid down for handing over the charge of their properties to the orphans.

The first of these is the attainment of puberty,

The second is that of mental maturity - i.e. the capacity to manage their affairs in a sound and appropriate manner. There is full agreement among Muslim jurists with regard to the first condition. As for the second condition, Abu Hanifah is of the opinion that if an orphan does not attain mental maturity after he has attained puberty, the guardian of the orphan should wait for a maximum of seven years after which he should hand over the property to its owner regardless of whether he has attained maturity or not.

The guardian is entitled to remuneration for his service. The amount of this remuneration should be such as is deemed to be fair by neutral and reasonable people. Moreover, the guardian is instructed that he should take a fixed and known amount by way of remuneration, that he should take it openly rather than secretly, and that he should keep an account of it.

(4:10) Behold, those who wrongfully devour the properties of orphans only fill their bellies with fire. Soon they will burn in the Blazing Flame.

We now go to the law of inheritance

Inheritance is considered as an integral part of Shariah Law. Muslims **inherit** from one another as stated in the Qur'an. Hence, there is a legal share for relatives of the decedent in his estate and property.

God's instructions concerning the inheritance of your children are that the males share will be equal to that of two females.

If there are two daughters their share is two thirds of the estate. If there is only one daughter her share is half.

If there are children then the parents get one sixth of the estate each; if there are no children and the parents are the only heirs then one third goes to the mother.

Debts take precedence over a bequest and bequests may not be given to those who inherit by law.

A man inherit half of his wife's estate if they have no children but if they have a child he inherits a fourth.

Wives will inherit a fourth of their husband's estate if they have no children but if they do they will inherit an eighth.

If there are no parents or children a single sibling inherits a sixth of the estate but if there is more than one sibling they share a third.

These are the rules set by God and those who obey Him and Prophet Muhammad will be admitted to gardens under which rivers flow, but those who disobey will abide in the Fire.

ADULTERY IN ISLAM

In Islam, like in other monotheistic religion and in compliance with all universal norms of morality, adultery is condemned.

The Qur'an firmly forbids adultery in this verse: "Those who commit adultery, men or women, give each of them a hundred lashes" Qur'an 24: 2.

It is noteworthy that the Qur'an does not stipulate stoning as punishment but rather

"a hundred lashes" that remains an exclusively dissuasive sanction.

It should be equally noted that both men and women are penalized for adultery, unlike what is generally assumed, namely that only women are blamed and responsible for adultery.

What about the stoning of Men and women in such cases???

Notably, there is no verse that talks about stoning either men or women or for committing adultery.

Believe or not it wasn't Islam that prescribed this punishment but it was the Mosaic law of Jewish communities living in the Medina at that time.

The Qur'anic sanction prescribed for adultery - for both men and women - is the "flogging," a measure introduced as a corporal deterring punishment to replace the practice of stoning.

VERSE 15 IN SURAH NISA STATES:

The verse says: "Those who commit adultery of your women - bring against them four [witnesses] from among you. And if they testify, confine the guilty women to houses until death takes them or Allah ordains for them [another] way."(Qur'an 4:15).

"Keeping" women in their homes can be considered a means of protecting them from becoming victims of the society".

So what does the Qur'an say of those who falsely accuse women

"And those who accuse chaste women and then do not produce four witnesses - lash them with eighty lashes and do not accept from them testimony ever after. And those are the defiantly disobedient" ; Qur'an 24; 4

This Qur'anic measure makes accusation of this nature extremely difficult, if not impossible. The proof of adultery requires the presence of four eyewitnesses who, according to the Muslim law, must have witnessed that act and relate the same descriptions, which is virtually impossible.

The new measure remains extremely difficult to implement since it is conditioned by the testimony of four people of good faith to validate the accusation of adultery. The obligation to provide four eyewitnesses is a drastic measure, which makes proving the adulterous act very hard to prove.

The Qur'an is very strict regarding false testimonies and punishes those who present false testimonies with the same penalty as that of adulterers: flogging along with the loss of all of their civil rights.

The Qur'an therefore attempts to establish a very reformist vision in order to change the social norms of the time by invalidating the Hebrew law of stoning and educating Muslims to respect the private life of individuals.

WOMEN'S RIGHTS

(4:19) Believers! It is not lawful for you to become heirs to women against their will. It is not lawful that you should put constraint upon them that you may take away anything of what you have given them; (you may not put constraint upon them) unless they are guilty of brazenly immoral conduct. Live with your wives in a good manner. If you dislike them in any manner, it may be that you dislike something in which Allah has placed much good for you.

This means that the relatives of the husband should not treat the widow of the deceased as if she were a part of the inheritance and begin imposing their will on her. Upon the death of her husband a woman becomes independent. As soon as her legally-prescribed period of waiting ends, she is free to go to wherever she likes and to marry anyone she wishes.

Prior to the revelation of this verse,

If a man died, his relatives used to have the right to inherit his wife, and one of them could marry her if he would, or they would give her in marriage if they wished, or, if they wished, they would not give her in marriage at all, and they would be more entitled to dispose her, than her own relatives. So the above Verse was revealed in this connection.

Lets look at the Family Unit in Medina at the time Surah Nisa was revealed.

Today the single unit of a family is most defined as a committed relationship between two people.

During the period of revelation the family unit was based on a Patriarchal System. The man was on top of the hierarchy, thereby bestowing him the status of the only decision maker.

As a result, every woman was completely at the grace of her spouse as there were no legal laws protecting her. If, for instance a woman did not conform to the man's needs and desires, he could easily abandon her.

Surah An-Nisa' was revealed to get rid of societal laws that oppressed women. This surah is aim at protecting Women's rights.

Surah Nisa tells us it is a husband's task to provide for his wife. A husband is not released from this responsibility even after the couple has divorced, until the former wife remarries. As such, the financial support of the family lies on the ex husband's shoulders, even if she is wealthy and receives a high salary.

In fact, what a woman earns she can keep for herself, while what a man earns he has to share with his wife and family.

This constitutes a part of the family law within Islamic law.

Now do we still think that Islam is backwards in the way women are treated, disrespected. Men who operate in these manner perhaps have never read the Qur'an, let alone understand it.

Women who may not be taken in wedlock.. Verse 23 explains this

WHATABOUT THE THOUGHTS OF THE CONSERVATIVES, THE HYPOCRITES AND JEWS ON ALL THESE REFORMS

Both the hypocrites and the conservatives were incensed at the reforms introduced by Islam, as these were opposed to their traditions and customs.

The reforms were numerous: a share of the inheritance was assigned to daughters; widows were liberated from bondage to the will of their husbands' families and were granted the freedom to marry whomever they wished after the expiry of the waiting-period ('iddah); marriage with one's step-mother and with two sisters together was prohibited; foster-father's marriage with either the divorced or widowed wife of his adopted son was declared lawful.

The Jews, on the other hand, had woven a complex network of laws and regulations for themselves.

The Qur'anic injunctions simply infuriated them and as soon as they came to know of any Qur'anic law, they vehemently denounced it. They expected the Qur'an to endorse and validate all the legal deductions and all the superstitions and myths of their forefathers, and to treat them as an integral part of the law of God. If the Qur'an would not do so then they would refrain from recognizing it as the Book of God.

PLEURALISM IN ISLAM

In the Jahiliyah period there was no limit on the number of wives a man could take. The result was that a man sometimes married as many as ten women and, when expenses increased because of a large family, he encroached on the rights either of his orphan nephews or other relatives. It was in this context that God fixed the limit of four wives and instructed the Muslims that they may marry up to four wives providing they possessed the capacity to treat them equitably.

A person who avails himself of this permission granted by God to have a plurality of wives, and disregards the condition laid down by God to treat them equally has not acted in good faith with God. In case there are complaints from wives that they are not being treated equally, the Islamic state has the right to intervene and redress such grievances.

WHEN RELATIONSHIPS BREAKS DOWN

Whenever the relationship between a husband and a wife starts to break down, an attempt should first be made to resolve the dispute at the family level, before it is aggravated and leads to the disruption of the matrimonial tie.

The procedure to be followed is that two persons, one on behalf of each family, should be nominated to look into the matter together and devise means whereby the misunderstanding between the spouses may be brought to an end.

Who should nominate these mediators? God has not specified this so as to allow people full freedom to choose the most convenient arrangement.

The parties would be free, for instance, to decide that the mediators be nominated either by the spouses themselves or by the elders of their respective families.

In order words when family relationships are breaking hold a family court. Don't give up on the marriage easily. But if you cant reconcile your differences then it is a blessing to terminate that marriage.

THE RIGHTS OTHER PEOPLE HAVE OVER YOU.

THE RIGHTS OF THE CHILD

Allah Almighty commanded us (Muslims) to give honor, respect and obey our parents in entire life except when it comes to the disobedience of Allah (SWT). Islam raised the status of parents and made it obligatory for Muslims to obey their parents with love and respect. It is the right of parents to be loved and respected but as we all know rights also come with responsibilities and duties.

Parents' responsibilities for the upbringing and care of their children are mentioned in many verses of Holy Qur'an and hadiths.

Allah Almighty said in Holy Qur'an about the responsibilities of parents in these words: **"O you, who have believed, protect yourselves and your families from a Fire whose fuel is people and stones..."** (Qur'an, 66:6).

Question is how we can save our families from this fire?

The answer is very simple we have to show them right path as described by Allah Almighty in Holy Qur'an and Sunnah of Prophet Muhammad (Pbuh). We need to teach the difference between right and wrong to our children.

Children are joys of life as well as sources of pride, seeds of arrogance, the cause of distress and allurement. Therefore, we need to be very focused and careful about their upbringing. Children are dependent on their parents and Islam clearly emphasized on their responsibility on forming the child's personality.

Islam pays particular attention to the upbringing children in a proper manner. Children have the rights to be fed, clothed, education and protected until they reached to adulthood. These rights are for both girls and boys there is no difference between their rights. We can say that children are a trust given to the parents. Parents will be held accountable for this trust on the Day of Judgment. Parents are responsible for the moral, ethical and the basic and essential religious teachings of their children which is their responsibility.

Allah Almighty says in Holy Qur'an: **"And those who believed and whose descendants followed them in faith – We will join with them their descendants, and We will not deprive them of anything of their deeds. Every person, for what he earned, is retained..."** (Qur'an 52:21)

Children's responsibility is not only on father but also on mother as mentioned by Prophet Muhammad (Pbuh) in one of his hadith in these words: **"Take care! Each of you is a shepherd and each of you shall be asked concerning his flock; a leader is a shepherd of his people, and he shall be asked concerning his flock; and a man is a shepherd of the people of his house, and he shall be asked concerning his flock; and a woman is a shepherd of the house of her husband and over their children, and she shall be asked concerning them"** (Al-Bukhari).

The parents' right to respect from their children is dependent upon the children's right to loving care and guidance of their parents. The future of children depends on the teachings given to them by their parents.

Some basic rights of children are mentioned below:

Children have the right to be fed, clothed, education, protection until they reached to adulthood. Protection means protection against moral and physical harm.

Parents should give a good name to their child.

It's the responsibility of parents to develop the child's personality in all fields.

In Islam education is not limited to bookish knowledge but includes moral and religious training also. It means healthy all-round growth of child's personality by giving them both religious and bookish knowledge or we can say worldly knowledge. It is famous hadith of our beloved Prophet Muhammad (Pbuh) in which He (PBUH) said: **"The best of you is one who gives a good education (intellectual and moral) to his children"**.

Children need to be loved, kissed and special treatment by their parents. Parents should treat their children with love and leniency but in some cases where they need strictness, it is also allowed.

This means that parents should not spend all that they have their own comforts and luxuries but must make a board for children's progress after the parents die.

Parents should teach children Islamic manners and etiquettes in accordance with the beautiful example of the Prophet Muhammad (Pbuh).

Parents should also give them learning to read and recite the Qur'an from an early age when the child's memory finds it easy.

It also includes the development of the regular performance of Prayer between the ages of 7 and 10.

The respect that parents impart to their children will help them to become respectable, responsible, kind, friendly, obedient, patient, humble and honorable children and human being for their entire life.

In short, it is the duty of the parents to keep in mind the following things mentioned above concerning their children so that they may not be corrupted under the influence of undesirable suggestions. Parents should teach their children Islamic teachings as well as worldly so that they get success in this life and hereafter too.

THE RIGHTS OF THE PARENTS

In Holy Qur'an respect of parents is mentioned about eleven times, Allah Almighty has mentioned in every instance to recognize and to appreciate love and care that your parents gave to you. It is obligatory for us (Muslims) to show the unconditional kindness, respect, and obedience to our parents. Just like it is beyond our means to fulfill the rights of Allah (SWT) and to thank Him for all His rewards in their integrity, similarly, we can never thank our parents adequately for their efforts which they have done for us. The only thing that we can do is to acknowledge our shortcomings and submit ourselves, in obedience and loyalty, before our parents. In Holy Qur'an, Allah Almighty says: **"And We have enjoined on man (to be good) to his parents. In travail upon travail did his mother bear him, and in two years was his weaning. Show gratitude to Me and to thy parents; to Me is thy final goal."** (Qur'an, 31:14)

Every Muslim must show kindness and mercy to his parents throughout their lives. It is obligatory on children to show love, respect, and gratitude to their parents. Always speaks to parents gently and respectfully. Our Parents as a team provided for all our needs: Physical, Educational, Psychological, and in many instances, Religious, Moral, and Spiritual. It becomes obligatory for us to show the utmost Kindness, Respect, and Obedience to our Parents.

"Worship Allah and associate nothing with Him, and to parents do good, and to relatives, orphans, the needy, the near neighbor, the neighbor farther away, the companion at your side, the traveler, and those whom your right hands possess. Indeed, Allah does not like those who are self-deluding and boastful." *[Qur'an, 4: 36]*

The above mentioned Qur'anic verse demonstrates that apart from having complete conviction in Oneness of the Almighty, one has to fulfill privileges of one`s family members like parents and relatives, take care of orphans and the poor in surroundings, both close to and distant neighbors, and travelers etc. So, this one Ayah contains the comprehensive plan of executing ones responsibilities in any social order which start from one`s own family and is spread across the whole community. Regarding the high status and implementation of rights of a neighbor

Committing Suicide Is Strictly Forbidden in Islam

The act of suicide is a grave sin in Islam. Allah Almighty says in the noble Qur'an: "...And do not kill yourselves (nor kill one another). Surely, Allah is most merciful to you." (4:29)

People who contemplate suicide do so to escape the suffering and pain of this world. They mistakenly think that by ending their lives they will end all their sorrows. But what they don't know, according to the Islamic belief, is that by committing suicide their troubles have only just begun.

The Prophet Muhammad (peace be upon him) said,

"Whoever throws himself down from a mountain and kills himself will be in the fire of hell, throwing himself down therein for ever and ever. Whoever takes poison and kills himself, his poison will be in his hand and he will be sipping it in the fire of hell forever and ever. Whoever kills himself with a piece of iron, that piece of iron will be in his hand and he will be stabbing himself in the stomach with it in the fire of hell, for ever and ever." (Bukhari)

So not only will the person who commits suicide not find peace when they kill themselves but they will be tortured for eternity by their weapon of choice when they committed the initial deed. And they will never even hope to reach heaven.

The Prophet Muhammad (peace be upon him) said in an authentic hadith:

"There was amongst those before you a man who had a wound. He was in [such] anguish that he took a knife and made with it a cut in his hand, and the blood did not cease to flow till he died. Allah the Almighty said: My servant has himself forestalled me; I have forbidden him paradise."

Anyone who has ever read the noble Qur'an can see the simplicity of this world within its' sacred text. This world is a testing ground to see who is the best in faith so that they may reap the rewards in the next life to come. This world is full of tragedy, pain and heartbreak. Depression and suicide are common maladies these days but killing oneself is never the answer. All humans must trust in Allah no matter what calamities befall them.

An excellent example of trusting in Allah's will and decree can be found in the story of the Prophet Ayub (Job). Prophet Ayub had everything. He was wealthy, married and had children. He was always obedient to Allah and his tongue was always wet with remembrances of Allah. One day the angels were talking that the Prophet Ayub was the best in the creation of Allah. Iblis, the devil, overheard and was immediately jealous. He set out to destroy the Prophet Ayub. However, Iblis was not capable of doing any harm to the Prophet Ayub except through Allah's will. Iblis asked Allah for the permission to do harm to Ayub and Allah allowed it because he knew that his servant was faithful and he wanted Iblis to see for himself.

Iblis destroyed all of Prophet Ayub's wealth, property and caused a building to collapse, which killed all of his children inside. Iblis then caused him to have a grave skin disease, which caused him severe pain and made society shun away from him.

All he had left was his wife and his faith in Allah. But even his wife succumbed to the wiles of Iblis and left Ayub alone to suffer. Through all of this, Prophet Ayub did not blame Allah almighty or even ask to be spared from his torture which lasted for a full seven years. He continued to have patience and trusted in Allah. However, now alone in the world he turned to Allah to seek his mercy, which is revealed in the Holy Qur'an.

"And (remember) Ayub? When he cried to his Lord: 'Verily, distress has seized me, and You are the most merciful of all those who show mercy'. So we answered his call, and we removed the distress that was on him, and we restored his family to him (that he had lost), and the like thereof along with them, as a mercy from ourselves and a reminder for all who worship Us." 21:83-84)

Through his faith he had everything restored to him Prophet Ayub was rewarded for his immense faith and trust in Allah. His health and wealth were restored and his wife even came back to him.

THE FORBIDINCE OF INTOXICANTS IN ISLAM

Islam dealt with the problem of alcohol and intoxicants in an excellent way. The information relating to the prohibition of alcohol in Islam is to be obtained directly from the word's of Allah alone in the *Qur'an* as well as from the saying of the Holy Prophet Muhammad (*peace be upon him*) in the *Hadith*. The prohibition of alcoholic beverages is mentioned three times in the Holy *Qur'an*.

In *Surah* Al-Baqarah, Allah says:

"They question thee about strong drinks and games of chance. Say: In both is great sin, and (some) utility for men; but the sin of them is greater than their usefulness." *Al-Qur'an* 2:219

There is a great sin in wine drinking and one of the things that Allah forbade is sins. The last portion of the verse tells us that there is greater harm in wine and gambling than the benefit. No sane man will approach or do anything that has a greater harm than benefit for him.

In *Surah* An-Nisa, Allah says:

"**O ye who believe! Draw not near unto prayer when ye are drunken, till ye know that which ye utter...** "*Al-Qur'an 4:43*

Islam regards prayers as a monologue between a Muslim and the Creator of the universe. So he is prohibited to approach this monologue while he is drunk. He must purify himself first before he approaches *Salat*. He must be pure in mind and body, therefore, he must be sober. He must be clean in clothes too.

In *Surah* Al-Maidah, Allah says:

"**O ye who believe! Strong drinks and games of chance and idols and divining of arrows are only an infamy of Satan's handiwork. Leave it aside in order that ye may succeed. Satan seeketh only to cast among you enmity and hatred by means of strong drink and games of chance, and turn you from remembrance of Allah and from (His) worship. So will ye not then abstain?**"*Al-Qur'an* 5:90-91

THE RULING ON MAKING WUDU IN THE ABSENCE OF WATER

Tayammum is also an act of worship consisting of wiping the forehead and the two hands. It is a substitute for *wudu* and ghusl. The Holy Qur'an says:

"O you who believe!... If you are sick, or on a journey, or one of you has come from toilet, or you have 'touched' (i.e., had intercourse with) your women and you cannot find water, then you should do Tayammum on the pure earth by wiping a part of your face and your hands." (4:43, also see 5:6)

Tayammum can be performed with clean earth and rub therewith your faces and hands. Allah does not want to place you in difficulty, but He wants to purify you, and to complete His Favour to you that you may be thankful.

— *Qur'an, Sura 5 (Al-Mai'da), ayat 6*

Chapter 5

Understanding S Maida

The name of the Surah – The Table Spread - is taken from verse 112:

> [And remember] when the disciples said, "O Jesus, Son of Mary, can your Lord send down to us a table [spread with food] from the heaven? [Jesus] said," Fear Allah, if you should be believers."

This Surah was revealed after the treaty of Hudaiybiyah at the end of 6 A. H. or the beginning of 7 A. H. It deals with problems that arose from this treaty. The continuity of the subject indicates that most probably the whole Surah was revealed as a single discourse at one and the same time.

1. The Surah deals with - Major Issues, Divine Law and Guidance
2. Lawful (Halal) and unlawful (Haram) in the matters of food.
3. Permission to eat the food of Ahl-al-Kitab (Jews and Christians).
4. Permission to marry women of Ahl-al-Kitab (Jews and Christians).
5. Regulations about bath, wudhu and Tayammum.
6. The fact that Salah and Zakah were also obligatory for Jews and Christians.
7. Invitation to Jews and Christians to become Muslims.
8. Those who do not judge by the Laws of Allah are declared to be unbelievers, wrong doers and transgressors.
9. Warning to guard against corruption of power.
10. Punishment for rebellion, disturbing the peace and theft.
11. Absolute prohibition of drinking and gambling.
12. Rules when in the state of Ihram.
13. Miracles of Jesus - and the fact that he did not claim divinity.
14. Testimony of Jesus which he shall give on the Day of Judgement.

HISTORICAL CONTEXT OF REVELATION

Al-Ma'idah was revealed at the time when the last effort of the Qureysh to suppress Islam had been defeated in the Battle of the Ditch, and it had become obvious to the Arabs that no power could suppress the Islamic movement. Now Islam was not merely a creed which ruled over the minds and hearts of the people, but had also become a State which was regulating the lives of people. Therefore, there was a need to formulate Islamic civil and criminal laws in detail and enforce them through Islamic courts. New and reformed ways of trade and commerce were needed to replace the old. Likewise, Islamic laws of marriage and divorce, segregation of the sexes, and punishment for adultery, were needed to mould the social life of Muslims. This Surah provided the guidelines to the believers in some of these aspects of their lives so that their social behaviour, conversation, dress, way of life and culture could take a definite shape of its own.

The treaty of Hudaiybiyah was also signed in the same year which gave the Muslims not only peace in their own territory but, also respite to spread the Message of Islam in the surrounding territories. The Holy Prophet wrote letters to the rulers of Iran, Egypt, and Rome and to the Chiefs of Arabia, inviting them to Islam.

Now that the Muslims had become a ruling body, it was feared that power might corrupt them. At this period of great trial, Allah had admonished them repeatedly to stick to justice and to guard against the wrong behaviour of their predecessors, the People of the Book. Believers are enjoined to remain steadfast to the Covenant of Obedience to Allah and His Rasool. They should follow Allah's commands and prohibitions to save themselves from the evil consequences which were faced by the Jews and the Christians who had violated them. They have been instructed to avoid hypocrisy. In continuation of the instructions given in Surah An-Nisa' about the consolidation of the Islamic Community, the Muslims have been directed to observe and fulfill all their obligations. The Jews and the Christians are also admonished to give up their wrong attitudes towards the Right Way and accept the guidance which is being taught by the Prophet Muhammad (peace be upon him).

WE HAVE THIS BEAUTIFUL VERSE IN SURAH MAIDA:

"This day, I have perfected your religion for you, completed My favour upon you, and have chosen for you Islam as your religion."

This, indeed, is the biggest favour from Allah to this Ummah, for He has completed their religion for them, and they, thus, do not need any other religion or any other Prophet except Muhammad (Pbuh). This is why Allah made Prophet Muhammad (Pbuh) the Final Prophet and sent him to all humans and Jinn. Therefore, the permissible is what he allows, the impermissible is what he prohibits, the Law is what he legislates and everything that he conveys is true and authentic and does not contain lies or contradictions.

It means accept Islam for yourselves, for it is the religion that Allah likes and which He chose for you, and it is that with which He sent the best of the honourable Messengers and the most glorious of His Books.

Imam Ahmad recorded that Tariq bin Shihab said, "A Jewish man said to Umar bin Al-Khattab, "O Leader of the Believers! There is an ayah in your Book, which is read by all of you (Muslims), and had it been revealed to us, we would have taken that day (on which it was revealed) as a day of celebration." Umar bin Al-Khattab asked, "Which is that ayah?" The Jew quoted Ayaat 3.

Ali radhiAllahu anhu says that this ayah is almost the last ayah of the Qur'an, no ayah dealing with ahkaam was revealed after that. The only exception here is that of some ayat of persuasive nature which have been identified as having been revealed after this ayah. After the revelation of this ayah, the Prophet sallAllahu aalyhi wa sallam lived for only eighty one more days.

Verses 1-6 Legislation of contracts, offerings to God, pilgrims, and inviolable months, food, ritual bath, ablution, and dry ablution

Fulfil your obligations.

1. O ye who believe! fulfil (all) obligations. Lawful unto you (for food) are all four-footed animals, with the exceptions named: But animals of the chase are forbidden while ye are in the sacred precincts or in pilgrim garb: for Allah doth command according to His will and plan.

2. O ye who believe! Violate not the sanctity of the symbols of Allah, nor of the sacred month, nor of the animals brought for sacrifice, nor the garlands that mark out such animals, nor the people resorting to the sacred house, seeking of the bounty and good pleasure of their Lord. But when ye are clear of the sacred precincts and of pilgrim garb, ye may hunt and let not the hatred of some people in (once) shutting you out of the Sacred Mosque lead you to transgression (and hostility on your part). Help ye one another in righteousness and piety, but help ye not one another in sin and rancour: fear Allah. for Allah is strict in punishment.

3. Forbidden to you (for food) are: dead meat, blood, the flesh of swine, and that on which hath been invoked the name of other than Allah. that which hath been killed by strangling, or by a violent blow, or by a headlong fall, or by being gored to death; that which hath been (partly) eaten by a wild animal; unless ye are able to slaughter it (in due form); that which is sacrificed on stone (altars); (forbidden) also is the division (of meat) by raffling with arrows: that is impiety. This day have those who reject faith given up all hope of your religion: yet fear them not but fear Me. This day have I perfected your religion for you, completed My favour upon you, and have chosen for you Islam as your religion. But if any is forced by hunger, with no inclination to transgression, Allah is indeed Oft-forgiving, Most Merciful.

4. They ask thee what is lawful to them (as food). Say: lawful unto you are (all) things good and pure: and what ye have taught your trained hunting animals (to catch) in the manner directed to you by Allah. eat what they catch for you, but pronounce the name of Allah over it: and fear Allah. for Allah is swift in taking account.

5. This day are (all) things good and pure made lawful unto you. The food of the People of the Book is lawful unto you and yours is lawful unto them. (Lawful unto you in marriage) are (not only) chaste women who are believers, but chaste women among the People of the Book, revealed before your time, - when ye give them their due dowers, and desire chastity, not lewdness, nor secret intrigues if any one rejects faith, fruitless is his work, and in the Hereafter he will be in the ranks of those who have lost (all spiritual good).

6. O ye who believe! when ye prepare for prayer, wash your faces, and your hands (and arms) to the elbows; Rub your heads (with water); and (wash) your feet to the ankles. If ye are in a state of ceremonial impurity, bathe your whole body. But if ye are ill, or on a journey, or one of you cometh from offices of nature, or ye have been in contact with women, and ye find no water, then take for yourselves clean sand or earth, and rub therewith your faces and hands, Allah doth not wish to place you in a difficulty, but to make you clean, and to complete his favour to you, that ye may be grateful.

You are forbidden to hunt while you are on pilgrimage, but when you have completed the rites of pilgrimage you may hunt. Do not let your hatred for some people make you to break the law. Help one another to do what is right and do not help one another towards sin.

You are forbidden to eat carrion, blood, pig's meat, any animal over which any name other than Allah's has been taken, and anything sacrificed on altars. Also, any permissible animal that is strangled, or is a victim of a violent blow or fall, or is gored or savaged by a beast of prey, is also forbidden unless you are able to slaughter it before its death.

Today I have perfected your religion for you, completed My blessing upon you, and chosen for you Islam as your religion. If any of you is forced by hunger to eat forbidden food, with no intention of doing wrong, then God is most forgiving!

The food of the Jews and Christians is lawful for you as your food is lawful for them. So are chaste Jewish and Christian women if you marry them, not taking them as lovers or secret mistresses.

Allah does not wish to place any burden on you: He only wishes to cleanse you and perfect His blessing on you, so that you may be thankful.

Verses 7 — 26 God's covenant, favours, and command of doing justice, some conditions of the People of the Book, Moses' experience with the Jews, Adam's two sons, and inviolability of the human soul

7. *And call in remembrance the favour of Allah unto you, and His covenant, which He ratified with you, when ye said: "We hear and we obey": And fear Allah, for Allah knoweth well the secrets of your hearts.*

8. *O ye who believe! stand out firmly for Allah, as witnesses to fair dealing, and let not the hatred of others to you make you swerve to wrong and depart from justice. Be just: that is next to piety: and fear Allah. For Allah is well-acquainted with all that ye do.*

9. *To those who believe and do deeds of righteousness hath Allah promised forgiveness and a great reward.*

10. *Those who reject faith and deny our signs will be companions of Hell-fire.*

11. *O ye who believe! Call in remembrance the favour of Allah unto you when certain men formed the design to stretch out their hands against you, but (Allah) held back their hands from you: so fear Allah. And on Allah let believers put (all) their trust.*

12. *Allah did aforetime take a covenant from the Children of Israel, and we appointed twelve captains among them. And Allah said: "I am with you: if ye (but) establish regular prayers, practise regular charity, believe in my apostles, honour and assist them, and loan to Allah a beautiful loan, verily I will wipe out from you your evils, and admit you to gardens with rivers flowing beneath; but if any of you, after this, resisteth faith, he hath truly wandered from the path or rectitude."*

13. *But because of their breach of their covenant, We cursed them, and made their hearts grow hard; they change the words from their (right) places and forget a good part of the message that was sent them, nor wilt thou cease to find them- barring a few - ever bent on (new) deceits: but forgive them, and overlook (their misdeeds): for Allah loveth those who are kind.*

14. *From those, too, who call themselves Christians, We did take a covenant, but they forgot a good part of the message that was sent them: so we estranged them, with enmity and hatred between the one and the other, to the day of judgment. And soon will Allah show them what it is they have done.*

15. *O people of the Book! There hath come to you our Messenger, revealing to you much that ye used to hide in the Book, and passing over much (that is now unnecessary). There hath come to you from Allah a (new) light and a perspicuous Book,-*

16. *Wherewith Allah guideth all who seek His good pleasure to ways of peace and safety, and leadeth them out of darkness, by His will, unto the light,- guideth them to a path that is straight.*

17. In blasphemy indeed are those that say that Allah is Christ the son of Mary. Say: "Who then hath the least power against Allah, if His will were to destroy Christ the son of Mary, his mother, and all every - one that is on the earth? For to Allah belongeth the dominion of the heavens and the earth, and all that is between. He createth what He pleaseth. For Allah hath power over all things."

18. (Both) the Jews and the Christians say: "We are sons of Allah, and his beloved." Say: "Why then doth He punish you for your sins? Nay, ye are but men, - of the men he hath created: He forgiveth whom He pleaseth, and He punisheth whom He pleaseth: and to Allah belongeth the dominion of the heavens and the earth, and all that is between: and unto Him is the final goal (of all)"

19. O People of the Book! Now hath come unto you, making (things) clear unto you, Our Messenger, after the break in (the series of) our apostles, lest ye should say: "There came unto us no bringer of glad tidings and no warner (from evil)": But now hath come unto you a bringer of glad tidings and a warner (from evil). And Allah hath power over all things.

20. Remember Moses said to his people: "O my people! Call in remembrance the favour of Allah unto you, when He produced prophets among you, made you kings, and gave you what He had not given to any other among the peoples.

21. "O my people! Enter the holy land which Allah hath assigned unto you, and turn not back ignominiously, for then will ye be overthrown, to your own ruin."

22. They said: "O Moses! In this land are a people of exceeding strength: Never shall we enter it until they leave it: if (once) they leave, then shall we enter."

23. (But) among (their) Allah.fearing men were two on whom Allah had bestowed His grace: They said: "Assault them at the (proper) Gate: when once ye are in, victory will be yours; But on Allah put your trust if ye have faith."

24. They said: "O Moses! while they remain there, never shall we be able to enter, to the end of time. Go thou, and thy Lord, and fight ye two, while we sit here (and watch)."

25. He said: "O my Lord! I have power only over myself and my brother: so separate us from this rebellious people!"

26. Allah said: "Therefore will the land be out of their reach for forty years: In distraction will they wander through the land: But sorrow thou not over these rebellious people.

Allah tells us to be just in our dealings.

Allah is aware of all of our secrets. Then Allah tells us about justice, equating it to righteousness.

Part of the covenant with which Allah requires it to deal with other people on the basis of absolute justice. This must not be clouded by feelings of love or hatred, or by feelings, interests, or relations of any kind. No influences are ever allowed to tilt the balance of justice, especially when believers are mindful that Allah watches over them and knows what lies at the bottom of their hearts.

Justice means meting out to a person that treatment which he deserves – no more and no less. In his dealings, he should follow the dictates of justice and not his desires. He should be bound by this principle to the extent that he should adhere to justice even when dealing with his enemies; even when grievances and bitter memories are apt to divert him from the path of justice.

This verse continues to cultivate this spirit of justice and tolerance among the Muslim community, and to weaken feelings of hostility, prejudice and revenge.

The covenant God had accepted from the Children of Israel stated a specific condition and stipulated certain penalties in case of default. After explaining the circumstances leading to the confirmation of this covenant, the surah mentions its terms, conditions and penalties.

A pledge was taken from the Children of Israel by their prophet that they would lead a godly life, and twelve chiefs from their twelve tribes were appointed to keep a watch over them. The pledge taken from the Children of Israel was they would make themselves godly by offering salat (prayers), that they would discharge the rights of others in the shape of zakat (obligatory charity), align themselves on the side of Allah by supporting His prophets, and spend their assets in support of the struggle for the religion of God. It was only after undertaking all this and after establishing a collective system among themselves for ensuring the continued fulfillment of these duties that they were entitled to Allah's company and support. One attains Paradise by performing good deeds and not due to any racial relationship.

It was a covenant made with the twelve captains of the Israelites, representing all twelve tribes descending from Jacob, or Israel. Each tribe descended from one of Jacob's sons. The terms of the covenant are outlined as follows:

When Allah says to any group of people, **"I shall be with you"**, He gives them a great promise. He who has Allah on his side suffers no opposition. Whoever and whatever stands against him is of no consequence. Moreover, whoever is with Allah will not go astray. To be with Allah is sufficient to ensure the right guidance and the proper support. Anyone who is sure to be on Allah's side will never suffer worry or misery. He is reassured and blessed with unfailing happiness. He need not ask for anything better than what he already has.

But Allah does not give this blessing of being with them as a special favour or a personal gift. This comes only after its conditions are fulfilled. It is, indeed, a contract that outlines conditions and specifies penalties. The first condition is to attend to prayer. This is more than merely offering prayers. It means that prayers should become a manifestation of a true relationship between man and his Lord. This makes prayer an educative element which purifies man's behaviour and dissuades him from committing any blatant sin or gross indecency.

Second is charitable payment, in recognition of Allah's favour for having given us what we have and by way of acknowledgement of the fact that whatever we may own belongs to Allah. The payment of zakat, or charity, is a manifestation of our obedience to Allah with regards to how to dispense with the money He has given us.

The next condition is to believe in Allah's Messengers making no distinction between them. Every single one of them was sent by Allah to preach the same message. Therefore, to deny any single one of them is to deny them all and to disbelieve in Allah, who had sent them all. Moreover, believing in them must not be a mere mental exercise. To truly believe in them is to be actively involved in supporting them in order to ensure that they succeed in their mission.

In addition to zakat, giving generously to support Allah's cause is mentioned as a loan given to Allah. It should be pointed out here that it is Allah who owns what we have, but He gracefully describes what we pay to further His cause as a loan given to Him.

These were the conditions of the covenant Allah accepted from the Children of Israel. The reward for the fulfilment of these conditions was to forgive them their sins. Human beings will always err, no matter how keen they are to do what is right. Therefore, the forgiveness of sins is a great reward and a manifestation of Allah's endless grace. The reward also includes admission into Heaven which is described in the Qur'ān as **"gardens through which running waters flow."**

The penalty for failing to honour one's pledges is specified at the end of this verse: **"But any of you who, after this, rejects the faith will indeed have strayed from the right path."** Hence, he can have no guidance and no way of return. The pledge had already been made, the guidance already provided, the way shown, and the penalty specified. Nothing can be of any benefit anymore.

Such was the covenant Allah accepted from the captains of the Children of Israel on behalf of their communities. They all accepted it, which made it a covenant applicable to every single individual among them, and one with the whole nation they constituted.

Allah also relates to His Messenger (peace be upon him) and to the Muslim community that He accepted a covenant from those who described themselves as Christians, but they, too, were unfaithful to their covenant and suffered the consequences.

This verse begins with a particularly significant description: "Likewise, from those who said: **'We are Christians', We have accepted a firm covenant."** This mode of expression tells us that they simply professed to be Christians without giving practical credence to their claims. The essence of their covenant was to believe in God's oneness. Yet it was in regard to this very issue that deviation crept into the history of Christianity. It is this central clause in their covenant which became the forgotten part of what they had enjoined. When it was forgotten, every deviation became possible and enmity broke out between the numberless sects and churches of Christianity, old and new. Allah tells us that their enmity and hatred will continue until the Day of Resurrection when they will be shown a clear image of what they have done in this life.

Those people who received revelations in the past found it rather hard to accept that a Prophet who did not belong to them should call on them to submit themselves to God. This Prophet belonged to a nation of illiterate people whom they used to despise, on account of their being unlettered while they themselves had Divine Scriptures. Allah wanted to bestow a great honour on those unlettered people and, therefore, He chose from among them the individual who was to become the last of all Prophets. He also gave them His final message, addressed to all mankind. He taught those unlettered people to become the ones with the highest standard of knowledge on earth. This transformation made them the ones with the highest beliefs, the most consistent and sound way of life, the most complete system and legal code, the soundest social set-up and the most sublime standard of morality. All this was part of the grace Allah bestowed on them when He chose Islam to be their faith. Those unlettered people could not have aspired to be the guides for humanity without this grace they received from Allah. Indeed, they never had and will never have anything to offer humanity except for what their faith gives them.

In this Divine address to the people of earlier Scriptures, it is made clear that they are called upon to accept Islam, believe in Prophet Muhammad (Pbuh) and support him, as this has been part of their covenant which Allah accepted from them. They are clearly told that God Himself is a witness that this Prophet who could not read and write was His Messenger to them as well as to the Arabs and to all mankind. There is no denying the fact that his message was given to him by God, and no claim can be admitted that his message was addressed to the

Arabs only; it is, indeed, addressed also to the people of earlier revelations: **"People of earlier revelations, Our Messenger has come to you to make clear to you much of what you have been concealing of the Scriptures, and to forgive you much."** He has sent a Messenger to you, and his role is to open things up to you so that you see them in their reality. You can thus see how he brings out into the open what you have conspired to suppress of the basic truth of the revelations given to you.

This applies to both the Christians and Jews. The Christians suppressed the very basic and fundamental principle of faith, namely, the concept of God's oneness, and the Jews suppressed many Divine legislations such as the punishment of adulterers with stoning and the total prohibition of usury. Both the Christians and the Jews also suppressed the news of the future mission of the unlettered Prophet, **"whom they find mentioned in the Torah and the Gospel in their hands." (7: 157)**

The nature of what the last Messenger has been given, the role it is destined to play in human life and its practical effect are then explained: **"There has come to you from God a light and a clear Book."** Perhaps nothing expresses the nature of the Qur'ān and the Divine message of Islam more accurately and comprehensively than stating that it is "a light". In his heart of hearts, in everything in his life, in his evaluation of things, events and people, a believer realises as soon as he accepts the truth of faith that he has a light that makes everything clear to him. Everything brightens up in front of him. No longer is he confused about anything; no longer does he suffer any hesitation before taking a serious decision; no longer is he travelling an unmarked road and no longer is he uncertain of his direction. His goal is clear. His way towards it is straight and he is certain of his footsteps. Two qualities describe the message which was given to the noble Messenger: **"a light and a clear book"**

It has been Allah's pleasure to choose Islam as the religion for mankind. Anyone who follows what Allah has been pleased to choose for him and accepts it with pleasure will be guided by Allah **"to the paths of peace"**. How true and accurate this description is. What this faith imparts to life as a whole is peace, in the broadest sense of the term. It is peace within the individual, the community and the whole world. It is peace with one's conscience, with one's mind and body. It is peace within the home and family, society and the community and with humanity at large. It is peace with life, the universe and with the Creator, Allah.

It is a true fact that through this religion of Islam Allah guides anyone who seeks His pleasure by following it **"to the paths of peace"** in all the aforementioned aspects of life. No one can appreciate how profound a blessing this is except a person who has experienced what life is as a Muslim.

To claim that Jesus Christ is God is a blatant blasphemy. To say that the Jews and the Christians are God's beloved sons is a false fabrication. Such claims are pressed by people of earlier revelations who have suppressed the clear essence of the concept of God's oneness. The last Messenger, Prophet Muhammad (peace be upon 'him), was sent to put it back in its clearest form, so that those who have strayed away from it may turn back.

The message Jesus (peace be upon him) conveyed as given to him by his Lord was the message of God's absolute oneness which has been given to every messenger. Total submission to God alone as the only God and the Lord of the universe was the attitude adopted by every messenger. This clear faith, however, later became distorted after pagans adopted Christianity, retaining some traces of their old pagan beliefs which they were keen to introduce into the faith based on God's oneness. As time passed, these deviant beliefs became an integral part of the whole faith.

These deviant beliefs were not introduced all at the same time. Ecclesiastical councils introduced them at different intervals until they eventually produced this singularly confusing mixture of legends and concepts that defies even those of its advocates who try to give a logical interpretation of it.

The basic concept of God's oneness was preached after Jesus (peace be upon him) by his disciples and their followers. The Gospel of Barnabas, one of many written at the time, speaks of Jesus Christ as a Messenger of God. Internal differences then broke out, with some maintaining that the Christ was not different from other messengers sent by God. Others acknowledged that he was a messenger but they claimed that he had a special relationship with God, while a third group said that he was the son of God because he was created without a father. Nevertheless, he was one of God's creation. A different group claimed that he was God's son, and that he was not created; he shared with the Father the quality of being eternal.

In ayaat 27 – 32,

27. Recite to them the truth of the story of the two sons of Adam. Behold! they each presented a sacrifice (to Allah.: It was accepted from one, but not from the other. Said the latter: "Be sure I will slay thee." "Surely," said the former, "(Allah) doth accept of the sacrifice of those who are righteous.

28. "If thou dost stretch thy hand against me, to slay me, it is not for me to stretch my hand against thee to slay thee: for I do fear Allah, the cherisher of the worlds.

29. "For me, I intend to let thee draw on thyself my sin as well as thine, for thou wilt be among the companions of the fire, and that is the reward of those who do wrong."

30. *The (selfish) soul of the other led him to the murder of his brother: he murdered him, and became (himself) one of the lost ones.*

31. *Then Allah sent a raven, who scratched the ground, to show him how to hide the shame of his brother. "Woe is me!" said he; "Was I not even able to be as this raven, and to hide the shame of my brother?" then he became full of regrets-*

32. *On that account: We ordained for the Children of Israel that if any one slew a person - unless it be for murder or for spreading mischief in the land - it would be as if he slew the whole people: and if any one saved a life, it would be as if he saved the life of the whole people. Then although there came to them Our apostles with clear signs, yet, even after that, many of them continued to commit excesses in the land*

We have the story of the two sons of Adam aalyhi salaam. It has many lessons and good counsels for the present and future generations; and under them, mention has been made of many religious injunctions. It tells us that the consequences of transgression, injustice and rebellion are dangerous.

Allah subhanahu wa ta'ala describes the evil end and consequence of transgression, envy and injustice in the story of the two sons of Adam, Habeel and Qabeel. One of them fought against the other and killed him out of envy and transgression, because of the bounty that Allah gave his brother and because the sacrifice that he sincerely offered to Allah was accepted. The murdered brother earned forgiveness for his sins and was admitted into Paradise, while the murderer failed, but was reprieved by Allah after sincere repentance.

Verse 27

"And recite to them the story of the two sons of Adam in truth..."

Verse 32

"Because of that, We ordained for the Children of Israel that if anyone killed a person not in retaliation of murder, or (and) to spread mischief in the land – it would be as if he killed all mankind, and if anyone saved a life, it would be as if he saved the life of all mankind."

Whoever kills an innocent soul it is as if he is killing the entire mankind. By killing one person the murderer is showing that killing people is okay. The punishment in the hereafter is going to be so serious that it'd be as if he has killed all people. Every human life is sacred. When a person kills one man that would not end there. This one murder will lead to many murders. Therefore, law and order must be maintained.

Verses 33-40 Ordained punishments, punishment of highway robbery, fearing God and drawing close to Him versus disbelieving in Him, punishment of theft, and repentance

33. The punishment of those who wage war against Allah and His Messenger, and strive with might and main for mischief through the land is: execution, or crucifixion, or the cutting off of hands and feet from opposite sides, or exile from the land: that is their disgrace in this world, and a heavy punishment is theirs in the Hereafter;

34. Except for those who repent before they fall into your power: in that case, know that Allah is Oft-forgiving, Most Merciful.

35. O ye who believe! Do your duty to Allah, seek the means of approach unto Him, and strive with might and main in his cause: that ye may prosper.

36. As to those who reject Faith,- if they had everything on earth, and twice repeated, to give as ransom for the penalty of the Day of Judgment, it would never be accepted of them, theirs would be a grievous penalty.

37. Their wish will be to get out of the Fire, but never will they get out therefrom: their penalty will be one that endures.

38. As to the thief, Male or female, cut off his or her hands: a punishment by way of example, from Allah, for their crime: and Allah is Exalted in power.

39. But if the thief repents after his crime, and amends his conduct, Allah turneth to him in forgiveness; for Allah is Oft-forgiving, Most Merciful.

40. Knowest thou not that to Allah (alone) belongeth the dominion of the heavens and the earth? He punisheth whom He pleaseth, and He forgiveth whom He pleaseth: and Allah hath power over all things.

The principle on which Allah has created the system of this world is that everybody should discharge his duty and noone should unnecessarily interfere in the sphere of others. Human beings have been given clear instructions through prophets, but they have been given a free will with which to act righteously or to rebel. Those who declare war against Allah and His prophet are terrible criminals. Such people indulge in acts of terrorism. For them there is a terrible punishment in this world and an all-consuming fire in the Hereafter.

The greatest achievement for man is nearness to Allah. The way to attain this nearness is through *taqwa* (fear of God or piety), i.e. becoming a worshiper or devotee of Allah through fear of Allah and struggling to make efforts for His cause. He has to surrender his ego, tolerating every difficulty and unpleasantness; he moves ahead towards Allah.

The punitive system in Islam for social crimes has two special aspects: one is punishment for a man's crime and the other is the deterrent effect of that punishment. However, if the criminal is truly repentant, seeks Allah's pardon and completely refrains from such misdemeanours in future, then Allah may forgive him in the Hereafter.

Verses 41-50 Obligation to judge by what God has revealed, Jews and the Torah, Jesus and the Gospel, Muhammad and the Qur'an

41. O Messenger. let not those grieve thee, who race each other into unbelief: (whether it be) among those who say "We believe" with their lips but whose hearts have no faith; or it be among the Jews, - men who will listen to any lie,- will listen even to others who have never so much as come to thee. They change the words from their (right) times and places: they say, "If ye are given this, take it, but if not, beware!" If any one's trial is intended by Allah, thou hast no authority in the least for him against Allah. For such - it is not Allah's will to purify their hearts. For them there is disgrace in this world, and in the Hereafter a heavy punishment.

42. (They are fond of) listening to falsehood, of devouring anything forbidden. If they do come to thee, either judge between them, or decline to interfere. If thou decline, they cannot hurt thee in the least. If thou judge, judge in equity between them. For Allah loveth those who judge in equity.

43. But why do they come to thee for decision, when they have (their own) law before them?- therein is the (plain) command of Allah. yet even after that, they would turn away. For they are not (really) People of Faith.

44. It was We who revealed the law (to Moses): therein was guidance and light. By its standard have been judged the Jews, by the prophets who bowed (as in Islam) to Allah's will, by the rabbis and the doctors of law: for to them was entrusted the protection of Allah's book, and they were witnesses thereto: therefore fear not men, but fear me, and sell not my signs for a miserable price. If any do fail to judge by (the light of) what Allah hath revealed, they are (no better than) Unbelievers.

45. We ordained therein for them: "Life for life, eye for eye, nose for nose, ear for ear, tooth for tooth, and wounds equal for equal." But if any one remits the retaliation by way of charity, it is an act of atonement for himself. And if any fail to judge by (the light of) what Allah hath revealed, they are (No better than) wrong-doers.

46. And in their footsteps We sent Jesus the son of Mary, confirming the Law that had come before him: We sent him the Gospel: therein was guidance and light, and confirmation of the Law that had come before him: a guidance and an admonition to those who fear Allah.

47. Let the people of the Gospel judge by what Allah hath revealed therein. If any do fail to judge by (the light of) what Allah hath revealed, they are (no better than) those who rebel.

48. To thee We sent the Scripture in truth, confirming the scripture that came before it, and guarding it in safety: so judge between them by what Allah hath revealed, and follow not their vain desires, diverging from the Truth that hath come to thee. To each among you have we prescribed a law and an open way. If Allah had so willed, He would have made you a single people, but (His plan is) to test you in what He hath given you: so strive as in a race in all virtues. The goal of you all is to Allah. it is He that will show you the truth of the matters in which ye dispute;

49. And this (He commands): Judge thou between them by what Allah hath revealed, and follow not their vain desires, but beware of them lest they beguile thee from any of that (teaching) which Allah hath sent down to thee. And if they turn away, be assured that for some of their crime it is Allah's purpose to punish them. And truly most men are rebellious.

50. Do they then seek after a judgment of (the days of) ignorance? But who, for a people whose faith is assured, can give better judgment than Allah.

These verses were revealed in the early years after the Prophet's settlement in Madinah where the Jews were part of its community.

In Madina there were two kinds of people who opposed the Islam – the hypocrites and the Jews. The hypocrites, feeling that the real Islamic mission was harmful to their success and purposes, merely put on a show of having adopted Islam. The Jews for their part, felt that the Islamic mission was pulling them down from their position. Therefore, they joined hands in running a campaign against Islam. They used to twist the meaning of the Prophet's words to defame him and his mission.

Their attitude was to accept only whatever suits their interests. Such people desert God and God deserts them.

Allah (limitless is He in His glory) consoles His Messenger (peace be upon him) and comforts him. He exposes the Jews and the hypocrites to the Muslim community. He directs His Messenger to the line of action he should adopt with them when they come to him for arbitration, after explaining to the Prophet what plots they have concocted before coming to him.

"We believe', while their hearts do not believe. Among the Jews are some who eagerly listen to falsehood, eagerly listen to other people who have not come to you. They tamper with words out of their context, and say, If such-and-such (a precept] is given you, accept it; but if you are not given it, then be on your guard."

Some reports suggest that these verses speak of a group of Jews who committed certain sins including adultery and theft, which carry specific punishments outlined in the Torah. The Jews, however, at least in the first place, had established different punishments, because they did not want to enforce the provisions of the Torah on those of them who were in power. They later wanted to waive these punishments of the Torah in all cases. They replaced them with other punishments. When some of them committed these sins at the time of the Prophet, they thought to seek his judgement. If he judged according to the lesser punishments, which they had legislated, they would enforce them and justify their action to Allah by saying that they had enforced the verdict of His Messenger. If he judged that they should be punished according to the Torah, they would refuse his judgement. They, thus, sent some of their people to seek his ruling. This, then, explains their statement, **"If such- and-such la precept] is given you, accept it; but if you are not given it, then be on your guard."**

They had indeed gone that far in playing games with Allah's law and in being dishonest in their dealings with Allah and His Messenger (peace be upon him). This is a stage which can be reached by any people who, having received Divine revelation, have long ignored their duties. In such a situation hearts are hardened and the light of faith is stifled. They say with their mouths, **'We believe', while their hearts do not believe."?**

Allah (glorified be He) says to His Messenger with regard to those who rush into disbelief and those conspirators who engage in such schemes that he should not be grieved by such people's actions. They seek to create confusion and they will fall victim to it, while he [i.e. God's Messenger] himself has no say in the matter and cannot help them through their test when they have brought confusion upon themselves: **"If God wants to put anyone to test, you shall not be able to avail him anything against God."** Such people have sunk their hearts into impurity, so Allah is unwilling to purify them: **"Such are the ones whose hearts God is not willing to purify."** He will cause them to suffer ignominy in this life and grievous suffering in the Hereafter: **"They will have disgrace in this world, and awesome suffering in the life to come."** He tells the Prophet not to worry about them, and not to be grieved by their disbelief. Their fate is sealed.

Allah has given the Prophet the choice whether to judge between them or to turn away from them, if they ask him for judgement. If he chooses not to pay any attention to them, they can harm him in no way. But if he chooses to judge between them then his must be a fair judgement, unaffected by their prejudices or their rushing into disbelief or by their plots and schemes: **"God loves those who deal justly."**

The Messenger (peace be upon him), Muslim rulers and judges deal directly with Allah in such matters and exert their efforts to establish justice in order to serve Allah because Allah loves those who deal justly. If people commit injustice or perjury or deviate from the truth, justice continues to carry its superior status. Fair judgement is not passed in order to please people but to please Allah. This is, indeed, the most effective guarantee provided by Islamic law everywhere and in all times.

Judgement according to Islamic law became compulsory, because the land of Islam does not enforce any law other than that of Allah. All people living there must refer their disputes to this law.

The punishments prescribed for adultery and theft are applicable to them, because they are stated in their Scriptures. Also enforceable are the punishments prescribed for rebellion against the legitimate authority, and for spreading corruption in the land. Such enforcement is necessary to guarantee the safety and security of the land of Islam and all its inhabitants, Muslims and non-Muslims alike. Such punishments cannot be waived in respect of anyone of those living in the land of Islam.

During that period in which the Prophet had the choice whether to judge between them or to ignore them, they used to come with some of their disputes to him.

An example of this is reported by `Abdullāh ibn `Umar: "Some Jews came to God's Messenger (peace be upon him) and told him that a Jewish man and a Jewish woman committed adultery. The Prophet asked them: 'What does the Torah say about stoning adulterers?' They said: 'We publicise their crime and punish them by flogging.' `Abdullāh ibn Sallām (a Jewish rabbi who had embraced Islam) said, 'This is a lie. The Torah prescribes stoning.' They brought the Torah and opened it up. One of them put his hand over the verse that mentioned stoning and read the preceding and the following verses. `Abdullāh ibn Sallām told him to lift his hand off. When he did, the relevant verse on the death punishment by stoning was there. They said, 'He (meaning `Abdullāh ibn Sallām) has told the truth. It specifies death by stoning.'

The Prophet gave his orders for the two adulterers to be stoned to death. I saw the man bending over the woman to shelter her from the stones." (Related by al-Bukhārī and Muslim.)

Those who claim to themselves or to others that they believe and still refuse to implement God's law in their lives or who are not satisfied when it is enforced on them do indeed make false claims. Their attitude is described in this definitive statement: **"For certain, they are not true believers."** It is not simply a question of rulers not implementing God's law, but also a question of ordinary people not being satisfied with God's law and judgement. Such dissatisfaction takes them out of the ranks of believers, no matter how emphatically they claim to believe.

Numerous references in the Qur'ān show that early religions, some of which might have been addressed to small communities, contained all three mutually complementary aspects in a fashion suitable to that particular community's stage of development. At this point, such complementarity in the three major religions, Judaism, Christianity and Islam, is outlined, starting with the Torah: **"Indeed, it is We who revealed the Torah, containing guidance and light."**

As revealed by Allah, the Torah was the Book providing guidance for the Children of Israel, lighting up the way they should follow in life in order to lead them to God's pleasure. It contained the essence of monotheistic faith, and a variety of worship rituals, as well as a code of law: **"By it did the prophets, who had surrendered themselves to God, judge among the Jews, and so did the divines and the rabbis: [they gave judgement] in accordance with what had been entrusted to their care of God's Book and to which they themselves were witnesses."**

The Qur'ān addresses the Muslim community with regard to judgements in accordance with revelations in general and the opposition people may show to such judgements. It also outlines the duty of everyone entrusted with the implementation of God's law and the punishment incurred by neglecting this duty: **"So, have no fear of men but fear Me; and do not barter away My revelations for a paltry price. Those who do not judge in accordance with what God has revealed are indeed unbelievers."**

Allah knows that enforcing His revealed law will be met with opposition in every period of time and in every community. Some people will not easily submit to it. Those who have power, tyrants and despots, and those who claim authority by right of inheritance will put up stiff resistance to it, because they realise that its enforcement will deprive them of the mask of Godhead they wear and acknowledge Godhead as totally belonging to God alone.

As Allah knows that opposition to His law will come from all these quarters, and that those to whose care His message is entrusted must face up to this opposition and make all the necessary sacrifices for its sake, He addresses them in these words: **"Have no fear of men but fear Me."** No fear of tyrants, exploiters or deluded masses should deter them from implementing God's law. It is God alone that they should fear, because fearing Him dispels all other fear.

Allah gave Jesus, son of Mary, the Gospel so that it may serve as a way of life and a code of law. The Gospel did not present new legislation, but rather introduced a few modifications into the law of the Torah. It, thus, confirmed this earlier law by endorsing it with a few modifications. In the Gospel, Allah gave guidance, light and admonition, but only **"to the God-fearing"**. It is the God-fearing who open their hearts to God's revealed Books and who find in them guidance, light and admonition. Hardened hearts, on the other hand, miss the meaning of the words and the essence of the directives. They neither appreciate the value of its words, benefit by the guidance and light provided, nor do they gain any new knowledge. The light is there, but it needs an open heart to benefit from it; guidance is available, but it only benefits a searching soul; and admonition is given but it is only picked up by a keen intellect.

This is a definitive statement, expressed in the clearest of terms. It takes extreme care to forestall any temptation to abandon even a small part of this law, regardless of the circumstances. When one reflects on this, one is bound to wonder how a person who claims to be a Muslim can abandon God's law in its totality, justifying his action by force of circumstance. How can he find it in himself to continue to claim that he is a Muslim after so doing? How can people call themselves Muslims when they have refused to acknowledge God's Godhead, turned their backs on God's law and denied its suitability for all situations!

"And to you, We have revealed the Book, setting forth the truth." Since it is revealed by God, the only One who has the authority to enact laws, then it certainly sets forth the truth. Everything that it contains of matters of faith, law, directives and stories are true.

Hence, it is the Book of the truth. Moreover, it confirms **"the Scriptures which had already been revealed before it and superseding them."** It, thus, provides the final version of the Divine faith. It is the final arbiter not only in this regard, but also with regard to the way of life mankind should follow, the legislation that should be implemented and the system that should be established. No modification is admissible. Any disagreement over any of these matters, whether between followers of Divine religions or between Muslims themselves, must be referred to this Book. No opinion advanced by any human being has any value unless it is supported by this final authority.

As this is an undeniable fact, it must have its practical implementation: **"Judge, then, between them in accordance with what God has revealed and do not follow their vain desires, forsaking thereby the truth that has come to you."** This command is addressed in the first instance to God's Messenger (peace be upon him) with respect to those of the followers of earlier religions who came to him for arbitration. But its import is not confined to this particular aspect. It is a general order, applicable till the end of time since there will never be a new messenger or a new message to modify anything in this final version of God's message to mankind.

This religion has been made complete, and through it God has perfected the grace He has bestowed on Muslims. Moreover, God has been pleased to choose this religion as a way of life for all mankind. As we have repeatedly said, no modification or amendment is possible or admissible. When God chose it for human life, He knew its inherent suitability. As God makes it the final arbiter, He knows that it benefits all mankind and that it can be implemented in all generations till the Day of Judgement. Anyone who seeks to modify it, let alone abandon it altogether, takes himself out of the fold of Islam altogether, even though he reiterates a thousand times his claim to be a Muslim.

Twice in this short passage God warns the Prophet (peace be upon him) against yielding to the desires of those who come to him for arbitration trying to tempt him away from any part of his revelations. At times, the thought may occur to some people that under certain circumstances, a certain provision of God's law may be modified or set aside. One such motivation could be the desire to establish a measure of unity among all sects and faiths living in the same country. Some people, however, may advocate a conciliatory attitude in matters which may not appear to be so fundamental.

Some reports suggest that the Jews in Madinah made an offer to the Prophet (peace be upon him) that they would follow him, if he agreed to waive certain provisions of the law including that of stoning adulterers. These reports suggest that the warning contained in these verses relate to that particular offer. It is perfectly clear, however, that the order given here has general application. The followers of this Divine faith may face similar temptations and similar offers. God chooses to give His final word in such matters and to leave no room for a compromise. He tells His Messenger that had He so willed, He would have made all mankind a single community. But He has chosen to give each community a code of law and a way of life in order to test them according to what He has given them. Each community will follow its own way but they will all return to God when He will hold them accountable for their actions and the method they had chosen to implement. He will tell them the truth over which they differ. As such, no compromise can be pursued in order to unite those who differ in method and way of life. Such a unification is out of the question: **"To every one of you We have given a code of law and a way of life. Had God so willed, He could have made you all one community; but (it is His wish) to test you by means of that which He has bestowed on you. Vie, then, with one another in doing good works. To God you shall all return. He will then make you understand all that over which you now differ"** As we clearly see, God has left no loophole. Even when a compromise may promise good results, such as national unity, it is inadmissible. God's law is too precious for any part of it to be sacrificed in return for something which God knows will never happen. People have been created with varying susceptibilities and different methods and ways. God has created them so for a particular purpose of His. He has offered them His guidance and called on them to vie with one another in doing good works. When they return to Him, He rewards them according to their deeds.

As Muslims engage in a fight to establish their new system as a living reality, the Qur'ān provides them with the necessary concept to create, in their subconscious, a sense of distinction between them and all those who do not belong to their community. This distinction does not preclude tolerance and kind treatment; for these come naturally to a Muslim. It only precludes a relationship of alliance, of the sort a Muslim owes only to God, His Messenger and the community of believers. All Muslims, in all generations, have this awareness and feel this distinction: **"Believers, do not take the Jews and the Christians for your allies. They are allies of one another."** The fact that they are allies of one another has nothing to do with any particular period of time because it is rooted in the nature of things. They have never been allies with the Muslim community in any land or in any period of history. One generation succeeded another, confirming the truth of this accurate statement. Ever since their collaboration in fighting the Prophet Muḥammad (peace be upon him) and the Muslim community in Madinah, they have maintained their own alliance in all parts of the world at all times. Never was there any exception to this rule. Never did this planet witness anything other than that stated in the Qur'ān as a universal fact. In the original Arabic text the mode of expression selected is the one which is normally used to state permanent facts.

As this is a permanent fact, its consequences are clearly stated. Since the Jews and the Christians are allies of one another, they can only be patronised by someone of their own kind. If someone from the Islamic camp establishes an alliance with them, he actually removes himself from the Muslim camp, abandons the basic quality of Islam and joins the other camp. For this is the natural and practical result: **"Whoever of you allies himself with them is indeed one of them."** He, thus, wrongs himself and wrongs the Divine faith of the Muslim community. Because of his wrongdoing, God puts him in the same group with the Jews and Christians to whom he has pledged his support and made himself an ally.

God neither guides him to the truth nor returns him to the Muslim ranks: **"God does not bestow His guidance on the wrongdoers."** This statement represents a very stern warning to the Muslim community in Madinah. Stern it certainly is, but not exaggerated. It simply describes the reality as it is. It is not possible for a Muslim to ally himself with the Jews and Christians and still retain his faith as someone who truly submits himself to God. He simply cannot keep his membership of the Muslim community which acknowledges alliances only with God and His Messenger, and with those who believe.

"Believers, do not take the Jews and the Christians for your allies. They are allies of one another Whoever of you allies himself with them is indeed one of them." It is the Qur'ān which has the final say. A Muslim should pay no heed to the attempts of those who try to weaken his resolve or water down his firm beliefs.

Verses 87-108 Good things which Allah has made lawful, ruling on oaths, wine, gambling, and some other prohibited practices, hunting, directions to the believers, testimony at the time of bequest

87. O ye who believe! make not unlawful the good things which Allah hath made lawful for you, but commit no excess: for Allah loveth not those given to excess.

88. Eat of the things which Allah hath provided for you, lawful and good; but fear Allah, in Whom ye believe.

89. Allah will not call you to account for what is futile in your oaths, but He will call you to account for your deliberate oaths: for expiation, feed ten indigent persons, on a scale of the average for the food of your families; or clothe them; or give a slave his freedom. If that is beyond your means, fast for three days. That is the expiation for the oaths ye have sworn. But keep to your oaths. Thus doth Allah make clear to you His signs, that ye may be grateful.

90. O ye who believe! Intoxicants and gambling, (dedication of) stones, and (divination by) arrows, are an abomination,- of Satan's handwork: eschew such (abomination), that ye may prosper.

91. Satan's plan is (but) to excite enmity and hatred between you, with intoxicants and gambling, and hinder you from the remembrance of Allah, and from prayer: will ye not then abstain?

92. Obey Allah, and obey the Messenger, and beware (of evil): if ye do turn back, know ye that it is Our Messenger.s duty to proclaim (the message) in the clearest manner.

93. On those who believe and do deeds of righteousness there is no blame for what they ate (in the past), when they guard themselves from evil, and believe, and do deeds of righteousness,- (or) again, guard themselves from evil and believe,- (or) again, guard themselves from evil and do good. For Allah loveth those who do good.

94. O ye who believe! Allah doth but make a trial of you in a little matter of game well within reach of your hands and your lances, that He may test who feareth him unseen: any who transgress thereafter, will have a grievous penalty.

95. O ye who believe! Kill not game while in the sacred precincts or in pilgrim garb. If any of you doth so intentionally, the compensation is an offering, brought to the Ka'ba, of a domestic animal equivalent to the one he killed, as adjudged by two just men among you; or by way of atonement, the feeding of the indigent; or its equivalent in fasts: that he may taste of the penalty of his deed. Allah forgives what is past: for repetition Allah will exact from him the penalty. For Allah is Exalted, and Lord of Retribution.

96. Lawful to you is the pursuit of water-game and its use for food,- for the benefit of yourselves and those who travel; but forbidden is the pursuit of land-game;- as long as ye are in the sacred precincts or in pilgrim garb. And fear Allah, to Whom ye shall be gathered back.

97. Allah made the Ka'ba, the Sacred House, an asylum of security for men, as also the Sacred Months, the animals for offerings, and the garlands that mark them: That ye may know that Allah hath knowledge of what is in the heavens and on earth and that Allah is well acquainted with all things.

98. Know ye that Allah is strict in punishment and that Allah is Oft-forgiving, Most Merciful.

99. The Messenger.s duty is but to proclaim (the message). But Allah knoweth all that ye reveal and ye conceal.

100. Say: "Not equal are things that are bad and things that are good, even though the abundance of the bad may dazzle thee; so fear Allah, O ye that understand; that (so) ye may prosper."

101. O ye who believe! Ask not questions about things which, if made plain to you, may cause you trouble. But if ye ask about things when the Qur'an is being revealed, they will be made plain to you, Allah will forgive those: for Allah is Oft- forgiving, Most Forbearing.

102. Some people before you did ask such questions, and on that account lost their faith.

103. It was not Allah who instituted (superstitions like those of) a slit-ear she- camel, or a she-camel let loose for free pasture, or idol sacrifices for twin-births in animals, or stallion- camels freed from work: It is blasphemers who invent a lie against Allah. but most of them lack wisdom.

104. When it is said to them: "Come to what Allah hath revealed; come to the Messenger.: They say: "Enough for us are the ways we found our fathers following." what! even though their fathers were void of knowledge and guidance?

105. O ye who believe! Guard your own souls: If ye follow (right) guidance, no hurt can come to you from those who stray. the goal of you all is to Allah. it is He that will show you the truth of all that ye do.

106. O ye who believe! When death approaches any of you, (take) witnesses among yourselves when making bequests,- two just men of your own (brotherhood) or others from outside if ye are journeying through the earth, and the chance of death befalls you (thus). If ye doubt (their truth), detain them both after prayer, and let them both swear by Allah. "We wish not in this for any worldly gain, even though the (beneficiary) be our near relation: we shall hide not the evidence before Allah. if we do, then behold! the sin be upon us!"

107. But if it gets known that these two were guilty of the sin (of perjury), let two others stand forth in their places,- nearest in kin from among those who claim a lawful right: let them swear by Allah. "We

affirm that our witness is truer than that of those two, and that we have not trespassed (beyond the truth): if we did, behold! the wrong be upon us!"

108. That is most suitable: that they may give the evidence in its true nature and shape, or else they would fear that other oaths would be taken after their oaths. But fear Allah, and listen (to His counsel): for Allah guideth not a rebellious people:

87. "O' you who have Faith! Do not prohibit the good things that Allah has made lawful to you, and do not transgress. Verily Allah does not like the transgressors."

Once the Prophet (Pbuh) was addressing his people about the Hereafter and the scenes of the gathering-place of Resurrection. The audience were so touched at heart and wept that some of them decided, from then on, not to consume any good food, to prohibit comfort unto themselves, to observe a fast, to abandon their wives, and to sleep at nights less than before.

They swore over that decision to be loyal to it. When the Prophet (Pbuh) was informed of it, he mustered people in the mosque and told them: "I eat food; I sleep at nights and do not abandon my wives. Our religion is not the creed of retreat and seclusion.

Some of them asked what they would do for the oaths they had taken. The subsequent verses were revealed saying that Allah does not call them to account for their vain (unintentional) oaths.

In the previous verse, the words were about the prohibition of unlawful things, while in this verse it has enjoined people to lawfully enjoying the merits of Allah. It says:

"And eat from the lawful and good things which Allah has provided for you;"

The only condition in this course is that you should avoid opposing the command of Allah in whom you believe.

"... and be in awe of Allah whom you have Faith in."

That is, your faith. Allah requires that you respect all his commandments both in enjoying the merits of Allah and observing moderation and piety.

In this verse, the general discussion is about the oaths which are taken upon the fields of making the lawful things into unlawful ones, and the like of them. These oaths, from this point of view, are divided into two sorts. At first, it says:

"Allah does not call you to account for your vain (unintentional) oaths....."

The objective meaning of 'vain oaths', as the commentators and jurisprudents have said, is the oaths that do not aim a definite goal and those that have not been taken intentionally and decidedly. Besides, the contents of such oaths are against the laws of religion.

The second sort is the oaths which are taken willfully, intentionally, decidedly, and earnestly. Referring to these kinds of oaths, in the continuation of the verse, the Qur'an says:

"... but he calls you to account for what you have pledged solemnly....."

And Allah charges you with a duty to fulfill these oaths.

Therefore, if someone takes an oath by Allah, it is obligatory to perform it according to his oath. So, if he breaches his pledge, one of the following three atonements is necessary to be performed by the one. At first, it says:

"... So its atonement is feeding ten paupers..."

Yet, in order that some people do not take this general ordinance so that they think they can give any low and worthless material of food as atonement, the Qur'an clearly explains the quality of this food, saying that it must be:

"... With the average of what you feed your own families....." The second is: to cloth ten needy persons with proper clothing. ***"... or clothing them....."***

The appearance of this verse, of course, indicates that the clothing should be of a sort which normally covers the body.

Yet it can be of various kinds according to the seasons and places in different periods.

The third is:

"....freeing a slave...."

Sometimes it happens that there may be some persons who are able to fulfill neither of the above two atonements. Therefore, next to stating these ordinances, it says:

"... But whoever does not find (the means to do so), should fast for three days....."

After that, as an emphasis, the Qur'an says:

"... That is the atonement of your oaths when you pledge..."

But, in order that no one might consider that by giving atonement, breaching the proper oaths is not unlawful, it says:

"... But guard your oaths..."

The purpose or this phrase is that you should be careful not to commit sins by breaching your oaths.

And, finally, at the end of the verse, in order that you might be grateful for these ordinances and commandments, which guarantee the happiness and felicity of both an individual and society, the Qur'an says:

"... Thus Allah makes His Signs clear for you in order that you might be thankful."

At the time of the advent of Islam, the Arabs customarily were intensively interested in poetry, wine, and fighting. The Divine revelations concerning the prohibition of wine were gradually conveyed.

The Qur'an, then, has referred to the benefits of gambling and wine (and also that their containing sin is greater than their benefits.

After that the verse was revealed enjoining not to establish prayer at the state of being intoxicated.

And, finally, the above verse was revealed which considered wine as an abomination, a Satanic action, and ordained that it is unlawful.

The verse enjoins to avoid not only drinking wine, but also approaching it. The reason of this ordinance is that a sound nutrition is effective in the prosperity of human beings. Therefore, it enjoins to avoid intoxication, so that you may be prosperous. The verse says:

"... So avoid it, that you may be prosperous."

Any kind of cooperation concerning wine, including its production, distribution, and consumption is prohibited.

The prohibition of drinking liquor and gambling, enjoined by Allah, is for the goodness and improvement of people's affairs both in this world and the Hereafter.

When the verse of prohibitions of gambling and drinking wine was revealed, there were some people who asked about their condition regarding to the time before that revelation or the condition of those who had not heard of that ordinance yet and were living in some far distances.

The verse answers them implying that those who have believed and have done good deeds but have not received this ordinance, if they have drunk wine or have devoured from the income of gambling, there is no sin on them. The verse says:

"On those who have Faith and do good deeds, there is no sin in regard to what they ate (before prohibition) ..."

Yet, this ordinance has conditioned that such people should be virtuous, have Faith, and do good actions. Here is the continuation of the verse:

"... so long as they are virtuous and faithful and do good deeds....."

This subject is repeated once more in the verse, when it says:

"... then still they be virtuous (upon prohibited things) and believe (in their prohibition)....."

And, for the third time this meaning is repeated, with a little difference, of course. It says:

"... then they are virtuous (due to prohibited things) and do good...."

So, at the end of the verse, it says:

"... and Allah loves the doers of good."

Each of these three senses of virtuousness refers to a stage of feeling responsibility and piety.

Verse 94 continues to elaborate on further prohibitions. This time hunting when one is in a state of ihram. It further speaks of the purpose of the sanctity of the kabaah, the sacred months, dedicated and garlanded cattle which must not be touched as the surah makes clear in its opening verses. This part concludes with the establishment of a clear standard of values for a Muslim society.

Like all the other sections of this long passage, this part opens with an address to the believers. They are then told that they are about to be set a test concerning game that has been prohibited to them while they are in the state of Ihram:

"Believers, God will certainly try you by means of game which may come within the reach of your hands or your spears, so that God may mark out those who truly fear Him in their hearts. Whoever transgresses after all this will have grievous suffering."
It is a very easy game that is brought within their vicinity. They could easily grab it with their hands, or with their spears.

The trial of the prohibition of hunting when in a state of ihram, was one of the numerous tests that the Muslim community successfully passed. The care Allah took of this Muslim community and its education is reflected in such tests. In this particular incident, Allah tells the believers of the purpose beyond His test:

"So that God may mark out those who truly fear Him in their hearts."

Being truly God-fearing, or fearing Him in one's heart, is the solid basis on which faith is established in a person's conscience.

Human beings do not see God, but they feel His presence in their hearts when they truly believe in Him. To them, He is beyond the reach of all their faculties of perception, but their hearts know and fear Him. The certainty of this great truth in a firm, unshakeable belief in Allah. A believer declares that **"there is no deity other than God"** without having seen Him.

Verse 96 is about seafood in the state of Ihram. It says:

"The games of the sea and its food are lawful for you....."

The objective meaning of 'food', mentioned in this verse, is the food that can be prepared from the hunted fish. The verse intends to make two things admissible. One of them is 'hunting', and the other is 'consuming the food made from the hunted things.'

Then, the Qur'an points to the philosophy of this ordinance, implying that this permission is for the sake that you and the travellers can enjoy it. It says:

"....provision for you and for the caravans....."

As an emphasis, the Qur'an returns to the former ordinance once more, and says:

"... but the game of the land is forbidden to you so long as you are in pilgrim garb...."

And, at the end of the verse, in order to emphasize upon all the ordinances that were mentioned, it says:

"... and be in awe of Allah toward whom you will be gathered."

The Philosophy of No Hunting when in the state of ihram!

We know that the performance of Hajj and 'Umrah is one of the worships that makes man aloof from the world of matter and brings him into an environment full of spiritualities.

In performing the rite of Hajj and 'Umrah, the ceremonies of the material life, fights and conflicts, hatreds, and material pleasures, will totally be put aside and the person reaches a kind of godly legitimated self-discipline. So, it seems that the prohibition of hunting, while being in a state of Ihram, is also for the same purpose.

The general attitude towards the Muslims had now changed since the revelation of the previous Surahs 3: Al-Imran (Family of Imran) and Surah 4: An-Nisa (The Women)

Islam had become a force and the Islamic State had extended to Najd on the east, to the Red Sea on the west, to Syria on the north, and to Makkah on the south. The set-back which the Muslims had suffered at Uhud had not broken their determination. It had rather spurred them to action. As a result of their continuous struggle and unparalleled sacrifices the power of the surrounding clans within a radius of 200 miles or so had been subdued. The conspiracies of the Jewish tribes - which had always threatened Madinah - were totally removed and the Jews in other parts of the Arabian Peninsula (Hijaz) had become tributaries of the State of Madinah. The last effort of the Quraysh to suppress Islam had been thwarted in the Battle of the Ditch.

Islam was no longer merely a creed which ruled over the minds and hearts of the people but had also become a State which dominated over every aspect of the life of the people who lived within its boundaries. This had enabled the Muslims to live their lives without any hindrance in accordance with their beliefs.

Another development had also taken place during this period. The Muslim state had developed in accordance with the principles of Islam. It identified the Muslims clearly from the non-Muslims in their moral, social and cultural behaviour. Mosques had been built in all territories, prayer had been established and a leader (Imam) for every habitation and clan had been appointed. The Islamic civil and criminal laws had been formulated in detail and were being enforced through the Islamic courts. New and reformed ways of trade and commerce had taken the place of the old ones. The Islamic laws of marriage and divorce, of the segregation of the genders, of the punishment for adultery and slander and the like had cast the social life of the Muslims in a special mould. Their social behaviour, their conversation, their dress, their very mode of living, their culture etc., had taken a definite shape of its own. As a result of all these changes, the non-Muslims could not expect that the Muslims would ever return to their former ways. Before the treaty of Hudaibiyah, the Muslims were so engaged in their struggle with the non-Muslim Quraysh that had little time to propagate their message. This was resolved by what was apparently a defeat but in reality a victory at Hudaibiyah. This gave the Muslims not only peace in their own territory but also respite to spread their message in the surrounding territories. Accordingly, the Prophet addressed letters to the chiefs of Arabia, the rulers of Persia, Egypt and the Roman Empire inviting them to Islam. At the same time the missionaries of Islam spread among the clans and tribes and invited them to accept the Divine Way of God. These were the circumstances at the time when al- Ma'idah was revealed.

Verses 109-110: Questioning messengers on the Day of Resurrection about the people's responses, reminder of miracles of Jesus and the story of the table, dialogue between Jesus and His Lord on the Day of Resurrection, good consequences of the truthful

> *109. One day will Allah gather the apostles together, and ask: "What was the response ye received (from men to your teaching)?" They will say: "We have no knowledge: it is Thou Who knowest in full all that is hidden."*

> *110. Then will Allah say: "O Jesus the son of Mary! Recount My favour to thee and to thy mother. Behold! I strengthened thee with the holy spirit, so that thou didst speak to the people in childhood and in maturity. Behold! I taught thee the Book and Wisdom, the Law and the Gospel and behold! thou makest out of clay, as it were, the figure of a bird, by My leave, and thou breathest into it and it becometh a bird by My leave, and thou healest those born blind, and the lepers, by My leave. And behold! thou bringest forth the dead by My leave. And behold! I did restrain the Children of Israel from (violence to) thee when thou didst show them the clear Signs, and the unbelievers among them said: 'This is nothing but evident magic.'*

The scene is full of life: "On the day when Allah will gather all [His] messengers and ask them:

"What response did you receive?" Messengers are human. They know what they see and feel with their senses, but they have no knowledge of what lies beyond. They had called on their peoples to follow Divine guidance. Some responded positively while others turned away. A messenger does not know the full truth. He can only tell by appearances; it is Allah who knows the full truth and what is concealed. Those messengers are now in the presence of Allah and, among all human beings, they know Allah best, fear Him most and are too modest to speak out, in His presence, on the basis of their limited knowledge when He knows all.

This is an awesome interrogation, on the day when all creatures are gathered, the Supreme Company is present and all humanity is looking on. This is a confrontation, when all humanity is put face to face with the Messengers, and especially the unbelievers who are now arrayed before those Messengers to whom they used to ridicule.

The Messengers are now in Allah's presence stating how the community responded to their messages.

This verse is a full account of the various aspects of grace bestowed by Allah on Jesus (Prophet Isa,PBUH) and his mother, Mary (Maryam). To start with, he was supported by the Holy Spirit in his infancy. Then, he was talking to people from the cradle, absolving his mother of all suspicion raised around her on account of his miraculous birth. He was born without knowledge of reading and writing, but Allah gave him that knowledge, as He imparted to him wisdom in order to deal with different situations in the best way. Allah also taught him the Torah which had been given to the Children of Israel and the Gospel which Allah gave him to confirm the Torah.

Furthermore, Allah gave Jesus several miraculous things that no human being could accomplish without Allah's support. Thus, he could fashion a bird shape of clay and breathe into it, and all at once it became a living bird. He cures a person born blind, by Allah's leave, when medicine does not know how to give eyesight to such a person. Allah, who gives human beings their faculty of seeing, is able to open a blind person's eyes to see the light. Jesus also cured the leper without using any medicine. Jesus was able to restore life to the dead, by God's leave. The One who initiates life is able to restore it at any tune.

Allah further reminds Jesus of His favours when He extended His protection to him against the Israelites who, when he produced all these miracles, denied him claiming that they were plain sorcery. On the one hand they did not wish to deny the miracles, witnessed by thousands of people, and yet they were too stubborn to submit to the message they imparted. Allah protected him and they were unable to kill or crucify him. Allah simply gathered him and elevated him to Himself. Another reminder to Jesus speaks of how Allah inspired the disciples to believe in Him and His Messenger, Jesus, and they do so, appealing to him to bear witness to their acceptance of the faith and total self-surrender to God.

Here Jesus is reminded of all these in the presence of the Supreme Company and in front of all mankind, including those people who exaggerated his status and attributed to him what was not his. When these favours are held in front of him, those who gave him a status far beyond his own humanity will see and hear, and, in consequence, they will be humiliated in the full sight of all humanity.

Verses 112 — 120

112. Behold! the disciples, said: "O Jesus the son of Mary! can thy Lord send down to us a table set (with viands) from heaven?" Said Jesus: "Fear Allah, if ye have faith."

113. They said: "We only wish to eat thereof and satisfy our hearts, and to know that thou hast indeed told us the truth; and that we ourselves may be witnesses to the miracle."

114. Said Jesus the son of Mary: "O Allah our Lord! Send us from heaven a table set (with viands), that there may be for us - for the first and the last of us - a solemn festival and a sign from thee; and provide for our sustenance, for thou art the best Sustainer (of our needs)."

115. Allah said: "I will send it down unto you: But if any of you after that resisteth faith, I will punish him with a penalty such as I have not inflicted on any one among all the peoples."

116. And behold! Allah will say: "O Jesus the son of Mary! Didst thou say unto men, worship me and my mother as gods in derogation of Allah.?" He will say: "Glory to Thee! never could I say what I had no right (to say). Had I said such a thing, thou wouldst indeed have known it. Thou knowest what is in my heart, Thou I know not what is in Thine. For Thou knowest in full all that is hidden.

117. "Never said I to them aught except what Thou didst command me to say, to wit, 'worship Allah, my Lord and your Lord'; and I was a witness over them whilst I dwelt amongst them; when Thou didst take me up Thou wast the Watcher over them, and Thou art a witness to all things.

118. "If Thou dost punish them, they are Thy servant: If Thou dost forgive them, Thou art the Exalted in power, the Wise."

119. Allah will say: "This is a day on which the truthful will profit from their truth: theirs are gardens, with rivers flowing beneath,- their eternal Home: Allah well-pleased with them, and they with Allah. That is the great salvation, (the fulfilment of all desires).

120. To Allah doth belong the dominion of the heavens and the earth, and all that is therein, and it is He Who hath power over all things.

In the above verses we learn about the story of the Ma'idah, the name of which this Surah bears, <u>Surat Al-Ma'idah</u>. This is also among the favours that Allah granted His servant and Messenger, Eesa, accepting his request to send the Ma'idah (table spread) down, and doing so as clear proof and unequivocal evidence.

THE TABLE-SPREAD

One day Prophet Isa asked his supporters to fast for 30 days. They agreed and began their fast.

On the completion of the fast they follow the prophet to the desert. There were always many people who followed the prophet. Some were sick people hoping to be cured.

But there were also a group of disbelievers who followed the prophet to mock and jeered at him.

They had also fasted and asked the prophet to send something special from the sky to break their fast. There were thousands of people and they wanted the spread to be sufficient for the entire gathering. They saw this as an impossible task for the prophet and was convinced that he will not be able to deliver.

But they were wrong!!

Prophet Isa went in a quiet corner and prayed to Allah. His prayers were answered. There was a table spread of food that descended from the sky. It was covered with a cloth. The prophet removed the cloth and saw the most mouthwatering food.

The people gasped in amazement. There were seven big fish, seven loaves of bread, seven bottles of vinegar, honey and an abundance of fruits. The beautiful aroma of the food filled the air. The people had never smelt anything so wonderful before.

The prophet asked the disbelievers to eat first as they were the ones who asked for the food. But they refused and stated they will not touch the food until the prophet and his followers ate.

All the sick and infirmed people ate first. Allah provided the people with another miracle. The sick people got cured.

The news of this miracle spread fast and thousands of people from the city came for this feast, and the food never ran out. This itself was another miracle.

After forty days, Allah directed the prophet that only the poor must be allowed to eat from the feast.

But this didn't happen. The rich pretended to be poor and kept on feasting.

The poor was asked not to take away any of the food to be saved for the next day. They didn't listen either.

The Table spread was lifted back to the sky where it came from.

This miracle remained in the people's minds for years and there were continued conversation about this miracle from Allah.

Verse 116 -120 Allah addressing the Christians

These verses present in detail a scene taking place on the Day Of Judgement.

Allah swt with gather all his prophets and ask about the response they had from their people.

Allah subhanahu wa ta'ala will ask Eesa aalyhi salaam if he commanded his people to worship him and his mother. He will be reminded of all the miracles he had performed by the permission of the Almighty: speaking to people from the cradle, knowledge of the Scripture, the Torah, and the Gospel, and wisdom, making birds out of clay that would turn alive when Eesa aalyhi salaam breathed into them, healing the blind and the leper, bringing the dead back to life, protection when people tried to harm him when he showed them signs, and the disciples believing in him and devoting themselves to God.

> 117. "Never said I to them aught except what Thou didst command me to say, to wit, 'worship Allah, my Lord and your Lord'; and I was a witness over them whilst I dwelt amongst them; when Thou didst take me up Thou wast the Watcher over them, and Thou art a witness to all things.
>
> 118. "If Thou dost punish them, they are Thy servant: If Thou dost forgive them, Thou art the Exalted in power, the Wise."
>
> 119. Allah will say: "This is a day on which the truthful will profit from their truth: theirs are gardens, with rivers flowing beneath,- their eternal Home: Allah well-pleased with them, and they with Allah. That is the great salvation, (the fulfilment of all desires).
>
> 120. To Allah doth belong the dominion of the heavens and the earth, and all that is therein, and it is He Who hath power over all things

Eesa aalyhi salaam will of course plead innocence. His response will be had he done done then Allah swt, knower of everything would have known.

Eesa aalyhi salaam will annouce that he only call on his people to worship the one God and that he is no more than a servant of Allah swt. He will then disclaim any responsibility for what they did after the end of his time on earth. He will conclude that its Allah decision whether he punish or forgive them.

"This is the Day when the truthful will benefit from their truthfulness." This is God's word at the end of that interrogation beheld by all creatures. It is the final and decisive word. It is coupled with the reward that befits truthfulness and those who are truthful.

Chapter 6

Towards Understanding Surah Al- Anaam

Name taken from Verses 136 138 and 139 where superstitions regarding lawfulness and unlawfulness of some cattle are discussed.

136 And the polytheists assign to Allah from that which He created of crops and livestock a share and say, "This is for Allah," by their claim, "and this is for our partners [associated with Him]." But what is for their "partners" does not reach Allah, while what is for Allah – this reaches their "partners." Evil is that which they rule.

The circumstances in which Sural Al Anaam was revealed.

This Surah was revealed in Makkah. It is one of the longest Makki Surahs and first of the Makki Surahs in Qur'an's compilation order. According to a tradition of Ibn Abbas: Asma, a daughter of Yazid and a first cousin of Hadrat Muaz-bin Jabl says:

"At the time of the revelation of this Surah, the Holy Prophet was mounting on a she-camel and I was holding her nose string. The she camel started to feel the weight so profoundly that it seemed as if her bones would break under it. As per traditions, the whole Surah was revealed at one sitting at Makkah.

Looking at the period of History when this surah was revealed.

This period of history was an exceedingly difficult time for the Muslims. They were facing a lot of antagonism and persecution from the Quraish. It was during this time that the first Hijrah took place.

The Holy Prophet (Pbuh) also suffered two great loses. His two greatest supporters Abu Talib and Hazrat Khadija had passed away.

Verses 1– 10

1. *Praise be Allah, Who created the heavens and the earth, and made the darkness and the light. Yet those who reject Faith hold (others) as equal, with their Guardian-Lord.*

2. *He it is created you from clay, and then decreed a stated term (for you). And there is in His presence another determined term; yet ye doubt within yourselves!*

3. *And He is Allah in the heavens and on earth. He knoweth what ye hide, and what ye reveal, and He knoweth the (recompense) which ye earn (by your deeds).*

4. *But never did a single one of the signs of their Lord reach them, but they turned away therefrom.*

5. And now they reject the truth when it reaches them: but soon shall they learn the reality of what they used to mock at.

6. See they not how many of those before them We did destroy?- generations We had established on the earth, in strength such as We have not given to you - for whom We poured out rain from the skies in abundance, and gave (fertile) streams flowing beneath their (feet): yet for their sins We destroyed them, and raised in their wake fresh generations (to succeed them).

7. If We had sent unto thee a written (message) on parchment, so that they could touch it with their hands, the Unbelievers would have been sure to say: "This is nothing but obvious magic!"

8. They say: "Why is not an angel sent down to him?" If we did send down an angel, the matter would be settled at once, and no respite would be granted them.

9. If We had made it an angel, We should have sent him as a man, and We should certainly have caused them confusion in a matter which they have already covered with confusion.

10. Mocked were (many) apostles before thee; but their scoffers were hemmed in by the thing that they mocked.

The first verse of this Surah points to the system of existence, the second verse hints to the creation of man; and the third verse refers to the deeds and behaviour of human beings.

Verse 2 is telling us of our creation – from clay. And it is the darkness of this clay that we are taken to the light of active life. Allah has appointed two kinds of time for humankind. The first term is that of death and the second term appointed is the resurrection.

This powerful opening to the surah addresses man's heart and mind, pointing out the evidence derived from creation and from life. The creation of the heavens and the earth, their organization according to a clear system, and the creation of life — the most important aspect of which is human life, all pointing to a creator and the oneness of that creator. Allah's oneness is the core topic of the whole surah. It is what the Qur'an aims to establish.

In answer to those who consider a separate god for every type of thing, such as god of rain, god of war, god of peace, god of sky, and the like of them, the verse says:

"And He is Allah in the heavens and in the earth!..."

It is obvious that the One Who dominates everywhere and in whose authority is the devise of everything, the Omnipresent, knows all the secret and concealed things. So, it is such that in the next sentence, the verse says:

"... He knows your secret and your open, and He knows what you earn."

Verse 4 points to the pagans' mood of obstinacy, heedlessness, and arrogance against the truth and the signs of Allah. It implies that they are so obstinate and disrespectful that whatever signs they see they immediately turn away from it:

"There never came unto them any Sign from the Signs of their Lord but they turned away from it."

Then, the next verse points to the consequence of this very action of theirs, and says:

"So they indeed belied the truth when it came unto them....."

It is in a case that if they contemplated carefully over the Divine verses, they would see the truth very well, and recognize it and believe in it. The verse continues saying:

"... therefore very soon the (bitter) tidings will come to them of what they used to mock at."

The truth has come to them from the Creator of the heavens and the earth, who has brought into being darkness and light and created man out of clay. It is He alone who is God in the heavens and on earth, and who has full knowledge of all that people keep secret or do openly, as well as all that they earn. What has come to them from Him is the truth, and they have rejected it, insisting on describing it as false, turning away from Divine revelations and deriding the call to faith. Hence, they are told to watch for the true information which is certain to come to them concerning that which they used to scorn.

Their attentions and minds are drawn to the calamities that befell past nations which, like them, rejected the truth. They even had some knowledge of those nations and what happened to them in the remains of the people of Aad and Thamud. The Arabs of Makkah used to pass by these remains when they went on their winter and summer journeys to Yemen and Syria. They also passed by the destroyed towns of the Prophet Lot's people, Sodom and Gomorrah, and were aware of the tales that were in circulation concerning what happened to those people. They should, therefore, reflect on these peoples' fate.

Those earlier generations were well established in the land and given power which was much greater than that enjoyed by the Quraysh.

Allah also sent them rain which brought into their lives fertility, growth and abundance. But they disobeyed their Lord and were subsequently destroyed by Him. Allah then raised up another generation to take over and wield power. No matter how powerful a community may be, Allah can easily inflict severe punishment on them. When those people were destroyed, the earth did not feel their absence since another generation was raised in their place. Life continued as if nothing had happened.

Some of pagans used to say that they might believe when a written paper accompanied with an angel was sent down to them.

They are only being unreasonably stubborn. Such an attitude allows no consideration of any evidence or proof. Had Allah chosen to send down the Qur'ān to His Messenger by means other than revelation, which they cannot see, and put it on paper which they can feel and see, and had they touched this paper with their own hands, they would still reject the evidence of their own hands and eyes. They would emphatically claim: **"This is nothing but plain sorcery."**

The disbelievers protested why there were not sent down an angel with the Prophet (Pbuh) so openly that they could see him and, consequently, they might attest his prophet hood.

"And they said: 'Why has not an angel been sent down to him?...'"

Then, to show that their disobedience has reached its climax, the verse implies that had *Allah* sent down an angel as they wished, they would not have believed:

"... And if we had sent down an angel, the matter would have certainly been determined, and then they would not be granted any respite."

Then the verse continued that even if the Prophet were an angel, he would appear in the guise of a man so that they could see him. This matter would cause people to be led into an error whether he is a human being or an angel.

"And had We appointed him (Our Messenger) an angel, We would certainly have made him as a man, and We would certainly have made confused to them what they (now) make confused."

Verse 10 is soothing the Messenger of Allah (Pbuh). Allah is reassuring him that former prophets were also mocked. The consequence of that is that the mockers will be confronted with not only the chastisement of the Hereafter but also the Divine wrath in the present world. Their own dangerous plots will bring their downfall.

Verses 11 – 18

11. Say: "Travel through the earth and see what was the end of those who rejected Truth."

12. Say: "To whom belongeth all that is in the heavens and on earth?" Say: "To Allah. He hath inscribed for Himself (the rule of) Mercy. That He will gather you together for the Day of Judgment, there is no doubt whatever. It is they who have lost their own souls, that will not believe.

13. To him belongeth all that dwelleth (or lurketh) in the night and the day. For he is the one who heareth and knoweth all things."

14. Say: "Shall I take for my protector any other than Allah, the Maker of the heavens and the earth? And He it is that feedeth but is not fed." Say: "Nay! but I am commanded to be the first of those who bow to Allah (in Islam), and be not thou of the company of those who join gods with Allah."

15. Say: "I would, if I disobeyed my Lord, indeed have fear of the penalty of a Mighty Day.

16. "On that day, if the penalty is averted from any, it is due to Allah's mercy; And that would be (Salvation), the obvious fulfilment of all desire.

17. "If Allah touch thee with affliction, none can remove it but He; if He touch thee with happiness, He hath power over all things.

18. "He is the irresistible, (watching) from above over His worshippers; and He is the Wise, acquainted with all things."

The following verse, (11) has taken another method of awakening the arrogant disbelievers. It tells the Prophet (Pbuh):

"Say: Travel in the earth..."

This verse is telling the prophet to say to the pagans to look at the previous nations who had rejected their prophets. Their punishment. They are warned. They will see the result of their misdeeds on the Day of Judgement.

The surah then refers to all creatures in terms of time, as it has referred to them in terms of place in the preceding verse. It states that Allah, limitless is He in His glory, owns them all, has full knowledge of them and hears everything they say and do.

"To Him belongs whatever takes its rest in the night or in the day. He alone hears all and knows all."

It implies having complete and perfect knowledge of all these creatures and all that is said about them by the unbelievers. The establishment of this fact of Allah's ownership of everything is given here as a prelude to the statement that God has mastery over everything and all creatures.

Say, "Indeed I fear, if I should disobey my Lord, the punishment of a tremendous Day."

This verse is a faithful portrayal of the feelings of Prophet's in respect of the commandments he received from Allah, and how he truly feared his punishment. To be spared that punishment is considered an act of grace bestowed by Allah.

The Messenger of Allah (Pbuh) once said:

"By Allah in whose hand is my soul, no one of people may enter into Paradise (merely) by his own deed."

They asked him:

"Even you, O' Messenger of Allah?" The Prophet (Pbuh) answered:

"Even I, unless Allah shelters me with His mercy and grace."

The Holy Prophet then put his hands on his head and recited the above-mentioned verse.

"Whoever is spared of it (the Divine retribution) on that Day, He has certainly been merciful to him, and that is the manifest triumph."

Everybody is threatened to fall in danger. Saving from the Divine punishment demands a particular grace from the side of Allah.

Hopes should be to Allah, and fears should also be from Allah, since the origin of all affairs is the same. It is not such that the goodness come from one source and vices originates from another source.

"And if Allah touches you with affliction, none can remove it but He; and if He touches you with good, then He is All-Powerful over all things."

Why does man allow himself to sink into paganism when he has been forbidden to do so? Why does he not do what he is commanded to do, namely to submit himself to God? Why does he expose himself to the grievous torment which follows upon such disobedience? Does he think that people will come to his help if he experiences misfortune? Or does he hope to receive kindness from them? All this can only be granted to him by Allah, who has supreme power and who can cause everything to happen and who holds sway over all His creatures. It is He alone who grants and denies people's wishes according to His wisdom and His knowledge of their conditions.

Here we see how the Qur'an penetrates the depth of the human soul to touch on its latent desires and innermost fears. It brings all this into the open and subjects it to the light of faith which distinguishes good from evil. It presents the issues clearly and defines the nature of Allah succinctly.

19. "Say: 'What thing is the greatest in testimony?' Say: 'Allah! He is witness between me and you, and this Qur'an has been revealed to me that I may warn you thereby, and whomever it reaches. Do you indeed testify that there are other gods with Allah? ' Say: ' I do not testify '. Say:, He is only One God, and verily I am quit of that which you associate (with Him) '."

The pagans of Mecca demanded proof from the Prophet (Pbuh) for his prophet hood. They did not accept the prophecy of the Messenger of Allah (SWT) and told him that even the Jews and the Christians did not know him as a divine prophet.

Then Allah reveals verse 19 foretelling of a bright and promising future for Muslims

Ayat 20 to 30

20. Those to whom We have given the Book know this as they know their own sons. Those who have lost their own souls refuse therefore to believe.

21. Who doth more wrong than he who inventeth a lie against Allah or rejecteth His signs? But verily the wrong-doers never shall prosper.

22. One day shall We gather them all together: We shall say to those who ascribed partners (to Us): "Where are the partners whom ye (invented and) talked about?"

23. There will then be (left) no subterfuge for them but to say: "By Allah our Lord, we were not those who joined gods with Allah."

24. Behold! how they lie against their own souls! But the (lie) which they invented will leave them in the lurch.

25. Of them there are some who (pretend to) listen to thee; but We have thrown veils on their hearts, So they understand it not, and deafness in their ears; if they saw every one of the signs, not they will believe in them; in so much that when they come to thee, they (but) dispute with thee; the Unbelievers say: "These are nothing but tales of the ancients."

26. Others they keep away from it, and themselves they keep away; but they only destroy their own souls, and they perceive it not.

27. If thou couldst but see when they are confronted with the Fire! They will say: "Would that we were but sent back! Then would we not reject the signs of our Lord, but would be amongst those who believe!"

28. Yea, in their own (eyes) will become manifest what before they concealed. But if they were returned, they would certainly relapse to the things they were forbidden, for they are indeed liars.

29. And they (sometimes) say: "There is nothing except our life on this earth, and never shall we be raised up again."

30. If thou couldst but see when they are confronted with their Lord! He will say: "Is not this the truth?" They will say: "Yea, by our Lord!" He will say: "Taste ye then the penalty, because ye rejected Faith."

31. Lost indeed are they who treat it as a falsehood that they must meet Allah, - until on a sudden the hour is on them, and they say: "Ah! woe unto us that we took no thought of it"; for they bear their burdens on their backs, and evil indeed are the burdens that they bear?

The Qur'an mentions on several occasions that the people who received earlier revelations, i.e. the Jews and the Christians, recognize the Qur'an and the truthfulness of the Prophet Muhammad's message as well as the fact that the Qur'ān was revealed to him by Allah. At times, the people of these earlier revelations are confronted by this fact because of their hostile attitude towards the Prophet and Islam. At other times, the Arab idolaters are told this so that they realize that the people of earlier revelations, are fully aware of the nature of revelation, recognize the Qur'an and that the Prophet Muhammad (peace be upon him) tells only the truth when he states that Allah revealed it to him in the same way as He bestowed messages from on high to earlier prophets.

"Who is more wicked than one who invents a falsehood about Allah or denies His revelations? The wrongdoers shall never achieve success."

Reference is made here to the idolators. Idolatry is an act of injustice perpetrated against the truth. It is an offence against Allah's right to be worshipped alone, without partners, and against oneself as it leads the perpetrator to ruin. It is also an offence against mankind who are thus led away from the path of submission to Allah. As such, idolatry is a great injustice, as it is described by the Lord of all the worlds. Neither idolatry nor the idolaters will, however, achieve any success: **"The wrongdoers shall never achieve success."** Here Allah is stating the full facts and the end result of idolatry and the idolaters.

There are numerous forms and types of idolatry and idolaters and the partners they associate with Allah. People worshipping statues, stones, trees, etc. is by no means the only form of idolatry. In essence, associating partners with God is to acknowledge any one of the qualities attributable to God alone as belonging to others as well, whether such quality relates to His conduct or control of events, destinies, or to the offering of worship rituals, or to the enactment and implementation of man-made laws. All these are forms of idolatry practised by different groups of unbelievers who associate different forms of partners with God.

The Qur'an describes all these forms as polytheism or idolatry. It portrays scenes from the Day of Judgement which depict many of these and show that the destiny and punishment of different types of idolatry are the same in this life and in the life to come.

The sūrah goes on to describe how some of the unbelievers stubbornly block their minds as they listen to the Qur'ān. Having resolved to reject it altogether, they argue with the Prophet alleging that the Qur'ān is nothing but fables told by the ancients. They turn away from it and they forbid others to listen to it. Having depicted the attitude they adopt in this life, the Qur'ān describes their miserable state as they are made to stand before the fire of hell, facing the horror of their destiny, powerless, and without support. The only thing they can do is wish to go back to life in order to change those views and practices which led them to this horrible end. Their wishes, however, are rejected as petty and childish.

Here, we have two contrasting scenes: the one in this life is characterized by stubborn rejection, while the other, in the hereafter, is a situation of profound regret. They are portrayed in such a way so as to help awaken human nature that has been left to rust for a long time. If only human nature would open up to the Qur'ān and reflect on its message, it would gain the chance to be spared a fearful destiny.

"**Some of them listen to you. But over their hearts We have laid veils which prevent them from understanding what you say, and into their ears, deafness. Were they to see every sign, they would still not believe in it.**" This is a description of a particular type of people who listen but do not understand as if they do not have minds to help them comprehend, or ears to help them hear. This type of person may exist any time, anywhere. Their listening to what is being said has no effect whatsoever. Their ears do not function and their comprehension is sealed, so that the meaning of what they hear does not register with them.

"**Were they to see every sign, they would still not believe in it. When they come to you to contend with you, the unbelievers say: This is nothing but fables of the ancients.**" Their eyes are open, but they do not seem to see, or what they see delivers no message to their minds. What has happened to them, then? What prevents them from responding when they have ears, eyes, and minds? God tells us: "**Over their hearts We have laid veils which prevent them from understanding what you say, and into their ears, deafness. Were they to see every sign, they would still not believe in it.**" It is God who has willed that their faculty of comprehension remains unable to grasp the truth and that their hearing does not function. We should try, then, to understand the wisdom behind God's will.

All indicators to the truth and pointers to the right way and to faith were displayed in front of the idolaters. The Qur'ān repeatedly drew their attention to countless signs and indications which they recognise within themselves and in the world around them. Had they only thought objectively about these, they would have awakened to the truth and responded to it. But they have made no effort to receive guidance. On the contrary, they suppressed their own nature, and in consequence, God placed a veil between them and proper guidance. They did not go to the Prophet with open hearts, ears and eyes in order to listen, see and reflect. They went to argue and dispute: **"When they come to you to contend with you, the unbelievers say: 'This is nothing but fables of the ancients.'"**

They were well aware that the Qur'an bears no resemblance to such fables or legends which speak of supernatural events that happen to heroes and deities and which constitute a part of the beliefs of idolatrous communities. In their attempts to justify their rejection of the message of Prophet Muhammad (peace be upon him), they give all types of false arguments. Since the Qur'an recited to them by the

Prophet contains stories about former prophets and their nations, as well as the fate of those who, in the past, denied God's messages, the unbelievers claimed that the Qur'an was no more than the fables of the ancients.

To give more credence to their false description of the Qur'ān and to turn people away from it, an individual named Malik ibn al-Nadr, had learnt some Persian epics about Rustom and other Persian legendary heroes. He used to sit at a short distance from the Prophet when he recited the Qur'an. After the Prophet Muhammad (peace be upon him) had finished, Malik ibn al-Nadr used to say to his audience: *"If Muhammad could tell you some fables of the ancients, I can tell you better ones."* He would then relate to them some of the epics and histories he had learnt, hoping that in this way, he could prevent them from listening to the Qur'an. **"They forbid [others] to listen to it and go far away from it. They ruin none but themselves, though they do not perceive it."**

All this effort which they exerted to refrain and prevent others from listening to the Qur'ān and allowing themselves not to be influenced by it or respond to it was a recipe for disaster: **"They ruin none but themselves, though they do not perceive it."** Whom would a person ruin if all his efforts were geared towards preventing himself and others from listening to proper guidance and following the right way that ensures salvation?

If you could but see them when they will be made to stand before the Fire!" Now they cannot turn away, use their argumentation, or repeat their falsehoods. If we were to see them ourselves in such a position, we would be sure to see something fearful. Their dearest wish would be: **"Would that we could return! Then we would not deny our Lord's revelations, but would be among the believers."** They know that the Qur'ān is God's revelation, and their desire to return to earth is such that they may have a second chance when they no longer deny these revelations. They claim that they would make sure that they would be among the believers.

Allah knows their nature very well and He is fully aware that they will stubbornly continue in their falsehood. He is also fully aware that it is only the fearsome situation in which they find themselves as they stand by the fire that causes them to utter such wishes and to make these promises. But the real situation is this: **"If they were to return to life, they would go back to that which they have been forbidden. They are indeed liars."** They are, thus, left to their miserable destiny. This answer confronts them with the truth as they endure their humiliation.

This is the eventual destiny of those who claimed that there was nothing beyond our present life and that they would never be raised up again. It is a miserable, shameful, humiliating destiny as they are brought before their Lord, having persistently denied that they would face Him. They cannot stir. They are depicted as if they were led by the neck until they are stood in that awesome surrounding, facing the questioning: **"Is this not the truth?"** What a humiliating question! There is only one possible reply: **"Yes indeed, by our Lord!"** Now they are face to face with their Lord, on the occasion that they most stubbornly refused to believe in.

VERSES 32 TO 39

32. *What is the life of this world but play and amusement? But best is the home in the hereafter, for those who are righteous. Will ye not then understand?*

33. *We know indeed the grief which their words do cause thee: It is not thee they reject: it is the signs of Allah, which the wicked contemn.*

34. *Rejected were the apostles before thee: with patience and constancy they bore their rejection and their wrongs, until Our aid did reach them: there is none that can alter the words (and decrees) of Allah. Already hast thou received some account of those apostles.*

35. *If their spurning is hard on thy mind, yet if thou wert able to seek a tunnel in the ground or a ladder to the skies and bring them a sign,- (what good?). If it were Allah's will, He could gather them together unto true guidance: so be not thou amongst those who are swayed by ignorance (and impatience)!*

36. *Those who listen (in truth), be sure, will accept: as to the dead, Allah will raise them up; then will they be turned unto Him.*

37. *They say: "Why is not a sign sent down to him from his Lord?" Say: "(Allah) hath certainly power to send down a sign: but most of them understand not.*

38. There is not an animal (that lives) on the earth, nor a being that flies on its wings, but (forms part of) communities like you. Nothing have we omitted from the Book, and they (all) shall be gathered to their Lord in the end.

39. Those who reject our signs are deaf and dumb,- in the midst of darkness profound: whom Allah willeth, He leaveth to wander: whom He willeth, He placeth on the way that is straight.

In these verses we see Allah subhanahu wa ta`ala comforting His Prophet and dispelling his grief at the denial he receives from the unbelievers. He is told that he has a good example in the cases of earlier messengers. They were denied and received hostile opposition, but they remained steadfast until Allah gave them victory. It states that the laws Allah has set in operation will not be changed, but they cannot be hastened either. If the Prophet cannot withstand their rejection, then he may try to bring them a miracle by his own human endeavour. Had Allah so willed, He would have brought them all to His guidance. But His will has so determined that those whose natural receptive faculties are not switched off will respond to divine guidance, while those who are dead will not make such a response. He will resurrect them and they will all return to Him. It also gives a lesson to the believers to remain steadfast in da`wah work and be patient in testing times.

VERSES 40 TO 49

Talk about both calamities and blessings.

Calamities serve as reminders that nothing lasts forever. Shaytan beautifies things for man to divert him from the right path and his main purpose of existence.

Here we also see examples of two groups of the people: those who believe in the

Message brought by the Messenger will have no fear and grief while the deniers will face a tormenting punishment.

Then we read about accountability and grace. First, Allah subhanahu wa ta`ala affirms that **the Messenger does not know the Unseen.** Then we read that **in Islam there is no distinction between rich and poor.**

52. Send not away those who call on their Lord morning and evening, seeking His face. In naught art thou accountable for them, and in naught are they accountable for thee, that thou shouldst turn them away, and thus be (one) of the unjust.

This verse was revealed as a response to the request from the Quraish when they ask the Prophet's uncle to trade all presence of Bilall and others in return for the elites to listen to the message.

In Islam there is No Distinction between Rich and Poor

Islam prohibits its followers from making money the sole focus of their life. When money and worldly things become the criterion for judging someone's character and status, the ones wealthy are considered high and noble whilst the poor ones are considered unworthy and low.

VERSES 50 TO 65

A response to the Mushrikeen has been given.

The Prophet salAllahu `alayhi wa sallam is absolutely certain and firm in his belief. Hence, he devotes himself to his faith, and takes his stand away from his people. His certainty that they are in deep error is as strong as his certainty of the truth that he is rightly guided. In the same passage, we learn about Allah's forbearance when He does not act on the unbelievers' requests for a physical miracle. Should He give them such a miracle and should they continue to disbelieve, their continued rejection of the truth would ensure their total destruction.

Only Allah knows the unseen, He knows everything that happens in the universe.

When the smallest leaf falls he knows about it. There is not even a grain deep in the darkness of the earth that Allah does not know about and has recorded it in a Clear Record. It is Allah who takes your souls at night when you sleep and returns them to you each morning to go on with your life. In the end you will return to Allah and He will tell you everything about your life.

VERSES 66 — 70

Prophet Muhammad (Pbuh) is told that he will not be responsible for people's erring ways. He is further instructed not to sit with them when they engage in idle talk about religion, taking it as a sport and fun, showing no due respect to it. His instructions are very clear: he has to remind and warn them, convey his message to them and explain to them what they will have to face on the Day of Judgment. However, he must realize that although they are his people, they belong to two different nations. No considerations of nationality, race, clan or family are of much value in Islam. It is faith that causes relationships to be established or severed. When the bond of faith is established all other bonds may establish their roots. When the bond of faith is severed, however, no other ties can be established.

VERSES 70 – 73

These verses denounce those who turn away from guidance to sink back into disbelief and their associating partners with Allah. They portray a man who is totally lost, bewildered, not knowing where to turn because he turned away from faith after believing in Allah. These verses emphasize that Allah's guidance is the only true guidance.

VERSES 74-94

These verses provides a vivid picture of the long procession of Prophets beginning with Prophet Noah and travelling down the ages until the time of the Prophet Muhammad (PBUH).

The common message of the stories of the Previous Nations is that Allah sent miracles to them. Despite these miracles, they did not believe and were destroyed.

Allah swt tells the Prophet (Pbuh) that if he was to send miracles to the pagans of Arabia and disbelieve prevailed, they too will be destroyed. The Prophet did not want this.

Nation of prophet Nuh/Noah (a.s):

Prophet Nuh (a.s) was sent to teach people the lesson of tauheed and to tell them to worship only Allah. Prophet Nuh (a.s) preached Islam over 950 years but only few followed his message. Nuh's people were engaged in worshiping false god in the form of statues. Then Allah sent his prophet to bring them to the right path.

Allah says:

"Indeed, We sent Nuh (Noah) to his people and he said: "O my people! Worship Allah! You have no other God but Him. Certainly, I fear for you the torment of a Great Day!"" [Al-A'raf 7: 59]

For many generations Nuh's people had been worshipping statues that they called gods. They believed that these gods would bring them good, protect them from evil and provide all their needs. They gave their idols names such as Waddan, Suwa'an, Yaghutha, Ya'auga, and Nasran, (These idols represented, respectively, manly power; mutability, beauty; brute strength, swiftness, sharp sight, insight) according to the power they thought these gods possessed.

Originally these were the names of good people who had lived among them. After their deaths, statues of them were erected to keep their memories alive. After some time, however, people began to worship these statues. Later generations did not even know why they had been erected; they only knew their parents had prayed to them. That is how idol worshipping developed. Since they had no understanding of Allah the Almighty Who would punish them for their evil deeds, they became cruel and immoral.

Prophet Nuh (a.s) warned them and invite them to worship only Allah, but they denied. They firstly denied prophethood of Nuh. As they said that he is also a man like us, he just want superiority on us that's why, he is doing this.

Allah says:

The leaders of his people said: "Ah! we see thee evidently wandering (in mind)." (Surat al-A'raf: 60)

"The chiefs of the disbeliveers among his people said: "We see you but a man like ourselves."' (11:27 Qur'an) Prophet Nuh (a.s) warned his people about the punishment of Allah. Allah says:

"We sent Nuh to his People (with the Command): "Do thou warn thy People before there comes to them a grievous Penalty."" (Surah Nuh: 1)

Nuh continued appealing to his people to believe in Allah hour after hour, day after day year after year. He admonished his people and called them to Allah day and night, in secret and openly. He gave them examples, explained Allah's signs and illustrated Allah's ability in the formation of His creatures. But whenever he called them to Allah, they ran away from him. Whenever he urged them to ask Allah to forgive them, they put their fingers in their ears.

They didn't listen and Allah told Nuh to prepare a large boat and collect pairs of every specie and every believer to make them safe from the disaster. Prophet Nuh (a.s) grieved for his people who will be punished.

It was revealed to Nuh: "None of thy people will believe except those who have believed already! So grieve no longer over their (evil) deeds." (Surah Hud: 36)

The ship was constructed, and Nuh sat waiting Allah's command. Allah revealed to him that when water miraculously gushed forth from the oven at Nuh's house, that would be the sign of the start of the flood, and the sign for Nuh to act.

The terrible day arrived when the oven at Nuh's house overflowed. Nuh hurried to open the ark and summon the believers. He also took with him a pair, male and female, of every type of animal, bird and insect. Seeing him taking these creatures to the ark, the people laughed loudly: "Nuh must have gone out of his head! What is he going to do with the animals?"

Slowly the level of water increased, and every non-believer died in the flood. Nuh's wife and his son who were non-believers did not join him and drowned. Not a single non-believer was left alive. Then the order to stop the rain and to retreat the water was given. But flood had cleaned the non-believers from the land.

Nation of prophet Lut (a.s):

Prophet Lut (as) was sent as a messenger to one of prophet Ibrahim's (as) neighbouring communities. These people, as the Qur'an tells us, practiced a perversion unknown to the world up till then, namely sodomy. When Lut (as) told them to give up this perversion and brought them Allah's warning, they denied him, refused his prophethood, and carried on with their perversion. In the end, these people were destroyed by a dreadful disaster.

This city was filled with evil. Its residents robbed and killed travellers. Another common evil among them was that men performed the unnatural act of sodomy (after the city of Sodom). It was practiced openly and unashamedly.

It was at the height of these crimes and sins that Allah revealed to Prophet Lut (PBUH) that he should summon the people to give up their indecent behaviour, but they were so deeply sunk in their immoral habits that they were deaf to Lut's preaching. Swamped in their unnatural desires, they refused to listen, even when Lut warned them of Allah's punishment. Instead, they threatened to drive him out of the city if he kept on preaching.

Allah says:

And his people gave no answer but this: they said, "Drive them out of your city: these are indeed men who want to be clean and pure!" (Surat al-A'raf: 80-82)

Lut (as) called his people to an obvious truth and warned them explicitly, but his people did not heed any warnings whatsoever and continued to reject him and to deny the penalty of which he told them. Receiving the above answer from his people, Lut asked for the help of Allah: He said: "O my Lord! help Thou me against people who do mischief!" (Surat al-Ankaboot: 30)

Upon Lut's (as) prayer, Allah sent two angels in the form of men. These angels visited Ibrahim (as) before coming to Lut (as). Giving Ibrahim (as) the good news that his wife would give birth to an infant, the messengers explained the reason for their being sent: the insolent people of Lut (as) were to be destroyed.

Angels came to Lut (a.s) as guest and stayed at his house. This news was spread in town by his wife who was non-believer and in some time the whole town was standing outside his home. They broke the door and came in. Angels said to Lut (a.s) that dont fear as we are angels and they cannot harm you. After listening that non-believers got feared and ran outside. The angels warned Prophet Lut (pbuh) to leave his house before sunrise, taking with him all his family except his wife.

Allah had decreed that the city of Sodom should perish. AN earthquake rocked the town. IT was as if a mighty power had lifted the entire city and flung it down in one jolt. A storm of stones rained on the city. Everyone and everything was destroyed, including Lut's wife. In the morning, his people were destroyed by the disaster of which Lut (as) had informed them in advance.

Allah says:

But the (mighty) Blast overtook them before morning, And We turned (the cities) upside down, and rained down on them brimstones hard as baked clay. Behold! in this are Signs for those who by tokens do understand. And the (cities were) right on the high-road. (Surat al-Hijr: 73-76)

People of A'd:

The people of 'Ad lived many years in the windswept hills of an area between Yemen and Oman. They were physically well built and renowned for their craftsmanship especially in the construction of tall buildings with lofty towers. They were outstanding among all the nations in power and wealth, which, unfortunately, made them arrogant and boastful. Their political power was held in the hand of unjust rulers, against whom no one dared to raise a voice.

They were not ignorant of the existence of Allah, nor did they refuse to worship Him. What they did refuse was to worship Allah alone. They worshipped other gods, also, including idols. This is one sin Allah does not forgive.

Allah wanted to guide and discipline these people so He sent a prophet from among them. This prophet was Hud (as), a noble man who handled this task with great resoluteness and tolerance.

Hud (as) condemned idol worship and admonished his people. "MY people, what is the benefit of these stones that you carve with your own hands and worship? In reality it is an insult to the intellect. There is only One Deity worthy of worship and that is Allah. Worship of Him and Him alone, is compulsory on you.

In Qur'an:

To the Ad People (We sent) Hud, one of their own brethren. He said: "O my people! worship Allah! ye have no other god but Him. (Your other gods) ye do nothing but invent!

Prophet Hud (as) told them "He created you, He provides for you and He is the One Who will cause you to die. He gave you wonderful physiques and blessed you in many ways. So believe in Him and do not be blind to His favors, or the same fate that destroyed Noah's people will overtake you." Hud (as) warned them.

With such reasoning Hud hoped to instill faith in them, but they refused to accept his message. His people asked him: "Do you desire to be our master with your call? What payment do you want?".Hud (as) replied them that he did not want their money nor reward from them.

Allah says:

O my people! I ask of you no reward for this (Message). My reward is from none but Him Who created me: Will ye not then understand?

Hud (as) tried to speak to them and to explain about Allah's blessings: how Allah the Almighty had made them Noah's successors, how He had given them strength and power, and how HE sent them rain to revive the soil.Hud's (as) people looked about them and found they were the strongest on earth, so they become prouder and more obstinate. Thus they argued a lot with Hud (as). Hud (as) taught them everything a prophet teaches to his nation. But they used to ask silly questions. Hud (as) used to answer them gently but they never followed his message.

Hud (as) warned them if they wont worship only Allah they will destroyed like Nuh's (as) nation. And they declared "we will be safe by our gods". Hud (as) told them that these idols will be the reason of your destruction.There is no one who harms or benefits any one except Allah.

The conflict between Hud (as) and his people continued. The years passed, and they became prouder and more obstinate, and more tyrannical and more defiant of their prophet's message.

Furthermore, they started to accuse Hud (as) of being a crazy lunatic. One day they told him: "We now understand the secret of your madness you insulted our gods and they harmed you; that is why you have become insane."

Almighty Allah repeated their words in the Qur'an:

"O my Hud! No evidence have you brought us, and we shall not leave our gods for your mere saying! And we are not believers in you. All that we say is that some of our gods (false deities) have seized you with evil (madness)." (11:53-54 Qur'an)

A drought spread throughout the land, for the sky no longer sent its rain. the sun scorched the desert sands, looking like a disk of fire which settled on people's heads. The drought increased, the trees turned yellow, and plants died.

A day came when they found the sky full of clouds. Hud's (as) people were glad as they came out of their tents crying: "A cloud, which will give us rain!" .But the weather changed suddenly from burning dry and hot to stinging cold with wind that shook everything; trees, plants, tents, men and women. The wind increased day after day and night after night.

Hud's (as) people started to flee. They ran to their tents to hide but the gale became stronger, ripping their tents from their stakes. They hid under cloth covers but the gale became stronger and still and tore away the covers. It slashed clothing and skin. It penetrated the apertures of the body and destroyed it. It hardly touched anything before it was destroyed or killed, its core sucked out to decompose and rot. The storm raged for 8 days and 7 nights.

Almighty Allah recounts:

Then when they saw it as a dense cloud coming towards their valleys, they said: "This is a cloud bringing us rain!" Nay but it is that torment which you were asking to be hastened! a wind wherein is a painful torment! Destroying everything by the command of its Lord! (46:24-25 Qur'an)

That violent gale did not stop until the entire region was reduced to ruins and its wicked people destroyed, swallowed by the sands of the desert. Only Hud (as) and his followers remained unharmed. They migrated to Hadramaut and lived there in peace, worshipping Allah, their true Lord.

Thamud (samood):

Prophet salih (as) was sent on people of thamud. People of thamud were also engaged in the same sins in which people of A'd were involved. Thamud rejected the warnings of Allah just as 'Ad did and perished in consequence.Thamud's denial of the warnings coming to them is an incident which is itself a warning to people of all ages. Prophet Salih (as) was sent to Thamud to warn them. Salih (as) was a recognised person within the Thamud society. His people, who did not expect him to proclaim the religion of truth, were surprised by his calling on them to abandon their deviation.

A small part of the community complied with Salih's (as) call, but most of them did not accept what he told. The leaders of the community in particular denied Salih (as) and took an antagonistic stand towards him. They tried to impede those who believed Salih (as) and tried to oppress them. They were enraged at Salih (as), because he called them to worship Allah. This rage was not specific only to Thamud; Thamud were repeating the mistake made by the people of Nuh (as) and by Ad' who had lived before them.

This is why the Qur'an refers to these three communities as follows:

Has not the story reached you, (O people!), of those who (went) before you? - of the people of Prophet Nuh, and 'Ad, and Thamud? - And of those who (came) after them? None knows them but Allah. To them came messengers with Clear (Signs); but they put their hands up to their mouths, and said: "We do deny (the mission) on which ye have been sent, and we are really in suspicious (disquieting) doubt as to that to which ye invite us." (Surah Ibrahim: 9)

Despite the Prophet Salih's (as) warnings, the people continued in their ways on overcome by doubts. But still, there was a group who believed in the prophethood of Salih (as) - and those were the ones who were saved along with Salih (as) when the great catastrophe came. The leaders of the community tried to oppress the group believing in Salih (as). Moreover, a certain group openly denied Salih (as). A group among those who rejected faith - supposedly in the name of Allah - made plans to kill Salih (as).

Saleh's people disbelieved and thought he was bewitched. Then they asked him to show them a sign from Allah that he was indeed a prophet. They pointed at a huge rock that was standing by itself, and proposed to him that he ask his God to create a she-camel out of it. They of course thought that it was a good way to dumbfound him and silence him. But Saleh, in turn, took a strong oath from them that if Allah provided them with this sign they would believe in him and follow him. He then fervently prayed to Allah to answer their request. The huge rock moved and split and from it came a wonderful she-camel, which was pregnant and soon to give birth. Allah provided the Thamud people this miracle which was also a test for them, to see if they obey His orders. In Qur'an:

Saleh told them: "O my people! This she-camel of Allah is a sign to you. Leave her to feed on Allah's earth, and inflict no harm on her, or a swift punishment will seize you!" (Hud, 11:64)

The she-camel and her young offspring lived among the Thamud people, she would drink from the water of the well for one day, and leave it to them the second day as Allah ordered:

"She has a right to drink (water), and you have a right to drink water, each on a day appointed," (Al-Shu'ara', 26:155).

Allah ordered Prophet Saleh to tell his people of the camel's rights, saying:

"And tell them that the water is to be shared between her and them. Each one's right to drink being established by turns," (Al-Qamar, 54:28).

On the day the she-camel was to drink from the well, she would have enough milk for all the people of Thamud who would milk her and fill all their containers. She would graze in the valley and she was so huge that when she came near their sheep, they would flee and leave the way for her, and the cattle would not come near the well on the day she would drink from it.

The Thamud people were very amazed and some of them believed and followed Prophet Saleh. It was clear that she was not a normal camel but was a miracle from Allah and a blessed animal. The disbelievers, however, were very much bothered by her for she was always reminding them of that oath

They plotted to kill her and get rid of her, so that way they would use the well every day. There were nine men in the city who were known for their mischief and crimes, and hence they were trusted with the mission of killing the camel. After making sure that all the disbelievers were in agreement to kill the she-camel, the men went out secretly by night to the well when she came to drink water. They hit her and killed her, then ran to kill the child but he ran away and vanish in the mountain from where she-camel came.

When saleh (as) heard of their horrible crime, Prophet Saleh (as) warned them saying:

"Enjoy yourselves in your homes for three days. This is a promise that will not be belied!" (Hud, 11:65).

This warning was an occasion for them to repent to Allah, but to the contrary, they not only disbelieved in the threat but also decided to kill Saleh as well.

After three days Angel Gabriel (as) shaked the walls of their homes and when they came out of their homes, he made a loud sound by which they were caused to death.Except saleh (as) and his believers.

The Pharaoh:

The pharaoh who ruled Egypt was a tyrant who oppressed the descendants of Musa (as). He used every means to demean and disgrace them. They were kept in bondage and forced to work for him for small wages or nothing. Under this system the people obeyed and worshipped the pharaoh, and the ruling class carried out his orders, thereby authorizing his tyranny and crazy whims.The pharaoh wanted the people to obey him only, and to believe in the gods of his invention. Perhaps, during that time, there were many classes of people who did not believe in or practice polytheism; however, they kept this to themselves and outwardly did as they were expected to do, without revolting or revealing themselves to anyone. Pharaoh came to know that a child will be born who will be cause of his destruction and death. He gave command to kill all the male children among the children of israel.

Ibn 'Abbas narrated: "Pharaoh saw in his vision a fire, which came from Jerusalem and burned the houses of the Egyptians, and all Copts, and did not do harm to the children of Israel. When he woke up, he was horrified. He then gathered his priests and magicians and asked them about this vision. They said: "This means a boy will be born of them and the Egyptian people will perish at his hands.' That is why Pharaoh commanded that all male children of the children of Israel be killed."

But that child was born. He was prophet Musa (as). Even he was cherished by pharaoh in his palace. But after the prophethood Musa (as) conveyed the message of Allah.

Musa (as) and Harun (as) went to pharaoh in obedience to Allah's command and conveyed to him the message of the religion of truth. They asked him to stop tormenting the Children of Israel and let them go with Musa (as) and Harun (as). It was unacceptable to pharaoh that Musa (as), whom he had kept near him for years and who most probably was to have been his successor on the throne, stood up to him and talked to him in this manner. For that reason, Fir'awn accused him of ingratitude.

In Qur'an:

(Fir'awn) said: "Did we not cherish thee as a child among us, and didst thou not stay in our midst many years of thy life? And thou didst a deed of thine which (thou knowest) thou didst, and thou art an ungrateful (wretch)!" (Surat ash-Shu'ara: 18-19

Out of pride and greed for power, pharaoh did not listen to what Musa (as) said. He tried to make fun of him, attempted to prove his power, and denied him. At the same time, he aimed to portray Musa (as) and Harun (as) as anarchists and accuse them of being politically motivated. Finally, neither Pharaoh nor the leaders of the people within his close circle, except for the magicians, obeyed Musa (as) and Harun (as). They did not follow the religion of truth shown to them. Therefore Allah first of all sent some disasters to them.

Pharaoh and his close circle were so deeply engaged in their polytheism and their idolatry, that is "the religion of their ancestors", that they never considered leaving it. Even the miracles of Musa (as) were not enough to make them move away from their superstitions. Moreover, they expressed this openly. They said: "Whatever be the Signs thou bringest, to work therewith thy sorcery on us, we shall never believe in thee." (Surat al-A'raf: 132)

Because of their conduct, Allah sent them a number of disasters as "separate miracles" to make them taste the torment in this world, before the eternal torment of the next world. The first of these was drought and scarcity of crops.

In relation to the subject, it is written in the Qur'an:

"We punished the people of Fir'awn with years (of droughts) and shortness of crops; that they might receive admonition." (Surat al-A'raf: 130).

However, instead of "taking heed" as they should have, they held all that had happened was because of ill fortune brought by Musa and the Children of Israel. They were overcome by such conviction because of their superstitions, disobedience and devotion to the religion of their ancestors and, as a result, they suffered great distress for years. Allah sent to them a series of disasters, and warned them. These disasters are described as follows in the Qur'an:

So we sent (plagues) on them: Wholesale death, Locusts, Lice, Frogs, and Blood: Signs openly self-explained: but they were steeped in arrogance - a people given to sin. (Surat al-A'raf: 133)

In pharaoh's time, this kind of chain of disasters appears to have occurred. According to this scenario, when the Nile was contaminated, fish also died, and the Egyptians were deprived of an important source of nutrition. Without predator fish, the frogs could initially breed freely in both ponds and the Nile and thus overpopulate the river, eventually escaping the anoxic, toxic, and putrefying environment by migrating to land, hence dying on land and decomposing along with the fish. The Nile and adjacent lands thus became fouled, and the waters became dangerous to drink or to bathe in. Moreover, the extinction of frog species causes bugs such as locusts and lice to reproduce excessively.

Finally, no matter how the disasters took place, and what effect they left, neither pharaoh, nor his people turned to Allah by paying heed, but they continued in their arrogance.

Musa (as) set out from Egypt with the Children of Israel who obeyed him. However, pharaoh could not accept their departure without his permission. He and his soldiers followed them. By the time Musa (as) and the Children of Israel reached the shore, pharaoh and his soldiers had caught up with them. Some of the Children of Israel, who saw this, began to complain to Musa (as). This weakness of the community is also described in the Qur'an in the following verse:

"And when the two bodies saw each other, the people of Musa said: 'We are sure to be overtaken.'" (Surat ash-Shu'ara: 61)

Allah revealed to Musa (as) that he should strike the sea with his rod. Upon this,

"it divided, and each separate part became like the huge, firm mass of a mountain." (Surat ash-Shu'ara: 63).

In ordinary circumstances, at the moment when pharaoh saw such a miracle, he should have understood that there was something extraordinary about the situation - that he was seeing Divine intervention. The sea opened for the people whom pharaoh wanted to destroy. Moreover, there was no guarantee that the sea would not close back after they passed across. Still, he and his army followed the Children of Israel into the sea. Most probably, Pharaoh and his soldiers had lost their ability to think reasonably because of their insolence and spite, and were unable comprehend the miraculous nature of the situation.

The Qur'an describes the last moments of pharaoh as follows:

We took the Children of Israel across the sea: Fir'awn and his hosts followed them in insolence and spite. At length, when overwhelmed with the flood, he said: "I believe that there is no god except Him Whom the Children of Israel believe in: I am of those who submit (to Allah in Islam)." (Surah Yunus: 90)

The People of Madyan:

The people of Madyan were Arabs who lived in the country of Ma'an, part of which today is greater Syria. They were a greedy people who did not believe that Allah existed and who led wicked lives. They gave short measure, praised their goods beyond their worth, and hid their defects. They lied to their customers, thereby cheating them. They led a very happy and a prosperous life. Due to Allah's grace and endowments, they were very wealthy. But instead of thanking Allah for His bounties, they turned greedy and started cheating and betraying people in business. They used to cheat in weighing goods i.e. when they sold goods they weighed less whereas while buying they asked for more. Fraud and deceit were commonplace and the one who was more expert in this field was considered more intelligent and wise.

Allah sent His Prophet Shoaib (as) armed with many miracles. Shu'aib preached to them, begging them to be mindful of Allah's favors and warning them of the consequences of their evil ways, but they only mocked him. Shu'aib remained calm as he reminded them of his kinship to them and that what he was doing was not for his personal gain.

In Qur'an:

"And to Madyan (We sent) their brother Shoaib. He said, O my people! Serve Allah, you have no god other than Him. Clear proof has indeed come to you from your Lord. Therefore give full measure and weight. And do not diminish to men their things and do not make mischief in the land after its reform. This is better for you if you are believers." (A'raaf: 85)

Shoaib (as) prohibited the people from committing such contemptible deeds, and also reminded them about Allah's chastisement. But people mocked at him and said, "You want us to worship as you worship? You expect us to leave the religion of our forefathers? You expect us to employ some other method in our trade? You want us to deal honestly and suffer losses? Never! Certainly we will never heed you! Since you have become old and also have children, we pardon you. Else we would certainly have stoned you to death'!

They seized the belongings of Shoaib (as) and his followers, then drove them out of the city. The Messenger turned to his Lord for help, and his plea was answered. Allah sent down on them scorching heat and they suffered terribly. On seeing a cloud gathering in the sky, they thought it would bring cool, refreshing rain, and rushed outside in the hope of enjoying the rainfall. Instead the cloud burst, hurling thunderbolts and fire. They heard a thunderous sound from above which caused the earth under their feet to tremble. The evil doers perished in this state of horror.

Chapter 7

Towards Understanding Surah Al Araf

The Surah is named after the story of the People awaiting on the "Elevations" between Paradise and Hell.

It comprises of 206 Ayat. It is the longest Meccan Surah. The basic theme of this Surah is Prophethood -All prophets came with the message and as Muslims we have to belief in all the Prophets.

The Surah then starts by telling us how Satan misled thousands of populations over time and gives us examples of some prophets who suffered to gain their lost companions to the right path.

This Surah tells us about the origin of our creations and what will happen on the Day of Judgement. It is the most detail Surah in the Qur'an of the Story of Aadam (PBUH) and Hawa.

A number of prophets is cited in this story:

Why the people in the Araf are referred to as Araf
Hazrath Hasan Basri says;

These are the people who were assigned by the command of Allah to allocate the companions of Hell and the companions of Paradise. I swear it is true, they might be among us today.

These are people who have equal amounts of good and bad deeds.

The Prophet said, "When the people of Paradise will enter Paradise and the people of Hell will go to Hell, rest will be told as, you are saved from Hell for your good deeds but did not deserve Paradise. But you are saved from Hell by My mercy, you may enter Paradise

Verses 1- 10

1. Alif, Lam, Mim, Sad.

2. A Book revealed unto thee,- So let thy heart be oppressed no more by any difficulty on that account,- that with it thou mightest warn (the erring) and teach the Believers).

3. Follow (O men!) the revelation given unto you from your Lord, and follow not, as friends or protectors, other than Him. Little it is ye remember of admonition

The Messenger of Allah (S) was afraid that the members of his tribe would accuse him as a liar, and then turn away from his statements, and hurt him. So Allah swt reveal verse two as a comfort for the Prophet.

Here Allah addresses Prophet Muhammad (PBUH) telling him not to feel any distress. He (Allah) reassures him that this book (the Qur'an) has been revealed as a warning and a reminder to those who believe.

These verses are also warning us not to follow anything other than the Qur'an, otherwise we will become sinners. It is evident that whoever is not the follower of the Qur'an is the follower of Satan. That is why Allah commands us to follow the Qur'an and avoid following other than it.

Allah is telling us to take warnings from the previous civilisations, the people of past nations. They were destroyed.

Some were taken at night, others when they rested in the heat of the day. When the punishment was upon them they admitted their wrongdoing.

6. *"Then certainly We will question those to whom (Our messengers) were sent, and certainly We will also question the messengers."*

7. *"Then certainly We will relate to them with knowledge for We were not absent."*

The previous verses reference what happened in this world. These verses are telling us about the hereafter.

Allah says: On the Day of Judgment, surely all people will be questioned, including: both the leaders, the nations and followers, both the good doers and the evildoers, and both the scholars and the imitators of them.

"Then certainly We will relate to them with knowledge for We were not absent."

On that Day, questioning is a kind of calling to witness, making confession and reprimand. But the fact is that there is nothing concealed to Allah to be discovered by question.

The weighing of our the deeds on that Day will be just. Those who scales are heavy (with good deeds) will be successful and those whose scales are light will be lost.

Those persons, whose scales are light, will be involved in an eternal punishment, because they have denied Allah's Signs and reasoning in their lives.

Allah is reminding us that he has created the earth for our sustenance but we were ungrateful. So this is the day of reckoning and we will face the consequences of our deed.

Verses 11 – 18 The story of Adam and Shaitan

These verses tell us about the creation of human life, angels and Iblis.

Allah, the almighty made the announcement of the forthcoming birth of mankind. The angels and Iblis were present.

The whole event is witnessed by the heavens and the earth and all that Allah has created. It is indeed a great event in the history of the universe.

When Allah blew the soul into this first creation of mankind, Adam, he ordered that all the angels and Iblis bow to him. Here we see clear evidence of the honour Allah has given to man,

All the angels prostrated in total obedience. As for Iblis, he wilfully disobeyed Allah, defying His orders.

Iblis is fully aware that it is Allah who is the Creator and Sustainer of all creation and yet he refuses to comply. He justify his disobedience by his own logic. And his logic! He is better that Aadam as he, Iblis, is made from the smokeless flame of the fire and Aadam from sounding clay.

Allah expelled him from the heavens to the earth. The evil and obstinate Iblis will never forget the reason behind this expulsion. Aadam. When Allah told him that he is destined for the hellfire, Iblis made dua to Allah to let him live until the end of the world. This dua was accepted.

Iblis wanted this long life to lead astray the Children of Aadam. In order words us. Us, whom Allah has bestowed His honour and who was the cause of Iblis's own tragedy and rejection. So, the sole purpose of his long life is to mislead us.

He lies await on the straight path, trying to turn away any human being who tries to pass along.

Allah has granted Iblis and his offspring the chance to lead people away from the right path. He has also given Adam and human beings in general the freedom of choice so that He can put them to the test. It is this choice which makes man a special type of creation: he belongs neither to the realm of angels who obey Allah in all situations nor to the world of satans who disobey Him all the time. Man has a totally different role to play.

Verses 19 – 25 Acceptance of repentance

Aadam and his wife, Hawa, were directed to live in Paradise and eat from wherever they will. However, they were commanded to steer away from a particular tree. The Qur'an remains silent about what kind of tree. It was necessary to identify something as forbidden so that the human race could learn that people must not exceed their limits. Humans must use their free will to control their desires so they can elevate themselves above the animal creation. Animals cannot control their desires. This is a quality that differentiate humans from animals.

Iblis whispered to them to eat the fruit of that forbidden tree. So Iblis is now putting his plan in action. We do not know how the whisperings of Shaitan took place.

Its worth mentioning here that the temptation from Shaitan relies on the weaknesses in human nature. However, such weakness can be transformed into strength through faith and remembrance of Allah. None of Shaitan's schemes can be of any effect with a believer who remains conscious of his Lord.

"He said to them: **'Your Lord has only forbidden you this tree lest you two become angels or immortals.'**" (Verse 20) He knew the inner desires of man who loves to be immortal or at least to have a very long life.

He swore to them that he only gave them sound advice and that he was sincere in that advice: *"And he swore to them:* **I am indeed giving you sound advice."** *(Verse 21)*.

They forgot what Allah had told them and yielded to Satan's temptation. The temptation was thus complete and yielded its bitter fruit. With their error, Satan brought them down from the level of obeying Allah to that of disobeying Him. Thus he caused their delusion: **"Thus he cunningly deluded them."** *(Verse 22)*

Their Lord called out to them: **"Did I not forbid you that tree and tell you both that Satan is your open enemy?"** *(Verse 22)*

We learn here that us humans have weaknesses which gives Shaitan the opportunity to delude us.

However, they cried out to Allah for forgiveness:

'Our Lord.' We have wronged ourselves; and unless You grant us forgiveness and bestow Your mercy upon us, we shall certainly be lost.'" *(Verse 23)*

They were forgiven.

This is one of man's main characteristics, establishing his bond with his Lord. This opening of the doors leading to his Lord involves recognition of his error, repentance, seeking forgiveness, feeling his own weakness, seeking Allah's help and mercy.

All of them:

Aadam and his wife, Iblis, fell down to earth where they began their fight fuelled with hostility. The battle rages between two natures, one of them devoted completely to evil while the other has a dual aspect which responds to good and evil. Thus the test begins.

Aadam and his offsprings are destined to remain on earth where they have the power to build it and to enjoy its comforts for a while. On earth they live and they die, before they are resurrected, when they return to their Lord at the end of their great journey. He then assigns them either to heaven or to hell.

The first round in the battle is over, but it is to be followed by numerous rounds. Man will also be victorious when he seeks help from his Lord and follows the path He has shown him. He will end up in defeat whenever he defers to his enemy.

Verses 26 – 32 A warning

Allah reminds the children of Aadam of His grace as He requires them to cover their nakedness with dress in order to protect their humanity against sinking to the level of animals. Everything He has facilitated for them is also an aspect of His grace. He reminds them of it *"so that they may reflect." (Verse 26)*

Again they are warned that Shaitan is a sworn enemy so be not deceived. The evil ones are allied to those who do not believe. Allah did not order immorality, thus what your forefathers did is not an excuse. Allah is reminding us here about our first parents, Aadam and Hawa first experience with Shaitan. Remember the first thing they did after eating the fruit from the forbidden tree was to cover themselves.

Let us look at the pagans Arabs tradition appearing nude in their tawaf rituals.

They performed ṭawāf around Allah's sacred house in the nude, accompanying their women. This they claimed Allah had ordered them to do, just as He had ordered their fathers:

What made their action worse was that they alleged that the practices of their fathers must be part of religion and must have been ordered by God.

This is a warning to human beings in general and most directly to the pagans whom Islam addressed at the time of its revelation. This warning makes it clear to them that they must not obey Shaitan in whatever laws they enact for themselves and any traditions they may observe.

In order to emphasize the urgency of His warning, their Allah tells mankind "Surely, he and his tribe watch you from where you cannot perceive them." (Verse 27) For this enables his enemy to direct him the way he wishes, when he has no real help or support and cannot resort to God's patronage since he is an unbeliever: "We have made the devils as patrons for those who do not believe." (Verse 27)

Allah commands the Prophet Muhammad (peace be upon him) to make it clear to them that their inventions are false. He is further ordered to declare that Allah's law is incompatible with indecency. Allah would not command anything that is indecent:

"Say: 'Never does God enjoin what is indecent. Would you attribute to God something of which you have no knowledge?'" (Verse 28)

At this point they are given a reminder and a warning. They should always remember that they will return to Allah after they have finished their present life which is meant as a test for them. When they return to Allah they will be in two groups: those who followed Allah's commandments and those who followed Satan.

This is a remarkable picture showing the starting point and the finishing line in the great journey of life:

"As it was He who brought you into being in the first instance, so also [to Him] you will return." (Verse 29)

Let us look at how we started this journey of life. In the beginning there were two groups. Our forefathers Aadam and Hawa in one group and Iblis in the other. In the end we will surely return to Allah swt in these groups. The believers and the sinners.

In the end they come back to their different destinations: "Some [of you] He will have graced with His guidance, whereas for some a straying from the right path will have become unavoidable. For, they will have taken satans for their protectors in preference to God, thinking all the while that they have found the right path." (Verse 30)

"Children of Adam, dress well when you attend any place of worship." (Verse 31) He also tells them to enjoy the wholesome provisions He has given them, without being extravagant: "Eat and drink but do not be wasteful. Surely He does not love the wasteful." (Verse 31)

Allah advises the children of Aadam to dress well, when and wherever they pray, and to eat and drink from what He has provided. However, He warns them not to be extravagant for He does not love those who do so.

Verses 33 — 41 The closed gates

In these verses Prophet Muhammad SWT is advised to tell the believers that Allah forbids disgraceful deeds, whether it is done openy or in secret.

33. Say: the things that my Lord hath indeed forbidden are: shameful deeds, whether open or secret; sins and trespasses against truth or reason; assigning of partners to Allah, for which

He hath given no authority; and saying things about Allah of which ye have no knowledge

Every nation's life span is set, it cannot be hastened nor can it be delayed. A reminder for us that our term is limited,

"For every community a term has been set. When [the end of] their term approaches, they can neither delay nor hasten it by a single moment." (Verse 34)

Unless we follow the messengers God Allah sent, then whatever we do in this life will be rejected.

"Children of Adam! Whenever there come to you messengers from among yourselves to relate to you My revelations, then those who are conscious of Me and live righteously shall have nothing to fear, nor shall they grieve." (Verse 35)

The gates of Heaven will not be opened to those who deny the verses or are arrogant towards them. Even if a rope was to be threaded through the eye of a needle they would not enter the Everlasting Garden. This is the punishment for the guilty and the evildoers.

Verses 42 — 58 A Day of Fulfilment (Judgment)

Those who believe and do good deeds are the people of the Garden. They will not be burdened with what they are unable to bear and the gates of Heaven will be open to them. They will praise Allah because of the Paradise they have inherited and will call out to the people of the Fire.

Their reply will be that they too have found the promise to be true. Next a caller will announce that the curse of Allah upon the wrongdoers. There will be a partition between both parties.

Then we will have the people of the Heights. They will recognise and call out to each other.

The inmates from Hell then beg for food and water from the inmates of Paradise, but their answer is that Allah has forbidden them sustenance. They will be forgotten just as they had forgotten the inevitability of this Day which is the fulfilment of what was promised in the Qur'an.

The Lord God created the universe and then rose over the Throne in a manner that suits His Majesty, so call upon him with humility, and invoke Him with fear and hope. He is the one who sends the wind and the rain bringing forth all kinds of fruit, likewise He will raise the dead. Vegetation emerges by the permission of Allah.

Verses 59 – 156 The stories of the Prophets

Story of Nuh/Noah begins with the prophet warning his people and then the community rejecting the message and facing a punishment.

Story of Hud: Hud lived with his people Aad, Aad were not ignorant of the existence of Allah, nor did they refuse to worship Him. What they did refuse was to worship Allah alone. They worshipped other gods, also, including idols. This is one sin Allah does not forgive. The Prophet Hud said to his people: "He created you, He provides for you and He is the One Who will cause you to die. He gave you wonderful physiques and blessed you in many ways. So believe in Him and do not be blind to His favours, or the same fate that destroyed Noah's people will overtake you.

"Story of Saleh: Saleh (meaning the good one in Arabic) was sent to an Arab tribe called Thamud, who were reported to be descendants of Noah.

They were vain people who took great pride in their fertile farmland and grand architecture. Prophet Saleh tried to call his people to the worship of One God, to Whom they should give thanks for all their bounties. He called upon the rich to stop oppressing the poor, and for an end to all mischief and evil.

Story of Shuaib: His people were greedy people who did not believe that Allah existed and who led wicked lives. Most of them were merchandisers and they gave short measure, praised their goods beyond their worth, and hid their defects. They lied to their customers, thereby cheating them.

Allah (God) sent his prophet Shu'aib armed with many miracles. Shu'aib preached to them, begging them to be mindful of Allah's favors and warning them of the consequences of their evil ways, but they only mocked him. Shu'aib remained calm as he reminded them of his kinship to them and that what he was doing was not for his personal gain.

Story of Musa/Moses and Haroon/Aaron: The pharaoh who ruled Egypt was a tyrant who oppressed the children of Israel (Bani Israel). He used every means to demean and disgrace them. They were kept in bondage and forced to work for him.

Under this system the people obeyed and worshipped the pharaoh, and the ruling class carried out his orders, thereby authorizing his tyranny and crazy whims.

Allah (God) sent his prophet Moses to save the Children of Israel from the pharaoh, he gave him great power to face the pharaoh and win over him. He succeeded and saved his people. And as soon as he went to listen to God's orders, they rejected his message even when Haroon/Aaron was present among them, this made Moses very mad about his brother but later he asked for mercy from the Almighty for him, his brother and those people, Allah accepted. Then the Surah says that every community or people that will come on earth will think that they are better than those before and thus better the examples cited above, but in fact those who will not believe in God, or got misled by Satan from the right path will have the same punishment, Hell, and people have to pay attention because Satan and his people can see you but you can't.

Verses 157 – 158 Mohammad in the Torah and Gospel

Allah Musa (PBUH) tells him something about the future and the community which will advocate the final version of His message.

This is an extremely important piece of news confirming that the Children of Israel had been given, most emphatically, confirmed information of the advent of the unlettered Prophet.

Both Prophets, Isa and Musa, may peace and blessings be upon them, informed The Children of Israel of his mission, description, the method his message would follow and the distinctive features of his faith.

Hence, the Children of Israel have received the most certain news that those who believe in this unlettered Prophet, honour and support him and follow the light that has been sent down with him *"shall indeed be successful."* (Verse 157)

This is, then, the final, universal message that is not confined to a particular community, area or generation. Earlier messages were limited to a certain community or a certain period of time which extended until the appearance of a new messenger. Every new message incorporated certain modifications of the divine law that took into account human progress. The final message is complete and perfect.

There will be no subsequent local messages for any particular community or generation. The last and final message responds to basic human nature, which means that it is suitable for all mankind. Hence, it was conveyed by the unlettered Prophet whose nature remained pure, refined only by the care he received from Allah. Hence, the Prophet's pure nature conveyed the naturally pure message, addressing the very nature that is common to all mankind: *"Say: 'Mankind, I am indeed Gods Messenger to you all.'" (Verse 158)*

Verses 159 — 168 Allah tells Prophet (Pbuh) to remind the Bani Israel of the disobedience of their forefathers

These verses describe the situation at the time of Prophet Musa (PBUH), and after him, which meant that there was among them a group who were keen to follow the truth and show its guidance and maintain justice. It was such people who received the Prophet Muhammad's message with ready acceptance, since they were informed in the Torah of his forthcoming appearance. The most notable of these was

`Abdullāh ibn Sallām (may God be pleased with him), a companion of the Prophet who stood up to the Jews in Madinah pointing out to them what the Torah says about the unlettered Prophet as well as the fact that Islamic law endorsed a number of Jewish laws.

Then comes information about historical events which the prophet related to the Bani Israel.

"We divided them into twelve tribes, each a community. And when his people asked Moses for water to drink, We inspired him 'Strike the rock with your staff' Twelve springs gushed forth from it, and each tribe knew its drinking-place. We caused the clouds to draw their shadow over them and sent down for them manna and quails, [saying]: **'Eat of the good things We have given you as sustenance.' Yet they could do Us no wrong, but they certainly wronged themselves."** *(Verse 160)*

161. And remember it was said to them: "Dwell in this town and eat therein as ye wish, but say the word of humility and enter the gate in a posture of humility: We shall forgive you your faults; We shall increase (the portion of) those who do good."

162. But the transgressors among them changed the word from that which had been given them so we sent on them a plague from heaven. For that they repeatedly transgressed.

They are told to enter a particular city. Allah makes lawful for them all its fruits and provision. The condition is as they enter they must submit themselves to Allah. In return for their obedience, Allah promised to forgive them their sins and to increase the reward of those among them who did well. But why would they disobey? There is no explanation other than the fact that deviation was in their nature:

"But the wrongdoers among them substituted other words for those which they had been given." (*Verse 162*)

At this point, Allah let loose against them a scourge from heaven. It was the same heaven from which He sent down manna and quails, and which carried the clouds that gave them shade and comfort: *"Therefore We let loose against them a scourge from heaven in requital for their wrongdoing."* (*Verse 162*)

Allah tells Prophet Muhammad (PBUH) to ask the Bani Israel about the town by the sea and what happened when they transgressed the laws of the Sabbath. They were tested because of their disobedience. On the Sabbath the fish came easily but did not appear on other days. Ask them also, Allah said, about the warners and why they preached to a people who surely would be destroyed or punished by God. The warners said they wanted to discharge their duty to Allah and they hoped some would take admonition. However, they disregarded the warning, continued with their behaviour and Allah said to them "Be thee detested apes".

Remind them also that Allah said he would raise against them those who would inflict them with grievous harm right up until the Day of Resurrection. Allah broke their unity as a nation and dispersed them all over the world. Some are righteous and others are not, they were tested with both blessings and misfortunes.

Verses 169 — 180 Including the covenant with the descendants of Adam.

This new generation of Israelites have certain characteristics that are described in the Qur'ān. They have inherited the Scriptures and learned them well. However, they did not take the Scriptures to heart.

This state of affairs was repeated time after time. Hence, the Qur'ān poses this rhetoric question:

"Have they not solemnly pledged through their Scriptures to say nothing but the truth about God? And have they not studied well what is in [the Scriptures]?" (*Verse 169*)

In their very Scriptures they pledged never to try to manipulate the provisions of divine law, or give them a false interpretation. They also vowed not to say anything about Allah but the plain truth. How is it possible, then, for them to claim that they will be forgiven when they are keen to indulge in every worldly pleasure that presents itself to them? How can they justify such indulgence by making a false statement about God, assuring themselves of His forgiveness, when they are well aware that God forgives only those who truly repent of their mistakes and resolve not to repeat them? This does not apply to them, because having studied the Scriptures well and known everything they contain, they remain ready to indulge in every fleeting pleasure of this low world.

"Surely the life in the hereafter is better for all who are God-fearing. Will you not use your reason?" **(Verse 169)** Indeed, the abode of the hereafter is the one to seek. Its value, as it is recognized by those who are God-fearing, is bound to tilt the scales

170. "And those who hold fast to the Book and establish the prayer, verily We do not waste the reward of the reformers."

This verse points to another group, opposite to the above-mentioned perverted group, who not only avoid any perversion and concealing the Divine verses, but also take hold of them and practice them minutely. The Qur'ān has called this group 'the reformers' of the world, and maintains an important reward for them. Concerning them, it says that surely Allah does not waste the great reward that they will have with Him. The verse says:

"And those who hold fast to the Book and establish the prayer, verily We do not waste the reward of the reformers."

The above-mentioned verse clearly indicates that, without taking hold of the Heavenly Books and Divine commandments, the fulfilment of the true reforms in the world is impossible. This meaning emphasizes this fact, once more, that religion is not something only related to the world of super nature or to the next world.

Religion is effective in the spirit of life for all human beings. It protects the interests of all humankind and it is alongside the execution of the principles of justice, peace, tranquillity and any concepts which are gathered in the vast meaning of the term 'reform'.

171. "And (remember) when We plucked the mountain (and held it) above them as if it were a canopy, and they supposed it was about to fall on them (when We told them:) 'Hold you firmly what We gave you and remember what is in it, that you may keep from evil'."

This is the last verse in this Surah which is upon the life of the Children of Israel.

It was taken at a time when Allah suspended the mountain over the Children of Israel's heads, just as though it was a shadow. For all intents and purposes, they thought it was going to fall on them. Just prior to that, they were reluctant to give any pledges, but when they experienced that supernatural event, they hastened to make their pledges. That should have prevented any relapse on their part. With such a miracle taking place before their eyes, they were ordered to take their pledges seriously, and to fulfil them conscientiously.

Ibn `Abbās, a companion of the Prophet who is renowned for his scholarship, reports: "Your Lord went over Adam's back with His hand, and out came every human being He would be creating until the Day of Resurrection. He took their pledges and made them bear witness about themselves, saying to them:

"Am I not your Lord? They replied 'Yes, indeed.'" **(Verse 172)**

Islam is the response to humanity search for meaning.

The purpose of creation for all men and women has been: To Know and worship the one God.

172. When thy Lord drew forth from the Children of Adam - from their loins – their descendants, and made them testify concerning themselves, (saying): "Am I not your Lord (who cherishes and sustains you)?" - They said: "Yea! We do testify!" (This), lest ye should say on the Day of Judgment: "Of this we were never mindful":

The Qu'ran teaches us that everyone human being is born conscious of God:

Ibn `Abbās, a companion of the Prophet who is renowned for his scholarship, reports: "Your Lord went over Adam's back with His hand, and out came every human being He would be creating until the Day of Resurrection. He took their pledges and made them bear witness about themselves, saying to them:

"Am I not your Lord? They replied 'Yes, indeed.'" **(Verse 172)**

Allah extracted all of Aadam's descendants who were yet to born, generation and generation, spread them out, and took a covenant from them. He address their souls directly, making them bear witness that He was their Lord. Since Allah made all human beings swear to his Lordship when he created Aadam, this oath is imprinted on the human soul even before it enters the foetus, so a child is born with a natural belief in the Oneness of God. This natural belief is called Fitra in Arabic.

173. Or lest ye should say: "Our fathers before us may have taken false gods, but we are (their) descendants after them: wilt Thou then destroy us because of the deeds of men who were futile?"

This law is a covenant that has been made between human nature and its Creator.

It is established in every single living cell from the moment it comes into existence. It predates God's messages and messengers. According to this covenant every cell testifies to the Lordship of the one God who has a consistent will that has established a single law to govern the whole universe as well as its own actions and reactions. With such a covenant made with human nature, no one can argue that he is unaware of God's revelations that explain the divine faith or that he knows nothing of God's messages that call on people to believe in His oneness. There is no validity in the argument advanced by anyone who says: "I was born into a family of unbelievers. Therefore, I had no chance of knowing the faith based on belief in God's oneness. I had to follow the footsteps of my forefathers who had erred and caused me to err. Therefore, the responsibility is theirs, not mine". Hence, the Qur'ānic comment on the testimony given by the offspring of Adam's children is stated most clearly.

175. Relate to them the story of the man to whom We sent Our signs, but he passed them by: so Satan followed him up, and he went astray.

This verse then gives an example of the practical effects of deviation. Abandoning Allah's revelations after having learnt them. The example is given of a person who has been given Allah's revelations However, he discards them, turning away, clinging to the life of this world and following his desire. This means that he neither fulfils his first covenant nor follows the revelations providing him with clear guidance. Hence, Satan overpowers him and he stands rejected by God, unable to enjoy security or peace. He is the loser in this world and the next.

176. If it had been Our will, We should have elevated him with Our signs; but he inclined to the earth, and followed his own vain desires. His similitude is that of a dog: if you attack him, he lolls out his tongue, or if you leave him alone, he (still) lolls out his tongue. That is the similitude of those who reject Our signs; So relate the story; perchance they may reflect.

Here we see a man on whom Allah bestows His grace, giving him His revelations and favouring him with knowledge to give him a perfect chance to follow the right path and to exalt himself. But he discards it all. The Qur'ānic description shows this man's action as if he is peeling Allah's guidance off his own body, as if those revelations form a skin that gives him his appearance. Therefore, discarding them requires a very strong action and the exercise of much effort. It is like taking the skin off of a person who is still alive. But this is an apt description, because believing in God is so essential to human existence as a skin to a living creature. Nevertheless, this man, given God's revelations, is exercising a strong effort to take off his protective shield in order to follow his desire and deviate from God's guidance. Thus he falls from the bright and sunny horizon in order to cling to the dark clay. He becomes easy prey for Satan, without any protection from his designs. Satan thus catches up with him and exercises his power over him.

We then look at a miserable and horrific scene in which this creature appears covered with mud, clinging to the earth, taking the shape of a dog that pants away whether he is driven off or left alone. All these scenes follow in quick succession and we follow the rapid change from one scene to the other with complete amazement. When the last scene of a dog always panting away is raised before our eyes, we have the highly significant comment on the whole panorama.

177. Evil as an example are people who reject Our signs and wrong their own souls

Can there be a more dismal example than that? Can there be a worse action than discarding guidance and pulling oneself away from divine revelations? Is there anything more disgraceful than clinging to the lowly life of this earth and succumbing to desires? Can any human being cause himself more wrong than the one who does this? By so doing, he tears apart that protective shield which could have ensured his safety. Instead, he leaves his soul easy prey for Satan and sinks to the level of animals, with all that it entails of worry and uncertainty. He is soon seen as a dog constantly panting away.

Every day we see new examples of such people everywhere and in all communities. Only a small minority cling to Allah's guidance and refuse to succumb to Satan or follow their desires. They seek Allah's support in order not to covet the trifling pleasures of this world that can be bestowed by those who are in power. Hence, the example given in the Qur'ān is not limited to a single case, but occurs in every society and in every generation.

178. Whom Allah doth guide,- he is on the right path: whom He rejects from His guidance,- such are the persons who perish.

This verse sets out the terms very clearly. According to this law, which has already been explained in detail, whoever has God's guidance is truly on the right path, and will surely attain his goal. He will be able to follow guidance to attain success and prosperity in the hereafter. Conversely, a person whom God lets go astray, in accordance with the same law, is indeed the loser, because he has lost everything and gained nothing, no matter how much he has in this life. All this accounts for nothing. We need only to remember that such a person has lost himself. What gain can such a person have after incurring such a loss?

179. Many are the Jinns and men we have made for Hell: They have hearts wherewith they understand not, eyes wherewith they see not, and ears wherewith they hear not. They are like cattle,- nay more misguided: for they are heedless (of warning).

Verses 169 – 180 Including the covenant with the descendants of Adam.

179. "Indeed We have created for Hell many jinn and humans; they have hearts with which they do not nderstand, and they have eyes with which they do not see, and they have ears with which they do not hear. They are as cattle, rather they are more astray. These are the heedless ones."

The Signs of Hellish People

In this verse and the follow on verses Allah tells us about the qualities of the people destined for the hellfire.

"Indeed We have created for Hell many jinn and humans..."

Allah has created all human beings pure and sinless, but, by means of their own evil deeds, some groups of them make themselves candidates for Hell. The end of these people is dark and inauspicious.

The qualities of the hellish group in three phrases. The first quality is that:

"...they have hearts with which they do not understand..."

Their second quality is that they have clear eyes for seeing the truth but they do not observe the feature of the facts and pass by them like some blind persons.

"...and they have eyes with which they do not see..."

Their third quality is that they have safe and sound ears, but they do not hearken to the truth and right words, and, like the deaf, they deprive themselves from hearing the divine truth. The verse says:

"...and they have ears with which they do not hear..."

Verse 180 follows this with a clear instruction to the believers to ignore those who deviate from the right path and go astray. At the time of the Prophet, those were the unbelievers who used to maintain idolatry in opposition to the Islamic message. They used to blaspheme against God's names, twist His attributes, and assign them to some of the idols they ascribe as partners to God. *"God has the finest names, so appeal to Him by these and stay away from those who blaspheme against His names. They shall be requited for all they do."* **(Verse 180)**

It is a community *"who guide others by means of the truth and with it establish justice."* (Verse 181)

Let us look at the description given to this community.

This community will continue to be always present. Its main characteristic is that those who belong to it *"guide others by means of the truth"*. (**Verse 181**) They call on people to accept the truth, and will never relinquish their task of advocating the truth. They are not happy to keep it to themselves, or to be inward looking. They try to publicize the truth they know, and guide other people to it. Thus, they have a role of leadership among those around them who have strayed away from this truth, and who have violated their covenant. They adopt a positive attitude, which is not limited to knowing the truth but goes beyond that knowledge in order to advocate the truth and guide to it.

But this is not all that they do about the truth. Their other characteristic is that they `establish justice' with the truth. This means that they go well beyond knowing the truth and advocating it, to take positive steps to implement the truth in human life and make it the criterion for judgement. The crux of the matter is that the truth has not been revealed only to remain a mere branch of knowledge studied by scholars, or even an admonition to point out the right path. The truth has been revealed so that people conduct their lives according to it. It should govern people's concepts so that these are moulded in accordance with it, and it should govern people's rites of worship so that these provide a practical image of the truth in as far as the relationship between human beings and their Lord is concerned. The truth has also been revealed in order to mould practical life so that all systems are in line with its principles and subject to the laws derived from it. It also shapes people's habits, traditions, moral values and behaviour, as well as their philosophical doctrines, culture and all branches of knowledge, providing the criteria to evaluate all these. When all this takes place, the truth is present in human life, and justice, which can only be based on the truth, is established. Thus, the establishment of the truth in human life is the task undertaken by this community, after having made the truth known and worked to guide other people to it.

"It is He who has created you all from a single soul, and out of it brought into being its mate, so that he might incline with love towards her." (**Verse 189**)

It is thus a single soul and a single nature, although it has different functions for the male and the female. These differences also serve as a means to make a man incline with love towards his wife and find comfort with her. This is the Islamic outlook on the nature of man and the role of marriage. It is a complete, integrated and honest outlook stated by this religion over fourteen centuries ago when other religions.

The original purpose of the meeting of a human couple is to provide love, comfort, and a settled happy life, which provides an ideal setting for the rearing of young children. It is in such a happy and loving environment that a new human generation is prepared to take over the task of promoting and adding to human civilization.

The story then begins, right at the first stage:

"When he has consorted with her, she conceives a light burden, which she carries with ease." (Verse 189)

The Qur'an employs a highly refined expression, particularly in the Arabic text, when it describes the initial relationship between a married couple, "When he has consorted with her." It selects such fine expressions to provide, and to impart refinement to the meeting itself so that it is not felt as merely physical. Conception is described as "light" in its initial stage, when a mother carries it with ease, practically unnoticed.

The second stage is then described:

"Then, when she grows heavy, they both appeal to God, their Lord: 'Grant us a goodly child and we will be truly grateful.'" **(Verse 189)**

Now that the pregnancy is ascertained, it gives great hopes to the parents-to-be. They now pin their hopes that the newborn will be healthy, pretty, cute, etc., bringing into reality all that parents wish to have in their children when they are still in the embryonic stage. With such hopes, pure human nature is awakened, and it turns to God acknowledging that He is the only Lord, and appealing to Him to bestow His grace. This they do because they truly feel that God is indeed the only source of strength, blessings and grace in the whole universe. Hence, they make their heartfelt appeal *"to God, their Lord: 'Grant Us a goodly child and we will be truly grateful.'"* (Verse 189)

The Qur'anic account describes the stages of deviation in human beings. The idolaters at the time of the Prophet Muhammad (peace be upon him), and prior to his time, used to pledge their children to serve their deities or be servants in temples and houses of worship. They did so in order to gain favour with God. Although at the beginning they used to turn to God alone, they then deflected from the summit of believing in God's oneness and fell into the depths of abject idolatry. In their error, they used to pledge their children to such idols and deities, hoping that by doing so their children would have a healthy life and would be protected against dangers. It is the same as some people do today when they make pledges to saints dedicating to them certain parts of their children's bodies. Some people may keep a boy's hair to grow, pledging that his first hair cut will be undertaken at the tomb or shrine of a saint, or they keep the boy uncircumcised until his circumcision is undertaken at such a tomb or shrine.

Yet these people acknowledge that God is one, but follow this acknowledgement with such idolatrous practices. Human beings remain the same.

"Exalted is God above anything people may associate with Him as partners." **(Verse 190)**

Rejected is all the idolatry they believe and practise.

It is only the Creator who deserves to be worshipped. The partners they associate with Allah can create nothing. Indeed, they themselves are created. How can they be raised to the status of deities? How come they assign to those deities a portion of themselves and their children? Power and authority are amongst the most essential attributes of Godhead. The One who can support His servants and protect them with His power is the One who deserves to be worshipped. All their alleged deities are powerless and without authority. How can they give them support when they cannot even help themselves? How are they to be treated as partners with God?

Hence, humanity today stands in the same old position and needs to be addressed by the Qur'ān anew. It needs someone to rescue it from its new jāhiliyyah, and present Islam to it; someone to take it from darkness into light and to save its hearts and minds from the new paganism and idolatry. This religion saved it the first time and it can certainly save it from the new folly into which it has sunk.

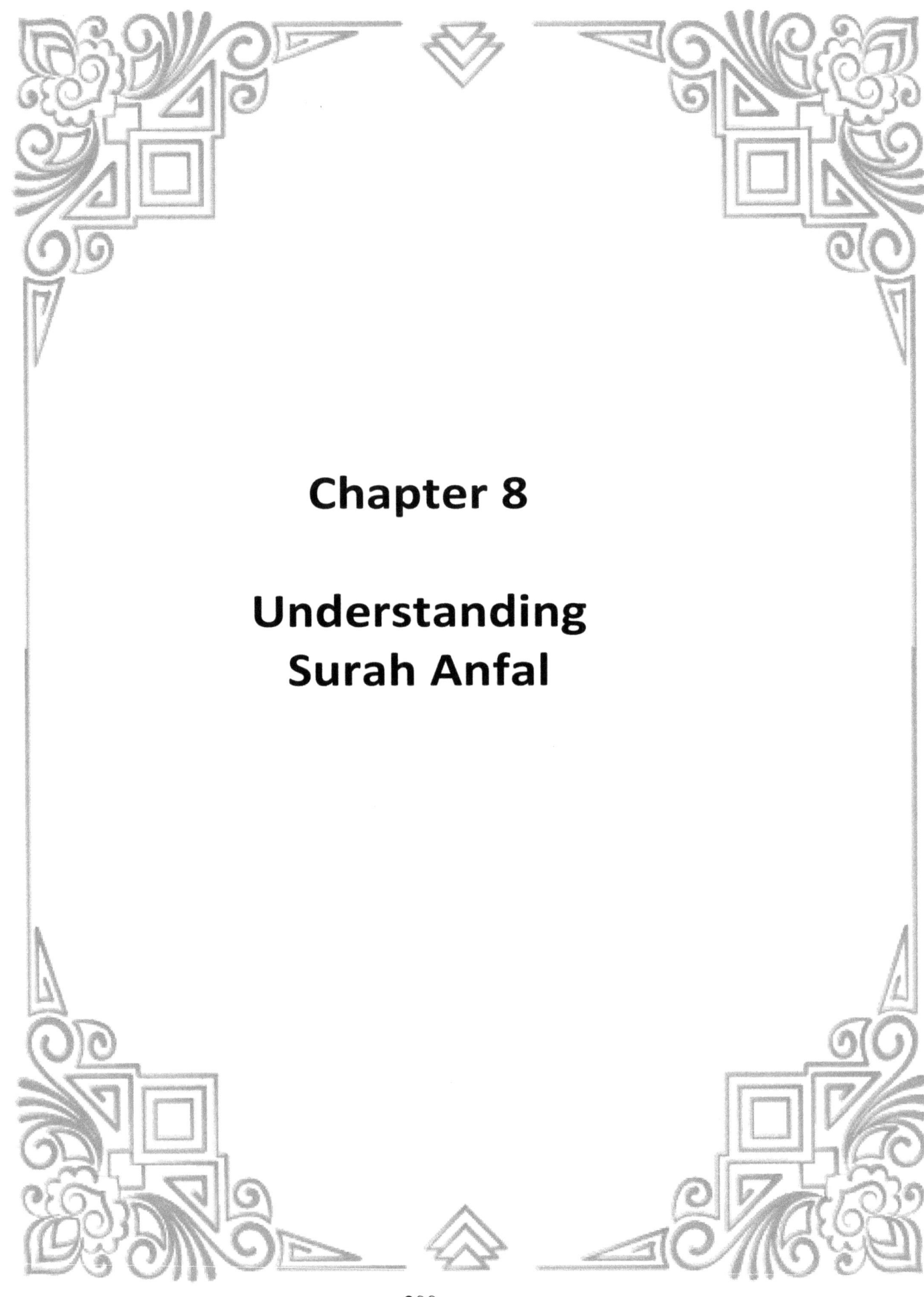

Chapter 8

Understanding Surah Anfal

This surah has 75 verses and is the 8th Chapter of the Qur'an.

Surah Anfal is one of the earliest of the Madani Surahs. It was revealed right after the battle of Badr.

The prisoners of war were still with the Muslims and they were wondering what to do them. In addition, they were unsure what to do with the **Spoils of the War.**

Anfal means the Spoils of War. So, what are the spoils of war?

After the Battle of Badr all of the armour, the horses, and all other possessions of the opposing army now basically belongs to the winning party, the Muslims.

There was now a controversy about who should get what share. This Surah came down regarding this issue.

The Spoils of War. Surah Anfal

This entire Surah from beginning to end is about the battle of Badr. So, Let's go to the battle of Badr.

Some information on the Battle of Badr.

The battle of Badr is the first major battle of the Muslims with the Quraish. It took place in the second year of hijrah in the month of Ramadan.

The Muslims have been persecuted for 13 years. Many of them were killed, many of them were forced to flee to Abyssinia, and then finally to Madina.

They suffered persecution, denied their basic freedom, many were killed. The prophet was attacked multiple times.

So now we are having the Muslims launching an attack back at the Quraish and they have every right to do so according to any law of any society.

Now they have the right to attack the economic lifelines of the Quraish.

The caravan of Abu Sufian.

A large caravan, headed by Abu Sufian was on its way up north to go to the Land of Syria. To reach Syria, they will now have to pass by Madina at some level because Mecca is South.

So when you are going north from Mecca you have to pass through Madina, and then you will get to the land of Syria.

Abu Sufian was in charge of the main annual goods, and that had so much fortune, like millions of dollars equivalent.

So, it was decided that they were going to attack the caravan of Sufian. There were about 310 volunteers.

However, Abu Suffian took a different route and sent word to the Quraish about the situation. This situation of the Muslims wanting to attack him.

The Quraish is not going to have this opportunity of further persecution of the Muslims go amiss.

Hence, they started preparing their army.

Included in their army are hired mercenaries, their slaves, armed guards, the best of armours and horses.

Over a thousand people marched towards where the caravan was.

Now, we have two camps here. Abu Sufian, with his annual fortune, and Abu Jahl with the army.

The prophet was told by Allah swt that he would have guaranteed victory over either one he chose to go into battle with.

Eventually the news was confirmed that Abu Sufian was out of range and Abu Jahl is coming with his army.

The prophet saw in a dream that Abu Jahl army were not many in numbers. This is not to discourage him as his army only comprise of 313 men.

It was confirmed that the Muslims will not attack the Caravan but they will engage in battle with Abu Jahl.

The prophet called a meeting on the plains of Badr. So lets see why this meeting was called.

Remember, their army only comprised of 313 people.

93 of them were the Muhajireen.

210 were from the Ansars, from Median.

Let's look at the position of the Ansar

The Ansars had taken an oath with the Prophet. They are obligated to defend the prophet's army if they were to be attacked in Madina. They were under no obligation to defend the prophet's army on the plains of Badr. That's not what they signed up for.

Our Rasool asked the Muhajireen:

"Would you protect the Muslims like you protect your family if Madina was to be attacked, and return you will be given Jannah?

This was the main purpose of calling this meeting. To enlist the help of the Ansars. He addressed the Muhajireen:

"What do you think we should do?

Shall we stand up and fight back or shall we retreat?"

One of the Mujahiroons stood up and gave a rising speech: "We are going to take them on."

A second one stood up and said the same. The Prophet asked for a third time.

They got confused as to why the Prophet is asking the same question for the third time.

Finally one of the leaders from the Ansar stood up and said: "Perhaps you want to know what the Ansars are going to do?" The Prophet agreed that it was indeed his intention.

So one of the Ansars, gave this famous response:

"Yah Rasoolulah. If you order us to plunge our horses into the sea, we will do so, if you ordered us to go into the sea we will do so, we will not say what the followers of Prophet Musa said:

"You go with your Lord and fight" He continued:

"We are with you wherever you are. We will fight in the Battle of Badr with your army."

As a result of this, the Ansars upgraded their contract to participate in any battles the Prophet engaged in.

The battle of Badr was a resounding victory for the Muslims.

The main leaders of the Quraish, Abu Jahl himself, and over 70 leaders of the Quraish were killed in the battle. The unbelievers fled and the Muslims captured 70 prisoners of war. This is also the first time this has happened and the surah Anfal will tell us of Allah's decision of what should become of these prisoners.

Also, for the first time Muslims have acquired a lot of wealth and so dispute arose, who gets how much, and that is why the Surah is called Surah Al Anfal, the spoils of war.

The surah begins with:

Verse 1

1. They ask thee concerning (things taken as) spoils of war. Say: "(such) spoils are at the disposal of Allah and the Messenger. So fear Allah, and keep straight the relations between yourselves: Obey Allah and His Messenger, if ye do believe."

From this ayah Allah is saying that it is up to Allah to say how it is going to be divided. This is something unique in this Ummah, the acquisition of war booty did not exist in the previous nations.

Our Prophet said:

"I have been given certain things no prophet before me was given and of them is the booty of war and no prophet before me were ever allowed these spoils".

This is the first time that Allah swt is allowing this for any ummah in any civilisation.

Verses 2 to 4:

2. For, Believers are those who, when Allah is mentioned, feel a tremor in their hearts, and when they hear His signs rehearsed, find their faith strengthened, and put (all) their trust in their Lord;

3. Who establish regular prayers and spend (freely) out of the gifts We have given them for sustenance:

4. Such in truth are the believers: they have grades of dignity with their Lord, and forgiveness, and generous sustenance:

Allah is describing the believers. The point here is that the majority of the booty will go to the warriors but Allah begins in Line No. 1 by saying:

"Look, it is up to Allah swt to decide and the believers should accept the decree of Allah".

Verse No 5:

5. Just as thy Lord ordered thee out of thy house in truth, even though a party among the Believers disliked it,

6. Disputing with thee concerning the truth after it was made manifest, as if they were being driven to death and they (actually) saw it.

Allah has brought you out from your home in truth. Some of the believers were reluctant to leave. They were arguing with you (the prophet) about the truth even when the matter was made clear. They thought they were being driven to the death and that's not what was happening.

Verse 7 - 8

7. Behold! Allah promised you one of the two (enemy) parties, that it should be yours: Ye wished that the one unarmed should be yours, but Allah willed to justify the Truth according to His words and to cut off the roots of the Unbelievers;-

8. That He might justify Truth and prove Falsehood false, distasteful though it be to those in guilt.

Here Allah is saying that remember that Allah promised you one of the two groups Abu Sufian or Abu Jahl, that you will be victorious, Allah promised that and you wanted the group that was Abu Sufian. You wanted the easy group. You wanted the group that had more money. But Allah wanted something else, Allah wanted to prove the truth and Allah wanted to defeat those enemies (The army of Abu Jahl). In order words your vision and your plans were limited, and you just wanted an easy victory with a large amount of money, but Allah wanted the truth of Islam to be established, and Allah wanted to send a message to the Quraish.

And this of course shows us a reality that we all know that the plan of Allah is infinitely more wise. We are always short sighted, we are blinded by our own greedy intentions, whatever they might be. But the plan of Allah is always the best plan.

So Allah says in verse number 8 that this was the plan of Allah in order to confirm the truth and nullify falsehood even if the unbelievers do not like it.

And so Allah swt is telling the believers that Allah knows what he is doing and Allah had the best plan and I promise you one of the two. You wanted the easier one but I had a higher goal for you and that was exactly what happened. As in the introduction, we know that the Battle of Badr was between the Muslims and the Army of Abu Jahl.

Verse No 9 to 16

9. Remember ye implored the assistance of your Lord, and He answered you: "I will assist you with a thousand of the angels, ranks on ranks."

10. Allah made it but a message of hope, and an assurance to your hearts: (in any case) there is no help except from Allah and Allah is Exalted in Power, Wise.

The battle of Badr was not won by only 313 Muslims but it was won by a battalion of angels that Allah had sent down. The Muslims would never have won over a thousand people who were better armed than them, who had more horses than them, who had a hired mercenary. Remember initially, the Muslims were not looking for a battle, they did not even had their full body armour. They were not ready for a war. So they were pleading to Allah to help.

The book of Seerah mentioned that the Prophet spent the whole night praying to Allah and in the morning of the battle, he was outside with his hands up for so long that the upper shirt he was wearing fell off. He was left bare chested. Abu Bakr came and took the shirt and put it on him and said:

"Enough yah rasoolulah, Allah has heard your dua and Allah will answer your prayer".

And this is what the verse is referencing:

"When you are beseeching your Lord, he answered you. And victory only comes from Allah.

The only one that can give us victory is Allah swt. And indeed Allah is the almighty and all wise.

Verse 11 to verse no 16

11. Remember He covered you with a sort of drowsiness, to give you calm as from Himself, and he caused rain to descend on you from heaven, to clean you therewith, to remove from you the stain of Satan, to strengthen your hearts, and to plant your feet firmly therewith.

12. Remember thy Lord inspired the angels (with the message): "I am with you: Give firmness to the Believers: I will instil terror into the hearts of the Unbelievers: Smite ye above their necks and smite all their finger-tips off them."

13. This because they contended against Allah and His Messenger. If any contend against Allah and His Messenger, Allah is strict in punishment.

14. Thus (will it be said): "Taste ye then of the (punishment): For those who resist Allah, is the penalty of the Fire."

15. O ye who believe! when ye meet the Unbelievers in hostile array, never turn your backs to them.

16. If any do turn his back to them on such a day - unless it be in a stratagem of war, or to retreat to a troop (of his own)- he draws on himself the wrath of Allah, and his abode is Hell,- an evil refuge (indeed)!

The night before the battle when people should be so nervous, Allah made them go to sleep so they had strength. You know when you are nervous, sleep is almost impossible. Even worse, when you are going to face a battle. You don't know whether you are going to lose or even die.

In that night before the battle, Allah swt said:

I made you drowsy as a security, as a peace, you slept completely the whole night and then in the next morning when you are marching, instead of the soft sand which was going to cover your feet l caused the rain to drizzle just enough, because too much rain would have made it muddy and you wouldn't have been able to walk, and without the rain it would be just the sand. I have just sent down the right amount of rain that would make the earth firm and your walking would be easier. And also you felt energize. You know with a little of rain you feel fresh, you feel nice, and so Allah swt is saying your feet and your hearts are becoming strong and subhannallah, when Allah sends his armies what can any mortal army do against the army of Allah.

Everything belongs to Allah, the wind, the air, the skies, the rain, the sand are all at the service of Allah. So, Allah facilitated this for the Muslims.

And then Allah spoke to the angels and Allah inspired the angels, and said:

"Go and attack the people of the Quraish" and indeed the angels terrified the people of the Quraish.

Verse No 17 – 19

17. It is not ye who slew them; it was Allah. when thou threwest (a handful of dust), it was not thy act, but Allah's: in order that He might test the Believers by a gracious trial from Himself: For Allah is He Who heareth and knoweth (all things).

18. That, and also because Allah is He Who makes feeble the plans and stratagem of the Unbelievers.

19. (O Unbelievers!) if ye prayed for victory and judgment, now hath the judgment come to you: If ye desist (from wrong), it will be best for you: If ye return (to the attack), so shall We. Not the least good will your forces be to you even if they were multiplied: for verily Allah is with those who believe!

Right before the battle when the Muslims could see each the Quraish at a long distance away, the prophet picked up some sand and pebbles and he threw it in the direction of the Quraish. The opposing army, the Quraish, felt the dust and the pebble into their face and into their eyes and were somewhat blinded for awhile and Allah is saying that:

"When you threw, you did not threw, but Allah threw. You just did a little bit but it was Allah swt who did the rest of it".

This really summarises the reality of Qadr. When we put our trust in Allah, when we believe in Qadr, it doesn't mean we do nothing, we do what we need to do and Allah will do the rest.

Allah affirms that he threw and then Allah is saying that your throw didn't have the impact, but it was Allah's.

And this in a nutshell what we believe about the reality of Qadr. And then Allah swt mentiones the reality of the Quraish in:

Verse 20 to 23

20. O ye who believe! Obey Allah and His Messenger, and turn not away from him when ye hear (him speak).

21. Nor be like those who say, "We hear," but listen not:

22. For the worst of beasts in the sight of Allah are the deaf and the dumb, those who understand not.

23. If Allah had found in them any good. He would indeed have made them listen: (As it is), if He had made them listen, they would but have turned back and declined (Faith).

Allah says that this is the worst of mankind. They are deaf, dumb and blind, they don't think, they are not understanding.

And then this is a very important verse, verse 23:

If Allah had deemed any good in them (the Quraish), if Allah knew that their hearts were pure, he would have caused them to hear and if he had allowed that hearing, then they would have been guided to Islam.

This shows us a very important point here. We believe in Qadr and we believe that Allah guides whosoever he wishes, and we believe whoever Allah does not guide will remain misguided. But this also shows that when people are sincere Allah will guide them. This is an especially important fact. Allah does not misguided, only the sincere. Its only those who are truly arrogant and are not worthy of being guided Allah misguides. The ones who want Allah, Allah will always choose him, but the one who doesn't and the one who doesn't have an ounce of good and who don't want to have good, that person will never be chosen.

Verse 28-29

28. And know ye that your possessions and your progeny are but a trial; and that it is Allah with Whom lies your highest reward.

29. O ye who believe! if ye fear Allah, He will grant you a criterion (to judge between right and wrong), remove from you (all) evil (that may afflict) you, and forgive you, for Allah is the Lord of grace unbounded

Allah is saying that you are now going to get a lot of wealth, and you must realise that your wealth and your children are a test for you and Allah possess an immense reward if you pass your test.

The Muslims were impoverished before the battle of Badr. This Battle would be their first financial success.

So Allah is telling the Muslims that all the money they are going to have and all their children are going to be a test for them.

And such is the case for us too. Allah is telling them and telling us: Make sure you pass the test.

And the rewards you are going to get from Allah are much better than the money and the wealth that you have in this world.

Verse 30

30. Remember how the Unbelievers plotted against thee, to keep thee in bonds, or slay thee, or get thee out (of thy home). They plot and plan, and Allah too plans; but the best of planners is Allah.

And remember when the people of the Quraish plotted against you, they tried to imprison you, they try to kill you, they try to expel you. This is about talking about the Hijrah when the Muslims were being persecuted, the prophet and his followers fled for their lives, and within a year victory has been given to you. They plan and Allah planned, and Allah is the best of planners.

Verses 32 and 33

32. Remember how they said: "O Allah if this is indeed the Truth from Thee, rain down on us a shower of stones from the sky, or send us a grievous penalty."

33. But Allah was not going to send them a penalty whilst thou wast amongst them; nor was He going to send it whilst they could ask for pardon

The Quraish were sarcastically mocking:

"Where is this punishment, where is this power of God that you are talking about. So the battle of Badr silence them and then Allah says:

"I am not going to destroy all of you, whilst the prophet is still alive amongst you, and as long as you are still asking for forgiveness there is hope of repentance. In order words the presence of the Rasool on this earth in enough of a blessing that Allah will lift up the punishment from the Quraish.

And then Allah is saying the Quraish repents, they will be forgiven, and this really shows the link of hope when you repent.

VERSE 36

36. The Unbelievers spend their wealth to hinder (man) from the path of Allah, and so will they continue to spend; but in the end they will have (only) regrets and sighs; at length they will be overcome: and the Unbelievers will be gathered together to Hell;

Here Allah is referencing the fund raising the Quraish did before the battle. They raised a lot of money and they invested a lot of money in this battle to fight against the Muslims, Allah says "what was the value in all of that.

Then in:

Verse 38

38. Say to the Unbelievers, if (now) they desist (from Unbelief), their past would be forgiven them; but if they persist, the punishment of those before them is already (a matter of warning for them).

Allah says that after all they have done if they stop, their path will be forgiven. If there is hope for the people who tried to kill the prophet and Allah is saying to them, if you stop, you repent, your past will be forgiven.

If they can be forgiven, then how any believer in Allah can lose hope and despair for the mercy of Allah for the sins they have committed. Allah forgives all sins with sincere repentance, so long as you don't return to sinning.

And then Allah reminds us in Verse 39

39. And fight them on until there is no more tumult or oppression, and there prevail justice and faith in Allah altogether and everywhere; but if they cease, verily Allah doth see all that they do.

40. If they refuse, be sure that Allah is your Protector - the best to protect and the best to help.

Allah is reminding the believers why they are fighting which is fight them until there is no oppression. They are the ones who are fighting you for worshipping Allah. They are the ones who are persecuting you from your land so fight them until there is no more persecution and the entire religion is established for the sake of Allah.

Verse 41

41. And know that out of all the booty that ye may acquire (in war), a fifth share is assigned to Allah, and to the Messenger, and to near relatives, orphans, the needy, and the wayfarer, if ye do believe in Allah and in the revelation We sent down to Our servant on the Day of Testing, the Day of the meeting of the two forces. For Allah hath power over all things.

This verse is an explanation of verse 1 where Allah swt tells us that the booty of the war belongs to Allah swt and his prophet. Basically, only Allah has the right to make that decision. And now Allah is telling us of his decision.

So verse 41 is an explanation of this. It's the legal answer of the shares.

4/5 of the spoils should be returned to the soldiers.

1/5 will go to the state. The state will then deal with it and gives it to the orphans, the poor, the widows.

Verse 42

42. Remember ye were on the hither side of the valley, and they on the farther side, and the caravan on lower ground than ye. Even if ye had made a mutual appointment to meet, ye would certainly have failed in the appointment: But (thus ye met), that Allah might accomplish a matter already enacted; that those who died might die after a clear Sign (had been given), and those who lived might live after a Clear Sign (had been given). And verily Allah is He Who heareth and knoweth (all things).

This verse is another reminder of the belief in Qadr. Allah is telling the believers that if both of you had planned this meeting, both of you wanted to participate in the battle of badr, and wanted to have a fight, you would have never done so. This is because disagreements would have happened – the timing, the place, the methodology, but Allah's plan was that you meet, Allah's plan that the battle of Badr takes place. Allah's plan was already predetermined, your planning could not have unplanned the plan of Allah swt.

So this is the point of verse 42.

Allah has willed this battle. It was the qadr of Allah. And Allah is saying if l had delegated this responsibility to the both of you, you would not have been able to do it, but Allah did it. It was Allah's will and even if you didn't plan it, it was the plan of Allah.

Verse 43, 44, 45, 46

43. Remember in thy dream Allah showed them to thee as few: if He had shown them to thee as many, ye would surely have been discouraged, and ye would surely have disputed in (your) decision; but Allah saved (you): for He knoweth well the (secrets) of (all) hearts.

44. And remember when ye met, He showed them to you as few in your eyes, and He made you appear as contemptible in their eyes: that Allah might accomplish a matter already enacted. For to Allah do all questions go back (for decision).

45. O ye who believe! When ye meet a force, be firm, and call Allah in remembrance much (and often); that ye may prosper:

46. And obey Allah and His Messenger. and fall into no disputes, lest ye lose heart and your power depart; and be patient and persevering: For Allah is with those who patiently persevere

Remember the day at Badr when the two armies met. It looked as if you would certainly fail, but God wanted to establish clear proof that He was on the side of the believers. In a dream Prophet Muhammad (AS) saw the disbelievers as few, because if Allah had shown him the disbelievers as many, he would have lost courage and rethink his decision to fight. Allah also made the believers appear as few in the eyes of the disbelievers so that He may establish a matter He had already ordained.

And in verse 44 Allah gave them another miracle. Both of you, the Quraish and the Muslims saw each other less than they actually were.

When you met, it made them appear less in your eyes and he made you appear in fewer in their eyes, so Allah can conclude a pre-determined matter.

So both sides are seeing the other side as fewer.

It was narrated that when the battle of Badr was beginning the Muslims turned to each other and said:

"These are not a thousand, how many do you think they are". Some say it looks like 100 and another said it looked less.

So they fought with more bravery and power as they saw the army much smaller. So it was a gift to the Muslims.

As for the Quraish, when they saw the Muslims less than their actual numbers, they became more foolish and more arrogant, marching to their defeat.

When the Muslims saw the Quraish fewer than their actual numbers, it made them fewer and stronger.

The same tactic of the opposing sides, have different results.

This is what Allah is saying that l gifted this to you. And this re-enforces that when Allah is on your side you are always the winner.

Then Allah instructs the believers to be firm in battle, to be mindful of Allah, and not to quarrel. Do not be full of conceit or bar others from the way of Allah. Satan gave the disbelievers false confidence, but when the battle began, he fled. He fears God.

Verse 47

47. And be not like those who started from their homes insolently and to be seen of men, and to hinder (men) from the path of Allah. For Allah compasseth round about all that they do.

Allah is saying that there should be complete unity and you do what you do for the sake of Allah. There must be no conceit or arrogance.

Verse 48

48. Remember Satan made their (sinful) acts seem alluring to them, and said: "No one among men can overcome you this day, while I am near to you": But when the two forces came in sight of each other, he turned on his heels, and said: "Lo! I am clear of you; lo! I see what ye see not; Lo! I fear Allah. for Allah is strict in punishment."

It was narrated that Ibn 'Abbaas (may Allah be pleased with him) said: Iblees came on the day of Badr bringing a troop of devils with him. I saw him in the form of a man from Banu Mudlij, in the form of Suraaqah ibn Maalik ibn Ju'sham. The Shaytaan said to the mushrikeen: No one of mankind can overcome you this day (of the battle of Badr) and verily, I will be your protector. Then when the people had drawn themselves up in battle array, the Messenger of Allah (blessings and peace of Allah be upon him) picked up a handful of dust and threw it in the faces of the mushrikeen, and they turned and fled. Jibreel came to Iblees and when he saw him, his hand was in the hand of one of the mushrik men. Iblees pulled his hand away, and turned and fled, he and his party. The man said: O Suraaqah, did you not say that you would protect us? He said: 'Verily! I see what you see not. Verily! I fear Allah for Allah is Severe in punishment.' That was when he saw the angels.

It was narrated by at-Tabaraani in his Tafseer (13/7).

Verses 49,50

49. Lo! the hypocrites say, and those in whose hearts is a disease: "These people,- their religion has misled them." But if any trust in Allah, behold! Allah is Exalted in might, Wise.

50. If thou couldst see, when the angels take the souls of the Unbelievers (at death), (How) they smite their faces and their backs, (saying): "Taste the penalty of the blazing Fire; Those that are arrogant say the believers are deluded, but if only you could see what happens when the angels take the souls of the disbelievers; they strike their faces, and they are destined for the fire.

Verse 51

51. "Because of (the deeds) which your (own) hands sent forth; for Allah is never unjust to His servants:

52. "(Deeds) after the manner of the people of Pharaoh and of those before them: They rejected the Signs of Allah, and Allah punished them for their crimes: For Allah is Strong, and Strict in punishment:

53. "Because Allah will never change the grace which He hath bestowed on a people until they change what is in their (own) souls: and verily Allah is He Who heareth and knoweth (all things)."

54. (Deeds) after the manner of the people of Pharaoh and those before them": They treated as false the Signs of their Lord: so We destroyed them for their crimes, and We drowned the people of Pharaoh: for they were all oppressors and wrongdoers.

55. For the worst of beasts in the sight of Allah are those who reject Him: They will not believe.

Verse 60

60. Against them make ready your strength to the utmost of your power, including steeds of war, to strike terror into (the hearts of) the enemies, of Allah and your enemies, and others besides, whom ye may not know, but whom Allah doth know. Whatever ye shall spend in the cause of Allah, shall be repaid unto you, and ye shall not be treated unjustly.

This is very interesting what Allah is saying here. The whole chapter has told us of so many miracles that Allah has gifted the Muslims. So many miracles were given to them.

Allah put them in a sound sleep the night before the battle, made the earth firm for them, he gave them the dream of reassurance, sent the angels down.

Now despite all of those miracles, Allah is telling the Muslims to prepare for battle as much as you can:

"Go out and train, make sure you have horses, make sure you have bows and arrows, make sure you have weapons".

This is very explicit and it shows us that Qadr and takwaful doesn't mean you just sit back and expect the miracles to happen. You have to do your utmost as much as you can.

It was narrated that our prophet said:

"The best strength is archery, meaning for that time frame, of that era – what is better than archery, archery is long distance, you are able to shoot arrows at a distance, whereas when you are fighting combat in a one in one.

The reality of taqwa is that we have to do the best that we can, as much as we can, then and only then Allah will help.

Verse 61

61. But if the enemy incline towards peace, do thou (also) incline towards peace, and trust in Allah. for He is One that heareth and knoweth (all things).

This verse was revealed in the pinnacle of conflict, between the Quraish and the Muslims, and here Allah is saying that if the unbelievers advance towards peace, then you also return that peace.

What does this shows us? That Isalm is certainly a religion of peace.

The Battle of Badr was as a result of what the Quraish has done to the Muslims for thirteen years. And therefore in Islam, the default is in peace. There is no denying this.

Verse 62, 63

62. Should they intend to deceive thee,- verily Allah sufficeth thee: He it is That hath strengthened thee with His aid and with (the company of) the Believers;

63. And (moreover) He hath put affection between their hearts: not if thou hadst spent all that is in the earth, couldst thou have produced that affection, but Allah hath done it: for He is Exalted in might, Wise.

Let the disbelievers escape if they can because they will not escape Allah, and prepare for war. Whatever is spent in the way of Allah will be repaid. If they incline towards peace make peace. Trust God because if they intend to deceive you, He will know.

All of the help came from Allah and he cause all of your hearts to be reunited. Allah is saying that have you spent everything on earth, have you spent all the money in the world to bring these groups of the believers, and to unite their hearts, you wouldn't have been able to do so. But Allah united their hearts, for Allah is indeed All mighty, and all wise.

What is Allah referencing here?

The feud between the Tribes of Aws and Khazraj. That feud was nasty and ugly. This feud has caused hundreds of their seniors of both sides to be killed.

So when Islam came along these two tribes they willing embrace it, and they saw in the prophet, someone who is a healer, someone who can unite, and that was exactly what had happened. So they invite the prophet to come and this is what Allah swt is referencing. That the aws and the Khzraj, these two tribes of Medina, they would have never some together under the same banner, never have viewed each other as brothers. These are the people we now know as the Ansars.

The muhajiroon from Mecca The aws Khazraj

All three of them became one team despite the fact that the Muhajiroon has no blood ties with the Ansars (the aws and the Khazraj) – they have a bitter feud that goes back two generations, and there is no way that would have come together but Allah brought them together. And this shows that whosoever Allah wants you to reconcile with then you can reconcile with. One of the ninety names of Allah is the one who brings friendships towards the hearts. Remember this verse, and anytime you have a problem with anyone, Allah can bring about a friendship like nothing else can.

Verses 64 to 66

64. O Messenger. sufficient unto thee is Allah, (unto thee) and unto those who follow thee among the Believers.

65. O Messenger. rouse the Believers to the fight. If there are twenty amongst you, patient and persevering, they will vanquish two hundred: if a hundred, they will vanquish a thousand of the Unbelievers: for these are a people without understanding.

66. For the present, Allah hath lightened your (task), for He knoweth that there is a weak spot in you: But (even so), if there are a hundred of you, patient and persevering, they will vanquish two hundred, and if a thousand, they will vanquish two thousand, with the leave of Allah. for Allah is with those who patiently persevere.

The believers are urged into battle. Twenty believers can overcome two hundred disbelievers, and if there are one hundred believers, they will overcome one thousand, and God lightens the hardship even more.

Here, Allah mentions certain aspects of numbers and ratios. What this means is that smaller numbers are going to overcome larger ones, if they are firm if they remain firm to their principles and faith.

Verse 67

67. It is not fitting for an apostle that he should have prisoners of war until he hath thoroughly subdued the land. Ye look for the temporal goods of this world; but Allah looketh to the Hereafter: And Allah is Exalted in might, Wise.

This is related to the famous dispute that happened over the prisoners of war, and this dispute goes back to the issues of what is to be done with the 70 people who were captured in the battle of Badr.

This is the first time that the muslims have these prisoners of war. The prophet called the sahaba. What can we do about these prisoners of war. There were differing opinions.

This is human nature, one group of sahaba looked at the positives of reconciliation, they opined that they are all part of one tribe and suggest that to forgive and release them and get some ransom.

Whilst the other group state that they need to send a message to the quraish – these people tried to kill us, we need to send a message that we cannot tolerate this. This is not acceptable, this is war, we need to end this by being harsh.

A good lesson to be learnt here. Sometimes mercy wins over harshness. When do you decide to be strict with the justice and when do you forgive? Other names of Allah, are Al aziz, Al hakeem, he is the one.

So the sahabas began differing among themselves what is to be done, one group said forgive and ransom and the other group said no.

And Allah swt revealed after the prophet decided to go with the first group.

Allah revealed this verse telling the prophet that he has made a decision that wasn't the best.

By sending the message to just ransoming them off seems like a sign of weakness. Ya rassoolulah, right now you have the upper hand.

But Allah said:

"I have forgiven you, lets move on. So he allowed and accepted the prophet decision.

So after the battle of badr the prophet allow all 70 of the prisoners to ransom themselves off by paying a certain amount. A point to note here is that each prisoner was given an appropriate for his wealth and this was amazing. The ransom was based on the financial status of the prisoners. The poor one will pay a smaller amount, and then the poorest of the poor who didn't have anything, the prophet set them free, with the condition that they teach 10 of the children of the Ansar how to read and write. So, education was even valued in the time of the Battle of Badr. They didn't have any money but had a skill and a talent so the prophet told them to teach some of the children of the Ansar.

But those who had the money, who had the means got ransomed and the more money they had, the higher was their ransom. Among the rich ones, were one of the uncles (Ibn Abbass) of the prophet and when the prophet state his price, he told his nephew that he did not have that money. The prophet responded to him by reminding him about the money he had hidden. Only him and his wife knew about this hidden treasure to be used only if something happened to him.

When Ibn Abbass heard this, he knew that the prophet must have heard it from Allah because that was a secret between him and his wife.

Verse 68,69

68. Had it not been for a previous ordainment from Allah, a severe penalty would have reached you for the (ransom) that ye took.

69. But (now) enjoy what ye took in war, lawful and good: but fear Allah. for Allah is Oft- forgiving, Most Merciful.

Allah is telling the prophet and the Muslims that they can take this treasure for the ransom, and remain conscious of Allah, for Allah is forgiving and merciful.

Verse 70

70. O Messenger. say to those who are captives in your hands: "If Allah findeth any good in your hearts, He will give you something better than what has been taken from you, and He will forgive you: for Allah is Oft-forgiving, Most Merciful."

"Oh prophet,

Say to those who you hold as prisoners:

"If Allah find any good in your heart, you will have better than what had been taken away. Allah will forgive you because Allah is forgiving and merciful. This verse in particular is in reference to Ibn Al Abbass and overall to all of the people of Badr who eventually converted.

This verse was particularly to Ibn Abbass, who said he knows that it applies to him because Allah took something from him and gave him back much more, and much better. He gave him Islam. Abbass indeed became a wealthy person after he embraced Islam.

Verse 70, once again Allah knows when there is good in your heart. This is a reality that we still apply to this day. Allah doesnot misguide the sincere. If Allah knows there is good in your heart Allah will give you back more than what has been taken away from you.

The final verses of the Surah

Verse 71 to 75

71. But if they have treacherous designs against thee, (O Messenger.), they have already been in treason against Allah, and so hath He given (thee) power over them. And Allah so He Who hath (full) knowledge and wisdom.

72. Those who believed, and adopted exile, and fought for the Faith, with their property and their persons, in the cause of Allah, as well as those who gave (them) asylum and aid, - these are (all) friends and protectors, one of another. As to those who believed but came not into exile, ye owe no duty of protection to them until they come into exile; but if they seek your aid in religion, it is your duty to help them, except against a people with whom ye have a treaty of mutual alliance. And (remember) Allah seeth all that ye do.

73. The Unbelievers are protectors, one of another: Unless ye do this, (protect each other), there would be tumult and oppression on earth, and great mischief.

74. Those who believe, and adopt exile, and fight for the Faith, in the cause of Allah as well as those who give (them) asylum and aid, - these are (all) in very truth the Believers: for them is the forgiveness of sins and a provision most generous.

75. And those who accept Faith subsequently, and adopt exile, and fight for the Faith in your company, - they are of you. But kindred by blood have prior rights against each other in the Book of Allah. Verily Allah is well-acquainted with all things.

These verses deal with protection, loyalty and alliances with the message very clear that believers need to be united. Their bonds are stronger than anything else, and those who do not believe in Islam, even if they fight among themselves, they will unite against Islam.

We see this even in our modern day times. These kinds of people will reunite against the Muslim ummah. So Allah is saying that the Ummah is divided and do not unite the unbelievers, causing a lot of fitnah and façade. This clearly shows us the importance of Muslim unity. The ummah is one body and the Qur'an keeps explicitly says because the Muslims were united in the battle of Badr, that's why they were successful.

In the battle of Uhud the Muslims did not unite, they differed among themselves and that led to their downfall. As we know the Muslims did not win or lose the battle.

Chapter 9

Towards Understanding Surah Tawbah

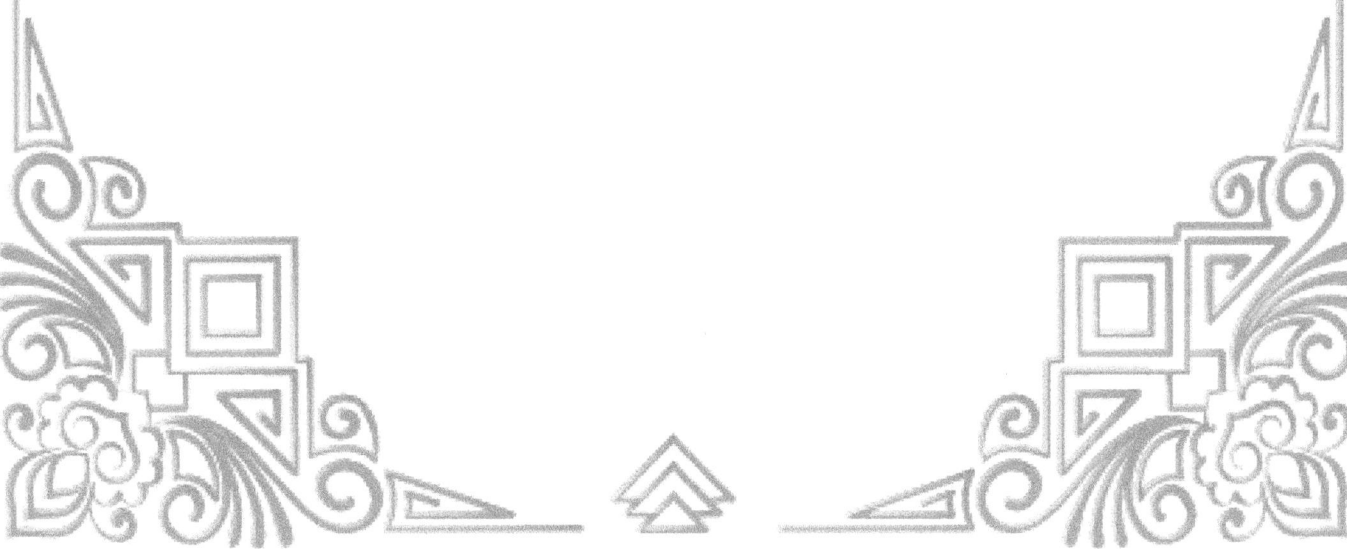

Background Surah Tawbab.

Surah Tawbah was revealed in the month Rajab after the battle of Tabuk. This is the only Surah in the Qur'an that doesnot begin with Bismillah Ir rahaman Ir Rahim. There are various reasons for this, is that it could be the continuation of the previous Surah, Surah Anfal. Two other reasons were that this surah was very harsh revealed in the context of two battles, and the third was that the prophet omit this Bismillaih.... When relating it to the transcribers.

Some notes on the conquest of Mecca:

Before the conquest of Mecca, several events took place. In 628CE, the Prophet set out from Medina with 1400 men to perform Hajj. Before entering the prophet sent a message to the Meccans about their intentions of performing their pilgrimage, and they hadnot not come to engage in warfare. However, they were prevented from entering. But an agreement was reached between the Muslims and the Quraish by establishing a Peace treaty. This treaty was called the treaty of Hudaybiyyah.

Some of the terms of the Treaty was that the Mulims would return the following year to perform their pilgrimage. They would clear the city so that the Muslims would perform their pilgrimage peacefully.

There would be a ten year peace agreement, hence preventing any further bloodshed.

If a member of the Quraish wants to accept Islam and move to Medina, they willnot be allowed. But if a Muslim in Medina wants to return to idolism, they he will be permitted to return to Mecca.

However, two years later there was a violation of the agreement.

One of the tribes who were allies with the disbelieving Meccans attacKed a tribe that was allied with the Muslims.

This is the incident Surah Tawbah is referring to when the opening verses stated the cancellation of all agreements with those who violated the terms.

By 630 CE, the Muslims are now become a formidable power, and the prophet led 10,000 men to conquer Mecca.

Once the Prophet reached Mecca the Quraish surrendered.

The above information is necessary to aid understanding of Surah Tawbah.

Themes of the Surah

Cancellation of the Treaties with those who Arabs who repeatedly broke them, but honour those who remained loyal

The battle of Hunain

The Battle of Tabuk

Only Muslims should be keepers of the Kabaah

Honesty – the Story of IBN Kab Malik in the context of those who did not join the prophet in the battle of Tabuk

The value of time – referencing Kab ibn Malik

Mockery – those who mock the poor in the context of the fundraising for the battle of Tabuk

Arrogance – leading oneself into a false sense of security in context of the battle of Hunain

The hypocrites who lie and break their promises

Unity of the Muslims – in the context of the hypocrites in Madinah wanting to divide the Ummah

The paradox of war and peace

In the beginning of this Surah, Allah swt issue a very harsh warning to the disbelievers who have waged a bloody battle against Islam. A warning was issued to them to stop their fitnah and their trouble making, if not the muslims will put an end to it. The prophet left Mecca nine years ago as a refugee. But now, nine years later he is not a refugee. He has established Medina as a state. He is the statesman, he is the founder of a new nation, a new culture, a new civilization, a new army. An army that was capable of challenging the might of Quraish. So before teaching Meccans a lesson and put them in their place, the policy of the prophet was to preach to them first, to send a warning to them. Islam is not about bloodshed, Islam is about peace and harmony. Islam only resorts to fighting when there is other option to bring peace and to put an end to fitnah.

VERSES 1 TO 4

1. A (declaration) of immunity from Allah and His Messenger, to those of the Pagans with whom ye have contracted mutual alliances:-

2. Go ye, then, for four months, backwards and forwards, (as ye will), throughout the land, but know ye that ye cannot frustrate Allah (by your falsehood) but that Allah will cover with shame those who reject Him.

3. And an announcement from Allah and His Messenger, to the people (assembled) on the day of the Great Pilgrimage,- that Allah and His Messenger dissolve (treaty) obligations with the Pagans. If then, ye repent, it were best for you; but if ye turn away, know ye that ye cannot frustrate Allah. And proclaim a grievous penalty to those who reject Faith.

4. (But the treaties are) not dissolved with those Pagans with whom ye have entered into alliance and who have not subsequently failed you in aught, nor aided any one against you. So fulfil your engagements with them to the end of their term: for Allah loveth the righteous.

Surah Tawbah in the first verse is issuing a warning to the polytheist. A four month ultimatum was given. The polytheist will either accept Islam or they will have to leave the Arabia and its surrounding plains and settle somewhere else.

All treaties, they have before are now cancelled. But Allah is fair and just and the Prophet was told that the treaty must not be nullified without informing those disbelievers first.

This would indeed be a difficult task as from previous experiences of the hostility of the Meccans, bearer of such such news can be killed.

WHO WILL DELIVER THIS MESSAGE

Our holy prophet (AS) dispatched Hadrat Abu Bakr and Hadrat Ali to deliver this message to the Meccans. Allah commanded that the treaty must not be broken without informing the Meccans first.

Now lets go to Verse 5

But when the forbidden months are past, then fight and slay the Pagans wherever ye find them, an seize them, beleaguer them, and lie in wait for them in every stratagem (of war); but if they repent, and establish regular prayers and practise regular charity, then open the way for them: for Allah is Oft-forgiving, Most Merciful.

This is a verse that has caused a lot of controversy in Islam. The haters of Islam and the extremist love this verse to justify their actions.

This is what happens when verses of the Qur'an are cherry picked and used out of context.

The Qur'an is a book that is taken in its whole message. You cannot pick and chose verses out of context and apply to what you think is your situation. This is the biggest mistake of both the haters of Islam and the Militant misguided extremists groups.

They open up the Qur'an without any knowledge of the life of the Prophet (AS), without understanding the context, without reading the sunnah and they cherry pick.

This surah has verses that is very easy to misunderstand if they are not put into context.

Straight after this verse we have

Verse 6:

6. If one amongst the Pagans ask thee for asylum, grant it to him, so that he may hear the word of Allah. and then escort him to where he can be secure. That is because they are men without knowledge

Verses 5 and 6, are related to the respite period of four months given to the polytheists to either vacate Arabia or accept the message of Islam. It is certainly not advising Muslims to seek out others of different fate and kill them. And that is the danger in cherry picking verses.

In verse 6 we see that Allah is saying if they asked for asylum they must be escorted to a safe place where they can hear the world of Allah.

And then Verse 11, reinforces this

11. But (even so), if they repent, establish regular prayers, and practise regular charity, - they are your brethren in Faith: (thus) do We explain the Signs in detail, for those who understand.

But if the idolators start praying and gives charity they became the brothers of the Muslims in faith.

Allah says in multiple verses in this surah to embrace Islam. But the message is if they refused and insist in remaining idol worshippers they have four months respite before being expelled from the region.

And this is the context in which **Verse 5** was revealed.

This verse was meant as an ultimatum. This verse was never applied. No one was ever killed because of this verse.

TIME TO PONDER AND REFLECT

As Muslims you many very well be asked about these verses. Your own children might even posed these questions to you. Knowledge of our deen is very important. We have a responsibility to know every aspect of our faith so we can give clear and accurate to others without the understanding.

Verse no 17 to 19:

17. It is not for such as join gods with Allah, to visit or maintain the mosques of Allah while they witness against their own souls to infidelity. The works of such bear no fruit: In Fire shall they dwell.

18. The mosques of Allah shall be visited and maintained by such as believe in Allah and the Last Day, establish regular prayers, and practise regular charity, and fear none (at all) except Allah. It is they who are expected to be on true guidance.

19. Do ye make the giving of drink to pilgrims, or the maintenance of the Sacred Mosque, equal to (the pious service of) those who believe in Allah and the Last Day, and strive with might and main in the cause of Allah. They are not comparable in the sight of Allah. and Allah guides not those who do wrong.

It is not befitting that those who worship idols take care or maintain the masjid of Allah swt. The masjid, the Kabab is a sacred place, it's the house of Ibrahim and Allah is telling us here, its not befitting, it is not appropriate that those who worship idols, should be the ones in charge.

Verse 23,24

23. O ye who believe! take not for protectors your fathers and your brothers if they love infidelity above Faith: if any of you do so, they do wrong.

24. Say: If it be that your fathers, your sons, your brothers, your mates, or your kindred; the wealth that ye have gained; the commerce in which ye fear a decline: or the dwellings in which ye delight - are dearer to you than Allah, or His Messenger, or the striving in His cause;- then wait until Allah brings about His decision: and Allah guides not the rebellious.

This surah mentions verses that states the importance of strengthening the ties of the ummah.

Verse 24, that if your parents and your children, your siblings and your spouses, your relatives, and the wealth that you have acquired, the homes that you love, if all of these worldly matters are more beloved to you, than striving in the cause Allah and his messengers, then wait until judgement day. Allah does not guide the sinful people.

This verse shows us the issues of priorities. For a muslim all of these aspects, your wealth, your family, your children, your spouses, your relatives. These worldly things are not our end goal. Of course, they are a part of our lives, but we must integrate our worldly affairs to the higher cause of the worship of Allah swt. We must utlise our wealth also, for the sake of Allah.

So, **verse 24** is talking about-getting your priority right.

TIME TO PONDER AND REFLECT

Time to look at our own priorities!! How do we spend our wealth? Do you know that we can give charity not only by monetary means. Do we seek out the needy in the community? Do we look for opportunities to do things for the sake of Allah?

Do we seize opportunities to use our home, the home that Allah blessed us to give dawah? I know we are in lockdown now. But before lockdown, many of the sisters have been using this opportunity to invite others from the Sisters circle to gain

Islamic knowledge. We must remind ourselves constantly about prioritizing. Look at what Allah has given you and ponder whether we are doing enough.

The next passage from 25 to 26

25. Assuredly Allah did help you in many battle-fields and on the day of Hunain: Behold! your great numbers elated you, but they availed you naught: the land, for all that it is wide, did constrain you, and ye turned back in retreat.

26. But Allah did pour His calm on the Messenger and on the Believers, and sent down forces which ye saw not: He punished the Unbelievers; thus doth He reward those without Faith.

Allah mentions the battle of Hunain.

Allah swt mentions a very important lesson for all of us in the battle of Hunain.

The battle of Hunain took place after the conquest of Mecca. It took place when the Muslims had one of the largest army, 12, 000 people. It was between the Muslims **and** the Badawi / Bedouin tribe of Hawazin and the tribe of Thaqif.

The Muslims, because of their numbers, the strength of their army deluded themselves into thinking that victory will be easy for them.

"We have this strength and power".

The tribes of Hawazin and Thaqif set up a trap and the Muslims walked into that trap. Many of them faltered and fled until the prophet stood up and summoned them to return.

They eventually won this battle.

But there was a time when they thought they were going to loose, and Allah references this in the Qur'an.

"On the day of Hunain when your numbers impressed you, when you thought that just because you have a large army that you were never going to defeated".

TIME TO PONDER AND REFLECT

The core **lesson** of **Hunain** is, undoubtedly, to never overlook the real most important reason for victory: **Allah.**

A victory does not come from numerical strength. Similarly, victory should not make a man conceited and defeat should not make a man hopeless.

The Victory Over the Quraish

The tremendous victory of Islam over the Quraish and the huge conversions to Islam at the conquest of Makkah amazed the disbelievers and lead many tribes to Islam.

Others, like the Hawazin and the Thaqif were dominant tribes from the lush fortified city of Taif were not happy. They watched in horror as the ending of idolatry was drawing near. The Hawazin were the old enemies of the Quraish. They regarded themselves as their rivals in power and prestige. The submission of the Quraish to the rising power of Islam had made them undisputed champions of paganism. Now they began to harbour hopes of bringing the Muslims to their knees and to build their fame upon the declining prestige of the Quraish. So they schemed with other pagan leaders and decided to battle against muslims under the command of Malik bin `Awf, in the month of Shawwal, 8th A.H.

Although, as mentioned above the Muslims suffered a temporary defeat at the beginning of battle of Hunain it eventually it ended in a decisive victory for the Muslims.

Many from these tribes accepted Islam, and repented, having all prior sins wiped out.

The Muslims as the winners of this battle acquired lots of spoils of war, hence, apart from being victorious in the battle they also accumulated lots of wealth.

TIME TO PONDER AND REFLECT
KEY LESSONS TO LEARN FROM THE BATTLE OF HUNAIN

It is important that one should do homework before starting any new task and gain the correct information, as it is essential for success.

Muslims became complacent due to their reliance on numbers; that was one of a setback of this battle. Though, it was natural to have that confidence after the conquest of Makkah. But there is a difference between being complacent and not taking right measures to protect one's gains that established over the years.

Temporary defeat strengthened the faith of Muslims which had the lesson that both victory and defeat come from Allah. Whether one is a new Muslim or old, he should not rely on means only, instead, one must put Allah above every other secondary consideration.

The core lesson of Hunain is, undoubtedly, to never overlook the real most important reason for victory: Allah. A victory does not come from numerical strength. Similarly, victory should not make a man conceited and defeat should not make a man hopeless.

The resilience and determination of the leader has a deep influence on the followers to lead them to victory. It can change the face of battles by strengthening the hearts of weaker followers. The statement of the Prophet (Pbuh) that he was a true prophet showed his firmness and self-confidence.

Prophet Mohammed (Pbuh)condemned the killing of a slave woman and reminded Khalid bin Walid not to kill any defenseless person. This is the mark of difference what Islam teaches and gives the superior code of conduct even in warfare.

Muslims can acquire weapons from non-muslims to protect their interests.

However, leadership should remain in the hands of muslims.

There are certain patterns of all battles. In many cases, it was the intervention of Allah SWT that took out muslims from the crisis. Because it is Allah's promise to protect His messenger and believers, though some companions were killed during the combats, Allah protected many so that message continued to spread.

Behind the distribution of booty in favour, the new converts had the wisdom to keep them in the fold of Islam, as many of them were leaders and wealthy people. They were new to the faith and this was the first spoil of war that came into their hands. Their faith was not as strong as the earlier companions of the Prophet. Prophet Muhammed (Pbuh) was unable to win them without any material reward. Wealth is many times the single and only factor that can remove the enmity of an enemy. He gave them wealth initially and would later work on their hearts and convert them to people strong in faith. It proved true as these same men became strong muslims and were instrumental in taking Islam to the rest of the world.

When the Prophet (Pbuh) heard about the rumors related to Ansaars, he immediately dispelled them by addressing the issue. He did not allow enemies to further build on a misconception and sow the seeds of hatred. His sequence of questions and his choice of words provide an incredible model of leadership. He not only convinced them of his honesty and kindness but also further strengthened his relationship with them.

The response of the Ansaars to the Prophet's speech was a vivid statement of their confidence and love for him. They knew that it was because of Allah and His Prophet (Pbuh) that saved them from a life of disgrace and difficulty. It brought them honour and they would always give their lives, wealth, and children in the service of Islam.

(Taken from "The Biography of Muhammad Sallallahu Alaihi Wasallam")

THE BATTLE OF TABUK (Brief Summary)

They did not wish to strive in Allah's way with their wealth and their selves; and they said (to the others), "Do not go in the heat". Say (O Muhammad), "The fire of Hell is fiercer in heat"; if only they could understand.

Surah at-Tawbah, 9:81

Islam, with all its conquest, is now becoming a superpower and the powerful Byzantine Empire (Roman Empire) is now beginning to feel very threatened.

Now, in the 9th year of the Muslim calendar, the Byzantine forces converged on the borders of Syria. They wanted to attack the Muslim territories.

Prophet Muhammad (Pbuh) heard about it and started a fund-raising campaign. He urged affluent Muslims to make significant donations. A number of them who were unable to make donations or volunteer were so unhappy that Allah (SWT) sent down a revelation exempting them from the obligation of joining the expedition. There were other Muslims who refused to join the expedition despite being in good health and having ample funds. They told the Prophet (Pbuh) that they would not go out in such intense heat.(Surah Tawbah refers to them as the Munafiqoon-the hypocrites)

Despite these setbacks, the Prophet (Pbuh) was able to gather a force of 30,000 fighters — the largest Muslim fighting force so far — and marched to Tabuk. The army crossed deserts and baked plains, and had very little water because they camped in lands which once belonged to the Thamud. Eventually their thirst was so great that Allah (SWT) sent down torrents of rain to aid them.

When the Muslim forces reached Tabuk, there were no Byzantines there: by that time, they had abandoned the border towns, so the Prophet (Pbuh) gave orders for the return march. However, this daring venture made such an impression on the pro-Byzantine tribes in northern Arabia that they shifted their allegiance from Constantinople to Madinah, in the same way that the conquest of Mecca had cleared opposition from those regions.

Allah mentions in

Verse no 39

39. Unless ye go forth, He will punish you with a grievous penalty, and put others in your place; but Him ye would not harm in the least. For Allah hath power over all things.

And this is a big eye opener for us.

What Allah is saying if you do not do your job 1 will bring another group that does do their job. If you don't live up to the commands of Allah swt.

40. If ye help not (your leader), (it is no matter): for Allah did indeed help him, when the Unbelievers drove him out: he had no more than one companion; they two were in the cave, and he said to his companion, "Have no fear, for Allah is with us": then Allah sent down His peace upon him, and strengthened him with forces which ye saw not, and humbled to the depths the word of the Unbelievers. But the word of Allah is exalted to the heights: for Allah is Exalted in might, Wise.

If you do not help him then Allah will help him.:

THE STORY OF WHEN THE PROPHET WAS EXPELLED FROM MECCA

During the year of the Hijrah, the idolators tried to kill, imprison or expel the Prophet (Pbuh), who escaped with his friend and Companion, Abu Bakr to the cave of Thawr. They remained in the cave for three days so that the pagans who were sent in their pursuit, returned (to Makkah), and they proceed to Al-Madinah. While in the cave, Abu Bakr was afraid the pagans might discover them for fear that some harm might touch the Messenger (Pbuh). The Prophet (Pbuh)kept reassuring him and strengthening his resolve, saying, (O Abu Bakr! What do you think about two, with Allah as their third)

TIME TO PONDER AND REFLECT

This really is giving us the very simple point that when you stand up and help the religion you are not helping in that sense, anyone but yourself. Allah doesn't need you. Your work is not what Allah needs. Allah is saying, if you all abandon him (The Prophet), l will take care of him. I don't need you, Your help is for your own good. It is for you to pass your test. Allah does not need you. You need Allah swt. So Allah is reminding the Munafiqoon, that when you give these excuses, you are making these excuses among yourselves, it is not as if Allah needs your help.

Verse 75 to78

75. Amongst them are men who made a covenant with Allah, that if He bestowed on them of His bounty, they would give (largely) in charity, and be truly amongst those who are righteous.

76. But when He did bestow of His bounty, they became covetous, and turned back (from their covenant), averse (from its fulfilment).

77. So He hath put as a consequence hypocrisy into their hearts, (to last) till the Day, whereon they shall meet Him: because they broke their covenant with Allah, and because they lied (again and again).

78. Know they not that Allah doth know their secret (thoughts) and their secret counsels, and that Allah knoweth well all things unseen?

Allah says, some hypocrites give Allah their strongest oaths that if He enriches them from His bounty, they will give away alms and be among the righteous. However, they did not fulfill their vows or say the truth with their words. The consequence of this action is that hypocrisy was placed in their hearts until the Day they meet Allah the Exalted, on the Day of

Resurrection. We seek refuge with Allah from such an end. Allah said, (...because they broke that (covenant) with Allah which they had promised to Him) He placed hypocrisy in their hearts because they broke their promise and lied. In the Two Sahihs, it is recorded that the Messenger of Allah (Pbuh) said,

(There are three signs for a hypocrite: if he speaks, he lies; if he promises, he breaks the promise; and if he is entrusted, he betrays the trust.) Allah said, (Know they not that Allah knows their secret ideas, and their Najwa,) Allah states that He knows the secret and what is more hidden than the secret; is that he has full knowledge of what is in their hearts, even when they pretend that they will give away alms, if they acquire wealth, and will be grateful to Allah for it. Truly, Allah knows them better than they know themselves, for He is the All-Knower of all unseen and apparent things, every secret, every session of counsel, and all that is seen and hidden.

They also laughed and mocked at those who donate dates, because they had nothing else.

Reference of the Above verses to the Fund-raising that the Prophet held for the battle of Tabuk.

There were those who did not have the means to help. They had no money. They just gave some dates. And then there were others who made a covenant with Allah promising that when they become rich they will be so generous with their charities. When they did have the means by the permission of Allah, they became very miser and refused to help.

Allah is telling us that he penalizes them with hypocrisy in their hearts and they will answer for their actions on the Day of Judgement.

Don't they know that Allah knows their planning, Allah know their secrets, and Allah knows their planning, and Allah is the knower of the unseen.

TIME TO PONDER AND REFLECT

These verses represent another tactic of the hypocrites. Are we also guilty of what these verses are referencing?

That's the purpose of Allah telling us these stories. We need to make sure that we do not associate with the tactics and mannerisms of the hypocrites.

Another tactic that they use and this is a unfortunately common occurrence amongst some groups of Muslims.

Lets now look at verse 79

79. Those who slander such of the believers as give themselves freely to (deeds of) charity, as well as such as can find nothing to give except the fruits of their labour,- and throw ridicule on them,- Allah will throw back their ridicule on them: and they shall have a grievous penalty.

This verse is referring to the scenario that the people who contributed the dates were mocked at by the hypocrites.

Allah tells us these events of the past so that we can ponder and reflect.

TIME TO PONDER AND REFLECT

This verse is terrifying.

You know why?

Many of us have these thoughts.

I will give charity, l will pray when l reach the age of…?

I will become the best Muslim when l come into some money.

Allah tells us these stories in the Qur'an so we don't make the mistakes of the people in the past.

These groups of hypocrites, they made a promise with Allah— the day l become rich, l will become charitable. Then when Allah made them rich, they turn around and became very miserly. Allah tells us that he has classed them as the Munakiqoons, the hypocrites, and they will have their recompense on the day of judgement.

Our generosity is not related to money, its related to the heart. If your heart is generous, you will be generous.

Even if you cannot give money like our prophet says, your smile is charity.

The minute we put these barriers up like - when l reach a particular age l will become righteous, when l cross this hurdle l will become righteous. These are all excuses. Do not fall into the traps of Shaitan.

Verse 79 is also referencing us. Hypocrisy is also when you find faults in other people. Unfortunately, there are many who find faults with anyone who is doing good and being charitable.

Now let us look at the following **two verses:**

117. Allah turned with favour to the Prophet, the Muhajirs, and the Ansar,- who followed him in a time of distress, after that the hearts of a part of them had nearly swerved (from duty); but He turned to them (also): for He is unto them Most Kind, Most Merciful.

118. (He turned in mercy also) to the three who were left behind; (they felt guilty) to such a degree that the earth seemed constrained to them, for all its spaciousness, and their (very) souls seemed straitened to them,- and they perceived that there is no fleeing from Allah (and no refuge) but to Himself. Then He turned to them, that they might repent: for Allah is Oft- Returning, Most Merciful.

The above verses are related to the story of Kab Ibn Malik. Because of his honesty Allah revealed those verses.

The Prophet commanded that all abled body male to fight in the Battle of Tabuk

The story of Kab Ibn Malik.

The Battle of Tabuk exposes the pretenders who didn't want to fight in the Battle of Tabuk. The weather was very hot and it was at a time when the business community of Madina was ready to harvest their palm dates. So they made up feeble excuses under various pretext not to take part in the battle. But Allah took the veil off their faces and these verses were revealed condemning their actions.

However, there were three among them who had genuine excuses and Kab Ibn Malik were among them.

The Story of Kab Ibn Malik

I never had better means and more favourable circumstances than at the time of this expedition. And by Allah, I had never before possessed two riding-camels as I did during the time of this expedition. Whenever Messenger of Allah (PBUH) decided to go on a campaign, he would not disclose his real destination till the last moment (of departure). But on this expedition, he set out in extremely hot

And so this is the story of Kab Ibn Malik. He was very eager to participate in the Battle of Tabuk. He was in a very favourable. He had two camels, was in good health. But he lured himself into a false sense of security and delayed leaving with the prophet and his arm. He felt that he was strong and young and would catch up with him. And when he decided to leave it was too late.

When the Prophet returned from this expedition those who did not join the expedition went to the prophet with their excuses. They all lied except Kab Ibn Malik and two others.

Kab Ibn Malik did not lie nor did he give any flimsy excuse and he spoke the truth and was sincerely repentant. So the Prophet (PBUH) told him to wait for Allah's decree and he ordered that he and along with two others were to be boycotted by the people of Madinah

TIME TO PONDER AND REFLECT

The Story of Kab teaches us about the effects of procrastination (delaying, putting something off) can have on us. It can, in fact, rob us of so many opportunities to do good. Because Kab delayed preparing, he missed out on the rewards of fighting for the sake of Allah.

Always make good use of your time.

A Great Lesson to learn from this story is that we must not make excuses in front of Allah swt and we should not try to justify our sins. Iblis could have repented but he did not while Adam AS admitted his sin and sought the forgiveness of Allah swt and so he was forgiven. Similarly, Kab did not make excuses but accepted his fault. He cried his heart out when he was boycotted by the people of Madina and by Prophet Muhammad SAW. He repented and Allah accepted his repentance

THE CONCLUSION:

The sūrah addresses the Prophet, showing him what attitude to take when people turn away from him and his message. It points to the source of power which gives him all the protection he needs. To Him belong all power, dominion, greatness and honour. His support is sufficient for everyone who seeks His patronage.

The sūrah which concentrates mainly on fighting and striving for God's cause is thus concluded with the directive to rely on God alone, trust Him and seek His powerful support. After all **"He is the Lord of the Mighty Throne."**

Chapter 10

Towards Understanding the Message Of Surah Yunus

STARTING SURAH YUNUS

Although the name of the Surah is Surah Yunus, this prophet has only been mentioned once in the surah, in verse 98. Surahs Al Saffat (Chapter 37) and Surah Al Anbiyah (Verse 21) are where the story Prophet Yunus can be found.

Historical context and the circumstance in which Surah Yunus was revealed.

This surah was revealed in Mecca. Let us look at the conditions of the Muslims in that time period.

The Prophet (peace be upon him) was ridiculed and those who converted to Islam were persecuted and tortured. The people of Quraysh boycotted the Muslims for three years, and the Muslims suffered from sickness, hunger, and poverty. A boycott document was written, which stated that no business or trade of any sort would be done with the boycotted tribes, nor would any food be allowed to reach them. Furthermore, no one would marry anyone from their tribes or have social interactions with them.

In the same year, Prophet Muhammad (peace be upon him) lost his two strongest supporters and sources of comfort, his wife, Khadijah, and his uncle, Abu Talib.

Without the protection from his uncle, Abu Talib, in Makkah, Prophet Muhammad (peace be upon him) needed to reach out and seek support beyond the city of Makkah. He (peace be upon him) wanted to spread the message to the people of Taif, in hopes that they would believe and accept the message of Islam. He trekked from Makkah to Taif to invite the people to belief in One God.

Prophet Muhammad (peace be upon him) met with the chiefs of the major tribe in Taif, Thaqeef tribe. He (peace be upon him) told them about Islam, worshipping only one God, and leaving idol worshipping. They rejected his message and insulted him. Not only did they refuse to listen to his message, but they unleashed the children of their tribe to throw stones at him and drive him out of their town. With people jeering at him as his ankles bled, he ran out, finding shelter in an empty orchard.

Alone, bleeding, and rejected, he (peace be upon him) rests on a rock and prays to Allah. He (peace be upon him) is so compassionate and merciful, he does not ask Allah to punish the people of Taif or to execute revenge against them.

At that moment, Angel Jibreel came to Prophet Muhammad (peace be upon him) and told him that if he wished, Allah could order an angel to collapse the two mountains surrounding the people of Taif and crush them.

How did Prophet Muhammad (peace be upon him) react to those who had insulted him and threw stones at him?

He opted for mercy not violence towards them. He was not overcome with rage or hate. Instead of seeking revenge against the people of Taif, he said to Angel Jibreel, "I rather hope that Allah will raise from among their descendants people who will worship Allah the One, and will not ascribe partners to Him."

We look to Taif today and we come to appreciate our Prophet's vision, patience, and mercy. Today Taif has a population of 1,200,000 people, predominantly Muslim. Taif is the summer capital of Saudi Arabia, and it is known for its grapes, pomegranate, figs, roses, and honey. Anyone living in Saudi Arabia loves to visit Taif for its cooler weather and the beautiful scenery of its mountains.

When reading the history, the incident of Taif is often mentioned only with negative connotations. This is understandable because it was one of the most painful and hurtful incidents in the Prophet's lifetime, but actually some good did come out of it on that day, and the message of Islam did not fall entirely on deaf ears. Someone did accept the message of Islam at that time in Taif, but he is not always mentioned in the books on the Prophet's life.

When Prophet Muhammad (peace be upon him) sat on the rock, raising his hands to Allah, the two owners of the orchard saw him and so they sent their slave with a bunch of grapes to give to the Prophet (peace be upon him).

The slave's name was Addas and he was a young Christian man. When Addas gave the Prophet the grapes, he heard the Prophet say, "In the name of Allah," before he ate. Addas was surprised and curious because he never heard anyone say such words before. The Prophet asked Addas where he was from and Addas answered that he was from Nineveh.

The Prophet (peace be upon him) said, "The land of Jonah the Just, son of Matta." The young man was bewildered that this man, Muhammad, knew of Prophet Jonah.

After informing the Prophet that he was a Christian, Addas then asked the Prophet who he was and how he had such knowledge.

The Prophet (peace be upon him) said, "Jonah is my brother. He was a prophet and I am a prophet."

Addas was amazed; he knew that this man indeed had to be a prophet. Addas kissed the Prophet's head and hands and he immediately accepted Islam. So, the Prophet's mission to

Taif was not totally unfruitful. One man, Addas, had whole heartedly embraced Islam after meeting and speaking with the Prophet (peace be upon him).

The lesson we can take from this incident is to never belittle any effort or act of goodness. Persevere and do your part. Work sincerely and do what you know is right, regardless of what the outcome may be, and sooner or later, the results will come.

It is also worthwhile here to mention that there is a verse in Surah Qalam:

"So wait with patience for the Command of thy Lord, and be not like the Companion of the Fish, when he cried out in agony. Had not Grace from his Lord reached him, he would indeed have been cast off on the naked shore, in disgrace. Thus did his Lord choose him and make him of the Company of the Righteous." from Qur`an, *Al*-Qalam, **Surah 68:48-50**

Here, we can see that the first Prophet introduced to Prophet Muhammad (AS) was Prophet Yunus. Surah Qalam was the third surah revealed to the prophet, and Allah is kind of telling him of the difficulties he will face.

Allah swt revealed three surahs in this time period one after the other – Surah Yunus, Surah Hud and Surah Yusuf.

There is a link between the name of the surah and the message of the surah.

Surah Yunus is named after the great Prophet Yunus. What is interesting about this surah is that Prophet Yunus (AS) is only mentioned once, in **Verse 98.**

So why is this surah named after him and what is so special about him. Well, Prophet Yunus is the only prophet who we know of, whose entire community accept Islam after he came out from the belly of the whale.

Each of the other prophets went through lots of struggles trying to convince their people to become Muslims. Some of them became Muslims, and some rejected the faith, or all of then rejected their prophets and then the punishment of Allah came upon them.

So its almost as though Allah swt is telling the Quraish that "this is your chance to return to Allah, just like the people of Yunus did, or suffer the faith like those who were destroyed.

Allah talks about his greatness in this Surah.

Now lets look at verses 1 to 13.

The Surah begins with Alif, Lam, Ra. These letters are one of the miracles of the Qur'an and only Allah knows their meanings. Also, you will find that surahs that have such beginnings are linked to a prophet.

Surah Yunus discusses the main logical proofs about the truth of Islam.

Proof about Allah's greatness.

THEME 1

Allah is telling us that it is he who created the heavens and the earth in six days, and is firmly established on the throne (of authority), regulating and governing all things.

These verses are also telling us and the Quraish that there is nothing in the creation of Allah Almighty which has no purpose. Everything is created with a certain specific purpose. At the same time, the Qur'an also makes it clear that everything on earth has been created for man and for the benefit of man.

It talks about the natural world and the signs around it, which should be sufficient miracles for us to understand and appreciate the power of and majesty of Allah.

Verse no, 4 tells us:

That Allah is the one that made the sun a bright light, a lamp and has made the moon a noor, a light, and has stationed them on a path.

He has stationed the sun and the moon to be at a particular time so that we can be able to count the number of years, to calculate the time around us. This is one of the many verses of the Qur'an that Allah swt links the sun and the moon with time.

Now just about these massive objects in motion in the solar system at supersonic speed.

Now, let us look at the solar system.

The Sun is the largest planet that Allah created, large enough to fit million of earths. It moves at 250 km per second. This is supersonic speed.

Just imagine, every second, this massive ball of flame is going through the universe. The moon is going around a third of that speed and the sun, the moon and the earth, are in such perfect synchronisation and harmony.

Allah is saying that we derive time from their accuracy. These massive objects are going at such enormous speed and they are so precise that they do not crash into each other.

These are the powers of Allah swt, the control of these massive celestial objects which are so accurate down to a millisecond. We derive the accuracy of our time- our seconds, our minutes, our hours, our days, weeks, months and years from the movement of the sun and the moon.

And this is what Allah swt is telling us. And asking the question:

"How can you deny the creator of the sun and the moon, the synchronizer of all that is in the heavens and the earth".

One of the main themes in this surah is that man always remember Allah in times of stress, in times of difficulties, and once that period is over they neglect Allah.

THEME 2

Verses 12 states that:

When a difficulty touches man, he starts praying seeking Allah's help, standing, sitting or lying down. Whatever state he finds himself in he is constantly seeking the help of Allah swt.

And as soon as relief comes he goes back to his normal state, forgetting the existence of his creator.

Allah is telling us and the Quraish these things so that we can take heed and to realise that there will be consequences for such actions.

We always need Allah. We don't only need Allah when calamity strikes, this is just an illusion. So these are warnings that we must take heed of. To make this journey in this world, we need Allah swt in all moments in our lives.

And a point to note here is we must not forget the role of Shaitan. When we are in good times, Shaitan causes us to forget, and only remember Allah at times of adversity.

Another theme here is the characterisation of the Qur'an, the descriptions of the Qur'an and Prophet Muhammed is the true prophet..

THEME 3

- The Prophet is a true prophet send by Allah

- The Qur'an is the world of Allah.

These are depicted by some remarkably interesting verses:

Verse No 16

16. Say: "If Allah had so willed, I should not have rehearsed it to you, nor would He have made it known to you. A whole life-time before this have I tarried amongst you: will ye not then understand?"

The prophet is appealing to the Quraish to believe in his prophethood. He is telling them that he has lived a lifetime among them and was not known for these types of revelations. He is telling them that Allah has revealed these verses to him, these messages to him.

So he proving his point by reminding the people of his characteristics of honesty and sincerity, and that these revelations began overnight.

In verse 37, there is the verse of challenge

37. This Qur'an is not such as can be produced by other than Allah. on the contrary it is a confirmation of (revelations) that went before it, and a fuller explanation of the Book - wherein there is no doubt - from the Lord of the worlds.

This Qur'an could have never had been manufacture by anyone but Allah, and the Qur'an is a confirmation of what had come before. There is no doubt in it that it is from the lord of the universe.

Verse 38

38. Or do they say, "He forged it"? say: "Bring then a Sura like unto it, and call (to your aid) anyone you can besides Allah, if it be ye speak the truth!"

Allah is saying if they think that this Qur'an is a fabrication then he is challenging them to produce one like it with the help from other beside Allah.

Anytime we are in doubt, anytime we feel spiritually lost we only have to open the book of Allah.

Look at what Allah says in **Verse 57**

57. O mankind! there hath come to you a direction from your Lord and a healing for the (diseases) in your hearts,- and for those who believe, a guidance and a Mercy. This verse summarizes the description of the entire Qur'an:

An advise has come that touches the inner soul of mankind, it has come from the Lord, a healing, a cure for what is in the heart, and a guidance and mercy for all mankind.

Its saying that anytime we have any spiritual disease, the Qur'an is the cure for it. That's why it is so important for us to have a continual relationship with the Qur'an.

We need to recite the Qur'an daily, even it is just five minutes per day. Let's open up the book of Allah and recite it. The Qur'an is food for our soul, just like the food we eat for our body, the Qur'an feeds the soul, it's a shifa, a guidance and a mercy. Its better than all of the wealth we possess, we cannot find the inner peace and the satisfaction that the Qur'an will give.

THEME 4

Verse 62-65

THE FRIENDS OF ALLAH

Who are they?

The awliya (friends of Allah), these close friends of Allah are very much so scattered amongst the people, you don't know who they are, and that's what makes this so interesting.

You don't know who is a wali, friend of Allah, is. In fact, some of the awliya of Allah themselves don't know that they're awliya of Allah; they don't quite understand how much Allah loves them and how they could have ascended in those ranks.

There are three ways, that the scholars mentioned, to attain that special friendship with Allah, the one that the Prophet Muhammad (peace be upon him) narrated in a hadith Qudsi that Allah has said:

"Whosoever takes that special friend of mine as an enemy, I will wage war on him".

May Allah let us be the friend of Allah, and not the one having war waged upon them.

That's very beautiful and very scary at the same time because again the awliya, friends of Allah, are hidden.

Ali said:

"Allah has hidden two things amongst his people. He has hidden his pleasures in his good deeds, so you don't know which of the good deeds is the one that unlocks his pleasure. And Allah has hidden his Awliyah, his special friends amongst his people."

3 Things That Allow A Person To Attain That State of Awliyah

1. Fulfil the Obligations and Do Good

You fulfil the obligations and you do good until you taste the sweetness of that good, which is the pleasure of Allah, and that becomes your unique driving force in life.

You don't come close to Allah with anything more beloved than doing your obligations: praying on time, fasting, doing the things that Allah tells you to do.

And then you get closer to Him with nafl. You taste the sweetness of the obligations and now you start to do the voluntary deeds until Allah loves you with that exclusive special love.

And when Allah loves you that way, He becomes the hearing with what you hear, the sight with which you see, the hand with which you strike, the way that you walk. You become entrenched in that pleasure of Allah and seeking that pleasure of Allah; and it becomes your exclusive driving force.

The pleasure of Allah is what drives you through all of your good deeds so that you keep on doing more and more, and you can't get enough of it. Because you tasted the sweetness of prayer, now five times it's not enough anymore; you tasted the sweetness of fasting, Ramadan is not enough anymore; you tasted the sweetness of Hajj, Hajj is not enough anymore…

So Allah unlocks these things for you, and you taste the pleasure of those good deeds and that becomes the driving force.

2. The Sincerity of Your Repentance

This is a more sudden one. A person makes the sincere repentance to Allah, for Allah, because of Allah; and the pleasure of Allah in that repentance completely removes the effect of the pleasure of that disobedience to Allah.

So that's where you find those hadiths about a person who is in major sin and then suddenly switches; the pleasure of Allah overwhelms any type of pleasure they used to get from that disobedience. And now they are calibrated in that way, and they immediately rise in status with Allah.

3. When Allah Tests You With a Major Tragedy

Allah takes away something from you, and through that tragedy you do *ihtisab*, which is to seek the reward (Allah's pleasure). And you try to seek that pleasure from Allah, and that's what seized you through that tragedy. That again becomes the way that you contextualize all of your tragedies and all of your tribulations; that a person would reach that status of *wilaya* (friendship).

(Omar Suleiman)

https://youtu.be/nNUAOgRvNS0

LESSONS TO BE LEARNT FROM CIVILIZATION OF THE PAST

FROM VERSES 71 TO VERSES 104

Here we have three stories in succession, one after the other.

The stories of:

Prophet Noah,

Musa and Firawn,

Prophet Yunus.

Allah swt is presenting three case studies to the people of the Quraish.

And asking them… "Which of these do you want to be":

The People of Nuh (AS)…. All the disbelievers were drowned

The People of Musa (AS)…. The believers were saved and the unbelievers drowned.

The people of Yunus (AS)… verse 98

Everyone chose Islam and all the people were saved.

Verses 104 onwards……

The last five verses of this surah beautifully summarize the entire surah and the entire religion of Islam.

These verses are saying:

"Yah rassoolulah, tell all mankind:

If you are in doubt as to what my religion is, of what I am preaching,

If you are in doubt that this religion is from Allah swt,

Then say:

I will not worship those who you worship,

I only worship Allah who gave you life, will cause you to die, and who shall cause you to be resurrected to him.

THE STORY OF PROPHET YUNUS

Prophet Yunus was sent as a Prophet to the people of a city called Nineveh, about 230 miles north-west of modern day Baghdad in Iraq. The people were steeped in wickedness, and Prophet Yunus exerted his utmost in guiding them to the Straight Path, but his people belied him. Prophet Yunus warned them of the coming of the punishment of Allah in three days, and in his wrath and anger, and without the specific permission and command of Allah Subhanah, he impatiently departed the place and boarded a ship to go far away from the disbelievers and the coming punishment of Allah!

Incidentally, after his departure, the people of Yunus realized their mistake and repented before the scourge of Allah came upon them; and the Merciful Lord forgave them.

But because Prophet Yunus showed impatience, and departed his place of mission without the permission and command of Allah, he was put in a severe trial by his Lord. To make a long story short, Yunus boarded the ship, and as Allah would have Willed, the river became violent to such an extent that the people of the ship threw away all its weight to keep the ship afloat! But the ship was still in danger of capsizing, and as was the norm in those days, they cast a lot, and the name of

Prophet Yunus was casted as the one who should be thrown into the river to lighten the load of the ship. When Prophet Yunus was thrown into the river, a huge fish swallowed him, and he stayed in the belly of the fish for three days and it was from the depths of the river, that the Prophet Yunus humbly implored his Lord to forgive him his error of impatience; and the Merciful Lord forgave him, and the fish cast him on a naked shore, and he returned back to his people.

(The whole story of Prophet Yunus is described in detail in the Holy Qur'an in Chapter 37 Surah Saafaat verses 139-148).

LESSONS TO BE LEARNT FORM SURAH YUNUS

"And had he not been of those who exalt Allah, he would have remained inside its belly until the Day they are resurrected." [Qur'an, 37:143-144]

The life and story of Prophet Yunus remain one of the most powerful in helping us understand the notions of patience, vulnerability, and faith – his trials and faith in Allah should stand as an inspiring reminder to us all on how to truly worship Allah alone.

The vulnerability of letting our emotions get to us, the fear of isolation and death, and the power of a simple but truly heartfelt prayer to Allah are all a part of the story of Prophet Yunus – so here are five lessons from the Holy Qur'an on the story of Prophet Yunus:

1. Don't let anger consume you

"And [mention] the man of the fish, when he went off in anger and thought that We would not decree [anything] upon him." [Qur'an, 21:87]

At the end of the day, we are all human – meaning that it is often easy to succumb to our emotions and frustrations. Here, the Holy Qur'an reminds us of the dangers of letting our anger consume us, and that for every rash action taken out of anger there will always be consequences.

2. No matter the darkness, always pray for the light of Allah

"And he called out within the darkness, 'There is no deity except You; exalted are You. Indeed, I have been of the wrongdoers.'" [Qur'an, 21:87]

Despite our mistakes and shortcomings, part of what makes the example of Prophet Yunus so empowering to us today is the vulnerability and purity of his heart – the Qur'an tells us that despite our mistakes and past deeds, it is never too late to sit down and pray for forgiveness and the mercy of Allah as Prophet Yunus did.

3. Allah is always merciful

"So We responded to him and saved him from the distress. And thus do We save the believers." [Qur'an, 21:88]

Chapter 11

Towards Understanding Surah Hud

Many stories in the Qur'an demonstrate the nature of Allah, some sections teach us about Paradise and Hell and still other parts of Qur'an teach us lessons. We can learn such valuable lessons from the Stories of the Prophets and their people in Surah Hud (Chapter 11)

Surah Hud deals with the histories of the following prophets - Noah, Hud, Salih, Abraham, Lot and Shu'ayb (peace be upon them all). The cruel and persecuting enemy – the Quraish - is warned of the fate that befell previous people. In Surah Tawbabh and Surah Yunus the the historical context in which these Surahs were revealed was discussed. Just a reminder -Surah Tawbah, Yunus, Hud and Yusuf were surahs revealed one after the other to console the Prophet Muhammad (AS). Him and his followers were severely tortured and persecuted in this time period.

So we would have known nothing about these stories had Allah not revealed it to His messenger. It is a favour upon us that we have the Qur'an. There is absolute no doubt regarding it's authenticity, so we know that every single thing mentioned in it is 100% accurate.

What is the purpose of these stories?

For us to draw a lesson from them for ourselves.

What lesson do we take from the story of Nuh AS which we have related? It was a consolation to the Prophet PBUH.

Allah swt revealed to the Prophet (AS)

"Bear patience O Muhammed SAW! The makkans will trouble you just as the nations of the past troubled their Prophets. Look at Nuh AS, he was a da'ee (caller) for 950 years with very little response. At times decades went by with not a single person turning to Allah.

THE STORY OF THE PEOPLE OF NUH(AS) NOAH

There is a big gap between Prophet Idris and Prophet Noah. Prophet Idris is the Great Grandson of Prophet Seth, the only child of Adaam (AS) who wasn't a twin.

So this is how Shaitaan started to set his traps in that long [period of when there was not prophets].

After Prophet Idris (AS) died, there were a group of very righteous men who continued to support and guide the people spiritually in the worship of Allah swt. They were indeed very holy men.

When these holy men died, Shaitaan saw his opportunity to mislead the children of Adam to the hellfire. He told the people to make statues of these holy men just to act as a reminder.

Shaitaan sets his traps gradually. When this generation died he influenced the people to worship these statues, telling them that these were the Gods of the previous generations. And that is how idol worshipping started.

And now this brings us to the story of Prophet NUH. (Noah)

According to the history of the People of the Book (this refers to the Jews, and Christians, so called by Allah because they received revealed Books - the *Tawrah*, *Zabur* and *Injil*. These names are translated Torah, Psalms, and Gospels respectively, but these Books are are corrupt and not in the original form it was revealed). Of the revealed Books, only the *Qur'an* remains exactly as it was revealed),

For many generations Noah's people had been worshipping statues that they called gods. They believed that these gods would bring them good, protect them from evil and provide all their needs. They gave their idols names such as *Waddan*, *Suwa'an*, *Yaghuthah*, *Ya'augah*, and *Nasran*. These idols represented, respectively, manly power; mutability, beauty; brute strength, swiftness, sharp sight, insight according to the power they thought these gods possessed.

Allah *the Almighty* revealed:

"They (idolaters) have said, 'You shall not leave your gods nor shall you leave *Wadd*, nor *Suwa*, nor *Yaghuth*, nor *Ya'uq* nor *Nasr*.'" *Al-Qu'ran* 71:23

Originally these were the names of good people who had lived among them. After their deaths, statues of them were erected to keep their memories alive. After sometime, however, people began to worship these statues. Later generations did not even know why they had been erected; they only knew their parents had prayed to them. That is how idol worshipping developed. Since they had no understanding of Allah *the Almighty* Who would punish them for their evil deeds, they became cruel and immoral.

Ibn 'Abbas explained, "Following upon the death of those righteous men, Satan inspired their people to erect statues in the places where they used to sit. They did this, but these statues were not worshipped until the coming generations deviated from the right way of life. Then they worshipped them as their idols."

In his version, Ibn Jarir narrated, "There were righteous people who lived in the period between 'Adam and Noah and who had followers who held them as models. After their death, their friends who used to emulate them said: 'If we make statues of them, it will be more pleasing to us in our worship and will remind us of them.' So they built statues of them, and after they had died and others came after them, Iblis crept into their minds saying: 'Your forefathers used to worship them, and through that worship they got rain.' So they worshipped them."

Ibn Abi Hatim related this story, "Waddan was a righteous man who was loved by his people. When he died, they withdrew to his grave in the land of Babylonia and were overwhelmed by sadness. When Iblis saw their sorrow caused by his death, he disguised himself in the form of a man saying: 'I have seen your sorrow because of this man's death; can I make a statue like him which could be put in your meeting place to make you remember him?' They said: 'Yes.'

So he made the statue like him. They put it in their meeting place in order to be reminded of him. When Iblis saw their interest in remembering him, he said: 'Can I build a statue of him in the home of each one of you so that he would be in everyone's house and you could remember him?'

They agreed. Their children learned about and saw what they were doing. They also learned about their remembrance of him instead of Allah. So the first to be worshipped instead of Allah was *Waddan*, the idol which they named thus."

The essence of this point is that every idol from those earlier mentioned was worshipped by a certain group of people. It was mentioned that people made picture sand as the ages passed they made these pictures into statues, so that their forms could be fully recognized; afterwards they were worshipped instead of Allah.

It was narrated that 'Umm Salamah and 'Umm Habibah told Allah's Prophet Muhammad *sallallahu 'alayhi wa sallam* about the church called *Maria* which they had seen in the land of Abyssinia. They described its beauty and the pictures therein. He said, *"Those are the people who build places of worship on the grave of every dead man who was righteous and then make therein those pictures. Those are the worst of creation unto Allah."* [*Sahih Al-Bukhari*]

Worshipping anything other than Allah is a tragedy that results not only in the loss of freedom; its serious effect reaches man's mind and destroys it as well. *Almighty* Allah created man and his mind with its purpose set on achieving knowledge the most important of which is that Allah Alone is the Creator and all the rest are worshippers (slaves). Therefore, disbelief in Allah, or polytheism, results in the loss of freedom, the destruction of the mind, and the absence of a noble target in life. (By worshipping anything other than Allah, man becomes enslaved to Satan, who is himself a creature and becomes harnessed to his own baser qualities).

Into this environment Allah sent Noah with His message to his people. Noah was the only intellectual not caught in the whirlpool of man's destruction which was caused by polytheism.

Allah is His Mercy sent His messenger Noah to guide his people. Noah was an excellent speaker and a very patient man. He pointed out to his people the mysteries of life and the wonders of the universe. He pointed out how the night is regularly followed by the day and that the balance between these opposites were designed by Allah *the Almighty* for our good. The night gives coolness and rest while the day gives warmth and awakens activity. The sun encourages growth, keeping all plants and animals alive, while the moon and stars assist in the reckoning of time, direction and seasons. He pointed out that the ownership of the heavens and the earth belongs only to the Divine Creator.

Therefore, he explained to this people, there cannot have been more than one deity. He clarified to them how the devil had deceived them for so long and that the time had come for this deceit to stop. Noah spoke to them of Allah's glorification of man, how HE had created him and provided him with sustenance and the blessings of a mind. He told them that idol worshipping was a suffocating injustice to the mind. He warned them not to worship anyone but Allah and described the terrible punishment Allah would mete out if they continued in their evil ways.

The people listened to him in silence. His words were a shock to their stagnating minds as it is a shock to a person who is asleep under a wall which is about to fall and who is vigorously awakened. This person may be alarmed and may even become angry although the aim was to save him.

Noah's people were divided into two groups after his warning. His words touched the hearts of the weak, the poor, and the miserable and soothed their wounds with its mercy. As for the rich, the strong, the mighty and the rulers they looked upon the warning with cold distrust. They believed they would be better off if things stayed as they were. Therefore, they started their war of words against Noah.

First they accused Noah of being only human like themselves.

"The chiefs of the disbelivers among his people said: 'We see you but a man like ourselves."
Al-Qur'an 11:27

He, however, had never said anything other than that. He asserted that, indeed, he was only a human being; Allah had sent a human messenger because the earth was inhabited by humans. If it had been inhabited by angels Allah would have sent an angelic messenger.

The contest between the polytheists and Noah continued. The rulers had thought at first that Noah's call would soon fade on its own. When they found that his call attracted the poor, the helpless and common laborers, they started to verbally attack and taunt him, "You are only followed by the poor, the meek and the worthless."

Allah *the Almighty* told us:

"Indeed We sent Noah to his people (he said), 'I have come to you as a plain warner that you worship none but Allah, surely, I fear for you the torment of a painful Day.' The chiefs of the disbelievers among his people said, 'We see you but a man like ourselves, nor do we see any follow you but the meanest among us and they too followed you without thinking. And we do not see in you any merit above us in fact we think you are liars.'" Al-Qur'an 11:25-27

Thus, the conflict between Noah and the heads of his people intensified. The disbelievers tried to bargain: "Listen Noah, if you want us to believe in you, then dismiss your believers. They are meek and poor, while we are elite and rich; no faith can include us both." Noah listened to the heathens of his community and realized they were being obstinate. However, he was gentle in his response. He explained to his people that he could not dismiss the believers as they were not his guests but Allah's.

Noah appealed to them:

"O my people! I ask of you no wealth for it, my reward is from none but Allah. I am not going to drive away those who have believed. Surely, they are going to meet their Lord, but I see that you are a people that are ignorant. O my people! Who will help me against Allah, if I drove them away? Will you not then give a thought? And I do not say to you that with me are the Treasures of Allah nor that I know the unseen, nor do I say I am an angel, and I do not say of those whom your eyes look down upon that Allah will not bestow any good on them. Allah knows what is in their inner selves (regards to Belief). In that case, I should, indeed be one of the dhalimin (wrongdoers, oppressors etc)." Al-Qur'an 11:29-31

Noah refuted the arguments of the disbelievers with the noble knowledge of the prophets. It is the logic of intellect that rids itself of personal pride and interests.

The rulers were tired of Noah's arguments. Allah *the Exalted* related their attitude:

"They said, 'O Noah! You have disputed with us and much have you prolonged the dispute with us, now bring upon us what you threaten us with, if you are of the truthful." He said,

'Only Allah will bring it (the punishment) on you, if He will, and then you will escape not. And my advice will not profit you, even if I wish to give you counsel, if Allah's Will is to keep you astray. He is your Lord! And to Him you shall return.'" Al-Qur'an 11:32-34

The battle continued; the arguments between the disbelievers and Noah became prolonged. When all the refutations of the disbelievers collapsed and they had no more to say, they began to be rude and insulted Allah's Prophet:

"The leaders of his people said, 'Verily, we see you in plain error.'" Al-Qur'an 7:60

Noah responded in the manner of the Prophets:

"O my people! There is no error in me, but I am a Messenger from the Lord of the 'alamin (mankind, jinn and all that exists)! I convey unto you the Messages of my Lord and give sincere advice to you. And I know from Allah what you know not." Al-Qur'an 7:61-62

Noah continued appealing to his people to believe in Allah hour after hour, day after day year after year. He admonished his people and called them to Allah day and night, in secret and openly. He gave them examples, explained Allah's signs and illustrated Allah's ability in the formation of His creatures. But whenever he called them to Allah, they ran away from him. Whenever he urged them to ask Allah to forgive them, they put their fingers in their ears and became too proud to listen to the truth.

Allah *the Almighty* related what Noah faced:

"Verily, We sent Noah to his people saying, 'Warn your people before there comes to them a painful torment.'

"He said, 'O my people! Verily, I am a plain Warner to you, that you should worship Allah Alone, be dutiful to Him and obey me, He (Allah) will forgive you of your sins and respite you to an appointed term. Verily, the term of Allah when it comes, cannot be delayed, if you but knew.'

"He said: 'O my Lord! Verily, I have called my people night and day (secretly and openly to accept the doctrine of Islamic Monotheism), but all my calling added nothing but to their flight from the truth. Verily! Everytime I called unto them that You might forgive them, they thrust their fingers into their ears, covered themselves up with their garments, and persisted (in their refusal), and magnified themselves in pride. Then verily, I called to them openly (aloud); then verily, I proclaimed to them in public, and I have appealed to them in private, I said to them: 'Ask forgiveness from your Lord, Verily, He is Oft Forgiving; He will send rain to you in abundance, and give you increase in wealth and children, and bestow on you gardens and bestow on you rivers.'"

"What is the matter with you, that you fear not Allah (His Punishment), and you hope not for reward from Allah or you believe not in His Oneness. While He has created you in different stages."

Al-Qur'an 23:13-14

And:

"See you not how Allah has created the seven heavens one above another, and has made the moon a light therein and made the sun a lamp? And Allah has brought you forth from the dust of earth. Afterwards He will return you into it (the earth), and bring you forth (again on the Day of Resurrection) Allah has made for you the earth wide spread (an expanse) that you may go about therein broad roads.

"Noah said, 'My Lord! They have disobeyed me, and followed one whose wealth and children give him no increase but only loss. They have plotted a mighty plot. They have said, 'You shall not leave your gods, nor shall you leave *Wadd*, nor *Suwa*, nor *Yaghuth*, nor *Ya'uq* nor *Nasr*.' Indeed they have led many astray. O Allah! Grant no increase to the *dhalimin* (polytheists, wrongdoers, and disbelievers etc) save error.'

"Because of their sins they were drowned, then were made to enter the Fire and they found none to help them instead of Allah."

Al-Qur'an 71:1-25

Noah continued to call his people to believe in Allah for nine hundred fifty years. Allah *the Almighty* said:

"Indeed We sent Noah to his people and he stayed among them a thousand years less fifty years (inviting them to believe in the Oneness of Allah (Monotheism) and discard the false gods and other deities)."
Al-Qur'an 29:14

It happened that every passing generation admonished the succeeding one not to believe Noah and to wage war against him. the father used to teach his child about the matter that was between himself and Noah and counsel him to reject his call when he reached adulthood. Their natural disposition rejected believing and following the truth.

Noah saw that the number of believers were not increasing, while that of the disbelievers were. He was sad for his people, but he never reached the point of despair.

There came a day when Allah revealed to Noah that no others would believe. Allah inspired him not to grieve for them at which point Noah prayed that the disbelievers be destroyed. He said:

"My Lord! Leave not one of the disbelivers on the earth. If you leave them, they will mislead Your slaves and they will beget none but wicked disbelivers." Al-Qur'an 71:27

Allah accepted Noah's prayer. The case was closed, and He passed His judgment on the disbelievers in the form of a flood. Allah *the Exalted* ordered His worshipper Noah to build an ark with His knowledge and instructions and with the help of angels. *Almighty* Allah commanded:

"And construct the ship under Our Eyes and with Our Inspiration and address Me not on behalf of those who did wrong; they are surely to be drowned." Al-Qur'an 11:37

Noah chose a place outside the city, far from the sea. He collected wood and tools and began to day and night to build the ark. The people's mockery continued, "O Noah! Does carpentry appeal to you more than prophethood? Why are you building an ark so far from the sea? Are you going to drag it to the water or is the wind going to carry it for you?" Noah replied, "You will come to know who will be put to shame and suffer."

Allah *the Almighty* narrated:

"As he was constructing the ship, whenever the chiefs of his people passed by him, they made a mockery of him. He said, 'If you mock at us, so do we mock at you likewise for your mocking. And you will know who it is on whom will come a torment that will cover him with disgrace and on whom will fall a lasting torment.'" Al-Qur'an 11:38-39

The ship was constructed, and Noah sat waiting Allah's command. Allah revealed to him that when water miraculously gushed forth from the oven at Noah's house, that would be the sign of the start of the flood, and the sign for Noah to act.

The terrible day arrived when the oven at Noah's house overflowed. Noah hurried to open the ark and summon the believers. He also took with him a pair, male and female, of every type of animal, bird and insect. Seeing him taking these creatures to the ark, the people laughed loudly, "Noah must have gone out of his head! What is he going to do with the animals?"

Almighty Allah narrated:

"So it was till then there came Our Command and the oven gushed forth (water like fountains from the earth). We said: 'Embark therein, of each kind two (male and female), and your family, except him against

whom the Word has already gone forth, and those who believe.' And none believed him except a few." Al-Qur'an 11:40

Noah's wife was not a believer with him so she did not join him; neither did one of Noah's sons, who was secretly a disbeliever but had pretended faith in front of Noah. Likewise, most of the people were disbelievers and did not go on board.

The scholars hold different opinions on the number of those who were with Noah on the ship. Ibn 'Abbas stated that there were 80 believers while Ka'ab al-Ahbar held that there were 72 believers. Others claimed that there were 10 believers with Noah.

Water rose from the cracks in the earth; there was not a crack from which water did not rise. rain poured from the sky in quantities never seen before on earth. Water continued pouring from the sky rising from the cracks; hour after hour the level rose. The seas and waves invaded the land. The interior of the earth moved in a strange way, and the ocean floors lifted suddenly, flooding the dry land. The earth, for the first time was submerged.

Allah told the story thus:

"He (Noah) said, 'Embark therein in the Name of Allah will be its moving course and its resting anchorage. *Surely, my Lord is Oft Forgiving, most Merciful*.' So it (the ship) sailed with them amidst the waves like mountains, and Noah called out to his son, who had separated himself (apart), 'O my son! Embark with us and be not with the disbelievers.' The son replied, 'I will betake myself to a mountain, it will save me from the water.' Noah said, 'This day there is no saviour from the Decree of Allah except him on whom He has mercy.' And a wave came in between them so he (the son) was among the drowned.

"It was said, 'O Earth! Swallow up your water, and O sky, withhold (your rain)!' The water was diminished (made to subside) and the Decree (of Allah) was fulfilled (the destruction of the people of Noah). And it (the ship) rested on Mount Judi, and it was said, 'Away with the people who are *dhalimin* (polytheists, and wrongdoing)!'

"Noah called upon his Lord and said, 'O my Lord! Verily, my son is of my family! Certainly, Your Promise is true, and You are the Most Just of the judges.' He said,

'O Noah! Surely, he is not of your family; verily, his work is unrighteous, so ask not of Me that of which you have no knowledge! I admonish you, lest you be one of the ignorants.'

"Noah said, 'O my Lord! I seek refuge with You from asking You that of which I have no knowledge. And unless You forgive me and have Mercy on me, I would indeed be one of the losers.'

"It was said, 'O Noah! Come down (from the ship) with peace from Us and blessings on you and on the people of who are with you (and on some of their offspring), but (there will be other) people to whom We shall grant their pleasures (for a time), but in the end a painful torment will reach them from Us.' " Al-Qur'an 11:41-48

With the issue of the divine command, calm returned to earth, the water retreated, and the dry land shone once again in the rays of the sun. The flood had cleansed the earth of the disbelievers and polytheists.

Noah released the birds, and the beats which scattered over the earth. After that the believers disembarked. Noah put his forehead to the ground in prostration. The survivors kindled a fire and sat around it. Lighting a fire had been prohibited on board so as not to ignite the ship's wood and burn it up. None of them had eaten hot food during the entire period of the floor. Following the disembarkation there was a day of fasting in thanks to Allah.

The *Qur'an* draws the curtain on Noah's story. We do not know how his affairs with his people continued. All we know or can ascertain is that on his deathbed he requested his son to worship Allah alone, Noah then passed away.

'Abdullah ibn 'Amr ibn Al-'As narrated that the Prophet Muhammad *sallallahu 'alayhi wa sallam* said:

"When the death of the Messenger of Allah Noah approached, he admonished his sons,

'Indeed I would give you far reaching advice, commanding you to do 2 things, and warning you against doing 2 things as well. I charge you to believe that there is no god but Allah and that if the seven heavens and the seven earths were put on one side of a scale and the words 'there is no god but Allah' were put on the other, the latter would outweigh the former. I warn you against associating partners with Allah and against pride."Sahih Al-Bukhari

Lessons to be learnt from The People Of Prophet Nuh (AS)

We too need to be patient in life with our children, family members, relatives, friends and all human beings. It may take a long time to solve matters but never lose hope in the Mercy of Allah. When assistance comes, it will be worth the wait. Even when du'aas are made, keep repeating them and do not lose hope. One day when the time is right you will be amazed at the outcome of the du'aas. This requires a lot of patience – which is in fact a test from Allah, to confirm that one deserves what he has asked for.

With regards to animate objects, in Islam we are not allowed to hang pictures of people and other animate objects as this prevents the angels from entering the house. We shouldn't frame pictures and display them etc. Whether we understand the wisdom behind this or not is not important, we need to submit to the verse when we hear it!

THE STORY OF THE PEOPLE OF AAD AND THEIR PROPHET HUD (as)

These people were granted great physical strength by Allah and they were huge in stature.

The first people to engage in Shirk after Nuh AS's people were the people of Aad. These people lived in the coastal area between Yemen and Oman. The nearby mountains in which they carved their homes were known as Ah-qaaf which means sandy mountains. They were fair in complexion, very tall, well built, healthy, wealthy and very strong – even stronger than the people of Nuh AS. They built huge homes and their favourite buildings were massive tent-like structures. They used to compete with one another in these buildings and in wealth as though they had nothing to live for besides that. Nobody before them or after them has ever built or will ever build what they have built. Their infrastructure was amazing. Allah Almighty has described it in the Qur'aan as "unmatched" and "miraculous". They lived on the flat coastal land yet they built their homes by carving the nearby mountains. Their large homes and wealth together with their good health, huge bodies and other gifts they were granted made them arrogant. They felt that they would live forever. Allah had granted them crops and livestock in abundance as well as offsprings. They had rivers flowing with fresh drinking water. All their wealth and arrogance made them forget their duties and their ultimate return to Allah Almighty.

They became so arrogant that it drove them to say, "Who is stronger than us in any way?" Allah Almighty says in the Qur'aan in response to that question, "Do they not realise that Allah who created them in the first place is stronger than them!"

So Allah Almighty sent them a Messenger from amongst them to remind them to be grateful to Allah and to worship Him Alone. The more you have the more closer to the ground you should become. If it's good wealth it will make us humble and down to earth. So Hud AS was ordered to remind them that arrogance will lead them to disbelief and as a result Allah Almighty may take away whatever He has bestowed.

Hud AS said, "Oh My people! Worship Allah Alone for you have no god besides Him. Do you not fear Him?" The elite from amongst his people responded saying, "We regard you as silly and as a liar!" He said, "Oh My people! I am not silly but I am a prophet from the Lord of the worlds and I am an honest adviser to you! Has it surprised you that your Lord has sent you a reminder through a person from amongst you to warn you? Remember that He has made you heirs after Nuh AS and granted you more in terms of physical ability (than them). Remember the gifts of Allah upon you so that you may succeed."

As Hud AS continued to remind them, they felt that with their vast wealth they could bribe him out of his call. He told them that they were senseless in their trials since he would get his reward from Allah Alone. He told his people to turn to Allah in repentance so that they could be given more than they had and at the same time earn His Happiness. These reminders meant nothing to them. They were so well to do that they felt they were above every law of Allah's. They even began to oppress those who were weak and poor to the extent that they killed some of them.

Whenever Hud AS told them to obey Allah and fulfill the rights of fellow humans they would laugh at him saying that he was just an ordinary human being who ate the same food as them and drank from what they drink. They said they knew what they were doing and swore oaths that there was no life after death and that they had to live it up whilst they were breathing because life would only come once.

They said of Allah:

"Is he promising you that after you die and have disintegrated into sand and bones that you are going to be resurrected? Very far is that which you are promised! It is only the life of this world, we live, we die and we are not going to be resurrected!"

We too, sometimes the way we operate as if we are not going to be raised up again and stand before Allah! We say we believe in the resurrection but the way we lead our lives proves otherwise!

The people of Hud AS accused him of being a liar, of being mad and being possessed by a jinn just as the people of Nuh AS had accused Nuh!

Why all these accusations? Simply because the wealthy were not prepared to change their lifestyle.

Sometimes, we are so comfortable in our bad habits that when we are reminded we don't want to admit, accept and change. Instead we want to throw the warner out.

They built huge monumental homes on the mountains which they didn't live in, and they built other fine homes in the valley which they lived in. They built them to boast and brag and compete with each other as if they were going to live forever. There's nothing wrong to own a lot of wealth and live in good homes but we should also find ourselves in the houses of Allah.

Hud AS told them he asks of no reward from them. His reward lies with his Creator and Maker alone. They said they are only practicing that which their forefathers practiced, and questioned as to why is he going against them!

From this we learn that even if generations of ours have been involved in that which is incorrect, it does not mean we need to engage in the same after knowledge has come to us! Sometimes our own children will be the ones to correct us. As parents we need to acknowledge our error even if we are being corrected by our own children. At times they will be far ahead of us as far as deen is concerned. Don't be embarrassed of our children when they incline towards religion. Support and encourage them.

Hud AS continued reminding them of the countless favours Allah bestowed on them. They were blessed with so much cattle and offspring. They had 100's of children because of their lengthy lifespan. They had gardens like a paradise on earth.

Remember that when Allah swt granted you abundance of wealth and children, this doesn't mean He is pleased with you and if He has granted you a little it doesn't necessarily mean He is displeased with you. It all depends on the condition of your heart and your relationship with Allah.

After he called them for a very long period of time, they got tired of him. They said "Whether you warn us or not it is the same. These are tales of the past and we will never be punished the way you are telling us!"

This was the result of their pride. A hadeeth states,

"Whoever humbles himself for Allah's sake Allah will raise his status and whoever is proud Allah will disgrace him. They thought that no one could be stronger than them. Allah tells them, that the one who made them is definitely stronger and mightier than them!

Prophet Hud (AS) said to the people:

"Get all your forces and false gods and come together then plot against me to destroy me and then you will not be spared…. And if you do not, then too I have delivered the message I have been sent to you with, and (soon) Allah will replace you with other nations and you will never be able to affect Him."

Hud As then called out to Allah Almighty saying, "Oh Allah! Assist me regarding their disbelief!" The response came that very soon they will regret their misdeeds.

Meanwhile the people of 'Aad felt that nothing could go wrong with their lives. Their houses were very strong and built within the mountains. Their bodies were so healthy they had not seen illness. Their strength was so great they could repel any power that may try to attack or destroy them. Their wealth was so much that they felt there was no loss that would be too great for them to handle.

For the first time they experienced a severe drought. Hud AS warned them that this was the punishment of Allah, but they rejected his warnings. Then one day they became very happy upon seeing a huge dark cloud at a distance. The cloud was over their valleys where the crop was planted. They mocked at Hud AS saying that this was no punishment, it was the rain that had come.

To their surprise, the winds began to blow, an ice-cold freezing wind accompanied by a howling sound steadily heading their way; Hud AS together with his followers went into a secure place. Through Allah's Decree and Mercy the wind was ordered not to affect Hud AS and his followers. The wind suddenly grew so severe that it destroyed them all together with everything they ever had. The Qur'aan says that after seven nights and eight days of destructive wind the only thing that could then be recognized was the remains of their homes which were built within the mountains. The huge and powerful people looked like hollow, burnt, rotten uprooted tree stumps covered in the ground. Allah Almighty says, "This is how we treat those who transgress (beyond the bounds)." No sign of them was left. Hud AS lived after this incident with his people in Hadhramaut – in Yemen, where he later passed away.

VALUABLE LESSONS TO BE LEARNT

This teaches us that whenever Allah has granted us anything we should never allow it to make us arrogant. If this happens, it is just a matter of time – long or short – and devastating punishment may overtake us. Allah sends reminders to us very often and if we continue to ignore them, thinking we know what we are doing or that it is not going to affect us, we are indeed tightly in the clutches of shaitaan and treading the path of destruction. We should understand that it is Allah Alone who has given it to us and He can take it back anytime he wishes to do so.

At times wealth, health and other goodness are none other than a test from Allah for us for a short period of time only to see how we react and change when we have got everything. Then once the test is over, all is taken away – either in this world or upon death.

When death overtakes us neither will we take with us a single penny of ours nor will our excellent health during our lifetime come with us. What will help us is if we obeyed Allah during the short stay in the world even when we had everything. If we treated fellow human being's fairly and fulfilled their rights even when we knew that if we oppressed them, they would not be able to do anything about it and they would succumb to our power and wealth.

The Story of Saleh and the People of Thamud

The Qur'an tells us about some Prophets who are not mentioned in the Bible.

One of these is Prophet Saleh (peace be upon him). His story is interesting because Allah does not just tell it once in the Qur'an, but many times. And the story of Saleh is also in Surah Hud.

Prophet Saleh lived in the region of *Al-Hajr*, which was located along the trade route from southern Arabia to Syria. The city of "Madain Saleh" lies several hundred kilometers north of Madinah in modern-day Saudi Arabia, is named after him.

The rock dwellings in which the people lived are still to be seen there to this day. Saleh was called to preach a message to the people of Thamud.

According to the Qur'an, these people cultivated very rich fertile land, and they had become very vain because of their wealth. They also worshiped many gods, oppressed the poor in their midst and lived lives which were far from the kind of lives Allah wanted them to lead.

The Message

Saleh's message was very simple: He told his people to turn away from the bad behavior and to turn, instead, to the One God, Allah, who gave them all the good things they enjoyed.

Now that doesn't seem a very difficult message to grasp, does it? Yet the people of Thamud were very stubborn in their ways, and refused to accept the message which Saleh was bringing them.

Allah works in very strange ways, sometimes quite beyond our comprehension. The way Allah chose to speak to the people of Thamud was through the story of a camel!

This is, perhaps, the first thing we should note about the story of Saleh as it is told in the Qur'an. God can choose any way to convey His message to us.

We are often slow to understand, but He can speak to us through people and events, or He can even speak to us through the example of a camel. The fact that He tells us the story not once, but many times, is a sure sign that its message is important.

The story as told in the Qur'an goes like this. The people of Thamud were very vain and they refused to accept that Saleh was a messenger sent from God, so they asked him for a sign to prove his credentials. (Surah Hud -verse 62)

They asked him, in fact, not just for any sign, but something quite specific. They pointed at a huge rock that was standing by itself, and proposed to him that he ask his God to create a she-camel out of it.

Despite their obstinacy, Saleh did this, on the condition that they would believe in

God if he produced the she-camel from the rock, and to this they agreed.

Saleh then fervently prayed to God to answer their request. The huge rock moved and split, and from it came a wonderful she-camel, which was pregnant and soon to give birth. God provided the Thamud people with this miracle to test them, to see if they would obey His orders. Saleh told them in Surah Hud, verse 64:

64. "And O my people! This she-camel of Allah is a symbol to you: leave her to feed on Allah's (free) earth, and inflict no harm on her, or a swift penalty will seize you!"

The camel lived among people of Thamud, and soon gave birth to a calf. Some of the people accepted to believe in God because of what they had seen, and because of what they had promised.

Others, however, did not, and they began to hate the camel, as it reminded them of Saleh and of the promise they had made to him. It used to graze among their herds and drink from their water.

In fact, one day it would drink, and the next day the other animals would drink. Saleh told them to let it drink from the water of the well for one day, and leave it to them the second day as Allah ordered:

28. And tell them that the water is to be divided between them: Each one's right to drink being brought forward (by suitable turns).

Instead of convincing them to be kind to the animal, they actually chose to harm it. (7:75-7)

As if their disbelief was not enough, they also challenged Saleh to bring down the punishment of God upon them if he was, indeed, a Prophet.

Nine men amongst them, known for their mischief and prompted on by some of the women, went to the camel and its calf at night time, and they killed them both.

Saleh was angry at what they had done. The camel had surely done them no harm, he said.

65. But they did ham-string her. So he said: "Enjoy yourselves in your homes for three days: (Then will be your ruin): (Behold) there a promise not to be belied!"

Despite their scoffing and scorn for his message, the people were destroyed. (11:67- 8)

Saleh and the people who were left moved from that place, never to return.

Lessons From the Story

The message of Saleh must be important or God would not have repeated it so often in the Qur'an. So what does it tell us today? How can this episode of a camel teach modern men and women how to live?

Well, first of all it teaches us that we should not put God to the test, asking for signs and proofs from Him, when the whole of creation is surely one great sign of His goodness to the world. He has repeatedly sent His messengers to us, but we are very slow to believe.

It teaches us, also, not to disobey God, but to listen to His Prophets and messengers and be prompt to do what they say.

The story of Saleh teaches us an important fact about ourselves. We agree with God when things are going good for us, but then we go back on what we have promised to Him, turning back to our previous ways.

Think of how many times we have pleaded for such and such a thing, promising to do all manner of good things in return. When we get what we want, we tend to forget our promises very quickly.

THE STORY OF PROPHET LUT(LOT) AND HIS PEOPLE AND LESSONS LEARN

These lessons are as relevant today as they were in the time Qur'an was revealed or even further back in the history of humankind. The story of Prophet Lot in both the Bible and the Qur'an are remarkably similar. The story of Prophet Lut is one that is particularly pertinent to the 21st century yet people usually remember very little of the story.

The story of Lut has over the centuries been reduced to a morality tale, a parable warning people not to practice homosexuality. Usually all we hear is that Lut was a man of Allah living in the town of Sodom whose people practiced the unnatural act of homosexuality, Allah called such behaviour an abomination and destroyed the town but not before saving Lut and most of his family. However Lut's story is much more than that, it is a story filled with lessons for humankind. Let us take a glimpse into his life and see what messages we are able to find and learn from it.

Lesson 1

Allah destroyed Sodom for crimes and sins we see around us and accept every day.

We live in a world where murder is common, drugs are readily available and young girls fall pregnant outside of the bonds of marriage. Identities are stolen, sinful acts are called fun, and some streets are unsafe to walk down even in the middle of the day. Paedophilia is rampant, as is child pornography and human trafficking. Degenerate lifestyles are accepted and thought of as normal. Alcohol is easily available even to underage children and is responsible for many of society's ills. The people of Prophet Lut lived in a society very similar to our own.

The town of Sodom was corrupt through and through. The majority of people had no shame and considered sinful acts to be fun and frivolity. Sodom was a party town, criminals and criminal activity abounded, and those passing through the town risked robbery and physical abuse. Rape was considered normal, homosexuality was considered fun and travellers expecting hospitality usually got more than they bargained for. Sodom was the equivalent of the district we avoid at night, perhaps even the suburb police will not respond to in an emergency.

Lesson 2

To invite people to the truth with wisdom and kind words.

"Invite to the Way of your Lord with wisdom and fair preaching, and argue with them in a way that is better..." (Qur'an 16:125)

Allah sent Prophet Lot to this town with the message to worship Allah alone. He asked them to fear Allah and mend their evil ways saying, **"Will you not fear Allah and obey Him?**

Verily! I am a trustworthy Messenger to you. So fear Allah and obey me" (Qur'an 26:161 - 163). Lot spoke using mild words; he condemned the actions not the people themselves and encouraged them to seek forgiveness. There is surely a lesson for us in this. Lot spoke mildly to people Allah described as evil and disobedient, thus we should remember this when we are confronted with the evil acts people in the 21st century think of as fun. Condemn the act, not the person. This was also the way of Prophet Muhammad; he too would speak harshly about the action, not about the person who did the action.

Lesson 3

Allah is the All-Seeing.

Sadly however, in Sodom, Lut's words fell on deaf ears because the people were content with their corrupt ways and had no desire to curb them. The people of Sodom committed their sins openly and had no shame, they cared not whether anyone saw their sinful actions so it did not bother them that Allah was watching. No matter whether we try to disguise or hide our sins Allah sees everything, nothing can be hidden from the Almighty. Thus if we are ashamed of our actions and wish that Allah did not witness our behaviour it is probably time to rethink, and find a way to act that is more pleasing to Allah.

Lesson 4

Believers should be hospitable.

When the angels came into the town of Sodom they appeared to the people as very attractive male travellers. The first person they spoke to was one of Lut's daughters. She was afraid for them and asked that they wait for her father in order for him to see them to safety. When Lut met the strangers he could not convince them to bypass the town so he tried to keep them safe in his own home. Lut did not know that his guests were angels sent by Allah, yet he feared for them more than his own safety. When the men of Sodom rioted outside his house, demanding that the strangers be delivered into their hands, Lut opposed them.

The goodness in hospitality comes from giving for no other reason than to please Allah. The person you help may never be in a position to help you and in some cases he may even bring you harm, however in Islam hospitality is a triangular relationship between the host, the stranger and Allah. Providing sustenance to a stranger is part of a stranger's right over you - it is not a gift that you bestow, and the duty to provide it is owed to Allah not to the stranger.

The Story of Prophet Shuaib and the people of Midian

Prophet Shuaib, known in Biblical literature as Jethro. Many scholars believe that Shuaib was the elderly man who offered Moses safety, security and the hand of one of his daughters in marriage, when he fled Egypt. There are no authentic sources either confirming or denying this, however the Qur'an tells us that Prophet Shuaib was from the people of Midian, and it was there that Moses found refuge.

Combing the stories of both Prophets Moses and Shuaib we find that Prophet Shuaib was one of the few truly good and upright men of Midian. The people as a whole were bandits and robbers, deceiving one another and those who had the misfortune to pass through their townships and nomadic camps. For the most part they led a happy and prosperous life due to the bounties from God. However instead of being grateful they wanted to accumulate more and would lie and cheat in order to do so. They moved far away from the religion of God, many were atheists, whilst others worshipped woodland or nature gods.

As was the case with all the prophets of God, Prophet Shuaib's mission was to call his people to worship God alone and to follow His commandments. He tried to do so by reminding them of the graces and favours bestowed on them by God, but they were heedless. Those who had not completely abandoned belief worshipped in the incorrect manner of their forefathers and said to Shuaib, "Would you have us abandon the religion of our forefathers? Can we not do what we like with our own property", they sneered.

"And to the people of Midian We sent their brother Shuaib. He said: 'O my people! Worship God! You have no other God but Him'..." (Qur'an 7:85)

Islamic historian Ibn Kathir tells us that the people of Midian were the first people to impose fees and tolls on the people that passed through their territory. They insisted on a life of robbery and injustice even though Prophet Shuaib did his best to convince them that the punishment of God would befall them if they did not desist. They never exacted true measure and weight in their business dealings and Shuaib pleaded with them explaining that God would see them poor and destitute by taking away the bounties they had come to expect.

"...so give full measure and full weight and wrong not men in their things, and do not do mischief on the earth after it has been set in order, that will be better for you, if you are believers. And sit not on every road, threatening, and hindering from the Path of God those who believe in Him and seeking to make it crooked...'" (Qur'an 7:85-86)

Prophet Shuaib continued to remonstrate with his people; he insisted that he was not trying to better himself but he wanted what was best for them. He like all the others prophets that had come before him practiced exactly what he preached and asked no more from those whom he sought to guide than what he asked from himself. As is the way with disbelievers they did not practice what they preached and they mocked and belittled Prophet Shuaib.

"He said, 'O my people! Tell me if I have a clear evidence from my Lord and He has given me a good sustenance from Himself (shall I corrupt it by mixing it with the unlawfully earned money). I wish not, in contradiction to you, to do that which I forbid you. I only desire reform to the best of my power. And my guidance cannot come except from God, in Him I trust and unto Him I repent.'" (Qur'an 11:88)

Prophet Shuaib then went on to warn his people that were likely to suffer a similar fate to the people of Prophets Noah, Hud and Saleh. Destruction was the end product of their disobedience. **"...The people of Lot are not far from you" (Qur'an 11: 89)**, he admonished. Ibn Kathir said that this phrase means that the people of Midian committed vicious sins such as highway robbery, as did the people of Lot. Any other possible meanings for that phrase were also applicable because, he said, the people of Shuaib were close to the people of Lot in time, place and behaviour.

Shuaib's people were growing tired of his constant reproaches and said they would stone him if it were not for his family. This did not stop Shuaib from delivering his message calling for repentance. The leaders amongst the disbelievers asked Shuaib's followers to return to the religion of their forefathers but Shuaib supplicated to God calling on Him to protect the righteous amongst them. Shuaib and his followers were driven out of the town. The disbelievers went on with their ignoble lifestyles and thought no more of the warnings from Shuaib.

God however was well aware of Shuaib and his followers' righteous behaviour and all the efforts made to dissuade the disbelievers from their dishonesty and ungrateful behaviour. Shuaib warned of a terrible punishment and in no less than three different chapters, Qur'an mentions this punishment of the unrepentant people.

"...We saved Shuaib and those who believed with him, by mercy from Us. And an awful cry seized the wrong-doers, and they lay (dead), prostrate in their homes." (Qur'an 11: 94)

"So the earthquake seized them and they lay (dead), prostrate in their homes." (Qur'an 7:91)

"But they belied him, so the torment of the day of shadow (a gloomy cloud) seized them. Indeed that was the torment of a Great Day." (Qur'an 26:189)

Lessons learnt from Prophet Shoaib and his people

You are not allowed to cheat with measurement/in your business and lie to your customers about your products.

Your wealth is impure if you cheat in your business.

Shuaib (pbuh) told his people not to cheat in their businesses.

The stories of the prophets are examples to teach us of the punishments of when you disobey Allah (swt).

Shuaib (pbuh) reminded them of the previous prophets and warned them not to disobey Allah (swt).

Never challenge Allah to give you more tests or to send you a punishment.

This is extremely disadvantageous for you.

Surely, Allah (swt) is the One who you request justice from as He is merciful. When Shuaib (pbuh) did not see any hope, he asked for justice from Allah (swt). **You will surely get punishment for disbelieving in Allah.**

Chapter 12

Qur'an Towards Understanding The Story Of Prophet Yusuf - (Joseph)

We relate unto you (Muhammad SAW) the best of stories through Our Revelations unto you, of this Qur'an. And before this (i.e. before the coming of Divine Inspiration to you), you were among those who knew nothing about it (the Qur'an). — Qur'an 12[Yusuf]:3

The story of Joseph was revealed after an Israelite asked Prophet Muhammad, may the mercy and blessings of God be upon him, what he knew about Prophet Joseph. The story of Joseph was not known to the Arabs at the time and it was part of a test the Jews concocted to test Prophet Muhammad's claim to prophethood. Stories in the Qur'an are usually told in small bites and revealed over several chapters; the story of Joseph however, is different. It was revealed in one chapter, from the beginning to the end.

As stated in the previous two Surahs – Surah Tawbah and Surah Yunus, Surah Yusuf is the last of the three surahs to be revealed to console Prophet Muhammed (AS).

Just a recap.

The period of these revelations, a couple of years before the Hijrah, was a very bad time period for the Prophet and his followers. They were persecuted and tortured severely. At one time, there was a trade and social ban placed upon them. There was a written agreement which prevented the Muslims from engaging in trade and marriage to any of the neighbouring tribes. So, there was severe economic hardship. This resulted in the Prophet travelling further afield to Taif to spread the word of Islam. The residents of Taiff were just as cruel as the Meccans. He was jeered, tortured, children upon the direction of their parents stoned the prophet.

In addition, Prophet Muhammad (AS) lost two of his closest supporters, his uncle Abu Talib and his beloved wife Khadijah. The story of Joseph confirms unconditionally that God has total control over all affairs. It is a story of patience in the face of adversity and trust in the face of sorrow.

Going back to present day, these three Surahs can provide comfort to us in the trials we encountered in this temporary world.

So, that was historical context in which these three Surahs were revealed.

Verses 1-3 The best story

The first three verses in the surah tells us that the Qur'an is a book revealed to make things clear, it is revealed in the Arabic language and contains information that Prophet Muhammad (AS) did not know. This story is called the best of stories meaning that it contains information relevant to events happening at the time of revelation and it contains lessons for all humankind in any time period.

Verses 4-18 Dreams and deception

Joseph has a dream in which he sees the sun, moon and eleven stars prostrating before him. This is interpreted as men bowing down to him. He confides in his father who advises him to keep it secret from his brothers.

Joseph (Yusuf) and Benjamin (Beniameen) were the sons of Jacob's Yacub) second wife (Rachel). The older boys considered themselves men. They were older, they were stronger and saw in themselves many good qualities. Blinded by jealousy they plan to kill Joseph. One of the brothers convinces the other brothers to throw him in a well instead. They carry out their devious plan and using their father's worst fear (a wolf attack) and a blood-stained shirt, they try to convince him of Joseph's death. Meanwhile, Allah eases Joseph's fear. Allah inspires him that one day he will inform his brothers of their deed while they do not realize who he is. Joseph's father Jacob sensed treachery but turned to Allah and accepted the news with trust and patience.

Verses 19-22 Joseph is established in Egypt

Joseph is rescued from the well and sold into slavery. He is sold for a small price to an influential man from Egypt, who comments to his wife that Joseph may be of some service to them. Allah remarks that He established Joseph in the land and provided him with sustenance in order to teach him the interpretation of dreams. Allah has full power and control over all affairs but most people are blind to this. Joseph grows up in comfortable conditions and Allah bestows upon him good judgment and knowledge. He is in the house of a politician learning how to negotiate and make wise decisions.

Verses 23-30 The failed seduction

The wife of the Egyptian politician watches Joseph grow to manhood and is attracted to him. She tries to seduce him but he seeks refuge in Allah. The wife chases Joseph to the front door just as her husband is entering the house. The wife tries to blame Joseph but a member of the household points out that his shirt was torn from the back. The women of the city began to gossip about Joseph and the politician's wife.

Verses 31-35 Joseph prefers prison

After she hears the gossip, she invites the women to her house to show them how beautiful and attractive Joseph is. She hands each of them a knife and calls for Joseph to show himself.

The women are astounded and cut their hands. She explains that she tried to seduce him but he resisted. She threatens that if he does not obey he will go to prison. Joseph is afraid that he will let himself be seduced so he asks Allah to protect him, saying he would prefer prison to what the women are planning.

Verses 36-40 More Dreams

He is imprisoned along with two other men. The two other prisoners discuss their dreams with Joseph and ask him to interpret them. One of them said, 'I dreamed that I was pressing grapes'; the other said, 'I dreamed that I was carrying bread on my head and that the birds were eating it.' Joseph mentioned their next meal reminding them that Allah provides their sustenance then replies that he is able to interpret dreams because Allah has taught him to do so. He spells out his belief in Allah and in the Day of Judgement. Joseph asserts that his family, the family of Abraham, Isaac and Jacob hold the knowledge of the Oneness of Allah, and that his religion and family do not attribute partners to Allah. Most people however do not realise this.

Verses 41-42 Joseph languishes in prison

Joseph interprets the dream. One will serve wine to his master; the other will be crucified and the birds will peck at his head. Joseph asks the one to be saved to mention him (Joseph) to his master. But Satan makes the man forget and Joseph languishes in prison for more time.

Verses 43-57 Joseph's innocence is established

The King (of Egypt) asks his counsellors to interpret his dream. 'I dreamed about seven fat cows being eaten by seven lean ones; seven green ears of corn and [seven] others withered.' They were unable to do so and the ex-prisoner remembered Joseph. He ran to Joseph, Joseph interprets the dream and the King asks for Joseph to be brought into his presence. The ex-prisoner goes back to Joseph but Joseph asks him to ask his master (the King) about the women who cut their hands. The King establishes Joseph's innocence. Joseph says he wanted his master, the politician to know that he did not betray him or abuse his trust. Joseph appears before the King who offers him a position of high rank. Joseph asks to be put in charge of the storehouses. In this way Allah settles Joseph in the land. Allah points out that He grants mercy to whomever He wishes, and does not fail to reward good. The reward in the Hereafter, He points out, is the best.

Verses 58–66 A dream prediction fulfilled

Joseph's brothers present themselves asking for their measure of grain. Joseph recognizes them but they do not recognize him. He asks them to come again, this time with their younger brother. Without him they will not be permitted to have the grain. They reply that they will try to persuade their father and get his permission. Joseph tells his servants to put the goods his brothers traded for grain back in their saddle bags in order to make them eager to return. The brothers ask Jacob to let them take their younger brother but he is wary asking "Am I to entrust him to you as I did his brother before?" The brothers open the saddle bags and find their goods returned to them. Jacob says he will not send the boy unless the brothers swear they will do everything humanly possible to keep him safe. They gave their pledge and Jacob said, 'Our words are entrusted to Allah.'

Verses 67-76 The brothers return

Jacob advises his sons to not all enter the city by the same gate as a precaution but at the same time tells them that this will not help them against the will of Allah. All power is in Allah's hands, says Jacob.

The sons of Jacob present themselves to Joseph and he draws his youngest brother (Benjamin) aside and reveals his identity to him. Joseph gives his brothers their portion of grain but places his drinking cup in his youngest brother's pack. Someone calls out and accuses the caravan of thievery. 'What is lost?' the brothers ask. 'The King's drinking cup', is the reply, and 'whoever returns it will be given a camel's load of grain'.

The brothers respond that they did not come to make mischief. Joseph's men ask the brothers what penalty should apply if they are found to be lying. They answered, 'the penalty will be the enslavement of the person in whose bag the cup is found: this is how we punish wrongdoers.' Joseph did not want his brother punished under the laws of Egypt but wanted the opportunity to keep his brother with him while the others returned to their father Jacob. The bags are searched and the cup is found in the youngest brother's belongings. Allah explains that He devised a plan for Joseph and that He will raise the status of whomsoever He wills.

Verses 77-82

The brothers allude to Benjamin's brother (Joseph) being a thief, but Joseph controls himself and does not disclose his identity. The brothers beg that one of them be allowed to stay in his brother's stead; this is refused. Finally the eldest brother, remembering the pledge he gave to his father, vows to stay in Egypt until Jacob gives him permission to leave or Allah decides on another course of action. The remaining brothers return to their father Jacob saying, we tried to keep our pledge, but we could not have foreseen that your son would steal. Ask the people we travelled with if you need proof.

Verses 83-86

Their father said, 'No! Your souls have prompted you to do wrong!' He turned away from them saying 'Alas, my grief for Joseph!'. Jacob's eyes went white with grief (he was blind) and the brothers said, 'If you don't stop thinking about Joseph you will ruin your health or even die.' He said, "I only complain of my suffering and my grief to Allah, and I know from Allah that which you do not know'. When this new sorrow overwhelmed Jacob, his first reaction was to be patient. He knew, without a shred of doubt, that the affairs of his beloved youngest sons were controlled by Allah.

Verses 87-98

Jacob said, 'My sons, go and seek news of Joseph and his brother and do not despair of Allah's mercy– only disbelievers despair of Allah's mercy.' So they presented themselves before Joseph without knowing his real identity. They explained that misfortune had afflicted their family and asked Joseph to be charitable towards them. Allah, they said, rewards the charitable. Joseph replied by 'Do you now realize what you did to Joseph when you were ignorant?' The brothers were astounded and asked if he was Joseph and he said, 'I am Joseph'. They said Allah really did favour you over all of us; we were in the wrong. Joseph replied that no reproach would be on them and may Allah forgive them.

Joseph then handed them his own shirt telling them to lay it over their father's face and all would be well, then he asked them to come back altogether. Back at home Jacob was saying that he could smell Joseph, and those around him looked upon him with derision thinking him lost in an old illusion. When the shirt was placed on Jacob's face his eyesight returned and he said, 'Did I not tell you that I have knowledge from Allah that you do not have?' The brothers asked their father to ask Allah to forgive them and he replied that his Lord is the Most Forgiving and the Most Merciful.

Verses 99-101

Later when the whole family was presented before Joseph he drew his parents close to him and welcomed them telling them that, Allah willing they will be safe. They all bowed down to Joseph and he commented to his father that this was the fulfilment of the dream he had so long ago. Joseph said that Allah had been gracious towards him after Satan (Iblis) had sowed discord between him and his brothers. Joseph prays to Allah acknowledging his blessings and asking to live and die as a Muslim and be joined with the righteous.

The story of Joseph is a lesson for all of humankind. True patience and the ability to forgive are lofty characteristics worthy of inculcating.

Verses 102-111

That concludes the story of Joseph and in this final 10-verse epilogue Allah tells Prophet Muhammad, may the mercy and blessings of God be upon him, that this was the story of which he had no previous knowledge and that he was not present when the brothers made their evil plans. Allah then tells him that he cannot make the people believe no matter how much he desires to do so. Allah also mentions that Prophet Muhammad (AS) asks for no reward yet people ignore the signs in the heavens and the earth and only believe in Allah while joining partners with Him. How can they be so sure that an overwhelming punishment or the Last Hour will not come upon them when they least expect it? Can the people not see the lessons all around them; how can they travel and see the signs of what happens to the disbelievers and still not understand, do they not have a mind? Here is a lesson for those who understand, this is no fabrication; it a confirmation of the truth and an explanation for everything ('everything' refers to either the story of Joseph or the religion as a whole, or perhaps both).

In this chapter Allah was advising Prophet Muhammad that the road may be long and difficult but the ultimate victory belongs to those with God-consciousness and patience.

The noble Qur'an is a book unique in content and context. The narrative style revelation brings into play series of events from pre-creation to the end of time. The story of Prophet Joseph AS was outstanding among the stories of prophets mentioned in the Qur'an. Joseph was from the genealogy of Prophets. He was the son of Jacob, grandson of Is'haq and the great-grandson of Ibrahim (May Allah's blessing be with them all).

The story of Prophet Joseph is a compelling and highly fascinating story that encapsulates noble praise-worthy characters and a mix of human weaknesses. Allah narrates to us about his trouble, joy, and sorrow. We saw how jealousy, hatred, deception, and terror was unleashed against Joseph's personality. Yet, he conquered with patience, bravery, honesty, and reliance on Allah. This, in the long run, led him to be among the victorious.

Lessons to Be Learnt From This Story

It's good to have dreams, but it's best to keep them to yourself:

Verses 4 & 5

We all have visions and great ambitions in life. However, not everyone shares the same aspiration with us. In modern times, we take everything to social media not knowing that this breeds jealousy, fear of missing out and the evil eye. In an authentic narration, the Prophet (PBUH) warned us: ***"be discrete in what you want to achieve, for everyone who is blessed is envied"***. So keep your dreams between yourself and your Lord.

2. Allah gives blessing and honour to whom He Wills:

Verse 6

Allah in His Supreme knowledge has the best of plans for you despite the challenge of human interceptions. So, if Allah blesses your brother, don't be envious. If you do not have that blessing or favour, it doesn't mean you're neglected. Have faith and remain steadfast. Share in the joy of others and happiness will reach you too. No matter the circumstances, never work towards the downfall of others.

3. There's good in adversity if you persevere:

And they brought his shirt stained with false blood. He said: "Nay, but your ownselves have made up a tale. So (for me) ***patience is most fitting****. And it is Allah (Alone) Whose help can be sought against that which you assert. — Verse 18*

Sometimes, we go through hardship and trial. We almost lose hope and trust in Allah's plan. That's the exact time we need to seek help with patience and prayer. Prophet Jacob was patient with the fabricated news about the death of his son and Allah honoured him in the long run. So put your trust in Allah's plan express gratitude to Him.

4. Always return good and evil with good:

And she, in whose house he was, sought to seduce him (to do an evil act), she closed the doors and said: "Come on, O you." He said: "I seek refuge in Allah (or Allah forbid)! Truly, he (your husband) is my master! He made my stay agreeable! (So I will never betray him). Verily, the Zalimoon (wrong and evil-doers) will never be successful." — Verse 23

Sometimes Allah blesses us, yet we use that blessing in rebellious ways. When people are kind to you, try to pay back with kindness. Even when people mean harm to you, return their evil with good so you'd earn a reward from Allah.

5. Worldly pain is better than eternal punishment:

He said: "O my Lord! Prison is more to my liking than that to which they invite me. Unless You turn away their plot from me, I will feel inclined towards them and be one (of those who commit sin and deserve blame or those who do deeds) of the ignorant." — Verse 33

Never try to put your faith to test amidst temptation. It's better to walk away or face severe consequences of the worldly life, than to compromise and earn the punishment of the afterlife. Even a prophet was tempted by a woman and it only took the help of Allah for him not to fall. So who are you to dare?

6. If you ask, ask from Allah:

And he said to the one whom he knew to be saved: "Mention me to your lord (i.e. your king, so as to get me out of the prison)." But Shaitan (Satan) made him forget to mention it to his Lord (or Satan made ((Yoosuf (Joseph)) to forget the remembrance of his Lord (Allah) as to ask for His Help, instead of others). So (Yoosuf (Joseph)) stayed in prison a few (more) years. — Verse 42

We all go through challenges in life but when we need help who do we call upon? We sometimes think people have the ability to bring us good or harm. Whereas, everything has been predestined as mentioned in <u>the famous hadith of Abdulah ibn Abass.</u> So always remember to ask help from Allah first and be not heedless.

7. Never compromise your moral standards:

(The King) said (to the women): "What was your affair when you did seek to seduce Joseph?"

The women said: "Allah forbid! No evil know we against him!" The wife of the politician said: "Now the truth is manifest (to all), it was I who sought to seduce him, and he is surely of the truthful." — Verse 51

A believer doesn't compromise his moral standard for a piece of cake. No matter how long falsehood appears, the truth will always prevail. So if you're being tested by Allah, hang on but remember that the truth will be manifest and falsehood is bound to perish. For Allah makes not to be lost the reward of *the beleivers*.

8. In Allah Alone let the believers put their trust:

And he said: "O my sons! Do not enter by one gate, but enter by different gates, and I cannot avail you against Allah at all. Verily! The decision rests only with Allah. In him, I put my trust and let all those that trust, put their trust in Him." — Verse 67

Imagine after losing a loved one and betrayal from his offspring, Prophet Jacob still had an unshakable trust in Allah. We sometimes question the existence of the Creator when been tested. It's only when we fully believe and entrust our affairs in the hands of Allah; then and until then will we find solace in any condition we find ourself

9. Patience is a virtue that's hard to implement:

He [Ya'qub (Jacob)] said: "Nay, but your ownselves have beguiled you into something. So patience is most fitting (for me). May be Allah will bring them (back) all to me. Truly He! Only He is All-Knowing, All-Wise." — Verse 83

Amidst all the mysteries and agonies, prophet Jacob remained patient and steadfast. In the face of trials, we should try our utmost to endure and persevere. There's nothing that <u>patience falls upon except that it's beautiful</u>. So be patient and trust that Allah has the best of plans for you.

10. Forgive and show mercy to those who offend you:

He said: "No reproach on you this day, may Allah forgive you, and He is the Most Merciful of those who show mercy". — Verse 92

Even after all that his brothers put him through, Prophet Joseph forgave them. So as much as you can, forgive the evil people do to you. And do not look at yourself better when you do so. This will make you a more honourable person before Allah. In hope you would earn Allah's mercy through this righteous act.

Chapter 13

Towards Understanding Surah Al'arad

This surah is revealed in the early to middle Makkan phase.

The first verse enunciates the main theme of this Surah - The Message of Prophet Muhammad, may peace and blessings of Allah be upon him, is The Truth.

1. A.L.M.R. These are the signs (or verses) of the Book: that which hath been revealed unto thee from thy Lord is the Truth; but most men believe not.

This is the pivot on which the whole Surah turns. This is why it has been shown over and over again in different ways that the basic components of the Message, Monotheism (Tawhid), Resurrection and Prophethood are a reality: and the disbelievers should believe sincerely in these for their own moral and spiritual good. They have been warned that they shall incur their own ruin if they reject them for disbelief (Kufr).

However, the aim of the Surah is not merely to satisfy the minds but also to appeal to the hearts to accept the Faith. As such there is not just logical arguments but there is also sympathetic and earnest appeals. The intention of which is to win over their hearts of the disbelievers. The surah does this by contrasting the consequences of disbelief and the rewards of Faith. In other words there is heaven for the believers and hell for the non-believers.

How did the Surah gets its name? Lets look at verses 12 and 13.

In verse 12:

12. It is He Who doth show you the lightning, by way both of fear and of hope: It is He Who doth raise up the clouds, heavy with (fertilising) rain!

Allah is saying that it is he who shows us the lighting, causing you fear and hope. Some people when they see lightening, they are terrified, and others see hope as preceded by the lightning there is the much needed rain. And he is the one who produced the heavy clouds.

Surah Al Ar'ad translates as the surah of lightning. Why?

Verse 13:

13. Nay, thunder repeateth His praises, and so do the angels, with awe: He flingeth the loud-voiced thunderbolts, and therewith He striketh whomsoever He will..yet these (are the men) who (dare to) dispute about Allah, with the strength of His power (supreme)!

And the thunder praises its glory and so does the angels in awe of him. And he sends the thunderbolts striking them, even as they argue about Allah swt.

Our book of Tasfeer mentions a story that perhaps that one of the people at the time of the Quraish were being very arrogant and proud, mocking Allah swt and his messenger and then a thunderbolt, a lightening came and strike them. So Allah swt is referencing this.

As, with all surahs revealed in Mecca the main themes are Tawheed, Risallah-the affirmation of the Prophethood- and life after death.

One of the sub theme of the surah is to tell the Quraish and us to not be deceived by the glitter of falsehood of this world because it is inevitably fleeting, while the truth shines throughout the entire universe.

Verses 1 to 4

1. A.L.M.R. These are the signs (or verses) of the Book: that which hath been revealed unto thee from thy Lord is the Truth; but most men believe not.

2. Allah is He Who raised the heavens without any pillars that ye can see; is firmly established on the throne (of authority); He has subjected the sun and the moon (to his Law)! Each one runs (its course) for a term appointed. He doth regulate all affairs, explaining the signs in detail, that ye may believe with certainty in the meeting with your Lord.

3. And it is He who spread out the earth, and set thereon mountains standing firm and (flowing) rivers: and fruit of every kind He made in pairs, two and two: He draweth the night as a veil o'er the Day. Behold, verily in these things there are signs for those who consider!

4. And in the earth are tracts (diverse though) neighbouring, and gardens of vines and fields sown with corn, and palm trees - growing out of single roots or otherwise: watered with the same water, yet some of them We make more excellent than others to eat. Behold, verily in these things there are signs for those who understand!

Allah is affirming the prophethood of Prophet Muhammed (PBUH) and telling us and the Quraish to have full belief in it. In the previous Surah Yunus, Allah told the Prophet to draw to the attention of the disbelieving Quraish that his prophethood, his message came overnight. That he has grown up with them and was known as being trustworthy and sincere. So, why now he will talk about his prophethood and what was revealed to him if it wasn't the truth.

This surah begins by beautifully describing certain aspects of the creation.

The heavens above us that he has created without any visible support and Allah swt establishing himself upon his throne.

The verses then go on to tell us about the creation of the Universe with the Sun and the moon floating in their own orbits and to look at the signs which is so clear. Allah swt has clarified all of this so that we will have no doubt about meeting him in the hereafter.

Allah swt has filled the universe with signs to ponder and reflect upon.

Allah has made this earth so vast, he had placed mountain and rivers, meaning that the earth is not all the same.

Allah is drawing to our attention of the differences of the terrain of the earth by referring to the mountains and rivers that flows. Such contrast, that the earth is vast and not the same.

Then comes the variety of fruits that our creator makes available for us.

To expand on this, think about any fruit – bananas, apples, oranges, grapes etc, just look at the varieties. All of this, the beauty of the earth with its marvellous landscape and beautiful varieties of fruits have been made for us.

And after all the signs around us which clearly points to the existence of a Creator, the Quraish are stubbornly demanding for a miracle of their choice.

We are told that those who are denying the existence of a creator are destined for the hell fire.

And this is what we too need to reflect upon too.

Verses 5 – 15 God knows the obvious and the unseen

The arrogant and proud Quraish

5. If thou dost marvel (at their want of faith), strange is their saying: "When we are (actually) dust, shall we indeed then be in a creation renewed?" They are those who deny their Lord! They are those round whose necks will be yokes (of servitude): they will be Companions of the Fire, to dwell therein (for aye)!

6. They ask thee to hasten on the evil in preference to the good: Yet have come to pass, before them, (many) exemplary punishments! But verily thy Lord is full of forgiveness for mankind for their wrong-doing, and verily thy Lord is (also) strict in punishment.

7. And the Unbelievers say: "Why is not a sign sent down to him from his Lord?" But thou art truly a warner, and to every people a guide.

8. Allah doth know what every female (womb) doth bear, by how much the wombs fall short (of their time or number) or do exceed. Every single thing is before His sight, in (due) proportion.

9. He knoweth the unseen and that which is open: He is the Great, the Most High.

10. It is the same (to Him) whether any of you conceal his speech or declare it openly; whether he lie hid by night or walk forth freely by day.

11. For each (such person) there are (angels) in succession, before and behind him: They guard him by command of Allah. Verily never will Allah change the condition of a people until they change it themselves (with their own souls). But when (once) Allah willeth a people's punishment, there can be no turning it back, nor will they find, besides Him, any to protect.

12. It is He Who doth show you the lightning, by way both of fear and of hope: It is He Who doth raise up the clouds, heavy with (fertilising) rain!

13. Nay, thunder repeateth His praises, and so do the angels, with awe: He flingeth the loud-voiced thunderbolts, and therewith He striketh whomsoever He will..yet these (are the men) who (dare to) dispute about Allah, with the strength of His power (supreme)!

14. For Him (alone) is prayer in Truth: any others that they call upon besides Him hear them no more than if they were to stretch forth their hands for water to reach their mouths but it reaches them not: for the prayer of those without Faith is nothing but (futile) wandering (in the mind).

15. Whatever beings there are in the heavens and the earth do prostrate themselves to Allah (Acknowledging subjection),- with good-will or in spite of themselves: so do their shadows in the morning and evenings.

The arrogant and proud Quraish are challenging the Prophet (PBUH) to bring about the punishments that he is referring to rather than asking Allah for forgiveness. Allah is full of mercies and forgiveness but also stern in his punishment. Our Prophet is told to remind them that he is only a warner and nothing more, he cannot bring about punishment or miracles.

Our creator, the one who made us knows everything about our birth and what is in the wombs, he knows what is obvious and what is hidden in our heart.

Verse 13:

Our book of tasfeer mentions a story about this. One of the people at the time of the Quraish were being very arrogant and proud, mocking Allah swt and his messenger and then a thunderbolt, a lightening comes and strike him. So Allah swt is referencing this.

Here again to be reminded that the Chapter has its name from this verse.

Allah swt shows His signs in the sky;

For some the lightening causes fear and for other hope, as the preceding it will be the much needed rain.

The unbelievers dispute these signs. Prayer to Allah swt is the only true prayer, praying to false deities will elicit no response. Everything in the heavens and the earth prostrates to God, willingly or unwillingly.

Verses 16 – 27 Who are the believers?

16. Say: "Who is the Lord and Sustainer of the heavens and the earth?" Say: "(It is) Allah." Say: "Do ye then take (for worship) protectors other than Him, such as have no power either for good or for harm to themselves?" Say: "Are the blind equal with those who see? Or the depths of darkness equal with light?" Or do they assign to Allah partners who have created (anything) as He has created, so that the creation seemed to them similar? Say: "(Allah) is the Creator of all things: He is the One, the Supreme and Irresistible."

17. He sends down water from the skies, and the channels flow, each according to its measure: But the torrent bears away to foam that mounts up to the surface. Even so, from that (ore) which they heat in the fire, to make ornaments or utensils therewith, there is a scum likewise. Thus doth Allah (by parables) show forth Truth and Vanity. For the scum disappears like forth cast out; while that which is for the good of mankind remains on the earth. Thus doth Allah set forth parables.

18. For those who respond to their Lord, are (all) good things. But those who respond not to Him,- Even if they had all that is in the heavens and on earth, and as much more, (in vain) would they offer it for ransom. For them will the reckoning be terrible: their abode will be Hell,- what a bed of misery!

19. Is then one who doth know that that which hath been revealed unto thee from thy Lord is the Truth, like one who is blind? It is those who are endued with understanding that receive admonition;-

20. Those who fulfil the covenant of Allah and fail not in their plighted word;

21. Those who join together those things which Allah hath commanded to be joined, hold their Lord in awe, and fear the terrible reckoning;

22. Those who patiently persevere, seeking the countenance of their Lord; Establish regular prayers; spend, out of (the gifts) We have bestowed for their sustenance, secretly and openly; and turn off Evil with good: for such there is the final attainment of the (eternal) home,-

23. Gardens of perpetual bliss: they shall enter there, as well as the righteous among their fathers, their spouses, and their offspring: and angels shall enter unto them from every gate (with the salutation):

24. "Peace unto you for that ye persevered in patience! Now how excellent is the final home!"

25. But those who break the Covenant of Allah, after having plighted their word thereto, and cut asunder those things which Allah has commanded to be joined, and work mischief in the land;- on them is the curse; for them is the terrible home!

26. Allah doth enlarge, or grant by (strict) measure, the sustenance (which He giveth) to whomso He pleaseth. (The wordly) rejoice in the life of this world: But the life of this world is but little comfort in the Hereafter.

27. The Unbelievers say: "Why is not a sign sent down to him from his Lord?" Say: "Truly Allah leaveth, to stray, whom He will; But He guideth to Himself those who turn to Him in penitence,-

Allah ask the question:

Are the blind and the seeing equal? What is Allah swt telling us here. The blindness is referring to Spiritual Blindness, the blindness of the heart. One may be blessed with sight, with high levels of academia, but if he doesn't ponder and reflect on his existence then he is a blind person. So the one who knows the purpose of his creation and how he has to make the journey in this world is certainly different to the one who hasn't figure that out. And it is they who are the blind ones and are not equal to those who knows their purpose of life.

Allah then goes on to describe the believers and their ultimate rewards.

The believers understand the truth of the revelations and is not equal to someone who does not. (The blind)

The believers have common sense and fulfil the agreements they make in Allah's name and are afraid of the coming Reckoning. They pray, give in charity from what Allah has provided them with, and fend off evil with good.

And it is this category of people who will enter Paradise with their families (the ones who were righteous in this world) and the angels will welcome them to their wonderful home.

These are the ones who will have the best houses. They will be in this beautiful garden, surrounding by doors, with the angels entering through them to give their salaams. The Angels are praising them for their sabr, their patience, overcoming their trials on earth.

This is such good news for those who have lost their loved ones. Its painful now, its temporary and inshallah the reunion will be a permanent one.

May Allah swt bless us to be among those.

We are also reminded of another reality of this world. Allah gives to whoever he wants and restricts to whoever he wants. Allah is reminding us that he controls the amount of wealth that everyone has. There are some to whom he gives a lot and are others who have very little. However, it's a great responsibility to be in excess for it is all a test. And Allah tells us that among them are those who are fooled and take delight in this world with arrogance, and neglect the world of the hereafter, hence depriving themselves of the eternal life.

With all of their wealth and their intelligence they are among the blind ones.

In contrast the non- believers, the cursed will find themselves in a terrible home. This worldly life is brief compared to the life in the Hereafter.

Verses 28 — 34 Allah's promise

28. "Those who believe, and whose hearts find satisfaction in the remembrance of Allah. For without doubt in the remembrance of Allah do hearts find satisfaction.

29. "For those who believe and work righteousness, is (every) blessedness, and a beautiful place of (final) return."

30. Thus have we sent thee amongst a People before whom (long since) have (other) Peoples (gone and) passed away; in order that thou mightest rehearse unto them what We send down unto thee by inspiration; yet do they reject (Him), the Most Gracious! Say: "He is my Lord! There is no god but He! On Him is my trust, and to Him do I turn!"

31. If there were a Qur'an with which mountains were moved, or the earth were cloven asunder, or the dead were made to speak, (this would be the one!) But, truly, the command is with Allah in all things! Do not the Believers know, that, had Allah (so) willed, He could have guided all mankind (to the right)? But the Unbelievers,- never will disaster cease to seize them for their (ill) deeds, or to settle close to their homes, until the promise of Allah come to pass, for, verily, Allah will not fail in His promise.

32. Mocked were (many) apostles before thee: but I granted respite to the unbelievers, and finally I punished them: Then how (terrible) was my requital!

33. Is then He who standeth over every soul (and knoweth) all that it doth, (like any others)? And yet they ascribe partners to Allah. Say: "But name them! is it that ye will inform Him of something he knoweth not on earth, or is it (just) a show of words?" Nay! to those who believe not, their pretence seems pleasing, but they are kept back (thereby) from the path. And those whom Allah leaves to stray, no one can guide.

34. For them is a penalty in the life of this world, but harder, truly, is the penalty of the Hereafter: and defender have they none against Allah.

Those who believe finds contentment, peace and happiness in their hearts, and these are the ones that remembers Allah. And only through the remembrance of Allah the heart finds tranquillity.

Everyone hearts is troubled, is pained at one time or the other. The problems of this world comes to us from all directions. We have the worries and the grievances. We will not be human otherwise.

So what is the solution? Allah is giving it to us :

Its only through the remembrance of Allah will the heart finds tranquillity.

And the remembrance of Allah is through the salah, the Qur'an, the dhikr, making duas- making that spiritual connection to Allah.

So these verses are telling us and the disbelieving Quraish that the happiness does not lie in the accumulation of wealth.

Also this surah has a very important verse **– The topic of Qadr-predestination.**

Its telling us that Allah has written down everything that will happen to us.

It is possible to change the levels of qadr (our scholars have informed that there are five levels of qadr) -it goes from low to high. It is possible to change a lower level of qadr because of somethings we have done, because of a dua we have made, because of sadaka and charity we have given. Our prophet says – give charity on behalf of your sick it will cure them. When we give charity, inshallah it will have a spiritual impact. So Allah swt knew we would give charity and will have a positive impact on the person.

Verses 35 – 43 An invitation

35. The parable of the Garden which the righteous are promised!- beneath it flow rivers: perpetual is the enjoyment thereof and the shade therein: such is the end of the Righteous; and the end of Unbelievers in the Fire.

36. Those to whom We have given the Book rejoice at what hath been revealed unto thee: but there are among the clans those who reject a part thereof. Say: "I am commanded to worship Allah, and not to join partners with Him. Unto Him do I call, and unto Him is my return."

37. Thus have We revealed it to be a judgment of authority in Arabic. Wert thou to follow their (vain) desires after the knowledge which hath reached thee, then wouldst thou find neither protector nor defender against Allah.

38. We did send apostles before thee, and appointed for them wives and children: and it was never the part of an apostle to bring a sign except as Allah permitted (or commanded). For each period is a Book (revealed).

39. Allah doth blot out or confirm what He pleaseth: with Him is the Mother of the Book.

40. Whether We shall show thee (within thy life-time) part of what we promised them or take to ourselves thy soul (before it is all accomplished),- thy duty is to make (the Message) reach them: it is our part to call them to account.

41. See they not that We gradually reduce the land (in their control) from its outlying borders? (Where) Allah commands, there is none to put back His Command: and He is swift in calling to account.

42. Those before them did (also) devise plots; but in all things the master- planning is Allah's He knoweth the doings of every soul: and soon will the Unbelievers know who gets home in the end.

43. The Unbelievers say: "No apostle art thou." Say: "Enough for a witness between me and you is Allah, and such as have knowledge of the Book."

Also in these verses Allah is telling us of the rewards of the believers in the hereafter and the punishment of the unbelievers:

Those who remember Allah will have a reward that looks like this; flowing streams, everlasting fruit, and shade. But the unbelievers have nothing but the Fire. Those who accepted Islam from among the People of the Book (Jews and Christians) rejoice at the new revelations (Qur'an) but some from among the People of the Book deny parts of it.

Prophet Muhammad (PBUH) must say, "I have been commanded to worship Allah and associate nothing with Him, I invite you to do the same, and to Him will I return".

Some of the messengers before Prophet Muhammad had wives and children but none had the power to perform miracles without God's permission. In every time period there was a book (or revelation) and Allah confirms or erases whatever He wills because He is the source. Prophet Muhammad (PBUH) is told that he may not see in his lifetime the punishment that awaits them but that is of no consequence because his task is only to deliver the message. It is Allah who will call them to account.

Do they not see that Allah shrinks the borders of what they control? Allah's plan overcomes all plans.

Allah is also affirming in these verses that our prophet is a true prophet and even if the disbelievers of the Quraish and us reject him, our negation doesn't change the fact that he is the true prophet of Allah sent to deliver the message of truth.

LESSONS LEARNT FROM SURAH AL'ARAD

Allah is He who raised the heavens without pillars that you can see, and then settled on the Throne. And He regulated the sun and the moon, each running for a specified period. He manages all affairs, and He explains the signs, that you may be certain of the meeting with your Lord. Qur'an Surah Ar'Rad 2

Nothing on earth was created useless, for everything and everyone has a purpose. In life sometimes we forget our place and become lost. The sun has a purpose and so does the moon. We human beings are not just freaks of nature as darwin and atheist may want you to believe. Every day, the **Sun** sends us more energy than all energy producing mechanisms, created by humans, combined. This energy is not only good for making us warm. Through the process of photosynthesis, the **Sun** powers plants to recycle carbon dioxide we breath out into much-needed oxygen we breathe in. The sun at the heart of our solar system is a yellow dwarf star, a hot ball of glowing gasses. Its gravity holds the solar system together, keeping everything from the biggest planets to the smallest particles of debris in its orbit. Electric currents in the sun generate a magnetic field that is carried out through the solar system by the solar wind — a stream of electrically charged gas blowing outward from the sun in all directions.

The connection and interactions between the sun and Earth drive the seasons, ocean currents, weather, climate, radiation belts and aurorae. Though it is special to us, there are billions of stars like our sun scattered across the Milky Way galaxy. A major **purpose** is to light up the night. The **moon** reflects the sun's light on to us even when the sun is on the other side of the earth. The amount of reflected light depends on the **moon's** surface area, so we are fortunate to have a **moon** that is so large. **The gravitational pull of the moon controls the rise and fall of tides on Earth and slows the planet's rotation, while the phases of the moon serve as calendar markers for human beings.** High tides occur on the portion of the Earth closest to the moon and the portion farthest away. Low tides occur between those two points. The moon's pull slows the Earth's rotation in what astronomers describe as tidal braking. This effect adds 2.3 milliseconds to the length of a full day each century. As it collects energy from the Earth, the moon moves further away from the planet at a distance of 3.8 centimeters per year.

The lunar calendar is based on the time that elapses between full moons. For centuries, many civilizations acknowledged that the moon's cycles influence everything from the female menstrual cycle to planting and harvesting times for crops.

Over the years, many have claimed that there is a correlation between full moons and erratic or aggressive human behavior. However, studies on the subject have found no connection between the two.

As human beings transitioned from rural, agriculture-based lifestyles to more urban lifestyles, they have, as a group, grown increasingly unaware of the cycles of the moon.

Just looking at the purpose alone of the sun and moon shows how much Allah loves his creation. The next time you feel you don't have a purpose, read this surah and you will know that you were not put here by accident.

And it is He who spread the earth, and placed in it mountains and rivers. And He placed in it two kinds of every fruit. He causes the night to overlap the day. In that are signs for people who reflect.On earth are adjacent terrains, and gardens of vines, and crops, and date-palms, from the same root or from distinct roots, irrigated with the same water. We make some taste better than others. In that are proofs for people who reason. Qur'an Surah Ar'Rad 3-4.

Even in nature our creator place examples for us to understand the purpose of life. As human beings we are to pay attention to everything around us and observe the miracles of life.

Should you wonder—the real wonder is their saying: "When we have become dust, will we be in a new creation?" Those are they who defied their Lord. Those are they who will have yokes around their necks. Those are the inhabitants of the Fire, where they will remain forever. And they urge you to hasten evil before good, though examples have passed away before them. Your Lord is full of forgiveness towards the people for their wrongdoings, yet your Lord is severe in retribution. Those who disbelieve say, "Why was a miracle not sent down to him from his Lord?" You are only a warner, and to every community is a guide. Qur'an Surah Ar'Rad 5-7

Oh! how the ignorants like to say things about Allah because they have no faith and lack the ability to think and reflect. Those who reflect on life and nature can clearly see that we are divine creation and did not just pop up by accident. In the above ayat is talking about the ones who think that all there is to life is what we see. They have become unconscious because of their attachment to their own limited human thinking. They even want to challenge the creator by threating to bring calamity on them or show them some sign in the physical. In reality, even if they are shown signs and miracle, they will just take it as mere magic or delusion. People before them had been shown miracles after miracles, yet their heart was never convinced, or they might have a small temporary belief; but when they go away and group with the evil ones they begin to say, well maybe it just a coincidence. As Allah says in the Qur'an that they are deaf, dumb and blind and will never see the straight path. When you read something in Allah's revelation and do not understand it, it's better to pray for guidance than to remain ignorant and damn your own soul, by saying things about Allah that which you do not know.

The Messenger (S.A.W.) warned us about the seriousness of speaking. The prophet said, in an authentic *hadith* reported by Imams At-Tirmithi and Ibn-Majah, that, *"A person may say a word that is pleasing to Allah (S.W.T.) and he may not think much of it, but Allah (S.W.T.) will, (because of that word), bestow his pleasure upon him on the Day of Judgment, and a person may say a word that is displeasing to Allah (S.W.T.), and he may not think much of it, but Allah will have, (because of that word) put his wrath and anger on him on the Day of Judgment."*

God knows what every female bears, and every increase and decrease of the wombs. With Him, everything is by measure. The Knower of the Invisible and the Visible; the Grand, the Supreme.Qur'an Surah Ar'Rad 8-9

Nothing in this world is hidden or can be hidden from our Rabb (Lord). Every person, whether he conceal or reveals his thoughts, whether he skulks in darkness or goes about by day, all are under Allah's watch and ward.His grace encompasses everyone. He is the Supreme and has no partner or equal.

God does not change the condition of a people until they change what is within themselves. Qur'an Surah Ar'Rad 11

There is a saying that goes: "God help those who help themselves." If you want change in your life, then you need to begin to change the inside of yourself. Change always begins with you. God does not work for any human being, but rather he works with you to achieving success in this life. God does not reward laziness, he rewards those who get up and walk towards success. Trying to gain wealth without spiritual health is a slow slippery road to hell. You are not your own and you can't do anything by yourself because you have a creator that must be involve in every aspect of your life. If you are sick and tired of your life, then repeat the above ayat over and over again. You! have to decide change before God can intervene and help.

It is narrated on the authority of Amir al-Mu'minin (Leader of the Believers), Abu Hafs 'Umar bin al-Khattab (may Allah be pleased with him), who said: I heard the Messenger of Allah (peace be upon him), say:

"ACTIONS ARE ACCORDING TO INTENTIONS, AND EVERYONE WILL GET WHAT WAS INTENDED. WHOEVER MIGRATES WITH AN INTENTION FOR ALLAH AND HIS MESSENGER, THE MIGRATION WILL BE FOR THE SAKE OF ALLAH AND HIS MESSENGER. AND WHOEVER MIGRATES FOR WORLDLY GAIN OR TO MARRY A WOMAN, THEN HIS MIGRATION WILL BE FOR THE SAKE OF WHATEVER HE MIGRATED FOR."

If you don't have a clear intention about your life or where you want to be in the next days, months or years, then you will always fail. Remember that failure to plan is planning to fail! Intentions begins with how you feel about yourself and where you want to go. Nothing happens without a feel. A feeling of failure leads to failure and a feeling of success leads to success.

Allah (swt) informs us in the Qur'an through the words of His Khaleel, Prophet Ibraheem that, on the day of Judgment the whole of mankind will be in loss "except he who brings to Allah a sound heart (Al-Qalb As-Saleem)". This means it is indeed vital for us to know what a saleem (sound) heart is. Islam considers the human heart to be the most important organ in the body. What appears to be an ordinary organ is actually the seat of human feelings, desires, aspirations, intuitions, and belief. Prophet Muhammad (Pbuh) said,

"Surely, in the body there is a small piece of flesh; if it is good, the whole body is good, and if it is corrupted, the whole body is corrupted, and that is surely the heart." [Bukhari] Human hearts are of four kinds:

(1) **A heart that is polished as shiny as a radiating lamp.** This is the sound, healthy, and soft heart. It is the heart of the extremely pious believer. A heart that becomes rarer with the passing time. The light that radiates from it is the light of faith. This light shines through as righteous actions of the body.

(2) **A solid heart with a knot tied around it.** This is the corrupt, dead, and hard heart. It is the heart of a disbeliever. It is a heart that has rejected the truth after it reached him. Such a heart is sealed by Allah in punishment of its rejecting the clear truth. The solid heart is incapable of benefiting from the remembrance of Allah and accepting the call towards His message.

(3) **The upside down heart.** It is the heart of the hypocrite believer who outwardly claims to accept the truth but inwardly denies it for the petty gains of this life. It is also the heart of the Faasiq (the disobedient Muslim) who has not entered Islam completely. He persistently disobeys Allah by following some of His commands while leaving off others to fulfill his hearts' base desires. This heart perceives things inverted; it sees this world as more important than the hereafter. It craves and strives more for this world than worry and prepare for the hereafter.

(4) **The wrapped, blackened heart.** This is a diseased heart that is neither fully healthy nor completely dead. This heart has signs of hardness in it. It is the heart of a common Muslim and majority of them. There are several levels of hardness and different types of diseases. Some hearts are severely sick and hard while other are near healthy and soft. When a Muslim commits a sin a black dot is put on his heart.

If the Muslim repents sincerely by turning away from that sin and seeking forgiveness, the dot is removed and the heart returns to its previous state. If the heart keeps committing more sins without repenting from them the black spots on the heart increase till they cover the whole heart. This is the 'Raana' (stain) that Allah describes in the Qur'an, "on their hearts is the stain of the (ill) which they do!"

Chapter 14

Towards Understanding The Message Of Surah Ibrahim

This is a mid-era Makki surah.

The surah begins by masterly combining the power of the Qur'an, the reality of the next life and the truth of the Prophet (PBUH)

Verse 4

1. A. L. R. A Book which We have revealed unto thee, in order that thou mightest lead mankind out of the depths of darkness into light - by the leave of their Lord - to the Way of (Him) the Exalted in power, worthy of all praise

We have never sent a messenger, except that he speaks the language of his people, so he can clarify and explain things to them.

This is also especially important in present day. Every Muslim has a duty to spread the message of Islam. The operative word here is spread and not to convert. For Allah guides who he wills. If one turns to the creator and sincerely ask for guidance, then the right path will be illuminated for him. As, Allah sent his messengers with the language of his people, it is also important that we must also spread the message of Islam in a language that people understand.

Surah Ibrahim mentions very briefly several prophets: The prophets Nuh, Musa, We are informed in this surah that all of them were ridiculed, mocked and rejected. One of the main purposes of Surah Ibrahim is to console our Prophet Muhamma (Pbuh).

We must also be very aware that when we are walking in the footsteps of our prophet in spreading the message of Islam, we will also run the risks of being mocked and ridiculed. Hence, in this way this verse is also giving comfort to those in our present day.

This surah also tells us about the announcement our Lord has made to all mankind.

"And remember! Your Lord caused to be declared: If ye are grateful, I will add more unto you" (Qur'an, 14:5-7).

Gratitude is not only the heart and essence of Islam; it is also the key to attracting abundance, prosperity, peace, and success in one's life. We can say that Gratitude and Shukr are the most important aspects of Islam. We should always be thankful to Almighty Allah for all the blessings that has been given by Him. He is the Creator of this world and the Most Merciful.

From the verses we learn that gratitude is essential to Islamic character and that practicing gratitude in Islam is the means to greater prosperity. Gratitude for our health, wealth, breath, family, friends and most importantly for being a Muslim, from the Ummah of Prophet (Pbuh).

We show ingratitude when we moan about those things that we do not have. And this is what makes the heart discontented. So, let us start counting our blessings.

Also in the context of these verses as is verse no 10.

The next section verses **10 to 14…**

10. Their apostles said: "Is there a doubt about Allah, The Creator of the heavens and the earth? It is He Who invites you, in order that He may forgive you your sins and give you respite for a term appointed!" They said: "Ah! ye are no more than human, like ourselves! Ye wish to turn us away from the (gods) our fathers used to worship: then bring us some clear authority."

11. Their apostles said to them: "True, we are human like yourselves, but Allah doth grant His grace to such of his servants as He pleases. It is not for us to bring you an authority except as Allah permits. And on Allah let all men of faith put their trust.

12. "No reason have we why we should not put our trust on Allah. Indeed He Has guided us to the Ways we (follow). We shall certainly bear with patience all the hurt you may cause us. For those who put their trust should put their trust on Allah."

13. And the Unbelievers said to their apostles: "Be sure we shall drive you out of our land, or ye shall return to our religion." But their Lord inspired (this Message) to them: "Verily We shall cause the wrong-doers to perish!

14. "And verily We shall cause you to abide in the land, and succeed them. This for such as fear the Time when they shall stand before My tribunal,- such as fear the punishment denounced."

Lets look at verse 10.

The existence of Allah pervades all places.

Now lets ponder on the following, reflect and ask ourselves the question: Do we still need more proofs, miracles to believe in the existence of our Creator?

Everywhere in the universe points to the manifestations of Allah's creative artistry. Allah's infinite might and greatness surrounds us. All delicate structures and balances on Earth and all the countless physical and cosmic laws that pervade it, the milky was, the Solar System, the light emitted by the sun. the rate of expansion of the universe, the level of viscosity of water, Earth's position in the Milky Way, the distance between the earth and moon, the proportions of gasses in the atmosphere and countless other such physical data.

The other verses talked about the reality of the prophets being mocked, and their perseverance and patience. Anyone who is ridiculed or mocked for any aspect of religion and face derogatory comments because of their faith, remember the prophet faced much worse.

So what do we do when we are mocked for the sake of Allah?

One thing we must not do is to react with vulgarities

Mockery is the same as Ignorance.

The Qur'an tells us to be dismissive of people of ignorance. It asks us to not engage with them in any conversation, except perhaps to safeguard ourselves from greater harm.

In a nutshell, the message of the Qur'an is to ignore the ignorant.

In the next section of surah, the verse gives a vivid description of the day of judgement – those people who follow their icons, they will try to excuse themselves.

Verse 21

21. They will all be marshalled before Allah together: then will the weak say to those who were arrogant, "For us, we but followed you; can ye then avail us to all against the wrath of Allah." They will reply, "If we had received the Guidance of Allah, we should have given it to you: to us it makes no difference (now) whether we rage, or bear (these torments) with patience: for ourselves there is no way of escape."

This verse is very deep and is admonishing those who follow blindly. We are all blessed with common sense, intelligence.

Think of situations when you follow others blindly. This could be in religious matters, social matters. Follow the teachings of our prophet and put in practice what the Qur'an tells us. Lets live this worldly life in a manner that will benefit us in the hereafter.

Lets look at this scenario:

Committing shirk: Worshipping others than Allah. Then on that day the weak will say:

"If Allah would have guided us, then we would have guided you". Such an attitude will not save the leaders or the followers on the day of reckoning.

What about your famous popstars? You could be of the belief our famous pop starts are Muslims and they don't follow Islam. They are having lots of fun so we will follow them.

This verse is telling us that we must not follow anyone blindly.

Lets look at verse no 22.

22. And Satan will say when the matter is decided: "It was Allah Who gave you a promise of Truth: I too promised, but I failed in my promise to you. I had no authority over you except to call you but ye listened to me: then reproach not me, but reproach your own souls. I cannot listen to your cries, nor can ye listen to mine. I reject your former act in associating me with Allah. For wrong-doers there must be a grievous penalty."

We have all heard of our beloved Prophet's last sermon.

But did you know that even the hated Iblis will have a sermon? Allah the All Wise will permit Iblis to give his sermon on Judgment Day.

Certainly, you're wondering what could Iblis have to say that's that important that

Allah would allow it to be said before Iblis is thrown into Hell? Shaitaan will announce to the people:

Iblis will confess:

"All that l did was to call out to you, to invite you and you are the ones who came and answered my call. Now blame yourself, l can't help you and you can't help me

In order to secure our place in Jannah it is crucial for us to not only recognize our enemies but to be fully aware of their plan. We don't want to hear Iblis's sermon live on the day of judgement.

Verse 23

23. But those who believe and work righteousness will be admitted to gardens beneath which rivers flow, - to dwell therein for aye with the leave of their Lord. Their greeting therein will be: "Peace!"

Allah is saying that those who do good and those who believe will be admitted into gardens where rivers flow. They shall remain forever by the permission of Allah. Their greetings will always be peace. Everyone will be giving their salaams. The angels will be saying salaam to them, the people will be returning their salaams.

Verse 24-26

"Do you not see how Allah sets forth a parable? A goodly word like a goodly tree, whose root is firmly fixed, and its branches reach out to the heavens. It brings forth its fruit at all times, by the leave of its Lord; so Allah sets parables for people in order that they may receive admonition. And the parable of an evil word is that of an evil tree: it is torn up by the root from the surface of the earth, it has no stability" Ibrahim (Prophet Abraham)

Please watch your speech.

Think very carefully before you speak ill of someone, before you try to cause mischief in another person's life.

For when you do this you are worshipping Shaitaan and not Allah swt. As we are cleansing our heart preparing for our end, take heed of what Allah swt tells us so we can have a good chance of paradise.

1. A good word benefits mankind and spreads far

2. A good word is true and has solid foundation

3. It spreads far, both horizontally and vertically

4. It benefits people and it guides them to the truth

5. In contrast a bad evil word has no foundation and is easily torn, but it can harm and cause damage

6. When we use bad words it allows Satan to incite enmity and hatred among us

And in the next passage Allah swt recounts many of the blessings he has given us.

In verse 32 to 34

32. It is Allah Who hath created the heavens and the earth and sendeth down rain from the skies, and with it bringeth out fruits wherewith to feed you; it is He Who hath made the ships subject to you, that they may sail through the sea by His command; and the rivers (also) hath He made subject to you.

33. And He hath made subject to you the sun and the moon, both diligently pursuing their courses; and the night and the day hath he (also) made subject to you.

34. And He giveth you of all that ye ask for. But if ye count the favours of Allah, never will ye be able to number them. Verily, man is given up to injustice and ingratitude.

Allah mentions that he has caused the rain to fall and the fruit to come as a means of food for us. Allah swt has given us the power of using the ships in the ocean and every means of transportation. Ships are built by humans, but Allah is saying here that:

"I allowed you that power and therefore by extension every single vehicle and means of transportation we have we have is from Allah swt".

Allah has gifted us the intelligence, Allah has gifted us and the power to produce it. There are some people who have responded to the favours of Allah swt with ingratitude. They cause others to end up burning in the fires of Hell by encouraging the worship of false gods. Their pleasure will be in this life only, for they have no hope of Paradise. The believers must continue to pray and give charity openly and secretly now before it is too late. The Creator sends down rain, causes the plants to bear fruit, and allows the ships to sail safely across the seas and the rivers to benefit humankind. The sun and the moon and the alternation of the night and day – all created for the benefit of humankind. Everything has been provided yet most of humankind is ungrateful.

And here again lies the importance of being of remaining thankful to our provider.

Verses 35 – 41 Prophet Ibraheem

35. Remember Abraham said: "O my Lord! make this city one of peace and security: and preserve me and my sons from worshipping idols.

36. "O my Lord! they have indeed led astray many among mankind; He then who follows my (ways) is of me, and he that disobeys me,- but Thou art indeed Oft- forgiving, Most Merciful.

37. "O our Lord! I have made some of my offspring to dwell in a valley without cultivation, by Thy Sacred House; in order, O our Lord, that they may establish regular Prayer: so fill the hearts of some among men with love towards them, and feed them with fruits: so that they may give thanks.

38. "O our Lord! truly Thou dost know what we conceal and what we reveal: for nothing whatever is hidden from Allah, whether on earth or in heaven.

39. "Praise be to Allah, Who hath granted unto me in old age Isma'il and Isaac: for truly my Lord is He, the Hearer of Prayer!

40. O my Lord! make me one who establishes regular Prayer, and also (raise such) among my offspring O our Lord! and accept Thou my Prayer.

41. "O our Lord! cover (us) with Thy Forgiveness - me, my parents, and (all) Believers, on the Day that the Reckoning will be established!

The above verses tells us about the duas of Prophet Ibraheem (AS).

Prophet Abraham implored Allah swt to keep the city of Mecca secure and to keep himself and his descendants free from the sin of worshipping idols. He settled his family in the barren valley (Mecca) and prayed that they would establish the prayer and build a thankful community there. Allah knows what humankind reveals and what they conceal, nothing is hidden from Him. Prophet Ibraheem praises God for the birth of his sons, Ishmael and Isaac, in his old age and asks for forgiveness for the believers on the Day of Judgment.

Let's now discuss the significance of dua according to the Qur'an and hadith and then analyse its concept. The Qur'an 40:60 reads:

Call me! I will answer (Qur'an 40:60)

Note that the verse mentions, "call me!" not necessarily "ask me!" We usually think that dua means asking, but it does not necessarily involve requesting. It is a broader concept that includes all kinds of calling.

For us as the servants of Allah, the most important thing is to be able to communicate and be connected to our Lord. Not only can we not survive without Allah, but we cannot survive without being connected to Him.

Lets look at this scenario:

Allah is there, but He says, "I don't want to talk or listen to you or have anything to do with you." As Allah's servants, we cannot survive without His mercy and grace. Think about a little child, for whom it would be a great punishment, if his father or mother said, "I won't speak to you anymore." In their early years, children have no sense of independence. This is why it is mentioned in hadiths that whenever you promise your children, keep your promise, because they look at you as their lords who give them their sustenance.

You are their only hope, so never disappoint your children.

So, just as it is a great punishment for a small child to hear from his parents that they do not want to talk to him, for a person who realises his total dependence on Allah, it would be a severe punishment if Allah did not pay attention to Him.

For the person who understands that he is totally dependent on Allah, the main thing is to keep the line of communication with Him open. So the fact that Allah says,

Call me! I will answer (Qur'an 40:60)

Means

"You can call Me during the day or night, on weekdays or weekend; any time you call Me, I am available." Allah did not set different conditions and say, "If you want to call Me, you must call Me in such a time or place, with such and such conditions," He is so kind that He just says, "Call me! No matter when or where, I will answer to you."

42 – 52 Gives Us A warning and a message

42. Think not that Allah doth not heed the deeds of those who do wrong. He but giveth them respite against a Day when the eyes will fixedly stare in horror,-

43. They running forward with necks outstretched, their heads uplifted, their gaze returning not towards them, and their hearts a (gaping) void!

44. So warn mankind of the Day when the Wrath will reach them: then will the wrong-doers say: "Our Lord! respite us (if only) for a short term: we will answer Thy call, and follow the apostles!" "What! were ye not wont to swear aforetime that ye should suffer no decline?

45. "And ye dwelt in the dwellings of men who wronged their own souls; ye were clearly shown how We dealt with them; and We put forth (many) parables in your behoof!"

46. Mighty indeed were the plots which they made, but their plots were (well) within the sight of Allah, even though they were such as to shake the hills!

47. Never think that Allah would fail his apostles in His promise: for Allah is Exalted in power, - the Lord of Retribution.

48. One day the earth will be changed to a different earth, and so will be the heavens, and (men) will be marshalled forth, before Allah, the One, the Irresistible;

49. And thou wilt see the sinners that day bound together in fetters;-

50. Their garments of liquid pitch, and their faces covered with Fire;

51. That Allah may requite each soul according to its deserts; and verily Allah is swift in calling to account.

52. Here is a Message for mankind: Let them take warning therefrom, and let them know that He is (no other than) One Allah. let men of understanding take heed.

Allah swt knows exactly what the disbelievers do; He gives them respite until the Day when they will be staring around in horror. Prophet Muhammad (AS) is asked to warn humankind of the Day when they will beg for respite again. It will not be granted but they will be reminded that they were warned and presented with many examples of what would become of them. They had plans but their plans were never hidden from Allah swt.

Allah will not break his promise to the messengers. The people should be warned that a Day will come when the earth and the heavens will change into another earth and heavens and everyone who ever lived will stand before Allah. On this Day the guilty will be bound together in chains, their faces will be aflame and their bodies will be covered in tar. Everyone will be judged and every soul will get exactly what it deserves.

Wow!!! What powerful verses. What powerful message. Brothers and Sisters, we are still in the land of the living. We don't want to be caught out facing our creator will our scales overflowing with bad deeds. Lets make our changes now, whilst we still have time.

When the Angel of death approaches us we do not want to be asking for more time. We certainly wouldn't even be given a second extra.

Chapter 15

Understanding
The Message of Surah Hijr

Surah Hijr is a mid Meccan Surah. This Surah has 99 verses, and its name came from the verses 80 to 84. Hijr means rocky tract. Some scholars believe that this is referring to the people of Thamud who built their houses by carving the mountains.

The Themes of the Surah:

- Allah's boundless mercies to us.
- The plans Iblis has for us.
- People of past generations.

The Surah begins with the famous letters Alif Lam Rah. There are some scholarly opinions on the meanings of these letters. Some advice that whenever we have these disjointed letters then there will be prophets mentioned in the surah, and also included are verses where Allah swt is telling us about the miraculous nature of the Qur'an. But the majority opined that only Allah knows.

Lets now look at:

Verses 2 to 15 —

2. Again and again will those who disbelieve, wish that they had bowed (to Allah's will) in Islam.

The second verse in this surah makes it noticeably clear that a day will come when those who reject Islam wished they were Muslims. So, let us accept this certainty before that day comes, because when it comes it will be too late.

Verse 3

3. Leave them alone, to enjoy (the good things of this life) and to please themselves: let (false) hope amuse them: soon will knowledge (undeceive them).

Allah is telling us that there are those who failed to recognise the signs of our creator, they only value the life of this world. Their pleasures come from what this world has to offer.

4. Never did We destroy a population that had not a term decreed and assigned beforehand.

5. Neither can a people anticipate its term, nor delay it.

This is to refute the mistaken belief of the disbelievers that Prophet Muhammad (peace be upon him) was not a true Prophet because they had received no prompt punishment for their disbelief. It is like this: We have never seized a community at the first committal of kufr.

We prescribe a limit for every community to hear and understand the message and reform its ways. Then We tolerate its mischief and evil deeds up to that limit and allow it full freedom to do as it likes, and give it respite till the term expires.

No people can outstrip the term for its destruction, nor can it delay it.

6. They say: "O thou to whom the Message is being revealed! truly thou art mad (or possessed)!

7. "Why bringest thou not angels to us if it be that thou hast the Truth?"

8. We send not the angels down except for just cause: if they came (to the ungodly), behold! no respite would they have!

These verses describe the degrading way the disbelievers addressed the Prophet (Pbuh), when he had only presented to them the Qur'ān to bring them into light from darkness. The Qur'an, to reawaken them to face the facts instead of running after beguiling hopes. He also reminded them of Allah's law and its operation. But they ridiculed him and spoke to him with extreme impudence.

They wanted miracles, they wanted Angels to bring the revelation. But Allah is saying that even if Angels had descended, they would have taken human form, and so they will still deny the truth.

9. We have, without doubt, sent down the Message; and We will assuredly guard it (from corruption).

10. We did send apostles before thee amongst the religious sects of old:

Then in verse 9 and 10 Allah tells us about the miraculous nature of the Qur'an by directing us to the corruption of the other scriptures. All the other books have been entrusted to their followers to protect. All the prophets brought the same message but when the prophets died, their message became corrupted.

Allah tells us that the Qur'an will forever remain in its original form preserved in the exact language revealed to the Prophet Muhammad peace be upon him. Allah took charge of this preservation himself.

So now lets look at how the Qur'an has been preserved.

The Qur'an is the pure word of God. Not one word therein is not divine. Not a single word has been deleted from its text. The Book has been handed down to our age in its complete and original form since the time of Prophet Muhammad. From the time the Book began to be revealed, the Holy Prophet had dictated its text to the scribes. Whenever some Divine Message was revealed, the Holy Prophet would call a scribe and dictate its words to him. The written text was then read out to the Holy Prophet, who, having satisfied himself that the scribe has committed no error of recording, would put the manuscript in safe custody.

The Holy Prophet used to instruct the scribe about the sequence in which a revealed message was to be placed in a particular Surah (chapter). In this manner, the Holy Prophet continued to arrange the text of the Qur'an in systematic order till the end of the chain of revelations. Again, it was ordained from the beginning of Islam that a recitation of the Holy Qur'an must be an integral part of worship. Hence the illustrious Companions would commit the Divine verses to memory as soon as they were revealed. Many of them learned the whole text and a far larger number had memorised different portions of it.

Since its revelation, Muslims have strived to memorise the parts of the Qur'an or its entirety. Today, millions of Muslims have the entire Qur'an memorised by heart. Parts of it are also recited in the 5 daily prayers. Therefore, if someone tries to change the Qur'an, others will quickly catch it because they commit it to memory. A good example would be if someone tried to change the words to a national anthem or change the order of the alphabets. So many people have it memorised that it's impossible to change without others noticing. This exact Qur'an is read across the globe.

When Prophet Muhammad (peace and blessings of Allah be upon him) was sent, the original Tawraat (Torah) and Injeel (Gospel) had already been altered and distorted. Allah revealed the Qur'an to His Prophet Muhammad (peace and blessings of Allah be upon him), and guaranteed that He Himself would preserve it, as:

"Verily We: it is We Who have sent down the Dhikr (i.e., the Qur'an) and surely, We will guard it (from corruption)." [al-Hijr 15:9]

Verses 11 to 13 tells us:

11. But never came an apostle to them but they mocked him.

12. Even so do we let it creep into the hearts of the sinners -

13. That they should not believe in the (Message); but the ways of the ancients have passed away.

It is the same story. Just like when the unbelievers in the communities of old received God's messages, the same is the case with the unbelievers in your community. They all show the same attitude. (Present day community and the polytheist in Mecca).

"Thus do We cause it [i.e. this scorn of the revelation] to slip into the hearts of the guilty, who do not believe in it, although the ways of ancient communities have gone before them." (Verses 12-13)

We let it sink into their hearts as its truth is denied, subject to ridicule, because their hearts cannot receive it except in this way. This applies to all generations and communities, past, present and future.

Verses 14 and 15

14. Even if We opened out to them a gate from heaven, and they were to continue (all day) ascending therein,

15. They would only say: "Our eyes have been intoxicated: Nay, we have been bewitched by sorcery."

In these verses Allah is telling us that some people will not believe even though they know the stories of the people who came before them. Even if Allah swt had opened a gate in heaven they would believe themselves to be dazzled and bewitched as they watched themselves ascend.

Verses 16 — 25

16. It is We Who have set out the zodiacal signs in the heavens, and made them fair-seeming to (all) beholders;

17. And (moreover) We have guarded them from every evil spirit accursed:

18. But any that gains a hearing by stealth, is pursued by a flaming fire, bright (to see).

19. And the earth We have spread out (like a carpet); set thereon mountains firm and immovable; and produced therein all kinds of things in due balance.

20. And We have provided therein means of subsistence,- for you and for those for whose sustenance ye are not responsible.

21. And there is not a thing but its (sources and) treasures (inexhaustible) are with Us; but We only send down thereof in due and ascertainable measures.

22. And We send the fecundating winds, then cause the rain to descend from the sky, therewith providing you with water (in abundance), though ye are not the guardians of its stores.

23. And verily, it is We Who give life, and Who give death: it is We Who remain inheritors (after all else passes away).

24. To Us are known those of you who hasten forward, and those who lag behind.

25. *Assuredly it is thy Lord Who will gather them together: for He is perfect in Wisdom and Knowledge*

Allah created the heavens and made it beautiful by filling it with constellations. He protects it from the devils, and those who try to eavesdrop on the inhabitants of the heaven are followed by a fiery comet. Allah spread out the earth and set mountains into it. He caused vegetation of many kinds to grow in a balanced order. There is a means of sustenance for every living thing. There is nothing that Allah cannot send down in the appropriate measure. He sends the winds to fertilise the earth, the rain to provide water. Humankind has no control over this. It is Allah who controls life and death and He knows who has existed in the past and will exist in the future. In the end Allah will gather all of us together.

Lets expand on this further.

Lets look how everything is created in balance.

We need a balanced amount of nitrogen, oxygen and carbon dioxide. Any imbalance is enough to end the life. Allah created many ways to make sure this delicate balance is never disrupted. The Sun, plants which by the process of photosynthesis, soil and bacterial lives in soil make this balance possible. Other factors like rain, lightning, pressure and earth's core keep the gas rate in our atmosphere to the right conditions.

Even with a small disruption or disproportion in these facts- even in one of them, for instance if one of the bacterial which we can never see without a microscope stop functioning- the nitrogen cycle and carbon cycle which are critically important will stop instantly. This means the end of life.

Everything we see around us, including our body, is created with very delicate balances. There is harmony in the heaves and on the earth and this harmony continued to exist without any disruption for millions of years.

Allah who is the Great, the Most High creates this harmony.

Allah makes all the systems of the universe function and grow in perfect harmony, even though, we are not aware of it.

Sometimes we tend to forget simple things. We tend to take things for granted. Even the steps we take require a certain balance from the turning speed of Earth back to our nervous system, our heart, our brain, our skeletal system and gravity.

Allah regulates all affairs and has control over all things. How can anyone question whether we have a creator.

Verse 23

23. *And verily, it is We Who give life, and Who give death: it is We Who remain inheritors (after all else passes away).*

This verse then perfects the attribution of all matters to Allah alone, stating that life and death, the living and the dead, the resurrection and judgement belong to Him

The Power of Allah to Initiate and Renew the Creation

Here Allah tells us of His power to initiate creation and renew it. He is the One Who brings life to creatures out of nothingness, then He causes them to die, then He will resurrect all of them on the Day when He will gather them together. He also tells us that He will inherit the earth and everyone on it, and then it is to Him that they will return. Then He tells us about His perfect knowledge of them, the first and the last of them. He says *"And indeed, We know the first generations of you who had passed away…"*. Ibn Abbas said, "The first generations are all those who have passed away since the time of Adam. The present generations and those who will come afterward refer to those who are alive now and who are yet to come, until the Day of Resurrection.

VERSES 26 TO 44

26. And indeed, We created man from dried (sounding) clay of altered mud.

27. And the Jinn, We created earlier from the smokeless flame of fire.

28. *Behold! thy Lord said to the angels: "I am about to create man, from sounding clay from mud moulded into shape;*

29. *"When I have fashioned him (in due proportion) and breathed into him of My spirit, fall ye down in obeisance unto him."*

30. *So the angels prostrated themselves, all of them together:*

31. *Not so Iblis: he refused to be among those who prostrated themselves.*

32. *(Allah) said: "O Iblis! what is your reason for not being among those who prostrated themselves?"*

33. *(Iblis) said: "I am not one to prostrate myself to man, whom Thou didst create from sounding clay, from mud moulded into shape."*

34. *(Allah) said: "Then get thee out from here; for thou art rejected, accursed.*

35. "And the curse shall be on thee till the day of Judgment."

36. (Iblis) said: "O my Lord! give me then respite till the Day the (dead) are raised."

37. (Allah) said: "Respite is granted thee

38. "Till the Day of the Time appointed."

39. (Iblis) said: "O my Lord! because Thou hast put me in the wrong, I will make (wrong) fair-seeming to them on the earth, and I will put them all in the wrong,-

40. "Except Thy servants among them, sincere and purified (by Thy Grace)."

41. (Allah) said: "This (way of My sincere servants) is indeed a way that leads straight to Me.

42. "For over My servants no authority shalt thou have, except such as put themselves in the wrong and follow thee."

43. And verily, Hell is the promised abode for them all!

44. To it are seven gates: for each of those gates is a (special) class (of sinners) assigned

The Substances from which Mankind and Jinns were Created

Here Allah is telling us that we are created from clay and the jinns from the smokeless flame of the fire.

When Allah created Adam he told the angels to bow down before him (Adam) and they did. Ibliss, the shaytan refused. As a result, Iblis was cast out and cursed until the Day of Judgment. He asked for a reprieve until that Day and Allah granted it to him. The shaytan vowed to mislead humankind and make disobedience attractive to all of them.

But there is one category that he will not succeed in misleading.

The category:

This is the category of people who follow Allah. He can only reach those who follow the sinful path. So those who follow Allah, there is a barrier between him and Shaytan.

45. "Verily, the pious ones shall be amidst gardens and watersprings."

46. "(They will be addressed:) 'Enter you therein in peace, secure'."

47. "And We remove whatever rancour may be in their breasts. (They will be as) brothers upon coaches, face to face."

48. "No toil there shall afflict them in it, nor shall they be ever cast out of it."

In the above verses, Allah has stated eight heavenly rewards for the people of virtue. They are: gardens, springs, health, security, removal of all hatred, brotherhood, face to face coaches, being aloof from any kind of harm or toil, and immortality.

The Qur'an says:

"Verily, the pious ones shall be amidst gardens and watersprings." "(They will be addressed:) 'Enter you therein in peace, secure'."

In the previous verse, we read that except those sincere believers selected by Allah, all people will be targeted by the Satan's temptations. In these verses the Qur'an implies that if man does not reach the heights already achieved by those who are devoted and selected, but attains the objectives for the hierarchy of virtues, he will still be covered by the kinds of Divine blessings.

The Qur'an says:

"And We remove whatever rancour may be in their breasts. (They will be as) brothers upon coaches, face to face."

What is of importance in this stage is the assembling of all blessings in one unit. In this world one finds gardens in one place, while there may be no springs therein, sometimes there are streams to be found there but there is no security over there; at times all are present with together, though there may not be authenticity or sincerity furnished there.

At times, it happens that all those blessings are coupled with different kinds of hardships and are tedious to obtain. At other times, when all blessings are brought together, one has to abdicate them all and leave them behind. However, what differentiates Hereafter from this world is that all material, spiritual, social and psychological blessings are eternal in Heaven.

In verses 49 to 50 Allah made an announcement to all mankind.

49. Tell My servants that I am indeed the Oft-forgiving, Most Merciful;

50. And that My Penalty will be indeed the most grievous Penalty.

Here Allah swt is telling us that he is forgiving and merciful but he is also severe in his punishment.

Allah is just, and His justice necessitates that He reward those who obey and serve Him and punish those who disobey and rebel against Him. If Allah did not punish the sinful, wicked and evil people who deserve to be punished, it would not be justice. When punishment for wrongdoing is certain, it serves to deter potential offenders. In contrast, if Allah forgave everyone and punished no one, there would be no reason for legislation, ethics or even morality. Life on earth would be chaotic and nothing short of anarchy. True justice, with its true rewards and just penalties can only be found with Allah, and that is what He has promised.

Verse 51 to 72 tells us about the Prophets Abraham (AS) and Lut (AS), Shoaib (AS) Prophet Abraham was visited by three angels. He was afraid but they even though they greeted him with peace. They allayed his fears and told him that he would have a son. It was good news but he could hardly believe it because he was very old.

We must never despair of God's mercy.

Prophet Abraham asked the angels about the purpose of their journey and they replied that they had been sent to punish a guilty nation. Prophet Lut and his family were to be the only people saved from the wrath of Allah. Lut's wife however would not be saved, as she was among the disbeleivers. When the angels arrived they explained to Lut that he must leave with his family in the last hours of the night and told him to walk behind them, to protect them. They were instructed not to look back and that by morning all the sinners would have been eliminated.

In the meantime the people of the town rejoiced that Lot had guests. They wanted to commit homosexuality with these handsome looking men (who were actually angels who had come in the form of humans). They came to Lut's door and he begged them not to disgrace or shame him, even offering his daughters in marriage. But they continued blindly in their wild intoxication and before sunrise a mighty shrieking blast overcame them. The town was turned upside down and stones of baked clay rained down upon them. There is a sign in this for those who will listen and understand.

Then Allah mentioned the Forest Dwellers. These were believed to be the people of Prophet Shuaib, were also wrongdoers and God took retribution on them. Both places are still on the open road, plain for all to see. The people of the Rocky Tract, Al-Hijr, also denied their messenger and ignored Allah's signs. A mighty blast seized the them and even their homes built into the rocks could not save them.

Verses 85 – 99

85. We created not the heavens, the earth, and all between them, but for just ends. And the Hour is surely coming (when this will be manifest). So overlook (any human faults) with gracious forgiveness.

86. For verily it is thy Lord who is the Master-Creator, knowing all things.

87. And We have bestowed upon thee the Seven Oft-repeated (verses) and the Grand Qur'an.

88. Strain not thine eyes. (Wistfully) at what We have bestowed on certain classes of them, nor grieve over them: but lower thy wing (in gentleness) to the believers.

89. And say: "I am indeed he that warneth openly and without ambiguity,"-

The Hour will come (where the truth will become apparent), so Prophet Muhammad (AS) is advised to overlook and forgive their misbehaviour. Allah reminds us that we are given great blessings like the seven oft-repeated verses (the opening chapter of Qur'an) and the Qur'an, in which there is light and guidance. We are warned not to look at this world and its attractions, or the transient delights.

Prophet Muhammad (AS) is told to be kind to the believers and to tell the people that he is nothing except a warner and to deliver the message and turn away from those who associate others with God.

Allah tells Prophet Muhammad (AS) that knows how distressed he is by what the disbelievers are saying but that he should cure his distress by praising Allah, bowing before Him and worshipping Him until the certainty of death arrives.

90. (Of just such wrath) as We sent down on those who divided (Scripture into arbitrary parts),-

91. (So also on such) as have made Qur'an into shreds (as they please).

92. Therefore, by the Lord, We will, of a surety, call them to account,

93. For all their deeds.

94. Therefore expound openly what thou art commanded, and turn away from those who join false gods with Allah.

95. For sufficient are We unto thee against those who scoff,-

96. Those who adopt, with Allah, another god: but soon will they come to know.

97. We do indeed know how thy heart is distressed at what they say.

98. But celebrate the praises of thy Lord, and be of those who prostrate themselves in adoration.

99. And serve thy Lord until there come unto thee the Hour that is Certain.

Allah commanded the Prophet (Pbuh) to say if he warns them Allah has asserted the fact that He will send them that kind of chastisement which was sent to 'those who divided', the same ones who divided the Qur'an and the Divine verses into acceptable and none acceptable parts.

The Holy Qur'an says:

"And say: 'Verily I am the manifest Warner'."

"(We shall send them chastisement) as We sent down on the dividers."

They took up the Qur'an and accepted from it whatever was to their advantage and discarded whatever was to their disadvantage. But the true believers do not impose any kind of analysis, divisions or discrimination as regards the Divine commandments.

The verse says:

"Those who made the Qur'an into shreds."

There were some chiefs of the unbelievers who during the days of Hajj pilgrimage used to divide forces at the crossroads and entrance gates of Mecca in order to tell the travelLers that a person called Muhammad (Pbuh) has got certain claims and they should not listen to him. They introduced him as a soothsayer, a sorcerer, and a lunatic.

92. "So, by your Lord, We shall surely question them all (in the Hereafter),"

93. "As to what they used to do."

Following their state of unbelief as to the Qur'an and their dividing it, the Qur'an implies that they shall see the punishment for this evil act of theirs and will be questioned about it.

O' Mohammad (Pbuh) by your Lord We shall question them about it and We mean by interrogating them warning and blaming of them, that is, to convey to them this message as to why they committed sin. What proofs have they got to offer for having committed sins? They will then be target of all scandals.

The Qur'an says:

"So, by your Lord, We shall surely question them all (in the Hereafter),"

In this verse, Allah swears to Himself, presenting Himself as the Lord of Muhammad so as to prove his splendid position to the people. Then it continues saying:

"As to what they used to do."

The subject in question in this verse is: We ask them what they worshipped and what answer they would have to offer the prophets! They will have no answer!

94. *"Therefore, declare openly what you are bidden and turn you away from the polytheists."*

95. *"Verily We will suffice you against the scoffers,"*

96. *"Those who set up another god with Allah, so they will soon know (the truth)."*

The Prophet (Pbuh) engaged in preaching the message for three years in secret. Then the verse below was revealed.

"Therefore, declare openly what you are bidden"

He openly went on to call people to Islam. He told the people if they accepted his call the splendour of this world and the world hereafter would be all theirs.

The verse says:

"Therefore, declare openly what you are bidden and turn you away from the polytheists."

However, the polytheist ridiculed and mocked that the Prophet. They went to Abū-Talib, the uncle of the Prophet (Pbuh), to present their complaint to him.

They complained that Prophet Muhammad (Pbuh) was seducing their youths. The went on to say that if Prophet Muhammad was after wealth, wife and high position, they were ready to provide him with them all. The Prophet (Pbuh) told his uncle:

"Dear uncle! My words are the Divine messages and I shall never give up preaching."

The pagans requested Abu-Talib to surrender Muhammad to them, but he did not condescend to the request.

Anyway, Allah issues a decisive decree to the Prophet (Pbuh) in this noble verse, implying:

You are here by instruction, so do not let any weakness, fear and numbness overtake you when facing these obstinate pagans. Declare your mission openly.

Afterwards, to provide reinforcement for the heart of the Prophet (S), Allah reassures him that He will back him up as against those who ridicule him. Allah implies: We shall remove the evil of those who ridicule you and We shall perish them.

The verse says:

"Verily We will suffice you against the scoffers,"

Allah then describes /mustahzi'in/ (those who ridicule), as: They are the ones who designate counterparts for Allah, but they will soon face the consequence of their evil behaviour.

The verse says:

"Those who set up another god with Allah, so they will soon know (the truth)."

They are so ignorant that they create god-like figures out of stones and wood but their punishment will come.

97. *"And (O' prophet!) We certainly know your breast is straitened by what they say."*

98. *"Therefore, (to reinforce yourself), celebrate the praise of your Lord, and be of those who make prostration (unto Him)."*

99. *"And worship your Lord until the Certain comes to you."*

Allah consoles and elevate the spirit of the holy Prophet (Pbuh) in the noble verse:

"And (O' prophet!) We certainly know your breast is straitened by what they say."

Your delicate spirit and your very sensitive heart cannot withstand all those ill-intentioned words and blasphemous sentences, thus making you deeply depressed.

However, do not be disturbed; to remove the ill-effects of their nasty and inappropriate words, worship and praise your Lord, and remain one of those who prostrate.

The verse says:

"Therefore, (to reinforce yourself), celebrate the praise of your Lord, and be of those who make prostration (unto Him)."

For, such a gratitude shown, Allah will remove the ill-effects of their words.

Some Islamic traditions denote that whenever the Prophet (Pbuh) became sad, he used to establish prayer by which he would wipe out the effects of that grief from his mind.

Worshipping Allah is the highest level of education.

It wipes out and washes away all the dust of sinfulness and negligence from one's heart and soul, while inculcating supreme human values within him. It strengthens one's faith and awareness, and makes one responsible in his affairs.

We cannot make this journey of life without worshipping the one who created us.

Chapter 16

Towards Understanding Surah Nahl

Surah Nahl is the 16th Chapter of the Qur'an and is known as the surah of blessings, of favours.

SURAH NAHL MAIN TOPICS:

- Allah's Favours and blessings for mankind
- Allah Knows What You Conceal And What You Declare
- Benefits of the Cattle and Honey Bee,
- Last Day A Witness Will Be Called From Each Nation,
- Prophet Muhammad As A Witness Over All witnesses
- Satan/ Devil Effect Only Those With Weak Belief,
- The practice of the pagan Arabs burying their daughters alive

This Surah has 128 verses and was revealed in Mecca in a later stage of Prophet Muhammad (PBUH) preaching in Mecca. In this period the persecution of the muslims had become severe. Its revelation period is almost the same as that of Surah Raad and Ibrahim. Its name "Nahl" taken from verse 68.

So, to aid understanding read and understand this summary as Allah is speaking to the Qureshi and us.

Let us ask ourselves this question: What are we actually grateful for?

Many will answer this question by listing the material things we can see and touch. Yes, of course nothing wrong with that.

In this surah Allah swt awakens our dormant feelings and returns to us our forgotten realisations; reminding us of the many favours bestowed upon us, too many to enumerate.

Verse No 2:

2. He doth send down His angels with inspiration of His Command, to such of His servants as He pleaseth, (saying): "Warn (Man) that there is no god but I: so do your duty unto Me."

This verse is telling us the greatest blessing of all - the angels being sent down to deliver the revelation to the prophets, to warn mankind of the truth that there is no God except Him. Allah is making us realize that knowing this truth and receiving a message from the upper realm is in itself something wonderful. This word, this revelation, **this Qur'an is the most beautiful gift bestowed upon us.**

And following this, Allah speaks of these two favours:

Verse No 3 & 4:

3. He has created the heavens and the earth for just ends: Far is He above having the partners they ascribe to Him!

4. He has created man from a sperm-drop; and behold this same (man) becomes an open disputer!

Allah speaks of the creation of the universe, which encompasses all that is tangible around us, and then the favour of our very own creation.

Verses 5 to 9

5. And cattle He has created for you (men): from them ye derive warmth, and numerous benefits, and of their (meat) ye eat.

6. And ye have a sense of pride and beauty in them as ye drive them home in the evening, and as ye lead them forth to pasture in the morning.

7. And they carry your heavy loads to lands that ye could not (otherwise) reach except with souls distressed: for your Lord is indeed Most Kind, Most Merciful,

8. And (He has created) horses, mules, and donkeys, for you to ride and use for show; and He has created (other) things of which ye have no knowledge.

9. And unto Allah leads straight the Way, but there are ways that turn aside: if Allah had willed, He could have guided all of you.

Allah swt is telling us of the benefits of the animals he created for us.

The creation of the cattle for food, clothing and to carry burdens. The mules and donkeys to ride and other things that are beyond the comprehension of humankind. For some, Allah distinguishes the right path from the wrong paths and He could have done this for everybody had it been His desire to do so.

And this is a reminder, if you pray to Allah swt with sincerity you will be guided towards the right path.

Verses 10 – 21

10. It is He who sends down rain from the sky: from it ye drink, and out of it (grows) the vegetation on which ye feed your cattle.

11. With it He produces for you corn, olives, date-palms, grapes and every kind of fruit: verily in this is a sign for those who give thought.

12. He has made subject to you the Night and the Day; the sun and the moon; and the stars are in subjection by His Command: verily in this are Signs for men who are wise.

13. And the things on this earth which He has multiplied in varying colours (and qualities): verily in this is a sign for men who celebrate the praises of Allah (in gratitude).

14. It is He Who has made the sea subject, that ye may eat thereof flesh that is fresh and tender, and that ye may extract therefrom ornaments to wear; and thou seest the ships therein that plough the waves, that ye may seek (thus) of the bounty of Allah and that ye may be grateful.

15. And He has set up on the earth mountains standing firm, lest it should shake with you; and rivers and roads; that ye may guide yourselves;

16. And marks and sign-posts; and by the stars (men) guide themselves.

17. Is then He Who creates like one that creates not? Will ye not receive admonition?

18. If ye would count up the favours of Allah, never would ye be able to number them: for Allah is Oft-Forgiving, Most Merciful.

19. And Allah doth know what ye conceal, and what ye reveal.

20. Those whom they invoke besides Allah create nothing and are themselves created.

21. (They are things) dead, lifeless: nor do they know when they will be raised up.

Allah is telling us of his favour of the rain he sends down. It provides drinking water and it nourishes crops and fruit including olives, date palms and vines.

This is a sign for those who ponder.

Allah tells us of the benefits to us of the creation of the day, the night, the sun, the moon. These are signs for those who think.

Allah is telling us here beautifully how the things of the universe that He alone has created has helped us and will help us in our future.

The creation of the sun and the moon affords us the ability of us knowing about the day and night, the start of a day and the end of a day.

Because of this blessing we are able to determine the length of days through the sun and in turn the length of the months and years. Allah has given us this convenience to understand how the sun and moon works by telling us this specifically in the Qur'an, making the book the complete source of guidance.

Allah went on the in the following verses to tell us how he has filled the Earth with things of many different colours; these are signs for those seeking to learn a lesson from them.

And then the benefits of the sea and ships, and the mountains.

The sea is created as a source of food for us and ships we can use to sail on the sea.

Its only through the mercy of Allah swt humans can build the ships from the trees he created.

And what about the mountains! This our creator has set firmly on the ground for the earth's stability, and then the rivers and the paths with landmarks and the stars to help us guide through the land.

Lets ponder and reflect of the power and generosity of our creator. The blessings we have been sent we would not be able to count.

Allah tells us that he is Forgiving and Merciful and He knows what people keep hidden.

Then Allah ask the question in verse 17

17. Is then He Who creates like one that creates not? Will ye not receive admonition?

The deities that are invoked along with God are unable to create anything for they are creations themselves.

Verses 22 – 29

22. Your Allah is one Allah. as to those who believe not in the Hereafter, their hearts refuse to know, and they are arrogant.

23. Undoubtedly Allah doth know what they conceal, and what they reveal: verily He loveth not the arrogant.

24. When it is said to them, "What is it that your Lord has revealed?" they say, "Tales of the ancients!"

25. Let them bear, on the Day of Judgment, their own burdens in full, and also (something) of the burdens of those without knowledge, whom they misled. Alas, how grievous the burdens they will bear!

26. Those before them did also plot (against Allah's Way): but Allah took their structures from their foundations, and the roof fell down on them from above; and the Wrath seized them from directions they did not perceive.

27. Then, on the Day of Judgment, He will cover them with shame, and say: "Where are My 'partners' concerning whom ye used to dispute (with the godly)?" Those endued with knowledge will say: "This Day, indeed, are the Unbelievers covered with shame and misery,-

28. "(Namely) those whose lives the angels take in a state of wrong-doing to their own souls." Then would they offer submission (with the pretence), "We did no evil (knowingly)." (The angels will reply), "Nay, but verily Allah knoweth all that ye did;

29. "So enter the gates of Hell, to dwell therein. Thus evil indeed is the abode of the arrogant."

Verse 22

So (as for) those who do not believe in the hereafter, their hearts are ignorant and they are proud" (Qur'an 16:22).

Allah is telling us that he is One and those who do not believe in the Hereafter are arrogant and their hearts contain no faith.

By equating the concepts of ignorance with having pride, the Qur'an teaches us that to have pride itself is to be blatantly ignorant. We must not become those who from meaningless pride and arrogance become embarrassingly ignorant, and forget our true purpose in life: to worship Allah alone in everything that we do here on earth.

When they are asked about what Allah has revealed they say that it is nothing but fairy tales from the old days.

Isn't this reality reflected in our present day society!

On the Day of Resurrection they will bear their own burdens plus some of the burdens of those they led astray.

People from earlier times felt the punishment come upon them from out of nowhere. On the Day of Judgment they will be humiliated once again. Those with knowledge know that it will be a day of misery for the disbelievers. Those who die doing wrong will deny their wrongdoing but Allah is aware of what they were doing. So they enter Hell and will remain there in the evil home of the arrogant.

Verses 30 — 40

30. To the righteous (when) it is said, "What is it that your Lord has revealed?" they say, "All that is good." To those who do good, there is good in this world, and the Home of the Hereafter is even better and excellent indeed is the Home of the righteous,-

31. Gardens of Eternity which they will enter: beneath them flow (pleasant) rivers: they will have therein all that they wish: thus doth Allah reward the righteous,-

32. (Namely) those whose lives the angels take in a state of purity, saying (to them), "Peace be on you; enter ye the Garden, because of (the good) which ye did (in the world)."

33. Do the (ungodly) wait until the angels come to them, or there comes the Command of thy Lord (for their doom)? So did those who went before them. But Allah wronged them not: nay, they wronged their own souls.

34. But the evil results of their deeds overtook them, and that very (Wrath) at which they had scoffed hemmed them in.

35. The worshippers of false gods say: "If Allah had so willed, we should not have worshipped aught but Him - neither we nor our fathers,- nor should we have prescribed prohibitions other than His." So did those who went before them. But what is the mission of apostles but to preach the Clear Message?

36. For We assuredly sent amongst every People an apostle, (with the Command), "Serve Allah, and eschew Evil": of the People were some whom Allah guided, and some on whom error became inevitably (established). So travel through the earth, and see what was the end of those who denied (the Truth).

37. If thou art anxious for their guidance, yet Allah guideth not such as He leaves to stray, and there is none to help them.

38. They swear their strongest oaths by Allah, that Allah will not raise up those who die: Nay, but it is a promise (binding) on Him in truth: but most among mankind realise it not.

39. (They must be raised up), in order that He may manifest to them the truth of that wherein they differ, and that the rejecters of Truth may realise that they had indeed (surrendered to) Falsehood.

40. For to anything which We have willed, We but say the word, "Be", and it is.

Now here we have the contrasting verse where the believers are addressed.

When the righteous will be asked about what Allah sent down and they will describe it as good.

Allah tells us that the righteous have rewards in this world for but their home in the Hereafter is even better, it is an excellent abode. They will be rewarded with gardens under which rivers flow and they will have whatever they desire. When the pious people die the angels greet them with words of peace and show them into the gardens of reward.

Jabir, *may Allah be pleased with him*, reported that the Messenger of Allah, *may Allah's peace and blessing be upon him*, said:

"The inhabitants of Jannah will eat and drink therein, but they will not have to pass excrement, to blow their noses or to urinate. Their food will be digested producing belch which will give out a smell like that of musk. They will be inspired to declare the freedom of Allah from imperfection and proclaim His Greatness as easily as you breathe." Muslim

Commentary: Belching the vapours of musk means that after meals one would not feel heaviness and acidity. On the other hand, the belch will give out scented air, and the food will be digested by it. There will be no excrement or urine there.

Secondly, recitation of Allah's Name will ever remain on their tongues without the least effort like the way we breathe, without any effort whatsoever. In other words the food in *Jannah* would be so light and fine that there would be no disagreeable urine or excrement. On the other hand, there will only be fine smell like that of musk.

Abu Hurayrah, *may Allah be pleased with him*, reported that the Messenger of Allah, *may Allah's peace and blessing be upon him*, said, "Allah, the Exalted, has said: 'I have prepared for my righteous slaves what no eye has seen, no ear has heard, and the mind of no man has conceived.' If you wish, recite:

'No person knows what is kept hidden for them of joy as a reward for what they used to do.' "Al-Bukhari and Muslim, the *ayah* recited is *Al-Qur'an* 32:17

Commentary: About the gifts and pleasures of *Jannah*, here a *hadith* has been stated in the Words of Allah. The subject matter is confirmed from the Verse of the *Qur'an* given in the text of the *hadith*.

Abu Hurayrah, *may Allah be pleased with him*, also reported that the Messenger of Allah, *may Allah's peace and blessing be upon him*, said:

"The first group (of people) to enter Jannah will be shining like the moon on a full-moon night. Then will come those who follow them who will be like the most shining planet in the sky. They will not stand in need of urinating or relieving of nature or of spitting or blowing their noses. Their combs will be of gold and their sweat will smell like musk; in their censers the aloes-wood will be used. Their wives will be large eyed maidens. All men will be alike in the form of their father 'Adam, sixty cubits tall."

Allah tells us that the final abode of the disbelievers being the hell fire is as result of their actions. Allah is not being unjust to them but they were unjust to their selves. Then Allah goes on to describe their position in the hellfire:

They will be struck by the consequences of their actions and will be swallowed up by what they used to mock and ridicule.

On that day we will have no excuse as messengers were sent to every nation and their only duty was to warn.

Allah's promise to raise the dead to life is true. Everything will be made clear and the disbelievers will realise how wrong they were. When Allah intends anything to happen He need only say, "Be", and it is.

Verses 41 – 50

41. To those who leave their homes in the cause of Allah, after suffering oppression, - We will assuredly give a goodly home in this world; but truly the reward of the Hereafter will be greater. If they only realised (this)!

42. (They are) those who persevere in patience, and put their trust on their Lord.

43. And before thee also the apostles We sent were but men, to whom We granted inspiration: if ye realise this not, ask of those who possess the Message.

44. (We sent them) with Clear Signs and Books of dark prophecies; and We have sent down unto thee (also) the Message; that thou mayest explain clearly to men what is sent for them, and that they may give thought.

45. Do then those who devise evil (plots) feel secure that Allah will not cause the earth to swallow them up, or that the Wrath will not seize them from directions they little perceive?-

46. Or that He may not call them to account in the midst of their goings to and fro, without a chance of their frustrating Him?-

47. Or that He may not call them to account by a process of slow wastage - for thy Lord is indeed full of kindness and mercy.

48. Do they not look at Allah's creation, (even) among (inanimate) things,- How their (very) shadows turn round, from the right and the left, prostrating themselves to Allah, and that in the humblest manner?

49. And to Allah doth obeisance all that is in the heavens and on earth, whether moving (living) creatures or the angels: for none are arrogant (before their Lord).

50. They all revere their Lord, high above them, and they do all that they are commanded.

Verse 41

As for those who have forsaken their homes for the sake of Allah after enduring persecution, We shall certainly grant them a good abode in this world; and surely the reward of the Hereafter is much greater.[37] If they could but know (what an excellent end awaits)

This is to comfort the Muslim emigrants from Makkah to Habesha, who were forced to leave their homes because of the unbearable persecution they suffered at the hands of the disbelievers.

Some information about this migration

After the second emigration of Muslims to Habesha (Abyssinia), Abu Jahl and Abu Sufyan, the two warlords of pagans of Makkah, sent a delegation to Najashi asking him to expel the Muslims. The delegation brought many precious gifts for the king and his courtiers. They presented their claim in the court saying:

"O king, there is a group of evil persons from among our youth who have escaped to your kingdom. They practice a religion, which neither we, nor you know. They have forsaken our religion and have not embraced your religion. The respected leaders of their people — from among their own parents and uncles and from their own clans — have sent us to you to request you to return them."

The king looked toward his bishops, who had already been bribed, they said: "O king, they speak the truth. Their own people know them better and are better acquainted with what they have done. Send them back so that they themselves might judge them."

The king was angry with this response and said: "No, by God, I won't surrender them to anyone until I myself call them and question them about what they havebeen accused of."

Najashi invited the Muslims at the court and asked their leader Jafar: "What is this religion which you have introduced for yourself and which has served to cut you off from the religion of your people? You also did not enter my religion nor the religion of any other community."

Jafar stood and replied with full confidence: "O king, we were a people in a state of ignorance and immorality, worshipping idols and eating the flesh of dead animals, committing all sorts of abomination and shameful deeds, breaking the ties of kinship, treating guests badly and the strong among us exploited the weak.

"We remained in this state until Allah sent us a Prophet (peace be upon him), one of our own people whose lineage, truthfulness, trustworthiness and integrity were well-known to us. He called us to worship Allah alone and to renounce the stones and the idols, which we and our ancestors used to worship besides Allah.

"He commanded us to speak the truth, to honour our promises, to be kind to our relations, to be helpful to our neighbours, to cease all forbidden acts, to abstain from bloodshed, to avoid obscenities and false witness, not to appropriate an orphan's property nor slander chaste women.

He ordered us to worship Allah alone and not to associate anything with him, to uphold Salat, to give Zakat and fast in the month of Ramadan. We believed in him and what he brought to us from Allah and we follow him in what he has asked us to do and we keep away from what he forbade us from doing.

"Thereupon, O king, our people attacked us, visited the severest punishment on us to make us renounce our religion and take us back to the old immorality and the worship of idols.

"They oppressed us, made life intolerable for us and obstructed us from observing our religion. So we left for your country, choosing you before anyone else, desiring your protection and hoping to live in justice and in peace in your midst."

Najashi was impressed and was eager to hear more. He asked Jafar: "Do you have with you something of what your Prophet brought from God? Please read to me:" Jafar, in his rich, melodious voice recited for him a portion of Surah Maryam. Najashi stood up for Allah's words and said: Certainly this and what Jesus had brought come out of one source. He turned to the Makkan delegates and said angrily: I won't hand them to you and I'll defend them. Then he ordered his courtier to dismiss the delegation and to return their gifts to them. He then turned to Jafar and his group and said: "You're welcome; Your Prophet is welcome. I admit that he is the Apostle about whom Jesus had given good news. Live wherever you like in my country."

The pagan delegation returned to Makkah with their gifts in despair.

SOURCE OF INFORMATION: ARAB NEWS JOURNAL

Allah assures the believers that they will reach a happy end and to put their trust in him.

Allah is saying that all the messengers sent were human beings and the people of the scripture (Jews and Christians) know this, so ask them if you need to.

This verse is directed to the pagans in Arabia

Allah is now telling us that this Qur'an has come so that Prophet Muhammad (PBUH) can explain things clearly and the people can think and reflect.

Are those who do wrong sure certain that the punishment will not come upon them suddenly, or perhaps it will sneak up on them gradually. The disbelievers have not truly reflected on what Allah has created - everything humbly fulfilling its purpose, fearing Allah and doing what He commands.

Verses 51- 60

51. Allah has said: "Take not (for worship) two gods: for He is just One Allah. then fear Me (and Me alone)."

52. To Him belongs whatever is in the heavens and on earth, and to Him is duty due always: then will ye fear other than Allah.

53. And ye have no good thing but is from Allah. and moreover, when ye are touched by distress, unto Him ye cry with groans;

54. Yet, when He removes the distress from you, behold! some of you turn to other gods to join with their Lord-

55. (As if) to show their ingratitude for the favours we have bestowed on them! then enjoy (your brief day): but soon will ye know (your folly)!

56. And they (even) assign, to things they do not know, a portion out of that which We have bestowed for their sustenance! By Allah, ye shall certainly be called to account for your false inventions.

57. And they assign daughters for Allah. - Glory be to Him! - and for themselves (sons,- the issue) they desire!

58. When news is brought to one of them, of (the birth of) a female (child), his face darkens, and he is filled with inward grief!

59. With shame does he hide himself from his people, because of the bad news he has had! Shall he retain it on (sufferance and) contempt, or bury it in the dust? Ah! what an evil (choice) they decide on?

60. To those who believe not in the Hereafter, applies the similitude of evil: to Allah applies the highest similitude: for He is the Exalted in Power, full of Wisdom.

In these verses Allah is reminding us not to worship two deities because there is only One God who has dominion over everything in the heavens and the earth.

All blessings are from Allah and it is to Allah that the distressed person turns. Yet as soon as the relief comes some people turn to something other than Allah.

We are told that there will be consequences for such ingratitude.

Verses 57-59

"They ascribe daughters unto Allah, who is limitless in His glory — whereas for themselves (they would choose, if they could, only) what they desire for, whenever any of them is given the glad tiding of (the birth of) a girl, his face darkens, and he is filled with suppressed anger, avoiding all people because of the (alleged) evil of the glad tiding which he has received, (and debating within himself) Shall he keep this (child) despite the contempt (which he feels for it) or shall he bury it in the dust? Oh, evil indeed is whatever they decide.

They think they will have a good reward but their reward is Hell and they will be among the first to be sent there. The followers of Satan will face a painful punishment. The Qur'an was revealed in order to make the things they argue about clear and it is a guidance and a mercy for those who believe.

Islam stopped this evil practice.

Lets know see how the Prophet used to treat his daughters.

The Prophet (PBUH) had a special place in his heart for Fatimah (RA). Fatimah, of whom Aisha (RA) commented, "When the Prophet saw her approaching, he would welcome her, stand up and kiss her, take her by the hand and sit her down in the place where he was sitting."

The Prophet showed his daughter great respect and dignity, teaching her, as well as the men around him, and even us today what good treatment to our daughters looks like.

Verses 61-69

61. If Allah were to punish men for their wrong-doing, He would not leave, on the (earth), a single living creature: but He gives them respite for a stated Term: When their Term expires, they would not be able to delay (the punishment) for a single hour, just as they would not be able to anticipate it (for a single hour).

62. They attribute to Allah what they hate (for themselves), and their tongues assert the falsehood that all good things are for themselves: without doubt for them is the Fire, and they will be the first to be hastened on into it!

63. By Allah, We (also) sent (Our apostles) to Peoples before thee; but Satan made, (to the wicked), their own acts seem alluring: He is also their patron today, but they shall have a most grievous penalty.

64. And We sent down the Book to thee for the express purpose, that thou shouldst make clear to them those things in which they differ, and that it should be a guide and a mercy to those who believe.

65. And Allah sends down rain from the skies, and gives therewith life to the earth after its death: verily in this is a Sign for those who listen.

66. And verily in cattle (too) will ye find an instructive sign. From what is within their bodies between excretions and blood, We produce, for your drink, milk, pure and agreeable to those who drink it.

67. And from the fruit of the date-palm and the vine, ye get out wholesome drink and food: behold, in this also is a sign for those who are wise.

68. And thy Lord taught the Bee to build its cells in hills, on trees, and in (men's) habitations;

69. Then to eat of all the produce (of the earth), and find with skill the spacious paths of its Lord: there issues from within their bodies a drink of varying colours, wherein is healing for men: verily in this is a Sign for those who give thought.

He certainly can punish people for their wrongdoing. Had He chosen to do so, He would have brought everything down over their heads. But in His wisdom, He has decided to give them respite, for a definite term: If Allah were to take people to task for their wrongdoing, He would not leave a single living creature on the face [of the earth]. But He gives them respite for a set term. When their time arrives, they cannot delay it by an hour, nor can they hasten it. (Verse 61) Allah has created man and bestowed on him grace and blessings of all types. Man is the only creature on earth that spreads corruption, commits injustice, denies his Creator, allows tyranny within his own social set up and inflicts harm on other species. Yet despite all this,

Allah is merciful to him, gives him one chance after another, and never abandons him altogether. His wisdom goes hand in hand with His might; His grace with His justice. But human beings are short-sighted, deluded by the respite given them. They do not feel how graceful Allah is to them until His justice brings them to account at the end of the term He has appointed for them. But *"when their time arrives, they cannot delay it by an hour, nor can they hasten it."* (Verse 61)

What is even more amazing is that those who associate partners with Allah assign to Him what they dislike for themselves, whether daughters or other things. They then falsely claim that they will only have what is good in return for what they do and allege. The Qur'ān states what they shall have, and this differs widely from what they claim:

"They attribute to God what they hate [for themselves]. And their tongues assert the lie that theirs is the supreme reward. Without doubt, it is the Fire that awaits them, and they will be hastened on into it." (Verse 62)

Their claim that they shall have the supreme reward when they assign to God what they hate for themselves is the lie their tongues reflect. Before the verse is completed however, the Qur'ān places them face to face with the truth, namely, that their reward is undoubtedly the Fire. They deserve this because of what they have done in their lives: "Without doubt, it is the Fire that awaits them." (Verse 62) They will be sent directly to it: "And they will be hastened on into it." (Verse 62)

Those Arabs were not the first community to deviate from the path of the truth, nor were they the first to attribute to Allah what they did not accept for themselves. Other communities before them traversed the same deviation and false claims against Allah. Satan made their concepts and actions seem fair to them and they accepted his bidding. Thus he became their master. Allah, then, sent His Messenger to save them, show them the truth and judge between them in their disputes over their faith. He provided guidance to the believers and delivered a message that is an act of grace bestowed on them:

By God, We have sent messengers to various communities before your time, but Satan made their foul deeds seem fair to them. He is also their patron today. A grievous suffering awaits them. We have bestowed upon you from on high this book for no other reason than that you may make clear to them those issues on which they differ, and [to serve] as guidance and grace to people who believe. (Verses 63-64)

At this point, the surah reviews some of the aspects pointing to God's oneness in what Allah has created in the universe, and in the qualities and characteristics He has given man, as well as in the aspects of grace He has bestowed on him which none but Allah could have provided.

"And God sends down water from the skies, giving life to the earth after it has been lifeless. In this there is surely a sign for people who listen." (Verse 65)

Water is indeed the source of life for every living thing. This verse makes it the source of life for the whole earth, implying that this includes all that exists on earth. The One who transforms death into life is indeed the One who deserves to be God and to whom worship is addressed: "In this there is surely a sign for people who listen." They should indeed reflect on what they hear and listen to its message. In fact the Qur'ān repeatedly mentions the signs pointing to God and His authority, and how He brings life into what is dead. It draws people's attentions to this, because it provides irrefutable proof for anyone who reflects on what he sees and hears.

Another sign is derived from the creation of cattle and their lives:

"In cattle too you have a worthy lesson: We give you to drink of that [fluid] which is in their bellies, produced alongside excretions and blood: pure milk, pleasant to those who drink it." (Verse 66)

How is milk produced through the udders of cattle? It is made of what remains in the bellies of cattle after they have digested their food and the absorption of the excretions in the intestines to transform it into blood. The blood is then circulated to every cell in the body, but when it reaches the milk glands or the udder, it becomes milk through a fine process set by Allah. This is indeed an aspect of His fine and inimitable creation. Indeed the whole process that transforms the food intake into blood, and gives every cell what it needs of the blood's ingredients is a highly remarkable process. Yet this goes on all the time inside the body, just like the metabolism process. At every moment complicated processes of maintenance and destruction take place in this unique organism, which continue until the spirit departs from the body. No fair minded human being could contemplate such remarkable processes without feeling that every atom in his being glorifies the Creator. Even the most complex man-made apparatus fades into insignificance when compared to the human constitution or to any one of its systems or even its countless cells.

Indeed beyond the general description of the metabolism processes we find details that fill us with wonder. Within this process, the function of a single cell in the human body is remarkably wonderful.

All this has remained a secret until recently. This scientific fact mentioned in this sūrah about how milk is produced alongside excretions and blood was unknown to mankind. Indeed no contemporary of the Prophet could have ever imagined it, let alone described it so accurately. No self respecting human being could ever argue about this. The mention of one such fact is sufficient to prove that the Qur'ān is God's revelation. All mankind was at the time totally ignorant of such facts.

Such pure scientific facts apart, the Qur'ān carries within its own unique characteristics irrefutable proofs of its being revealed by Allah, provided we appreciate such characteristics as they truly are. However, one scientific fact like this, expressed with such accuracy, refutes all arguments advanced by those who are hardened in their rejection of the truth.

"And from the fruit of the date palms and vines you derive intoxicants and wholesome food. Surely in this there is a sign for people who use their reason." (Verse 67)

Such fruits come out of the life which is produced through the rain pouring down from the sky. From them people make wine and other intoxicating drinks, which were not forbidden at the time this surah was revealed. People also derive from such fruits wholesome food. The way this verse is phrased implies that intoxicants are unwholesome, which serves as a preliminary indication of their forthcoming prohibition. The verse describes the situation as it was in practice. It does not imply that wines and intoxicants were permissible. On the contrary it hints that they will soon be forbidden. "Surely in this there is a sign for people who use their reason." (Verse 67) People with reason are sure to realize that the provider of all these fruits and other provisions is God, the One who deserves to be worshipped.

Your Lord has inspired the bee: 'Take up homes in the mountains, in the trees and in structures people may put up. Then eat of all manner of fruit, and follow humbly the paths your Lord has made smooth for you. 'There issues from its inside a drink of different colours, a cure for people. Surely in this there is a sign for people who think. (Verses 68-69)

The bees work on the prompting of their nature which Allah has given them. It is an inspiration that they follow. The work the bees do is so detailed, accurate and well planned that the rational mind finds it difficult to contemplate. This applies to the building of the hives, the division of the work between the tees, and to their production of pure honey.

The bees take up home, according to their nature, in hills and mountains, in trees and in structures people put up for their vines or other plants. Allah has smoothed things for the bees through what He has planted in their nature and through the nature of the world around them. The verse states that honey provides a cure for people. Although this has already been fully explained by some medical experts, it is also true for the simple reason that the Qur'ān states it. This is what every Muslim should believe, based on the complete truth embodied in the Qur'ān. This is what the Prophet expressed very clearly.

Al-Bukhārī and Muslim relate on the authority of Abū Saʿīd al-Khudrī that "a man came to the Prophet telling him that his brother was suffering from diarrhoea. The Prophet told him: 'Give him a drink of honey.' The man did, then he came again and said: 'Messenger of God, I have given him honey, but his complaint has worsened.' The Prophet said to him: 'Go and give him a drink of honey.' The man went away again before returning the third time to say: 'Messenger of God, that has only aggravated his condition.' The Prophet said emphatically: 'God tells the truth and your brother's belly tells lies. Go and give him a drink of honey.' The man did just that and his brother took the drink and was cured." [Related by al-Bukhārī and Muslim]

This report is so significant because it demonstrates the Prophet's complete trust in the face of the patient's seeming deterioration when given honey to drink. But the situation ended with a clear confirmation of the truth stated in the Qur'ān. A Muslim should always have such complete trust in the truth of what the Qur'ān says, even though reality may appear to contradict it at times. In other words, what is stated in the Qur'ān is more truthful than apparent reality, which could easily change, giving way to a new reality that will confirm the Qur'ānic statement.

Your Lord has inspired the bee: 'Take up homes in the mountains, in the trees and in structures people may put up. Then eat of all manner of fruit, and follow humbly the paths your Lord has made smooth for you. 'There issues from its inside a drink of different colours, a cure for people. Surely in this there is a sign for people who think. (Verses 68-69)

We need to reflect a little on the fine harmony in portraying these blessings: the sending down of water from the sky, the production of milk alongside excretions and blood, the derivation of intoxicants and wholesome food from the fruits of date and vine trees, and the production of honey by bees. All are drinks produced from materials that possess totally different shapes and forms. Since the context is that of drinks, the only aspect of blessings related to cattle mentioned here is their milk. This adds to the harmony of the vocabulary employed in this panoramic scene. In the next passage we will see how the sūrah mentions the hide, wool and hair of cattle, because the context then is one of dwellings, homes and places of refuge. Hence the aspects of cattle mentioned there are those that fit that scene. This is an essential element of the artistic harmony evident in the Qur'ān.

Verses 70 – 81

70. It is Allah who creates you and takes your souls at death; and of you there are some who are sent back to a feeble age, so that they know nothing after having known (much): for Allah is All-Knowing, All-Powerful.

71. Allah has bestowed His gifts of sustenance more freely on some of you than on others: those more favoured are not going to throw back their gifts to those whom their right hands possess, so as to be equal in that respect. Will they then deny the favours of Allah.

72. And Allah has made for you mates (and companions) of your own nature, and made for you, out of them, sons and daughters and grandchildren, and provided for you sustenance of the best: will they then believe in vain things, and be ungrateful for Allah's favours?-

73. And worship others than Allah,- such as have no power of providing them, for sustenance, with anything in heavens or earth, and cannot possibly have such power?

74. Invent not similitudes for Allah. for Allah knoweth, and ye know not.

75. Allah sets forth the Parable (of two men: one) a slave under the dominion of another; He has no power of any sort; and (the other) a man on whom We have bestowed goodly favours from Ourselves, and he spends thereof (freely), privately and publicly: are the two equal? (By no means;) praise be to Allah. But most of them understand not.

76. Allah sets forth (another) Parable of two men: one of them dumb, with no power of any sort; a wearisome burden is he to his master; whichever way be directs him, he brings no good: is such a man equal with one who commands Justice, and is on a Straight Way?

77. To Allah belongeth the Mystery of the heavens and the earth. And the Decision of the Hour (of Judgment) is as the twingkling of an eye, or even quicker: for Allah hath power over all things.

78. It is He Who brought you forth from the wombs of your mothers when ye knew nothing; and He gave you hearing and sight and intelligence and affections: that ye may give thanks (to Allah..)

79. Do they not look at the birds, held poised in the midst of (the air and) the sky? Nothing holds them up but (the power of) Allah. Verily in this are signs for those who believe.

80. It is Allah Who made your habitations homes of rest and quiet for you; and made for you, out of the skins of animals, (tents for) dwellings, which ye find so light (and handy) when ye travel and when ye stop (in your travels); and out of their wool, and their soft fibres (between wool and hair), and their hair, rich stuff and articles of convenience (to serve you) for a time.

81. It is Allah Who made out of the things He created, some things to give you shade; of the hills He made some for your shelter; He made you garments to protect you from heat, and coats of mail to protect you from your (mutual) violence. Thus does He complete His favours on you, that ye may bow to His Will (in Islam).

Allah is telling us that it is he who created us and it is him who will cause us to die, and then went on to tell us about losing our faculties in old age. What powerful statements. Man thinks he will live and be healthy forever. This is a perpetual reminder of our true existence in this world. We will die. Death will come to us. If we live till old age then we will have health issues. Lets value the passage of time and prepare for our hereafter by making the journey of this world as Allah intended us to. Lets not be caught unaware on the day when there is no turning back.

In verse 78 Allah is saying to us:

The blessings of family.

Allah has gifted us spouses, and from the spouses he has given us children and grandchildren.

We must honour these gifts. Especially the gifts of children and parents in old age.

We emerge from our mother's wombs knowing nothing, but Allah provides us with hearing, sight and intelligence so we can be thankful to Him.

Allah has made the birds able to fly without falling. He provides humankind with shelter and warmth and everything we need for the term of our lives.

In verses 80 onwards Allah reminds us of the blessings of our homes.

Allah has gifted us our houses to be a place of peace and serenity. In our homes we find familiarity, contentment, peace.

Allah tells us that he has gifted us houses from the skins of animals- meaning tents. From these leathers and tents we can roll them up and carry them in our temporary travels.

Allah then says he gives us clothing from the animals. The fur that the people would wear to protect themselves from the cold.

Clothing that protects us in heat and cold, in times of war, (Referring to the amour). In all of these verses Allah is reminding us of the blessings he has bestowed upon us.

From the cattle- we eat some, we benefit from their milk, we use them for transport, we use their skins to make tents, houses, armours, to protect us in the heat, in the cold, in the times of war.

Chapter 17

Towards Understanding Surah Al-Israa

Surah Al- Israa was revealed in the last year before the Hijrah and concentrates on some important moral and spiritual principles. Like all the Meccan surah it stresses the oneness of Allah, the authority of the prophets, and the belief of life in the Hereafter.

The Surah has 111 verses.

Surah Al- Israa emphasizes that human beings always need divine guidance. Without the guidance of Allah, we end up in evil, sin and misery. Human beings must have good relations with each other and live in a society built on the principles of faith, justice and morality. The Surah talks about the evils of pride and arrogance and urges human beings to reflect on Allah's signs and be humble before Him in prayers.

Verse 1:

"How perfect is the one who took his slave in the middle of the night from the Sacred Mosque to the Mosque of Jerusalem the one whose surroundings we have made full of blessings in order to show him some of our miraculous signs, undoubtedly, he is all seeing, all hearing."

This verse explains in detail the journey from Makkah to Jerusalem that the prophet had endured upon within a small portion of the night. That is the first part of the topic… the night journey. Getting into literal translation, the first part of this Aya,

'How perfect is the one who took his slave in the middle of the night'. So here, the reader can see that Prophet Muhammad SAW, is not only declared in the Qur'an as the leader of the Muslims in Makkah, but now, he's being declared as the leader of Jerusalem as well, because as the Muslims believe, he had led the prayer to all of the previous messengers sent by Allah SWT, i.e., Noah, Abraham, Moses, Jesus, John, Adam, Joseph, etc.

The reason this is highlighted is that not only does that make Prophet Muhammad (Pbuh) the leader of Makkah and Jerusalem, but also the Imam to all the prophets that were sent before him. The next part of this Aya,

'The one whose surroundings we have made full of blessings' can be taken in a literal term and a metaphysical term. The literal meaning can be taken as its very lush, very green, very rich in vegetation, but additionally, Allah SWT blessed it with riches, profits, revelation, as we know, it is one of the places that Prophet Ibrahim (AS) set foot in. It's also the birthplace of Prophet Isa, the son of Maryam.

When this incredible account happened, the prophet had informed the people on what had occurred, firstly, to Jerusalem, then to the heavens, and then back. Back in those days, the journey from Makkah to Jerusalem was ventured over the span of a month. Some of the eyewitnesses that were there said that the hook lock on the door was still swinging by the time he got back. So that's one of the accounts of miraculous signs, in which, Allah had literally taken the prophet out of the realm of time, and brought him back.

From the past Surahs we know that Prophet Muhammad SAW had suffered immensely.

After 12 years of calling the people of Makkah to reject false idols and to worship the one God, Prophet Muhammad SAW was sorely tested by the year of grief, which was a series of unfortunate events for him. His uncle and caretaker, Abu Talib, whose kinship and protection had shielded him from the leaders of Makkah had passed away during this period. In that year, the pagans imposed severe sanctions on his tribe - Bani Hashem, by starving them, and making them social outcasts by expelling them from society.

In that same year, prior to the migration (Hijrah), following the death of his uncle, Prophet Muhammad (Pbuh) was once again devastated by the death of his wife for 24 years, Khadijah RAA. While the Meccans had closed all doors on the prophet, Allah SWT assures him that he didn't forsake him, rather he had opened up the doors of Paradise to him and ultimately resulting in the victory of Islam.

Allah SWT expresses in Surat Al-Israa',

"indeed with hardship comes ease".

By that, it is acknowledged that Muhammad SAW went through the most traumatic time of his life, and that event was followed by the most incredible accounts from his entire experience in the world.

Verses 2 to 8

2. We gave Moses the Book, and made it a Guide to the Children of Israel, (commanding): "Take not other than Me as Disposer of (your) affairs."

3. O ye that are sprung from those whom We carried (in the Ark) with Noah! Verily he was a devotee most grateful.

4. And We gave (Clear) Warning to the Children of Israel in the Book, that twice would they do mischief on the earth and be elated with mighty arrogance (and twice would they be punished)!

5. When the first of the warnings came to pass, We sent against you Our servants given to terrible warfare: They entered the very inmost parts of your homes; and it was a warning (completely) fulfilled.

6. Then did We grant you the Return as against them: We gave you increase in resources and sons, and made you the more numerous in man-power.

7. If ye did well, ye did well for yourselves; if ye did evil, (ye did it) against yourselves. So when the second of the warnings came to pass, (We permitted your enemies) to disfigure your faces, and to enter your Temple as they had entered it before, and to visit with destruction all that fell into their power.

8. It may be that your Lord may (yet) show Mercy unto you; but if ye revert (to your sins), We shall revert (to Our punishments): And we have made Hell a prison for those who reject (all Faith).

We gave Moses the book and made it a [source of] guidance for the Children of Israel, saying:

Do not take anyone for a guardian other than Me. You are the descendants of those whom We carried [in the ark] with Noah. He was a truly grateful servant of Ours. ' We made it clear to the Children of Israel in the book: 'Twice will you spread corruption on earth and will indeed become grossly overbearing.' When the prediction of the first of these came true, We sent against you some of Our servants of great might who wrought havoc throughout the land. Thus [Our] warning came to be fulfilled. Then We let you prevail against them once more, and We gave you wealth and offspring, and made you more numerous [than ever. And We said:] 'If you do good, you will be but doing good to yourselves; and if you do evil, it will be also against yourselves.' And when the second prediction came true, [We allowed your enemies] to disgrace you utterly, and to enter the Mosque just like [their predecessors] had entered it the first time, and to visit with destruction all that fell into their power. It may be that your Lord will have mercy on you; but if you revert [to your old ways], We shall revert [to punishing you]. Indeed We have made hell a place of confinement for the unbelievers.

The issue of 'making mischief on the earth twice' might probably be related to the two occasions of the Children of Israel: Once to the martyrdom of Sho'aia and the opposition of Armia, and the second occasion is concerned with the murder of Zakaryya and Yahya.

In the Torah, Allah warned the Children of Israel that they would spread corruption on earth twice and that they would gain power and be the masters in the Holy Land. Every time they held power and used it corruptly or spread corruption, Allah sent some of His servants against them who overpowered and destroyed them:

"*When the prediction of the first of these came true, We sent against you some of Our servants of great might who wrought havoc throughout the land. Thus [Our] warning came to be fulfilled.*" **(Verse 5)**

This was the first time: they gained power in the Holy Land and they established their strong state. But then they resorted to tyranny and corruption. As a result, Allah brought them face to face with some of His servants who combined great might with strong determination. They overran those who had erred and spread corruption, completely subjugating them.

After the Children of Israel were vanquished and suffered humiliation, they turned back to their Lord, mended their ways and applied the lessons they had learnt. In the meantime, their conquerors were blinded by victory and travelled along the same road of tyranny and corruption. As a result, the tables were turned. The vanquished were victorious again:

"Then We let you prevail against them once more, and We gave you wealth and offspring, and made you more numerous than ever." (Verse 6) History thus repeated itself.

Verses 9 – 21 - Those who trade the hereafter for this world.

9. Verily this Qur'an doth guide to that which is most right (or stable), and giveth the Glad Tidings to the Believers who work deeds of righteousness, that they shall have a magnificent reward;

10. And to those who believe not in the Hereafter, (it announceth) that We have prepared for them a Penalty Grievous (indeed).

11. The prayer that man should make for good, he maketh for evil; for man is given to hasty (deeds).

12. We have made the Night and the Day as two (of Our) Signs: the Sign of the Night have We obscured, while the Sign of the Day We have made to enlighten you; that ye may seek bounty from your Lord, and that ye may know the number and count of the years: all things have We explained in detail.

13. Every man's fate We have fastened on his own neck: On the Day of Judgment We shall bring out for him a scroll, which he will see spread open.

14. (It will be said to him:) "Read thine (own) record: Sufficient is thy soul this day to make out an account against thee."

15. Who receiveth guidance, receiveth it for his own benefit: who goeth astray doth so to his own loss: No bearer of burdens can bear the burden of another: nor would We visit with Our Wrath until We had sent an apostle (to give warning).

16. When We decide to destroy a population, We (first) send a definite order to those among them who are given the good things of this life and yet transgress; so that the word is proved true against them: then (it is) We destroy them utterly.

17. How many generations have We destroyed after Noah? and enough is thy Lord to note and see the sins of His servants.

18. If any do wish for the transitory things (of this life), We readily grant them - such things as We will, to such person as We will: in the end have We provided Hell for them: they will burn therein, disgraced and rejected.

19. Those who do wish for the (things of) the Hereafter, and strive therefor with all due striving, and have Faith,- they are the ones whose striving is acceptable (to Allah..

20. Of the bounties of thy Lord We bestow freely on all- These as well as those: The bounties of thy Lord are not closed (to anyone).

21. See how We have bestowed more on some than on others; but verily the Hereafter is more in rank and gradation and more in excellence.

Let us look at verse 9 and 10.

"Surely this Qur'ān shows the way to that which is most upright."

The Qur'an guides to that which is 'most upright' in relation to man's inner feelings and thoughts, outlining a clear faith, free of complication and ambiguity. Its guidance, frees the human spirit of the burden of myth and superstition, and releases human energy so that it is constructive, bringing benefit, providing a harmonious link between the laws that govern the universe and those governing human nature.

If we do not follow the guidance of the Qur'an, then we will not be able to make this journey of life as Allah intends us to.

Therefore, the Qur'an in this verse indicates that those who do not believe in the Hereafter and its great court of justice, and thus may not engage in performing decent and righteous acts, it unveils the fact that a painful chastisement has been prepared for them.

Verse 11 and in line with the previous discussions that one of the main causes of disbelief is lack of adequate study into the matters, and it is so because man is instinctively hasty.

Alluding to the matter, it declares:

"And man prays for evil as he prays for the good; and man is ever hasty."

In fact, the man's haste has its origin in his aspiration for acquiring greater amounts of benefits in a short pace. And also in contrast he expects the punishment to be instantly.

In an Islamic tradition quoted from the Messenger of Allah (S), he says:

"Haste brings forth the people's destruction; if the people did their jobs with deliberation, no one would annihilate."

So far the Surah has pointed to some of the signs Allah gave to His messengers, such as the Prophet's night journey, Noah's ark, Moses' book, and, above all, the Qur'an. Now the Surah is mentioning some of Allah's universal signs and relates these to people's actions.

The universal law that governs the succession of day and night is linked to numerous aspects of human life. It is linked with people's efforts in earning their living, and their knowledge of time and calculation.

The same universal law is linked to Allah's promise that He will not inflict punishment on anyone until He has sent His messengers. This link further applies to the law which governs the destruction of communities only after the affluent among them have been guilty of immense transgression. The law further relates to the diverse destinies of those who seek the pleasures of this world and those who prefer the good reward of the hereafter, and what Allah grants to both in this life and in the life to come. All these aspects follow a well-set system. Nothing takes place haphazardly.

"Whoever chooses to follow guidance does so for his own good, and whoever goes astray does so to his own loss. No soul shall be made to bear the burden of another." **(Verse 15)**

It is all individual responsibility. When one follows guidance, one reaps the fruits, and when one chooses error, one bears the consequences. None will bear or lighten the burden of another. Everyone will be questioned about their own actions and will have the reward for what they have done in this life. Close friends will be of no help to each other.

The same consistent and universal law that governs the succession of day and night also applies to the destruction of any community:

"When it is Our will to destroy a community, We convey Our command to those of its people who live a life of affluence. If they persist in sin, judgement is irrevocably passed, and We utterly destroy them." **(Verse 16)**

The affluent who enjoy wealth, servants, luxuries, comfort and power are prone to carelessness and decadence in their lives. They thus lead a life of corruption, transgress all limits, trample over values, desecrate sanctities and defile other people's honour. Unless they are taken to task for their misdeeds, they will spread corruption and indecency throughout their community. They will debase the sound values and principles which every community needs to observe in order to survive. Thus their corruption will lead to the loss of strength, vigour and means of survival by the whole community. It then becomes lifeless, and is soon overtaken by destruction.

This verse applies to the destruction of community that has erred in the past. Our erring community is also warned.

"Many generations have We destroyed since Noah's time. Suffice it that your Lord is well aware of His servants' sins, and observes them all." **(Verse 17)**

The one who wish to lead a life based solely on this world, looking up to nothing beyond this earth and its pleasures, will suffer the consequences of their actions. In the life to come, hell will be waiting for him because he will have deserved it. This is because those who do not aspire to anything beyond this world are keen to immerse themselves in its carnal pleasures. This however inevitably leads them to hell:

"As for those who care only for [the pleasures of] this fleeting life, We readily grant of it whatever We may please to whomever We will. In the end We consign any such person to hell, where he will burn disgraced and rejected." **(Verse 18)**

He is disgraced by his actions, rejected, suffering severe punishment. On the other side is a totally different picture:

"But those who care only for the life to come, strive for it as it should be striven for, and are true believers, are indeed the ones who will have their endeavours well rewarded." **(Verse 19)**

Someone who desires the rich reward of the life to come must pursue his goal diligently. He should fulfil the duties Allah requires of him. Moreover, he must have faith which serves as the basis of his pursuit for the life to come. Faith is not a matter that people attain through idle wishes, but it is rather an idea that is firmly held as a belief, and clearly endorsed by action. Pursuit of the hereafter does not deprive anyone of the wholesome pleasures of this life. It simply opens up wider horizons before us. Thus, enjoyment and pleasure are not the driving goal. There is no harm in seeking pleasure, provided however that one is not captivated or enslaved by it.

A life that seeks nothing more than the pleasures of this world is fitting only for worms, reptiles, insects, cattle and wild beasts. It is only the life that pursues the rewards of the hereafter that is fitting for man who has been the recipient of honour bestowed on him by Allah.

Verses 22 – 40 Some commandments

This section begins with:

22. Take not with Allah another object of worship; or thou (O man!) wilt sit in disgrace and destitution.

23. Thy Lord hath decreed that ye worship none but Him, and that ye be kind to parents.

Whether one or both of them attain old age in thy life, say not to them a word of contempt, nor repel them, but address them in terms of honour.

Placing Unity, monotheism, is the most fundamental principles of Islam, alongside with being kind and good towards one's parents.

Verse 23 refers to one of the clear examples for kindness to one's parents, implying when they need your care, do not spare them any act of kindness and do not despise them or scorn them by insulting them the least. That is, even stop uttering the slightest despising murmuring sound.

Do not shout at them, but speak to them in a calculated kind and highly esteemed manner.

The verse continues saying:

"...if one of them or both of them reach old age with you, do not say to them 'fie', nor repulse them, and speak to them a gracious word."

24. "And out of compassion, lower unto them the wing of humility, and say: 'My Lord! Have mercy on them both as they cherished me when I was little."

By the phrase: **'lower unto them the wing of humility'**, which is literally mentioned in the above verse, is the simile which refers to making oneself in the utmost sense of submissive gentleness towards one's parents. It makes one recall a bird which opens up its wings to provide shelter for its offspring.

The Almighty thus proclaims to cover your parents gently under your love and generosity by providing them with shelter and care as they provided you with shelter and care when you were little.

The verse says:

"And out of compassion, lower unto them the wing of humility..."

Imam Sadiq (as) in this regard said:

"That is, do not look at them except with compassion and kindness; do not raise your voice when talking to them above their voice; and do not raise your hand above theirs, and do not go before them when walking."

Therefore, pray for them and ask Allah to allocate His blessings and forgiveness to them before and after their death, for they have brought you up as a child.

Give your relatives their rights but also spend on the needy and the travelers.

Do not be wasteful, squandering your money. If you cannot assist needy people, then at least be courteous to them. Do not be miserly or extravagant, instead take a middle path. Allah gives abundantly to some and sparingly to others, He knows and observes everyone.

Do not kill your children because you think you cannot provide for them, it is a great sin. It is Allah who provides for them; they cannot cause poverty; that is the will of Allah.

Do not even come near to committing adultery.

Do not take a life, except within the laws of God. If anyone is killed unjustly, Allah has granted a right of retribution but do not be vengeful and take things too far.

Do not deal with the property of orphans except with good intentions. Honour your commitments because you will be questioned about them.

Conduct your business fairly, give full measure and do not balance your scales incorrectly.

Do not pursue that of which you have no knowledge - use your heart, eyes and ears to confirm the things you hear.

Do not walk about the earth arrogantly. A human being is just a small and weak creature; don't act as if you are something more than that.

The evil deeds mentioned above are hateful to Allah and He knows the wisdom in their prohibition. Again, do not set up something other than God to be worshipped or you will be thrown into Hell. Do not say that Allah has taken the angels as daughters. That is a monstrous statement with grave consequences.

Verses 41 – 52 Everything in the Heavens and in the Earth Glorifies Allah

41. We have explained (things) in various (ways) in this Qur'an, in order that they may receive admonition, but it only increases their flight (from the Truth)!

42. *Say: If there had been (other) gods with Him, as they say,- behold, they would certainly have sought out a way to the Lord of the Throne!*

43. *Glory to Him! He is high above all that they say!- Exalted and Great (beyond measure)!*

44. *The seven heavens and the earth, and all beings therein, declare His glory: there is not a thing but celebrates His praise; And yet ye understand not how they declare His glory! Verily He is Oft-Forbear, Most Forgiving!*

45. *When thou dost recite the Qur'an, We put, between thee and those who believe not in the Hereafter, a veil invisible:*

46. *And We put coverings over their hearts (and minds) lest they should understand the Qur'an, and deafness into their ears: when thou dost commemorate thy Lord and Him alone in the Qur'an, they turn on their backs, fleeing (from the Truth).*

47. *We know best why it is they listen, when they listen to thee; and when they meet in private conference, behold, the wicked say, "Ye follow none other than a man bewitched!"*

48. *See what similes they strike for thee: but they have gone astray, and never can they find a way.*

49. *They say: "What! when we are reduced to bones and dust, should we really be raised up (to be) a new creation?"*

50. *Say: "(Nay!) be ye stones or iron,*

51. *"Or created matter which, in your minds, is hardest (to be raised up),- (Yet shall ye be raised up)!" then will they say: "Who will cause us to return?" Say: "He who created you first!" Then will they wag their heads towards thee, and say, "When will that be?" Say, "May be it will be quite soon!*

52. *"It will be on a Day when He will call you, and ye will answer (His call) with (words of) His praise, and ye will think that ye tarried but a little while!"*

There are no deities alongside Allah. What they claim to be their God are no more than some of His creatures, be they stars, human beings, animals, plants and trees or other inanimate objects. All these turn to Allah submitting themselves to His will, in accordance with the law of nature.

These verses portray the whole universe, with all creatures living in it, under God's

Throne. They all turn to Allah glorifying Him:

"The seven heavens extol His limitless glory, as does the earth, and all who dwell in them. Indeed every single thing extols His glory and praise, but you cannot understand their praises. He is indeed Forbearing, Much Forgiving." **(Verse 44)**

Every single particle in this vast universe shares in this glorification. Indeed it comes alive as it praises and glorifies The creator. The scene shows the whole universe full of life and activity, sharing in a single action, addressing God in His exalted nature in a glorification that implies submission to His will and acknowledgement of His authority over everything.

It is a powerful and majestic scene in which we see every stone, large and small, every seed and leaf, every flower and fruit, every little shoot and every tree, every insect and reptile, every animal and human being, every creature that walks the earth, swims in the water or floats in the air, in short, all creatures in the whole universe glorifying Allah and turning to Him in submission. We are filled with awe as we sense that everything that comes within our vision or stays beyond it comes alive. 'Whenever we stretch our hands out to touch something, and whenever we put our feet to step over something, we feel that it is alive, glorifying God.

"Indeed every single thing extols His glory and praise," in its own way and language. *"But you [human beings] cannot understand their praises."* (Verse 44)

Human beings are limited by their own constitution which has a clay origin. This debars them from understanding the praises of other creatures. Had they listened with their hearts, directing them to appreciate the subtle laws that operate in the universe and make everything, large or small, turn to the Creator of all, they would have appreciated something of that praise. When human souls are purified and when they hearken to every animate and inanimate object as it addresses its glorification to God alone, they are better prepared to be in contact with the Supreme Society. They are better able to understand the secrets of the universe than those who limit themselves to the material world.

"He is indeed Forbearing, Much Forgiving." (Verse 44)

These attributes of Allah are mentioned here because of what seems clear of people's failing in their duties towards Him. Compared with this great show of submission to Allah in the whole universe, human beings seem to be in a singular position. Some associate partners with Allah, while others allege that He has daughters, and still others remain oblivious of their duty to praise and glorify Him. Infact human beings should have been the first among all creatures to acknowledge Allah, declare their submission to Him and extol His praises. Had it not been for Allah's forbearance and forgiveness, He would have hastened their punishment. But He allows them time, reminds and admonishes them because

'He is indeed Forbearing, Much Forgiving.'

The leaders of the Quraysh, the Prophet's own tribesmen who rejected his call, tried hard to prevent their hearts and souls from responding positively to the truth of the Qur'ān. As a result, Allah raised an invisible curtain between them and the Prophet, and placed coverings on their hearts preventing them from understanding it. Their ears were in a state similar to deafness, which meant that they could not understand its message.

When you read the Qur'ān, We place an invisible barrier between you and those who do not believe in the life to come. We cast a veil over their hearts which makes them unable to grasp its meaning, and their ears We make deaf. And so, when you mention your Lord in the Qur'ān as the One and only God, they turn their backs in aversion. We are fully aware of what they are listening for when they listen to you, and what they say when they speak to each other in private. The wrongdoers say:

'The man you follow is certainly bewitched.' See to what they liken you. They have certainly gone astray and are unable to find a way back [to the truth]. **(Verses 45-48)**

One report states that the elders of the Quraysh issued a general order telling everyone not to listen to the Qur'ān when they heard it being recited by Muslims. But the Qur'ān had its attraction even to the most outspoken enemies of Islam. Protected by the cover of darkness, three of those elders, Abū Jahl, Abū Sufyān and al-Akhnas ibn Sharīq sat just outside the Prophet's house, listening to the Qur'ān being recited from inside. Every one of them was on his own, thinking that no one would know about his action. As the day began to break, each took his way home, so that no one would find out. Soon, the three of them met. There was only one reason for their presence there at that particular time. Therefore they counselled each other against such action: "Should some of your followers see you," one of them said, "you would stir doubts in their minds."

The following night they did the same, and once again they met at the break of day. Again they counselled each other against their 'irresponsible' action. Nevertheless, the third night each of them went to sit outside the Prophet's home and listen to the

Qur'ān. When they met in the morning, they were ashamed of themselves. One suggested that they should each give their word of honour not to return. This they did before going home.

Later that morning al-Akhnas ibn Sharīq went to see Abū Sufyān at his home. He asked him what he thought about what he had heard Muḥammad reciting. Abū Sufyān said: "I heard things which I know and recognize to be true, but I also heard things whose nature I cannot understand." Al-Akhnas said that he felt the same. He then left and went to Abū Jahl's home to put the same question to him. Abū Jahl's answer was totally different. For once, he was candid and honest with himself and his interlocutor: "I will tell you about what I heard! We have competed with the clan of `Abd Manāf for honours: they fed the poor, and we did the same; they provided generous support to those who needed it and we did the same. When we were together on the same level, like two racehorses running neck and neck, they said that one of their number was a Prophet receiving revelations from on high! When can we attain such an honour? By God, we shall never believe in him."

They were averse to the very principle of God's oneness because they felt that it threatened their social position based on the myths that prevailed in those dark ages. In fact, the elders of the Quraysh were too intelligent not to realize the hollow nature of their beliefs as compared with the profound faith of Islam. They could easily appreciate the superb nature of the Qur'ān. Indeed their very nature motivated them to listen to it, but their pride caused them to take a hostile attitude to it. Thus they even fabricated allegations against the Prophet to justify their opposition:

'The wrongdoers say: 'The man you follow is certainly bewitched.' **(Verse 47)**

Such was what they said about the Qur'ān and the Messenger who recited it. They also denied resurrection and the life to come:

They say: *'When we are bones and dust, shall we be raised to life again as a new creation?' Say: 'Be you stones or iron, or some other form of creation which, to your minds, appears even harder [to bring to life]. They will say: 'Who is it that will bring us back [to life]?' Say:*

'He who created you the first time.' Thereupon they shake their heads [in disbelief] and ask:

'When will this be?' Say: 'It may very well be near at hand. On that day He will call you, and you will answer by praising Him, thinking that you stayed on earth but a very short while.' **(Verses 49-52)**

The concept of resurrection was the subject of a long controversy between the Prophet and the unbelievers. The Qur'ān relates much of this argument. Yet the whole issue is very clear and simple for anyone who contemplates the nature of life and death, resurrection and the gathering of all creation. The Qur'ān explains it in full on various occasions. Yet people could not take it in its simple and clear nature. They could not imagine how a person could be brought back to life after the body had decomposed: "They say:

'When we are bones and dust, shall we be raised to life again as a new creation?' **(Verse 49)**

They simply did not reflect on the fact that there was a time when they were not alive, yet they were brought to life. Nor did they appreciate that the second origination is simpler than the first. They did not fully understand that, as far as Allah is concerned, nothing can be described as 'easier' or 'more difficult'. Nor did they appreciate that the method of creation is the same in all cases. It is just that Allah issues His command for any creature to 'Be', and it comes into existence immediately. It is immaterial whether people consider something to be easy or difficult. When Allah wants it to happen, it will, without fail.

The reply comes in the form of an instruction to the Prophet to say to them:

"Be you stones or iron, or some other form of creation which, to your minds, appears even harder [to bring to life]." **(Verses 50-51)** The bones and dust may still have some traces or memory of life, but iron and stones seem even further away from life. Hence, they are told to be stones or iron or any other form that cannot ever be associated with life. Even if they are made of material that is least imagined to have life, Allah will bring them alive. They naturally cannot make themselves stones or iron or some other form of creation. This is given only by way of a challenge and reproach. Stones and iron have no feelings and cannot be inspired or influenced. This sounds as an implicit reference to their hardened nature.

The Qur'an explains things in many different ways but that makes some people turn even further away. If there really was some other deity, why does it not dethrone the Master of the Throne?! He is exalted and far above what they say about Him. Everything in the heavens and earth glorifies Him, but you do not understand how they glorify.

When you recite the Qur'an there is a barrier between you and those who do not believe in the Hereafter. They do not understand it and when God's Oneness is mentioned they turn away. God is aware of what they (the unbelievers of Mecca) want to hear (from Prophet Muhammad), and He knows that privately they call Prophet Muhammad a man bewitched. They dispute that they will be raised up after they become bones and dust. God says, even if they were stones and iron they would be bought back and tells Prophet Muhammad to say that. When they ask who will do this, say, the One who created you in the first place, and when they ask when this will take place remind them that this might well be very soon. On the Day you are raised up you will imagine that you had been dead for only a very short time.

The Surah then paints a speedy image of what happens when that event takes place, as it will indeed do:

"On that day He will call you, and you will answer by praising Him, thinking that you stayed on earth but a very short while." **(Verse 52)**

The image shows those people who were bent on denying the resurrection rising up to respond to the call that brings them back to life. As they do, they praise Allah in clear terms. They have nothing else to say apart from praising Allah. This is a strange response from those who were in denial of resurrection and the Day of Judgement altogether. They simply rise, saying nothing except: "Praised be God, praised be God." Thus this whole life is shown to be very brief, like a flickering light:

"You will answer by praising Him, thinking that you stayed on earth but a very short while." (Verse 52)

Describing this life in this way is sure to belittle its importance in the minds of those to whom this address is made. It is a very short life. Nothing of its effects is of a lasting nature. It is no more than a brief moment that has passed, accompanied by a brief enjoyment.

Verses 53 — 60 Good Speech

53. Say to My servants that they should (only) say those things that are best: for Satan doth sow dissensions among them: For Satan is to man an avowed enemy.

54. It is your Lord that knoweth you best: If He please, He granteth you mercy, or if He please, punishment: We have not sent thee to be a disposer of their affairs for them.

55. And it is your Lord that knoweth best all beings that are in the heavens and on earth: We did bestow on some prophets more (and other) gifts than on others: and We gave to David (the gift of) the Psalms.

56. Say: "Call on those - besides Him - whom ye fancy: they have neither the power to remove your troubles from you nor to change them."

57. Those whom they call upon do desire (for themselves) means of access to their Lord, - even those who are nearest: they hope for His Mercy and fear His Wrath: for the Wrath of thy Lord is something to take heed of.

58. There is not a population but We shall destroy it before the Day of Judgment or punish it with a dreadful Penalty: that is written in the (eternal) Record.

59. And We refrain from sending the signs, only because the men of former generations treated them as false: We sent the she-camel to the Thamud to open their eyes, but they treated her wrongfully: We only send the Signs by way of terror (and warning from evil).

60. Behold! We told thee that thy Lord doth encompass mankind round about: We granted the vision which We showed thee, but as a trial for men,- as also the Cursed Tree (mentioned) in the Qur'an: We put terror (and warning) into them, but it only increases their inordinate transgression!

53. "And say to My servants to speak what is best. Verily, the Satan sows dissensions among them. Verily the Satan unto man is an open enemy."

Here Allah is telling us to use the best of speech, and not to be rude and quarrelsomeness in words, it recalls the Satan's interference and inciting corruption amongst them.

The verse says:

"...Verily, the Satan sows dissensions among them..."

Do not remain heedless of the fact that Shiatan does not remain idle. The Satan is always round the corner, for he has always been an open enemy of mankind.

The verse continues saying:

"...Verily the Satan unto man is an open enemy."

Sometimes, the believers who had recently accepted the faith, following their previous ancient habits, used to provoke aggression against those who opposed them.

Moreover, those humiliating expressions of the dissidents towards the Prophet (Pbuh), some of which were mentioned in the previous verses, such as: sorcerer, insane, soothsayer, poet, etc... sometimes caused the believers to lose control of themselves and raise up against the opponents in a verbal attack, saying whatever they wanted.

The Qur'an seeks to hinder them from such things, persuading them to call with leniency and selection of softest words so as to prevent the Satan from inciting corruption.

Following on from the previous verse Allah is telling us that we must not humiliate others, not even calling the pagans as 'hell-inhabitants' while declaring oneself to be one of those who go to the Paradise, for such a manner leads to rebellion and sedition. Moreover, how on earth do we know about the happy ending of each of us? Allah is more knowledgeable; He excuses if He pleases and punishes if He pleases.

The verse says:

"Your Lord is more knowledgeable about you than yourself. He will have mercy on you if He pleases, or He will punish you (for your behaviour) if He pleases..."

In the end, concluding the verse, He addresses the Prophet (Pbuh) and, in order to console him for the extraordinary unease which he had suffered at the hands of the pagans as a result of their lack of faith, He says:

"...and We have not sent you as a warden over them."

So that you feel as the advocate of the people which compels you to make them definitely embrace the faith. It is your duty to openly take the message to them, and call them earnestly to the truth. If they embrace the faith, so much the better for them; otherwise, no harm will be done to you.

This verse, which begins with a definitive negation of the concept of Allah having a son or partner concludes with a challenge to those who associate partners with Allah. The challenge is simply that they should call on those partners to remove any harm that befalls them:

"Say: 'Call on those whom you claim (to be gods] besides Him, but they have no power to remove any affliction from you, nor can they shift it.'" **(Verse 56)**

No one can remove hardship or change its nature or recipient except Allah Himself. He alone is in control of the destinies of all creation.

Islam has one miracle to prove its truth. That is the Qur'ān. It is a book that maps a whole system of life, addressing both the mind and heart and meeting all the needs of human nature. It remains open to all generations to read and to believe in. It is valid for all time. A physical miracle is given to one generation, and its effects are limited to those who witness it. Yet the majority of those who witnessed such physical miracles did not believe in them. The example given here is that of the Thamūd who were given the miracle they sought. It came in the shape of a she-camel. Yet they transgressed and slaughtered the she-camel. Hence, Allah's warning came to pass and they were destroyed as a result of their denials that continued even after this clear, miraculous sign had been given them. All such signs were given by way of warning. They heralded the inevitable punishment, a punishment that was bound to be inflicted should rejection of the message continue.

Past history being such, it was necessary that the final message should not be accompanied by any physical miracle. This message is not meant for one generation; it is addressed to all future generations. It is a message that addresses the human mind with all its receptive faculties. It respects man's intellect and power of understanding.

The preternatural events that took place at the time of the Prophet, or happened to him, such as that of his night journey, were not meant as proof of his message. These were given as a test for his people.

We said to you that your Lord encompasses all mankind. We have made the vision which We have shown you, as also the tree cursed in this Qur'ān, only a trial for people. We seek to put fear in their hearts, but it only increases their gross transgression. **(Verse 60)**

Some of those who believed in the message preached by the Prophet Muhammad (peace be upon him) reverted to unbelief after he told them about his night journey. Others, however, became firmer than ever in their belief. Hence, it is true that what Allah showed His Messenger on that night was meant as 'a trial for men', so that they would reaffirm their faith. The Prophet is reminded that Allah encompasses all mankind. This was given to him as a promise from Allah, assuring him of ultimate victory. In the meantime, Allah would protect him against any evil scheme they might devise against him. He would come to no harm at their hands.

The Prophet told his people of Allah's promise and what he had seen in his true vision. This included the tree of zaqqūm which grows in hell. It is a tree which Allah cites as a warning to unbelievers. However, they continued to deny the message and whatever the Prophet said. Abū Jahl, the arch-enemy of Islam even ridiculed the tree, playing on the sense given by its name. He asked for dates and butter and mixed them together and ate them. He said to those around: "Come and eat. This is the only zaqqūm we know."

Of what use could any miraculous event be with such people, had it constituted proof of the Prophet's message, as was the case with some messengers before him? The whole event of his night journey and the warning about the tree of hell only caused them to become more insolent and to transgress even further.

Allah had not pre-determined to destroy them. Hence, He did not give them a physical miracle. It was His will to destroy those who continued to reject the truth of His message after they had been given miraculous evidence confirming it. The Arabs of the Quraysh were given more time. They were not subjected to the same fate that befell the peoples of Noah, Hūd, Ṣāliḥ, Lot and Shu`ayb. Some of those who rejected the message of the Qur'ān at first subsequently changed their mind, believed in Islam and were among its true servants. Others who died as unbelievers were the fathers of good believers. The Qur'ān — the miracle of Islam — continued to be a book open to future generations just like it was open to the generation of the Prophet's Companions. People who did not see the Prophet or his companions came to believe in it when they read it or heard it being read. It remains open to all future generations, a guide for many who are not yet born. Some future believers in the Qur'ān may be even stronger in faith and better servants of Islam than many in past generations.

Verses 61 – 65 Adam & Iblees

61. "And (remember) when We said to the angels: 'Prostrate unto Adam'; so they (all) did prostrate except 'Iblis who said: 'Am I to prostrate to the one You have created of clay?'"

Here, the Qur'an alludes to the unruliness of 'Iblis with regard to the Allah's command.

Dealing with this issue, just like the pagan Arabs, when we display qualities of arrogance, paganism, and unruliness, we are indeed followers of Iblees. The Qur'an points out as to how his fate ended; hence, the followers of the Shaitan will meet their doom in just the same way.

"And (remember) when We said to the angels: 'Prostrate unto Adam'; so they (all) did prostrate except 'Iblis…"

Iblees who had been overwhelmed by arrogance and pride, said:

"…who said: 'Am I to prostrate to the one You have created of clay?'"

Therefore, we repeatedly face the issue of the prostration of the angels in the Qur'an, and the unruliness of the Shaitan in this connection.

"…he was of the jinn…"

and has got an army:

"And the host of 'Iblis, all."

Allah's punishment is all-encompassing; the guilty will be provided with both the divine chastisement which is due to their own sins, and the punishment for misleading others in their entirety either.

The Satan, at first, removes man's instinct for monotheism by means of persuasion. Later, he seeks to invade him with his ammunitions and armies.

Shaitan does not just select one way for deceiving man. On the contrary, he usually entrenches man from all sides, using all forms of persuasions, dissuasions, promises, aspirations, temptations, and enticements.

Other cases of forming partnership with Shaitan, consist of: having forbidden sources of income, living on illegal money, adultery.

The verse says:

"And startle whomever of them you can with your voice, and collect your cavalry and infantry against them…"

Iblees possesses numerous aids and assistants who are of his own kind as well as from among mankind who help in seducing people. Some who are more powerful and speedier in act just like the mounting army; others are weaker and slower in action and behave just like infantry.

The verse, addressing the Iblees, continues saying:

"...and share with them in wealth and children and make promises to them..." Then the Qur'an warns that Iblees does not do anything else except deceiving them. The verse says:

"...and the Satan makes no promises to them except delusion."

Therefore, serving and worshipping the Lord provides one with insurance against satanic persuasions, temptations.

Verses 66 — 70 Humanity is ungrateful

Shaitan tries to inflict only evil on mankind, yet there are those who listen to his temptations, turning their backs on Allah's guidance. Allah is always merciful to them, provides them with help, support and guidance, facilitates their living, saves them from harm, removes their distress and responds to them when they pray to Him to lift their suffering and hardship. Yet despite all this, they turn away, denying Him and the message He has sent them:

Your Lord is He who makes ships go smoothly through the sea, so that you may go about in quest of His bounty. He is indeed most merciful to you. And when you are in distress at sea, all those you may call upon to help you will forsake you, except Him. Yet when He has brought you safe to dry land, you turn away. Indeed, bereft of all gratitude is man! **(Verses 66-67)**

These verses portray the scene of distress at sea by way of an example of hard times.

At sea, people realize much more quickly and keenly that they cannot do without Allah's help. Any boat or ship they use is no more than a little spot of wood or metal on the surface of an endless great sea. It is subject to the winds and currents that travel in different directions. They cling to life over this little spot, their vessel, which needs Allah's care more than anything else.

It is an inspiring image, the effects of which come more readily to anyone who has experienced it. People remember how, in their fear and apprehension, their hearts turn only to Allah, no matter how large their vessel is. At times when the wind is very strong and in high seas, even huge liners, designed to cross the oceans with ease and comfort, look vulnerable, like a feather blown away by the wind.

The Qur'an touches people's hearts as it shows them that it is Allah's hand that allows their ships to travel smoothly over the sea, so that they may seek Allah's bounty. Allah is indeed Most Merciful to man. It is Allah's grace that man's heart seeks most in such a situation of helplessness. The following verse then shows them the other extreme. After a smooth phase in their journey, they experience great turbulence in high seas. Enormous waves seem to carry their vessel and throw it around in every direction. They realize then that they have no real support and no saviour except Allah. They turn to Him in a sincere prayer, addressed to Him alone:

"And when you are in distress at sea, all those you may call upon to help you will forsake you, except Him." **(Verse 67)**

But man remains the same. When the hardship is over and he feels himself steady, moving easily on dry land, the experience he suffered disappears gradually from his mind, and as a result he forgets Allah. He then allows his desire to get the better of him and overshadow the beckoning of his uncorrupted nature:

"Yet when He has brought you safe to dry land, you turn away. Indeed, bereft of all gratitude is man!" **(Verse 67)**

This applies to all people except those who maintain their strong bond with Allah. Their hearts continue to have the light of right guidance.

At this point the Surah makes a direct and emotional address to people's consciences, depicting the danger they left at sea as though it were chasing them on land, or engulfing them again when they return to sea. It wants them to feel that safety and security can only be ascertained with Allah's protection. It cannot be guaranteed at sea or on land, with easy waves and moderate wind, or with a comfortable home or fortified shelter:

Can you feel so sure that He will not let a tract of the land cave in beneath you, or let loose against you a deadly stormwind? You will not find then anyone to protect you. Or can you feel so sure that He will not let you go back to sea again, and then let loose against you a violent tempest to drown you for your ingratitude? You shall not find then anyone to help you against Us. (Verses 68-69)

Allah has honoured mankind, favouring the human race over many of His creatures. He has honoured man when He created him in this particular fashion, giving him a nature that combines the characteristics of clay, from which he was made, and the spirit that was breathed into him. Thus he combines elements of heaven and earth in his constitution. Allah has also honoured man by placing in his nature such faculties that make him able to take charge of the earth, able to be active and make changes in it. Thus, human beings initiate and produce new things, combine things together and analyse complex matters in order to elevate life to the highest standard attainable.

Allah has also honoured man by making natural forces on earth subservient to his will and endeavour, and by making other natural forces operating in the universe helpful to him. A further aspect of the honour Allah has given man is seen in the reception given him when he was first created. It was a reception in which the angels prostrated themselves in a gesture of respect, because Allah Himself declared that man is to be honoured. Then there comes the additional honour when Allah states in His book, sent down from on high and which He guaranteed to remain intact for the rest of time, that man is given a position of honour.

We have indeed honoured the children of Adam, and borne them over land and sea, and provided for them sustenance out of the good things of life, and favoured them far above many of Our creatures. **(Verse 70)**

"And borne them over land and sea."

This is accomplished by making natural laws fit with human nature and its abilities. Had these laws been at odds with human nature, life would have been impossible to sustain on earth. Indeed, man is weak when his strength is measured against the natural forces that operate on land and sea, but man is given the ability to live on earth and to make use of its resources and treasures. This is all an aspect of Allah's grace.

"And provided for them sustenance out of the good things of life." (Verse 70)

Man tends to forget that whatever sustenance is given to him is indeed granted by Allah, because its different aspects become familiar to him. He only remembers the different forms of sustenance he is given when he loses access to them. It is then that he realizes the value of what he was given. But man's memory is short. He soon forgets again all God's blessings. He forgets what role the sun, air, and water play in sustaining human life. He forgets how important health is to him, and how he is given mobility, senses and reason, in addition to different types of food and drink. Indeed he is placed in charge of a complete world which includes countless blessings.

"And favoured them far above many of Our creatures." **(Verse 70)**

Indeed, Allah has favoured human beings by giving them mastery of this wide planet. Furthermore, He placed in their nature such abilities that make them unique among Allah's creatures.

Verses 71 – 84 The truth

71. One day We shall call together all human beings with their (respective) Imams: those who are given their record in their right hand will read it (with pleasure), and they will not be dealt with unjustly in the least.

72. But those who were blind in this world, will be blind in the hereafter, and most astray from the Path.

73. And their purpose was to tempt thee away from that which We had revealed unto thee, to substitute in our name something quite different; (in that case), behold! they would certainly have made thee (their) friend!

74. And had We not given thee strength, thou wouldst nearly have inclined to them a little.

75. In that case We should have made thee taste an equal portion (of punishment) in this life, and an equal portion in death: and moreover thou wouldst have found none to help thee against Us!

76. Their purpose was to scare thee off the land, in order to expel thee; but in that case they would not have stayed (therein) after thee, except for a little while.

77. (This was Our) way with the apostles We sent before thee: thou wilt find no change in Our ways.

78. Establish regular prayers - at the sun's decline till the darkness of the night, and the morning prayer and reading: for the prayer and reading in the morning carry their testimony.

79. And pray in the small watches of the morning: (it would be) an additional prayer (or spiritual profit) for thee: soon will thy Lord raise thee to a Station of Praise and Glory!

80. Say: "O my Lord! Let my entry be by the Gate of Truth and Honour, and likewise my exit by the Gate of Truth and Honour; and grant me from Thy Presence an authority to aid (me)."

81. And say: "Truth has (now) arrived, and Falsehood perished: for Falsehood is (by its nature) bound to perish."

82. We send down (stage by stage) in the Qur'an that which is a healing and a mercy to those who believe: to the unjust it causes nothing but loss after loss.

83. Yet when We bestow Our favours on man, he turns away and becomes remote on his side (instead of coming to Us), and when evil seizes him he gives himself up to despair!

84. Say: "Everyone acts according to his own disposition: But your Lord knows best who it is that is best guided on the Way."

One aspect of Allah's favour is to make human beings responsible for themselves, accountable for their actions. This is the first quality which distinguishes mankind and makes them worthy of their exalted position on earth: freedom of choice and individual responsibility. It is only fair that people should receive the results of their work and get their reward in the life to come, when everyone's record is considered:

One day We shall summon every community by their leaders. Those who are given their records in their right hands will read their records. None shall be wronged by as much as a hair's breadth. But whoever is blind in this world will be even more blind in the life to come, and still further astray from the path of truth. **(Verses 71-72)**

Those who pretended to be blind to the Hereafter will be worse than blind in the Hereafter. People tried to entice Prophet Muhammad (Pbuh) to fabricate revelations but Allah strengthened his heart. If he had inclined even a little towards them, he would have received a double punishment in this life and in the Hereafter. It was that way with all the Messengers. So establish the prayer from when the sun is at its zenith until the darkness of the night (four obligatory prayers fall during this time) and recite the Qur'an at the time of the Morning Prayer. The recitation at the time of dawn is always witnessed by the angels. Truth has come and falsehood has departed. The Qur'an was sent as a healing and a mercy for the believers but the disbelievers gain nothing from it except loss. Humankind can be strange; when Allah bestows favours upon him, he turns away instead of coming towards Him, and then when things go wrong he falls into despair. Everyone does things in their own way but Allah knows who is following the best way.

Verses 85- 96 A man with a message

85. They ask thee concerning the Spirit (of inspiration). Say: "The Spirit (cometh) by command of my Lord: of knowledge it is only a little that is communicated to you, (O men!)"

86. If it were Our Will, We could take away that which We have sent thee by inspiration:then wouldst thou find none to plead thy affair in that matter as against Us,-

87. Except for Mercy from thy Lord: for his bounty is to thee (indeed) great.

88. Say: "If the whole of mankind and Jinns were to gather together to produce the like of this Qur'an, they could not produce the like thereof, even if they backed up each other with help and support.

89. And We have explained to man, in this Qur'an, every kind of similitude: yet the greater part of men refuse (to receive it) except with ingratitude!

90. They say: "We shall not believe in thee, until thou cause a spring to gush forth for us from the earth,

91. "Or (until) thou have a garden of date trees and vines, and cause rivers to gush forth in their midst, carrying abundant water;

92. "Or thou cause the sky to fall in pieces, as thou sayest (will happen), against us; or thou bring Allah and the angels before (us) face to face:

93. "Or thou have a house adorned with gold, or thou mount a ladder right into the skies. No, we shall not even believe in thy mounting until thou send down to us a book that we could read." Say: "Glory to my Lord! Am I aught but a man,- an apostle?"

94. What kept men back from belief when Guidance came to them, was nothing but this: they said, "Has Allah sent a man (like us) to be (His) Messenger."

95. Say, "If there were settled, on earth, angels walking about in peace and quiet, We should certainly have sent them down from the heavens an angel for an apostle."

96. Say: "Enough is Allah for a witness between me and you: for He is well acquainted with His servants, and He sees (all things).

At this point the Surah mentions how some unbelievers questioned the Prophet about the soul and its nature. The consistent approach of the Qur'ān, which is indeed the best approach, is to answer people when they ask about matters that they need to know about and to give them answers that their faculties can understand and learn. It does not waste the intellectual faculties Allah has given them in pursuits that are of no use to them. Nor does it carry them over domains which they cannot comprehend. Hence, when they asked about the soul and its nature, the Prophet was instructed to tell them that such knowledge belonged to God alone. None other than Him has such knowledge.

'They question you about the soul. Say, 'The [knowledge of the nature of the] spirit belongs to my Lord alone. You, [mankind], have been granted but little knowledge.'" **(Verse 85)**

Such an answer does not present a barrier preventing the proper working of the human intellect. It simply directs such intellect to concentrate its efforts within the limits of its power and the domain where it can profitably function. It is worthless to roam endlessly in a maze. Similarly, it is pointless to spend one's mental energies pursuing what we are not equipped to comprehend. The spirit is one such pursuit. It belongs to the realm that lies beyond the reach of human perception. It is a secret Allah has kept to Himself. Compared to Allah's absolute knowledge, human knowledge is limited. The secrets of existence are too great to be understood by man's finite reason. It is not man's role to manage all the affairs of the universe, and as such, his powers are limitless. Instead he has been given such powers as are sufficient for him to control his own world and to fulfil his mission of building the earth and bringing it to the best standard possible within the limits of his faculties and knowledge.

Man has been able to achieve high standards with his inventive powers. However, he looks helplessly at the soul, unable to fathom its secrets, or to comprehend its nature. He does not know how the spirit comes to us and how it departs, where it comes from and to where it eventually goes. He knows nothing of the soul except the information Allah has given us in the revelations. This information provides knowledge that is certain, beyond doubt. It comes from the One who knows everything. Had it been His will, He would have deprived mankind of such knowledge, taking away what He revealed to His Messenger. But He does not do so as an act of grace:

"Had We so willed, We would have taken away that which We have revealed to you. In that case, you would not find anyone to plead with Us on your behalf except through the grace of your Lord. His favour towards you has been great indeed." (Verses 86-87)

Alternatively, they told him that they would not believe in him until "you have a garden of date-palms and vines, and you cause rivers to flow through it." (Verse 91)

Their conditions were so irresponsible that they even demanded that the Prophet inflict on them some punishment from the sky above, mockingly stating that the sky itself should fall upon them in pieces, just as he had warned would happen on the Day of Judgement. A similarly absurd condition was that he should bring Allah and the angels before them, so that they could support him and defend his case, like they themselves used to do in tribal arguments. Absurdity knows no limit, for they even asked him to take for himself a house of gold and similar precious metals. They further suggested to him that he should ascend to heaven as a proof of his special position. But even if he had done so, this too would not have been enough. For he was to bring back a book with him for them to read.

The childish absurdity of all these requests and conditions is clearly apparent. They are all arbitrary suggestions and widely different in scope and nature that they cannot be placed on the same level. How could residence in a luxurious house be considered of similar value to a person's ascension to heaven? And how can the digging up of a water spring be treated as equivalent to bringing Allah and the angels marching in ranks before them? However, to them these are all miraculous matters, so they can be grouped together. Should the prophet accomplish any of these miraculous events, they would consider believing in him and his message.

Verses 97 — 100 Resurrection

97. It is he whom Allah guides, that is on true Guidance; but he whom He leaves astray — for such wilt thou find no protector besides Him. On the Day of Judgment We shall gather, them together, prone on their faces, blind, dumb, and deaf: their abode will be Hell: every time it shows abatement, We shall increase from them the fierceness of the Fire.

98. That is their recompense, because they rejected Our signs, and said, "When we are reduced to bones and broken dust, should we really be raised up (to be) a new Creation?"

99. See they not that Allah, Who created the heavens and the earth, has power to create the like of them (anew)? Only He has decreed a term appointed, of which there is no doubt. But the unjust refuse (to receive it) except with ingratitude.

100. Say: "If ye had control of the Treasures of the Mercy of my Lord, behold, ye would keep them back, for fear of spending them: for man is (every) niggardly!"

He whom Allah guides is indeed rightly guided; whereas for those whom He leaves to go astray you cannot find anyone to protect them from Him. On the Day of Resurrection We shall gather them together, prone upon their faces, blind, dumb and deaf. Hell shall be their abode. Every time it abates We will increase for them its blazing flame. That is their reward for having disbelieved in Our revelations and said,

'When we are bones and dust, shall we be raised to life again as a new creation?' Do they not see that God, who has created the heavens and the earth, has power to create their like? He has beyond any doubt set a term for their resurrection. But the evildoers refuse to accept anything other than unbelief **(Verses 97-99)**

Allah has operated certain laws concerning His guidance and people's choice of error in preference to that guidance. He has allowed people to conduct their lives as they wish, but they remain subject to these laws and they will have to face the outcome. One of these laws is that human beings either follow Allah's guidance or turn away from it into error. The choice is made by man himself. Whoever deserves, on the basis of his efforts and actions, to receive Allah's guidance will definitely be guided aright. He is the one who will be truly guided as a result of his choice.

In the other camp we find those who deserve to be left in error because they turn away from Allah's revelations and blind themselves to all signs pointing the way to His guidance. Such people will have no one to protect them against Allah's punishment:

"You cannot find anyone to protect them from Him." **(Verse 97)**

On the Day of Judgement they shall suffer humiliation and will be resurrected in a terrible situation, 'prone upon their faces', lost as they will be 'blind, dumb and deaf' **(Verse 97)**

Verses 100 – 111 Truth in the form of the Qur'an

101. To Moses We did give Nine Clear Sings: As the Children of Israel: when he came to them, Pharaoh said to him: "O Moses! I consider thee, indeed, to have been worked upon by sorcery!

102. Moses said, "Thou knowest well that these things have been sent down by none but the Lord of the heavens and the earth as eye-opening evidence: and I consider thee indeed, O Pharaoh, to be one doomed to destruction!"

103. So he resolved to remove them from the face of the earth: but We did drown him and all who were with him.

104. And We said thereafter to the Children of Israel, "Dwell securely in the land (of promise)": but when the second of the warnings came to pass, We gathered you together in a mingled crowd.

105. We sent down the (Qur'an) in Truth, and in Truth has it descended: and We sent thee but to give Glad Tidings and to warn (sinners).

106. (It is) a Qur'an which We have divided (into parts from time to time), in order that thou mightest recite it to men at intervals: We have revealed it by stages.

107. Say: "Whether ye believe in it or not, it is true that those who were given knowledge beforehand, when it is recited to them, fall down on their faces in humble prostration,

108. "And they say: 'Glory to our Lord! Truly has the promise of our Lord been fulfilled!'"

109. They fall down on their faces in tears, and it increases their (earnest) humility.

110. Say: "Call upon Allah, or call upon Rahman: by whatever name ye call upon Him, (it is well): for to Him belong the Most Beautiful Names. Neither speak thy Prayer aloud, nor speak it in a low tone, but seek a middle course between."

111. Say: "Praise be to Allah, who begets no son, and has no partner in (His) dominion: Nor (needs) He any to protect Him from humiliation: yea, magnify Him for His greatness and glory!"

Miracles do not initiate faith in hardened hearts. Prophet Musa, for example, was given nine such clear signs, but Pharaoh and his people denied them until they suffered Allah's punishment.

"To Moses We gave nine clear signs. Ask the Children of Israel [about what happened]. When he came to them, Pharaoh said to him, 'Indeed, Moses, I think that you are bewitched.

'[Moses] said, 'You know full well that none other than the Lord of the heavens and the earth has revealed these eye-opening signs. Indeed, Pharaoh, I think that you are utterly lost.' So he resolved to wipe them off the face of the earth, but We caused him and all those who were with him to drown. Then We said to the Children of Israel, Dwell in the land. When the promise of the Last Day shall come to pass, We will bring you all together." **(Verses 101-104)**

This part of the history of Prophet Musa, may peace and blessings of Allah be upon him) and the Children of Israel is mentioned here because it fits with the context of the Surah. It started by mentioning the Aqṣā mosque in Jerusalem, and it then related a part of the history of the Israelites with Musa. This is followed by mentioning the hereafter when Pharaoh and his people will be brought forward.

This also fits with the scene of the hereafter and the one showing the end of those who deny resurrection, mentioned a little earlier in the Surah.

Musa' nine clear signs to which the Surah refers were his hand turning white, his staff, and the tests to which Pharaoh's people were subjected, such as drought, shortage of fruit, floods, locusts, ants, frogs and blood.

"Ask the Children of Israel' about what happened. They were witnesses to what took place between Moses and Pharaoh: "When he came to them, Pharaoh said to him: Indeed, Moses, I think that you are bewitched." **(Verse 101)**

"We have bestowed [this Qur'ān] from on high in truth, and in truth has it come down. We have sent you only as a herald of good news and a warner. We have divided the Qur'ān into parts so that you may recite it to people with deliberation. We have indeed bestowed it from on high step by step." (**Verses 105-106**)

The Qur'ān was revealed in order to educate a community and establish for it a system and code of life. This community would then carry it to all the corners of the earth in order to educate humanity on the basis of this perfect system. Hence the Qur'ān was revealed one part at a time, according to the practical needs of that community and the circumstances attending its first formative period. Education and the moulding of a nation and a community require time as well as practical experience. Thus the Qur'ān was not revealed as a theoretical doctrine or an abstract vision to be used for academic study and polemical argument. It was revealed part by part instead so that it could be implemented gradually during this formative period. This is indeed the reason for its gradual revelation, one part or passage at a time, not a whole scripture or code given at the outset.

The first generation of believers received it in this light. They approached it as directives to be implemented in practice, be the prohibitions, recommendations or obligations. They never approached it as something for moral or intellectual debate like poetry and literature, or for amusement like legends and stories. They allowed it to influence their daily lives to the full, bringing their feelings, perceptions and behaviour in line with it, and moulding their way of life in accordance with its teachings. They discarded whatever was in conflict with it of their values, norms and practices.

`Abdullāh ibn Mas`ūd, a learned Companion of the Prophet says: "When any of us learnt ten verses of the Qur'ān, one would not try to learn more until we had fully learnt their meaning and how to put them into practice."

Allah revealed the Qur'ān based on the truth:

"We have bestowed [this Qur'ān] from on high in truth." **(Verse 105)** *And its purpose is to establish the truth on earth: "And in truth has it come down."* **(Verse 105)** *Thus the truth is its fabric and ultimate aim, its substance and whole concern.*

Chapter 18

Towards Understanding Surah Kalf

This 110 verse chapter was revealed in Mecca. It takes its name from the story of the people who fell asleep in a cave, told in verses 9 to 26.

Surah al-Kahf is among the earliest revelations received by our Prophet SAW. In a hadith narrated by [Abdullah ibn Masud], the Prophet SAW states:

'Surah Bani Isra'il (Surah Isra), al-Kahf, Maryam, Ta Ha and al-Anbiya' are amongst my first earnings and my old property, and (in fact) they are my old property.'

So from this we learnt that Surah Kalf was amongst the earlier surahs revealed to our prophet.

The Blessings of Surah al-Kahf

There are numerous Hadiths that detail the blessings of Surah al-Kahf.

A man was reciting Surah al-Kahf and his horse was tied with two ropes beside him. A cloud came down and spread over that man, and it kept on coming closer and closer to him till his horse started jumping (as if afraid of something). When it was morning, the man came to the Prophet SWT, and told him of that experience. The Prophet SAW said, 'That was al-sakinah (tranquillity), which descended because of (the recitation of) the Qur'an.'

Ibn Hajar al-[Asqalani explains that al-sakinah referred here to the angels, because wherever angels go, peace and tranquillity descends. Sahih al-Bukhari, 5011

Another blessing of Surah al-Kahf is that it protects against the fitnah of Dajjal. As reported in the hadith of Abu al-Darda' t, the Prophet SAW said: 'He who memorises the first ten verses of Surah al-Kahf will be protected from the trial of the Dajjal. Sahih Muslim, 809.

It contains three stories and was revealed as a comfort to Prophet Muhammed (Pbuh) because the Muslims in Mecca were suffering ongoing torment and persecution at the hands of the ruling classes of Mecca.

Ibn Kathir and al-Tabarani mention in their respective tafsirs (commentaries) that the reason Surah al-Kahf was revealed was in response to specific questions raised by the Quraysh.

The Quraysh had never heard of a prophet from until the Prophet SAW began preaching. They therefore asked some of their elders to approach the Jewish community in the city of Yathrib (later to be renamed Madinah) and asked them what a prophet is and what are the signs of a true prophet.

Accordingly, a delegation from the Quraysh went to Yathrib where they spoke to the Jewish community there, stating that a man among the Quraysh is claiming to be a prophet, so how should the Quraysh know whether he is true or not. The Jews told them to test the Prophet SAW with three questions:

1. What is the story of the young men who fled seeking Allah's protection (i.e. the people of the cave)?

2. What is the story of the king whom Allah Swt blessed with the east and west (i.e. Dhu al-Qarnayn)?

3. What is the ruh (i.e. soul)?

The Jews added that the Prophet SWT should know the answers to the first two questions, but not the third question as no one knows what the ruh is apart from Allah. The delegation of Quraysh then returned to Makkah, and the questions were posed to the Prophet SWT. Our Prophet had become accustomed to Jibril a coming down at a certain time of the week, and in this instance it was the following day. Therefore, expecting Jibril's arrival at the usual time, the Prophet swt responded to the Quraysh that they should wait until the following day when he will be able to give them the answers to their questions. He was confident in Jibril's arrival and did not say insha'Allah. However, instead of coming the following day, Jibril delayed his visit; in some reports he came three days later and in other reports it was fifteen days later. The Quraysh were pleased at the delay, given it undermined the Prophet SWT. When Jibril did come, he came with Surah al-Isra', which is also known as Surah Bani Isra'il, and Surah al-Kahf. In these lessons from surah al-kahf 10 surahs were the answers to the questions. The account of the young men of the cave is at the beginning of Surah al-Kahf and that of Dhu al-Qarnayn is at the end.

As for the question of the ruh, it is found in Surah al-Isra'. Allah states in verse 85:

'They ask you about "the spirit". Say: "The spirit descends by the command of my Lord, but you have been given only a little knowledge."' This means we don't know what the ruh is.

To this day we cannot scientifically prove that there is a ruh and it is beyond our understanding.

Verses 1 – 13 A straightforward book

1. Praise be to Allah, Who hath sent to His Servant the Book, and hath allowed therein no Crookedness:

2. *(He hath made it) Straight (and Clear) in order that He may warn (the godless) of a terrible Punishment from Him, and that He may give Glad Tidings to the Believers who work righteous deeds, that they shall have a goodly Reward,*

3. *Wherein they shall remain for ever:*

4. *Further, that He may warn those (also) who say, "(Allah) hath begotten a son":*

5. *No knowledge have they of such a thing, nor had their fathers. It is a grievous thing that issues from their mouths as a saying what they say is nothing but falsehood!*

6. *Thou wouldst only, perchance, fret thyself to death, following after them, in grief, if they believe not in this Message.*

7. *That which is on earth we have made but as a glittering show for the earth, in order that We may test them - as to which of them are best in conduct.*

8. *Verily what is on earth we shall make but as dust and dry soil (without growth or herbage).*

9. *Or dost thou reflect that the Companions of the Cave and of the Inscription were wonders among Our Sign?*

10. *Behold, the youths betook themselves to the Cave: they said, "Our Lord! bestow on us Mercy from Thyself, and dispose of our affair for us in the right way!"*

11. *Then We draw (a veil) over their ears, for a number of years, in the Cave, (so that they heard not):*

12. *Then We roused them, in order to test which of the two parties was best at calculating the term of years they had tarried!*

13. *We relate to thee their story in truth: they were youths who believed in their Lord, and We advanced them in guidance:*

The first verse describes the Qur'an as a straight forward Book which leads us to the straight path.

With the second verse warning us of a severe punishment to those who do not accept the message, and at the same time giving good news to those who, do with the good news of everlasting reward.

Then the follow-on verse warns those who declare that Allah has taken a son when they have no evidence of such a monstrous lie. Prophet Muhammad SAW is told that he is in danger of worrying himself to death over the people who do not believe in his message.

However, the fact of the matter is the earth has been filled with attractive things in order to test people and in the end everything will be reduced to dust.

Verses 14 – 26 The sleepers in the cave – The Trial of Faith

14. We gave strength to their hearts: Behold, they stood up and said: "Our Lord is the Lord of the heavens and of the earth: never shall we call upon any god other than Him: if we did, we should indeed have uttered an enormity!

15. "These our people have taken for worship gods other than Him: why do they not bring forward an authority clear (and convincing) for what they do? Who doth more wrong than such as invent a falsehood against Allah.

16. "When ye turn away from them and the things they worship other than Allah, betake yourselves to the Cave: Your Lord will shower His mercies on you and disposes of your affair towards comfort and ease."

17. Thou wouldst have seen the sun, when it rose, declining to the right from their Cave, and when it set, turning away from them to the left, while they lay in the open space in the midst of the Cave. Such are among the Signs of Allah. He whom Allah, guides is rightly guided; but he whom Allah leaves to stray, - for him wilt thou find no protector to lead him to the Right Way.

18. Thou wouldst have deemed them awake, whilst they were asleep, and We turned them on their right and on their left sides: their dog stretching forth his two fore-legs on the threshold: if thou hadst come up on to them, thou wouldst have certainly turned back from them in flight, and wouldst certainly have been filled with terror of them.

19. Such (being their state), we raised them up (from sleep), that they might question each other. Said one of them, "How long have ye stayed (here)?" They said, "We have stayed (perhaps) a day, or part of a day." (At length) they (all) said, "(Allah) (alone) knows best how long ye have stayed here.... Now send ye then one of you with this money of yours to the town: let him find out which is the best food (to be had) and bring some to you, that (ye may) satisfy your hunger therewith: And let him behave with care and courtesy, and let him not inform any one about you.

20. "For if they should come upon you, they would stone you or force you to return to their cult, and in that case ye would never attain prosperity."

21. Thus did We make their case known to the people, that they might know that the promise of Allah is true, and that there can be no doubt about the Hour of Judgment. Behold, they dispute among themselves as to their affair. (Some) said, "Construct a building over them": Their Lord knows best about them: those who prevailed over their affair said, "Let us surely build a place of worship over them."

22. (Some) say they were three, the dog being the fourth among them; (others) say they were five, the dog being the sixth,- doubtfully guessing at the unknown; (yet others) say they were seven, the dog being the eighth. Say thou: "My Lord knoweth best their number; It is but few that know their (real case)." Enter not, therefore, into controversies concerning them, except on a matter that is clear, nor consult any of them about (the affair of) the Sleepers.

23. Nor say of anything, "I shall be sure to do so and so tomorrow"-

24. Without adding, "So please Allah." and call thy Lord to mind when thou forgettest, and say, "I hope that my Lord will guide me ever closer (even) than this to the right road."

25. So they stayed in their Cave three hundred years, and (some) add nine (more)

26. Say: "(Allah) knows best how long they stayed: with Him is (the knowledge of) the secrets of the heavens and the earth: how clearly He sees, how finely He hears (everything)! They have no protector other than Him; nor does He share His Command with any person whatsoever.

The first Story is the story of the people of the Cave.

In around 250 CE there ruled a Roman king called Daqyanoos (Decius) who would annually hold a gathering dedicated to the worshipping of idols. Many people would attend, dressed in their best clothing. However, one youth believed in the oneness of Allah, the teachings of Prophet Isa (JESUS) and shunned pagan worship. He rebelled against the practices that were happening in the society. He attracted another youth and then a few others to form a small group.

When the king heard of their rebellion, he became very angry and issued a command for them to be killed. In order to save their iman (faith) they fled and went into hiding. On their escape route they met a young farmer who owned a dog; they gave him da'wah, he accepted and decided to also join them. Eventually they came to a cave in which they made dua to Allah for ease. They decided to take rest there for a while, leaving the dog (named Qitmir) near the entrance as a guard.

Allah swt put them and their dog into a deep sleep.

Some say for 300 years, others say 309, but Prophet Muhammad (Pbuh) is told to say that only Allah knows exactly how long they were there, because He is the one who knows all the secrets of the heavens and the earth. There is no protector besides Allah and He does not let anyone share in His rule

When they woke up, they had no idea they slept for centuries and thought they had only slept a few hours. When they sent one of them to buy food, the shopkeeper was amazed to see such old coins and the reality of the time they had spent in the cave gradually came to light. The present ruling king, whom some scholars have identified as Tandoosees, was a believer who came on foot to see them and to find out more about their situation. *(Source of information – Ibn Ishaaq)*

Verses 27 – 31

Prophet Muhammad is told to recite what has been revealed to him and there is no authorisation to change anything in any way. Be content to be among those who seek Allah's approval and do not let the notable people of Mecca drive away the weak and humble among your followers. Tell them that now the truth has come; let the people choose whether to believe it or deny it. The wrongdoers will end up surrounded by Fire with nothing but a wretched drink or and a pain filled resting place. Good works will never be wasted; they will be rewarded with gardens of bliss with flowing streams. They will wear garments of silk and golden bracelets and recline on soft couches in a pleasant resting place.

Verses 32 – 44 – The trial of wealth

27. And recite (and teach) what has been revealed to thee of the Book of thy Lord: none can change His Words, and none wilt thou find as a refuge other than Him.

28. And keep thy soul content with those who call on their Lord morning and evening, seeking His Face; and let not thine eyes pass beyond them, seeking the pomp and glitter of this Life; nor obey any whose heart We have permitted to neglect the remembrance of Us, one who follows his own desires, whose case has gone beyond all bounds.

29. Say, "The truth is from your Lord": Let him who will believe, and let him who will, reject (it): for the wrong-doers We have prepared a Fire whose (smoke and flames), like the walls and roof of a tent, will hem them in: if they implore relief they will be granted water like melted brass, that will scald their faces, how dreadful the drink! How uncomfortable a couch to recline on!

30. As to those who believe and work righteousness, verily We shall not suffer to perish the reward of any who do a (single) righteous deed.

31. For them will be Gardens of Eternity; beneath them rivers will flow; they will be adorned therein with bracelets of gold, and they will wear green garments of fine silk and heavy brocade: They will recline therein on raised thrones. How good the recompense! How beautiful a couch to recline on!

32. *Set forth to them the parable of two men: for one of them We provided two gardens of grape-vines and surrounded them with date palms; in between the two We placed corn-fields.*

33. *Each of those gardens brought forth its produce, and failed not in the least therein: in the midst of them We caused a river to flow.*

34. *(Abundant) was the produce this man had: he said to his companion, in the course of a mutual argument: "more wealth have I than you, and more honour and power in (my following of) men."*

35. *He went into his garden in a state (of mind) unjust to his soul: He said, "I deem not that this will ever perish,*

36. *"Nor do I deem that the Hour (of Judgment) will (ever) come: Even if I am brought back to my Lord, I shall surely find (there) something better in exchange."*

37. *His companion said to him, in the course of the argument with him: "Dost thou deny Him Who created thee out of dust, then out of a sperm-drop, then fashioned thee into a man?*

38. *"But (I think) for my part that He is Allah, My Lord, and none shall I associate with my Lord.*

39. *"Why didst thou not, as thou wentest into thy garden, say: '(Allah)'s will (be done)! There is no power but with Allah.' If thou dost see me less than thee in wealth and sons,*

40. *"It may be that my Lord will give me something better than thy garden, and that He will send on thy garden thunderbolts (by way of reckoning) from heaven, making it (but) slippery sand!-*

41. *"Or the water of the garden will run off underground so that thou wilt never be able to find it."*

42. *So his fruits (and enjoyment) were encompassed (with ruin), and he remained twisting and turning his hands over what he had spent on his property, which had (now) tumbled to pieces to its very foundations, and he could only say, "Woe is me! Would I had never ascribed partners to my Lord and Cherisher!"*

43. *Nor had he numbers to help him against Allah, nor was he able to deliver himself.*

44. *There, the (only) protection comes from Allah, the True One. He is the Best to reward, and the Best to give success.*

45. *Set forth to them the similitude of the life of this world: It is like the rain which we send down from the skies: the earth's vegetation absorbs it, but soon it becomes dry stubble, which the winds do scatter: it is (only) Allah who prevails over all things.*

46. *Wealth and sons are allurements of the life of this world: But the things that endure, good deeds, are best in the sight of thy Lord, as rewards, and best as (the foundation for) hopes.*

47. One Day We shall remove the mountains, and thou wilt see the earth as a level stretch, and We shall gather them, all together, nor shall We leave out any one of them.

48. And they will be marshalled before thy Lord in ranks, (with the announcement), "Now have ye come to Us (bare) as We created you first: aye, ye thought We shall not fulfil the appointment made to you to meet (Us)!":

49. And the Book (of Deeds) will be placed (before you); and thou wilt see the sinful in great terror because of what is (recorded) therein; they will say, "Ah! woe to us! what a Book is this! It leaves out nothing small or great, but takes account thereof!" They will find all that they did, placed before them: And not one will thy Lord treat with injustice.

50. Behold! We said to the angels, "Bow down to Adam": They bowed down except Iblis. He was one of the Jinns, and he broke the Command of his Lord. Will ye then take him and his progeny as protectors rather than Me? And they are enemies to you! Evil would be the exchange for the wrong-doers!

51. I called them not to witness the creation of the heavens and the earth, nor (even) their own creation: nor is it for helpers such as Me to take as lead (men) astray!

52. One Day He will say, "Call on those whom ye thought to be My partners," and they will call on them, but they will not listen to them; and We shall make for them a place of common perdition.

53. And the Sinful shall see the fire and apprehend that they have to fall therein: no means will they find to turn away therefrom.

54. We have explained in detail in this Qur'an, for the benefit of mankind, every kind of similitude: but man is, in most things, contentious.

55. And what is there to keep back men from believing, now that Guidance has come to them, nor from praying for forgiveness from their Lord, but that (they ask that) the ways of the ancients be repeated with them, or the Wrath be brought to them face to face?

56. We only send the apostles to give Glad Tidings and to give warnings: But the unbelievers dispute with vain argument, in order therewith to weaken the truth, and they treat My Signs as a jest, as also the fact that they are warned!

57. And who doth more wrong than one who is reminded of the Signs of his Lord, but turns away from them, forgetting the (deeds) which his hands have sent forth? Verily We have set veils over their hearts lest they should understand this, and over their ears, deafness, if thou callest them to guidance, even then will they never accept guidance.

58. But your Lord is Most forgiving, full of Mercy. If He were to call them (at once) to account for what they have earned, then surely He would have earned, then surely He would have hastened their punishment: but they have their appointed time, beyond which they will find no refuge.

59. Such were the populations we destroyed when they committed iniquities; but we fixed an appointed time for their destruction.

Prophet Muhammad (Pbuh), was told to tell the people about the parable of two men both with beautiful gardens and land for cultivation.

One was rich and the other was poor. It is said that the poorer friend lived in the path of Allah, and contributed most of his assets towards charity, hence living a very simple and frugal existence.

The rich companion owned two lush gardens of grapes, date palms and cultivated crops. Allah caused rivers and streams to flow in between the two gardens, providing ample fresh water to irrigate the farmland. The two fertile gardens continuously yielded magnificent harvests without fail and thus became a reliable source of great income for its owner.

As with most human beings who are bestowed wealth and ease, the abundance of wealth made the richer companion arrogant and diverted him from the path of Allah. He took great pride in his abundant crops, financial and social strength, and the respect that he commanded from his peers.

He used to spend many hours in the two gardens, marvelling at his accomplishments, being boastful and arrogant: and these are attitudes which are very displeasing to Allah.

He frequently boasted of his wealth to his companion, rubbing into his companion's face, that the latter was not as successful as he was.

In asserting his superiority, he used to remind his companion:

"I am more than you in wealth and stronger in respect of men." (Al Qur'a n 18:34)

His boastful attitude also extended to his children, who outnumbered his companion's. His conceit, in calculating his material accomplishments, made him look down on the poor.

Eventually, he became so dazzled by his wealth, that arrogance, pride and disbelief blinded his heart. He felt secure and invincible with his vast possessions and the status they brought him.

He began to formulate the view that his garden was indestructible and would never perish.

He felt so secure in his materialistic cocoon that he even began to deny the coming of the Day of Judgment or the concept of resurrection before his Lord.

He rationalised that even if the Day of Judgment existed, he would be granted an even better garden in the afterlife.

His poorer companion tried to counsel him to be more grounded and humbler. He reminded his rich friend of his lowly origin.

And did his rich companion listened? No. He didn't. Quite the opposite.

His proudness and arrogance reached no end, he continued to strut proudly in his garden.

The poorer companion did not have riches, but he had contentment and peace within his heart.

He accepted this as the *qadr* of Allah, and that Allah in his infinite knowledge is the best of planner.

And alas!!! A time came when his garden was destroyed. He was not wealthy anymore. He had lost everything.

This story holds two great lessons. The first lesson is about the trial of wealth. A person must always be thankful for all the wealth and blessings of Allah and must believe that everything he has is from Allah the Almighty and he is in full power to take it back.

He tests people by means of wealth to see the impact it will have on them. Will they be thankful and help the less unfortunate or will arrogance and proud?

The second lesson that this story holds is that we must understand that the nature of material things. They are temporary. Everything in this world will end and nothing is permanent, and one must always thank Allah before it is too late. Even today Allah puts the Muslim ummah in various trials of wealth. We must always be thankful for what we have and not be too attached to the worldly things that we forget Allah and his mercies.

Verses 60 — 82 Moses and Khidr -TRIAL OF KNOWLEDGE

60. Behold, Moses said to his attendant, "I will not give up until I reach the junction of the two seas or (until) I spend years and years in travel."

61. But when they reached the Junction, they forgot (about) their Fish, which took its course through the sea (straight) as in a tunnel.

62. When they had passed on (some distance), Moses said to his attendant: "Bring us our early meal; truly we have suffered much fatigue at this (stage of) our journey."

63. He replied: "Sawest thou (what happened) when we betook ourselves to the rock? I did indeed forget (about) the Fish: none but Satan made me forget to tell (you) about it: it took its course through the sea in a marvellous way!"

64. Moses said: "That was what we were seeking after:" So they went back on their footsteps, following (the path they had come).

65. So they found one of Our servants, on whom We had bestowed Mercy from Ourselves and whom We had taught knowledge from Our own Presence.

66. Moses said to him: "May I follow thee, on the footing that thou teach me something of the (Higher) Truth which thou hast been taught?"

67. (The other) said: "Verily thou wilt not be able to have patience with me!"

68. "And how canst thou have patience about things about which thy understanding is not complete?"

69. Moses said: "Thou wilt find me, if Allah so will, (truly) patient: nor shall I disobey thee in aught."

70. The other said: "If then thou wouldst follow me, ask me no questions about anything until I myself speak to thee concerning it."

71. So they both proceeded: until, when they were in the boat, he scuttled it. Said Moses: "Hast thou scuttled it in order to drown those in it? Truly a strange thing hast thou done!"

72. He answered: "Did I not tell thee that thou canst have no patience with me?"

73. Moses said: "Rebuke me not for forgetting, nor grieve me by raising difficulties in my case."

74. Then they proceeded: until, when they met a young man, he slew him. Moses said: "Hast thou slain an innocent person who had slain none? Truly a foul (unheard of) thing hast thou done!"

75. He answered: "Did I not tell thee that thou canst have no patience with me?"

76. (Moses) said: "If ever I ask thee about anything after this, keep me not in thy company: then wouldst thou have received (full) excuse from my side."

77. Then they proceeded: until, when they came to the inhabitants of a town, they asked them for food, but they refused them hospitality. They found there a wall on the point of falling down, but he set it up straight. (Moses) said: "If thou hadst wished, surely thou couldst have exacted some recompense for it!"

78. He answered: "This is the parting between me and thee: now will I tell thee the interpretation of (those things) over which thou wast unable to hold patience.

79. "As for the boat, it belonged to certain men in dire want: they plied on the water: I but wished to render it unserviceable, for there was after them a certain king who seized on every boat by force.

80. "As for the youth, his parents were people of Faith, and we feared that he would grieve them by obstinate rebellion and ingratitude (to Allah and man).

81. "So we desired that their Lord would give them in exchange (a son) better in purity (of conduct) and closer in affection.

82. "As for the wall, it belonged to two youths, orphans, in the Town; there was, beneath it, a buried treasure, to which they were entitled: their father had been a righteous man: So thy Lord desired that they should attain their age of full strength and get out their treasure - a mercy (and favour) from thy Lord. I did it not of my own accord. Such is the interpretation of (those things) over which thou wast unable to hold patience."

This story took place when Prophet Musa (AS) led the Bani Israel at the other side of the red sea.

Once when Prophet Musa (AS) was addressing Bani Israel (children of Israel), he was asked: "Who is the most learned man among the people?"

He said:

"I am the most learned."

Allah admonished Musa as he did not attribute absolute knowledge to Him (Allah SWT). So Allah instructed him to go to the junction of the two seas where he would meet one who was more learned than Prophet Musa (AS).

That learned man at the junction of the two seas was Al-Khidr. When Musa met him and introduced himself, Al-Khidr asked:

"The Moses of Banu Israel?"

Musa replied in the affirmative.

Moosa (Moses) said to him (Khidr) "May I follow you so that you teach me something of that knowledge which you have been taught (by Allah)?" (Qur'an, Surah Kahf:66)

Al-Khidr replied:

"Verily! You will not be able to remain patient with me, O Moses! I have some of the knowledge of Allah which He has taught me and which you do not know, while you have some knowledge which Allah has taught you which I do not know."

Prophet Musa assured him that he would be patient and not disobey him in any matter. Both of them set out walking along the seashore. Soon a boat passed by and they requested the crew to take them on board. The crew recognized Al-Khidr and took them on board without fare.

Then a sparrow came and stood on the edge of the boat and dipped its beak once or twice in the sea. Al-Khidr said:

"O Moses! My knowledge and your knowledge have not decreased Allah's knowledge except as much as this sparrow has decreased the water of the sea with its beak."

Al-Khidr then removed one of the planks of the boat. Moses said:

"These people gave us a free lift but you have broken their boat and scuttled it so as to drown its people."

Al-Khidr replied:

"Didn't I tell you that you will not be able to remain patient with me?"

They proceeded further and found a boy playing with other boys. Al-Khidr killed him. The Qur'an describes that in this verse

Then they both proceeded, till they met a boy, he (Khidr) killed him. (Prophet Moosa) said:

"Have you killed an innocent person who had killed none? Verily, you have committed a great sin

Al-Khidr replied:

"Did I not tell you that you cannot remain patient with me?"

They went farther till they came to a town. They asked the people for food, but they refused.

In this town they found a wall which was on the point of collapsing. Al-Khidr repaired it with his own hands. Musa said:

"If you had wished, surely you could have taken wages for it."

Al-Khidr then replied:

"This is the parting between you and me."

Al-Khidr then explained all his actions.

He said that the ship which he had damaged, belonged to some poor people working in the sea.

The ruling king then was seizing every ship by force. So by making it defective, he had saved it for its owners.

As for the boy, his parents were believers, and there was a fear that the boy would oppress them by his rebellion and disbelief.

So Allah planned to take him away and give them another child instead who would be more righteous and kind.

As for the wall, it belonged to two orphan boys in the town. A treasure was hidden under it which also belonged to them; their father had been a righteous man, and Allah intended to safeguard their treasure. Building the wall ensured that the treasure would be protected till they reached maturity.

Al-Khidr concluded that he had not done anything of his own accord but had followed Allah's instructions.

In spite of repeated reminders from Khidr, and assurances from Prophet Musa (AS) that he would be patient and not question any of Khidr's actions, Musa forgot his promise and demanded immediate explanations for actions that seemed to him unjust

We can learn from this incident about the weakness of the human mind and limitations of human understanding and to put our trust in Allah and be firm in the belief that The Most Merciful, plans everything for our benefit which is not immediately visible to us.

Verses 83 – 102 Dhul Qarnayn – A Trial Of Faith

83. They ask thee concerning Zul-qarnain. Say, "I will rehearse to you something of his story."

84. Verily We established his power on earth, and We gave him the ways and the means to all ends.

85. One (such) way he followed,

86. *Until, when he reached the setting of the sun, he found it set in a spring of murky water: Near it he found a People: We said: "O Zul-qarnain! (thou hast authority,) either to punish them, or to treat them with kindness."*

87. *He said: "Whoever doth wrong, him shall we punish; then shall he be sent back to his Lord; and He will punish him with a punishment unheard-of (before).*

88. *"But whoever believes, and works righteousness,- he shall have a goodly reward, and easy will be his task as We order it by our Command."*

89. *Then followed he (another) way,*

90. *Until, when he came to the rising of the sun, he found it rising on a people for whom We had provided no covering protection against the sun.*

91. *(He left them) as they were: We completely understood what was before him.*

92. *Then followed he (another) way,*

93. *Until, when he reached (a tract) between two mountains, he found, beneath them, a people who scarcely understood a word.*

94. *They said: "O Zul-qarnain! the Gog and Magog (People) do great mischief on earth: shall we then render thee tribute in order that thou mightest erect a barrier between us and them?*

95. *He said: "(The power) in which my Lord has established me is better (than tribute): Help me therefore with strength (and labour): I will erect a strong barrier between you and them:*

96. *"Bring me blocks of iron." At length, when he had filled up the space between the two steep mountain-sides, He said, "Blow (with your bellows)" Then, when he had made it (red) as fire, he said: "Bring me, that I may pour over it, molten lead."*

97. *Thus were they made powerless to scale it or to dig through it.*

98. *He said: "This is a mercy from my Lord: But when the promise of my Lord comes to pass, He will make it into dust; and the promise of my Lord is true."*

99. *On that day We shall leave them to surge like waves on one another: the trumpet will be blown, and We shall collect them all together.*

100. *And We shall present Hell that day for Unbelievers to see, all spread out,-*

101. (Unbelievers) whose eyes had been under a veil from remembrance of Me, and who had been unable even to hear.

102. Do the Unbelievers think that they can take My servants as protectors besides Me? Verily We have prepared Hell for the Unbelievers for (their) entertainment.

We will look at why Surah Kalf was revealed – To answer the questions that the Unbelievers posed as a test to the Prophet (Pbuh) So this story starts with Allah swt giving information to the Prophet SAW about

Dhul Qarnayn

And they ask you, [O Muhammad], about Dhul-Qarnayn. Say, "I will recite to you about him a report." (verse 83)

Who exactly is Dhul-Qarnayn? It is popularly believed that Dhul-Qarnayn refers to Iskandar Dhul-Qarnayn or Alexander the Great of Macedonia. However, the historical details do not match, and further, Alexander the Great of Macedonia was not a believer in Islam whereas Dhul-Qarnayn was a pious believer. There are many theories of who this man was and in what era he lived. However, the precise identity of Dhul-Qarnayn is not described in the Qur'an and Hadith, and Allah did not provide us with the details for a wisdom that He knows. As with many other Qur'anic stories, Allah only reveals essential information to us, and if details are not revealed, then the knowledge of such details is inconsequential to our journey of iman and we should not enquire or debate any further about it.

What is known is that Dhul-Qarnayn was a man endowed by Allah with many talents and abilities, including military prowess, the ability to rule kingdoms, and extensive practical knowledge on many aspects of life. He was also a pious and steadfast Muslim who constantly contemplated over the signs of Allah and lived his days travelling from one destination to the next in order to establish justice in the land and alleviate the suffering of the people.

Indeed We established him upon the earth, and We gave him to everything a way. So he followed a way. (verses 84 – 18:85)

The Travels of Dhul-Qarnayn

Dhul-Qarnayn travelled extensively in his life. It is said that he ruled the earth from east to west, but it is noted that Allah only revealed part of this story to us. We therefore record what is revealed in the Qu'ran, and will not cite information which is not verified by authentic sources.

One of his travels brought him to the West, where he found the sun setting as if in a spring of dark mud. In this location he discovered a community who were living under oppressed conditions.

Until, when he reached the setting of the sun, he found it [as if] setting in a spring of dark mud, and he found near it a people. Allah said, "O Dhul-Qarnayn, either you punish [them] or else adopt among them [a way of] goodness." (verse 86)

So Dhul-Qarnayn went into the community and led them to the correct path and ways of life in accordance with the rulings of the Almighty. He liberated the community from the oppression that they were subjected to, inflicted punishment upon the oppressors, criminals and evildoers and aided the weak and oppressed until justice was established in the land.

He said, "As for one who wrongs, we will punish him. Then he will be returned to his Lord, and He will punish him with a terrible punishment. But as for one who believes and does righteousness, he will have a reward of Paradise, and we will speak to him from our command with ease." (verses 87 – 18:88)

Having completed his task, he and his army continued their journey, until one day, against the rising sun, he found a people who were backward and ignorant, living in the open without any shelter or protection against the sun.

Then he followed a way. Until, when he came to the rising of the sun, he found it rising on a people for whom We had not made against it any shield. (verse 90)

He educated the community there on what they needed to do. He shared and imparted his knowledge to them, taught them the skills required such as carpentry and agriculture, and then continued on his journey.

Thus. And We had encompassed [all] that he had in knowledge. (verse 91)

The next part of his journey is the most astounding, where he met a curious community, so far removed that he barely understood their language.

Then he followed a way. Until, when he reached [a pass] between two mountains, he found beside them a people who could hardly understand [his] speech. **(verses 92 – 18:93)**

They said, "O Dhul-Qarnayn, indeed (Ya'juj) Gog and Magog (Ma'juj) are [great] corrupters in the land. So may we assign for you an expenditure that you might make between us and them a barrier?" (verse 94)

Added Information on Gog and Magog

The story of Yajuj and Majuj is stated both in the Qur'an and hadith. Their appearance will be one of the signs of the end times. These events will transpire after the arrival of Dajjal, Mehdi and Isa-Jesus (alaihi salam). Both Qur'an and the hadith have clearly mentioned their existence, arrival and the aftermath of their arrival.

After Isa (as) will kill the Dajjal (False Masiah), Allah will inform Isa (as) of the coming of Yajuj and Majuj and order him to seek refuge in a mountain along with the believers. As Yajuj and Majuj will swarm in the land and keep causing destruction down the mountain, the believers will find it harder and harder to find food and water to survive. (Riyad al-Salihin, b19 #1)

The Prophet (sa) told us how arrogant they will become at their success, "They shoot their arrows into the heavens so they returned dyed with blood, and they say – crudely and arrogantly – 'We vanquished those in the earth, let us dominate the inhabitants of the heavens.'" (Tirmidhi 3153)

The Prophet (sa) is also reported to have said, "Yajuj and Majuj are sons of Adam. If they were allowed to come out, they would cause mischief and ruin people's lives, and not one of them would die before leaving behind one thousand or more of his offspring." (Tabaraani, qt in 'Areefi 368)

Their Destruction and Ultimate Abode Isa (as) will make dua to Allah to destroy them. Allah will send insects which will attach onto their necks, and they will all die. (Riyad al-Salihin, b19 #1)

Their ultimate abode is undoubtedly the Hellfire, given how they behaved on earth.

Verses 103 — 110 Worship is for Allah Alone

103. Say: "Shall we tell you of those who lose most in respect of their deeds?-

104. "Those whose efforts have been wasted in this life, while they thought that they were acquiring good by their works?"

105. They are those who deny the Signs of their Lord and the fact of their having to meet Him (in the Hereafter): vain will be their works, nor shall We, on the Day of Judgment, give them any weight.

106. That is their reward, Hell, because they rejected Faith, and took My Signs and My Messengers by way of jest.

107. As to those who believe and work righteous deeds, they have, for their entertainment, the Gardens of Paradise,

108. Wherein they shall dwell (for aye): no change will they wish for from them.

109. Say: "If the ocean were ink (wherewith to write out) the words of my Lord, sooner would the ocean be exhausted than would the words of my Lord, even if we added another ocean like it, for its aid."

110. Say: "I am but a man like yourselves, (but) the inspiration has come to me, that your Allah is one Allah. whoever expects to meet his Lord, let him work righteousness, and, in the worship of his Lord, admit no one as partner.

Prophet Muhammad SAW is told to tell the people that the person who loses the most, by his or her actions, is the one whose efforts are lost even though they think they are doing well.

Here reference is made to these who disbelieve in Allah's verses and signs, and deny that they will ever come face to face with Him. This disbelief renders their deeds worthless. All they will gain is Hell. On the other hand, those who believe and do good deeds will find themselves in the gardens of Paradise, where they will live forever and never have any desire to leave.

Then the last two verses – 109 and 110 summarised as:

If all the oceans were ink for writing, the ink would run dry before the words of Allah's attributes, grandeur, and knowledge were exhausted. Even if another amount of ink just like it were to be added it would not be enough.

Prophet Muhammad SAW is told to say that he is just a human being, the same as everyone else, and it has been revealed to him that Allah is One. Everyone amongst the people who fears their meeting with Allah should do good deeds and never let anyone else or anything share in the worship that is due to Allah alone.

Chapter 19

Towards Understanding Surah Maryam (Mary)

Surah Maryam comprise of 89 verses and has been given the name Maryam because Allah mentions the story of Maryam (as) and her family and how she gave birth to Isa miraculously. Aspects of the Surah

- To affirm the oneness of Allah and to negate that Allah has taken a son.
- It tells the Stories of Prophet Zachariyah (Zechariah) and his son Yahyah (John)
- The Story of Prophet Ibraheem and his father.
- The Day of Judgement

Some Background knowledge on Prophet Zachariyah (PBUH)

Centuries passed after the death of Sulaiman AS, and the Muslim kingdom rose and fell. The temple of Sulaiman AS disappeared over the generations, and in its vicinity, the modern day Bait-al Maqdis was erected.

The final group of Prophets and Messengers descended from Ishaq AS: Zakariya AS, Yahya AS and Isa AS are interlinked, both by blood relationship and by the proximity in time and location.

During this time, Bani Israel had reverted to their characteristics of stirring mischief amongst each other, and more seriously, they also started initiating blasphemy against Allah SWT. They claimed that Allah was stingy, *astaghfirullah al adzeem*, and that Allah withheld from them. These claims are the direct opposite of Allah's attributes of generosity. After all that Allah had given to them throughout the generations, this was how they displayed their thanks and gratitude towards Allah. These constant accusations provoked the anger of Allah upon them.

Their claims of stinginess are even contained in current Jewish and Christian scriptures. The original scriptures revealed to Musa AS and Daud AS had been manipulated to such an extent that they now assert that when Allah had completed the creation of the earth, He was too tired to rule the earth. This is why the Old Testament (which was originally based on the Taurat and Zabur, but has been manipulated and falsified by Bani Israel) claim that after the final day of creation, God took a rest – again, being total blasphemy as it depicted Allah as being incompetent instead of omnipotent.

Additionally, the Jews claimed that Allah had granted authority to the Jewish scholars to rule the earth, and to issue rulings which would supersede and override the teachings of Musa AS. Bani Israel had elevated itself to be the chosen people of Allah above other races, in direct contradiction of the teachings of racial equality in Islam.

Such was their immense arrogance that they claimed to know more than Allah, but there is nothing new in this pattern of behaviour. This is why, generation after generation, Prophets and Messengers were sent to Bani Israel to lead them to the right path, but within time, they would deviate until yet another Prophet was sent down to their community to guide them afresh. Yet, repeatedly, Bani Israel disobeyed from the smallest things to the largest issues, continuously rejecting the messages, signs and commands of Allah.

In the last era of the Prophets descended from Ishaq AS, their behaviour worsened and they even resorted to murdering the Messengers and Prophets.

THE GUARDIANSHIP OF MARYAM AS

During this time, there lived amongst Bani Israel a man by the name of 'Imran. He was so renowned for his piety that he was considered to be one of the best of the families of all time. He was not a Prophet or Messenger, but his household was so noble and elevated in Allah's kingdom that there is even an entire chapter in the Qur'an named after it. Surah Imran – Chapter 3.

'Imran had a pious wife, and her sister was married to Zakariya AS, a prophet.

The Qur'an does not provide accounts of Zakariya's AS childhood or youth. Hence, the story of Zakariya AS begins in his late adulthood, when he was elderly. He was a Prophet and Messenger of Bani Israel. He is a direct descendant of Daud AS and Sulaiman AS and his activities were centred in Bait-al Maqdis, where the temple of Sulaiman AS once stood.

It is confirmed by authentic Hadith that Zakariya AS was a carpenter. He led a simple life, and like majority of his brothers in prophethood, was of limited financial means.

Although he lived an austere life, Zakariya AS was constantly in a state of gratitude to Allah, and was intensely humble in his demeanour. Similar to his distant ancestor, Ibrahim AS, he and his wife had already reached an extreme old age without having any children.

What was happening in Mecca at the time of the revelation of the Surah.

This surah was revealed at a time when the Muslims suffered a lot of persecution from the disbelieving Quraysh. They became very frustrated as they could not stop the spreading of Islam. Because of this they became ruthless and subjected the Muslims to various forms of torture. When the persecution became unbearable the prophet gave permission for a group of Muslims to migrate to Abyssinia.

The ruler of Abyssinia was a very kind and just king. Initially, 10 men and 4 women migrated. After a few months, a larger group comprised of 83 men and 18 women followed.

When the Quraysh heard of this migration, they became enraged. They then came up with a plan.

A delegation of two men were sent with gifts to persuade the kind king An-Najashi to return migrants to Mecca.

They went to each ministers with their gifts and said:

"Verily, foolish youth from amongst us have come to the country of your king; they have abandoned the religion of their people and have not embraced your religion. Rather they have come with a new religion that neither of us knows. The noblemen of their people, from their fathers and uncles, have sent us to the king asking that he send them back."

The ministers accepted their bribes and agreed. They went to convince the king but the just king demanded that he hears the refugees' side of the story.

Al-Najāshī then summoned the new arrivals. Naturally, they became very anxious and consult with each other as to what to say. They all agreed to speak the truth and appointed Jaffar as their spokesperson.

Meanwhile, al-Najāshī called for his priests, who gathered around him with their scrolls spread out before them.

When the Muslims arrived Al-Najāshī began by asking them,

"What is this religion for which you have parted from your people? You have not entered into the fold of my religion, nor the religion of any person from these nations."

Jaffar addressed Al-Najāshī:

"O king, we were an ignorant people: we worshipped idols, we would eat from the flesh of dead animals, we would perform lewd acts, we would cut off family ties, and we would be bad neighbors; the strong among us would eat from the weak. We remained upon that state until Allah sent us a Messenger, whose lineage, truthfulness, trustworthiness, and chastity we already knew. He invited us to Allah – to believe in His oneness and to worship Him; to abandon all that we and our fathers worshipped besides Allah, in terms of stones and idols.

He commanded us to speak truthfully, to fulfil the trust, to join ties of family relations, to be good to our neighbours, and to refrain from forbidden deeds and from shedding blood. And he forbade us from lewd acts, from uttering falsehood, from wrongfully eating the wealth of an orphan, from falsely accusing chaste women of wrongdoing. And he ordered us to worship Allah alone and to not associate any partners with him in worship; and he commanded us to pray, to give zakāh, and to fast."

He enumerated for al-Najāshī the teachings of Islam.

He went on to say, "And we believe him and have faith in him. We follow him in what he came with. And so we worship Allah alone, without associating any partners with Him in worship. We deem forbidden that which he has made forbidden for us, and we deem lawful that which he made permissible for us. Our people then transgressed against us and tortured us. The tried to force us to abandon our religion and to return from the worship of Allah to the worship of idols; they tried to make us deem lawful those abominable acts that we used to deem lawful. Then, when they subjugated us, wronged us, and treated us in an oppressive manner, standing between us and our religion, we came to your country, and we chose you over all other people. We desired to live alongside you, and we hoped that, with you, we would not be wronged, O king."

Jaffar then recited Surah Maryam

Al-Najāshī began to cry, until his beard became wet with tears and said to the migrants:

"By Allah, this and what Mūsa (as) came with come out of the same lantern. Then by Allah, I will never surrender them to you, and henceforward they will not be plotted against and tortured."

Al-Najāshī addressed Jaffar:

"What do you say about ʿĪsa ibn Maryam?"

Jaffar said, "We say about him that which our Prophet came with – that he is the slave of Allah, His messenger, a spirit created by Him, and His word, which he bestowed on Maryam, the virgin, the batūl."

Al-Najāshī struck his hand on the ground and took from it a stick.

He then said, "'Īsa ibn Maryam did not go beyond what you said even the distance of the stick."

When he said this, his ministers spoke out in anger, to which he responded,

"What I said is true even if you speak out in anger, by Allah. (Turning to the Muslims, he said) Go, for you are safe in my land. Whoever curses you will be held responsible. And I would not love to have a reward of gold in return for me hurting a single man among you. (Speaking to his ministers he said) Return to these two (men) their gifts, since we have no need for them. For by Allah, Allah did not take from me bribe money when He returned to me my kingdom, so why should I take bribe money. The two left, defeated and humiliated; and returned to them were the things they came with (reported by Umm Salamah rahnu]

Verses 1-11 Story of Prophet Zakariyya (PBUH)

1. *Kaf. Ha. Ya. 'Ain. Sad.*

2. *(This is) a recital of the Mercy of thy Lord to His servant Zakariya.*

3. *Behold! he cried to his Lord in secret,*

4. *Praying: "O my Lord! infirm indeed are my bones, and the hair of my head doth glisten with grey: but never am I unblest, O my Lord, in my prayer to Thee!*

5. *"Now I fear (what) my relatives (and colleagues) (will do) after me: but my wife is barren: so give me an heir as from Thyself,-*

6. *"(One that) will (truly) represent me, and represent the posterity of Jacob; and make him, O my Lord! one with whom Thou art well-pleased!"*

7. *(His prayer was answered): "O Zakariya! We give thee good news of a son: His name shall be Yahya: on none by that name have We conferred distinction before."*

8. *He said: "O my Lord! How shall I have a son, when my wife is barren and I have grown quite decrepit from old age?"*

9. *He said: "So (it will be) thy Lord saith, 'that is easy for Me: I did indeed create thee before, when thou hadst been nothing!'"*

10. *(Zakariya) said: "O my Lord! give me a Sign." "Thy Sign," was the answer, "Shall be that thou shalt speak to no man for three nights, although thou art not dumb."*

11. *So Zakariya came out to his people from him chamber: He told them by signs to celebrate Allah's praises in the morning and in the evening.*

Surah Maryam started by telling us the story of Zakariyya (PBUH). He was the husband of Maryam's paternal aunt, Elizabeth. He was also one of the caretakers or custodians of Baitul Maqdis.

He and his wife had reached old age without having any children. He prayed to Allah swt for a child to carry on his legacy.

Verses 4 to 6

4. "O my Lord! infirm indeed are my bones, and the hair of my head doth glisten with grey: but never am I unblest, O my Lord, in my prayer to Thee!

5. "Now I fear (what) my relatives (and colleagues) (will do) after me: but my wife is barren: so give me an heir as from Thyself,-

6. "(One that) will (truly) represent me, and represent the posterity of Jacob; and make him, O my Lord! one with whom Thou art well-pleased!"

The Story of Prophet Zachariyah (PBUH) is also mentioned in many other places in the Qur'an:

"My Lord, grant me from Yourself a good offspring. Indeed, You are the Hearer of supplication." (Al Qur'an 3:38)

He also supplicated:

"O My Lord! Leave me not single (childless), though You are the Best of the inheritors." (Al Qur'an 21:89)

"My Lord! Indeed my bones have grown feeble, and grey hair has spread on my head, And I have never been unblest in my invocation to You, O my Lord! And Verily! I fear my relatives after me, since my wife is barren. So give me from Yourself an heir, who shall inherit me, and inherit (also) the posterity of Yaqub). And make him, my Lord, one with whom You are Well-pleased!" (Al Qur'an 19:4 – 19:6)

Before long, Allah responded to his prayer, confirming that his wife's barrenness had been cured and that they were to have a son who would also become a Prophet. Moreover, this son had the honour of being named by Allah himself, with a name that had never existed in mankind's history:

So We answered his call, and We bestowed upon him Yahya (John), and cured his wife (to bear a child) for him. Verily, they used to hasten on to do good deeds, and they used to call on Us with hope and fear, and used to humble themselves before Us. (Al Qur'an 21:90)

So the angels called him while he was standing in prayer in the chamber, "Indeed, Allah gives you good tidings of Yahya (John), confirming a word from Allah [meaning, the word of Isa AS later on] and [who will be] honorable, abstaining [from women], and a prophet from among the righteous." (Al Qur'an 3:39)

Nevertheless, Zakariya AS was astounded by the news. He burst out:

"My Lord, how will I have a boy when I have reached old age and my wife is barren?" The angel said, "Such is Allah; He does what He wills." (Al Qur'an 3:40).

This reaction is reminiscent of the earlier reaction given by his distant ancestor, Ibrahim AS when it was announced to him that he was to have a son. It was not a statement of disbelief, but rather an exclamation of surprise.

Zakariya AS continued:

"My Lord, make for me a sign." He said, "Your sign is that you will not [be able to] speak to the people for three days except by gesture. And remember your Lord much and exalt [Him with praise] in the evening and the morning." (Al Qur'an 3:41)

True to Allah's promise, his wife soon delivered a son, and he was named <u>Yahya AS (John)</u>.

Verses 12-15 Prophet John

12. (To his son came the command): "O Yahya! take hold of the Book with might": and We gave him Wisdom even as a youth,

13. And piety (for all creatures) as from Us, and purity: He was devout,

14. And kind to his parents, and he was not overbearing or rebellious.

15. So Peace on him the day he was born, the day that he dies, and the day that he will be raised up to life (again)!

Arabic scholars speculate that the name Yahya came from the root word "Hayaa" meaning life, because he brought life to his mother's barren womb. It is also said that the name was given because Allah elevated him in the earth with his faith and piety, and to be guided as a messenger. Allah blessed him with plenty of unique qualities that none other possessed.

Even as a child, Yahya AS did not fritter his time on silly things. Once, some children invited him to play with them. He replied that they were not created for play. This showed that from an early age, Yahya AS was single minded and serious about his purpose in life, which was to worship and serve Allah.

Unlike most other Prophets who received the revelation after they turned forty, Yahya AS was given sacred scriptures from a young age. From childhood, Yahya AS was given the upper hand in religious knowledge and wisdom, which reflected in his righteous qualities:

THE CHARACTER OF YAHYA AS

Yahya AS was, to his community, the best of characters: calm and deeply compassionate to both humans and animals. He was merciful and tender to everyone, and bore a deep love of all of Allah's creations. His manner was gentle and tranquil, and he was not quick to anger.

He was so pure in behaviour and thought that there was not a single action of his that disobeyed Allah. Even though Prophets and Messengers are allowed to take wives, he did not even desire for the pleasure of a woman's companionship because he did not want his heart or attention to be occupied by anyone other than Allah. He remained chaste throughout his life.

He refrained from any form of wrongdoing and his behaviour was so spotless that no one in the community could gossip or even speculate about him. Of him, Allah says:

And (made him) sympathetic to men as a mercy (or a grant) from Us, and pure from sins [i.e. Yahya] and he was righteous. (Al Qur'an 19:13)

He was also a dutiful son, and never once disobeyed his parents. He served and honoured them, being kind, patient and generous even as they became extremely old. In short, his character was flawless, never once transgressing, or showing even any signs of arrogance or disobedience.

And dutiful towards his parents, and he was neither an arrogant nor disobedient (to Allah or to his parents). (Al Qur'an 19:14)

Verses 16-22 Mary and her pregnancy with Jesus

16. Relate in the Book (the story of) Mary, when she withdrew from her family to a place in the East.

17. She placed a screen (to screen herself) from them; then We sent her our angel, and he appeared before her as a man in all respects.

18. She said: "I seek refuge from thee to (Allah) Most Gracious: (come not near) if thou dost fear Allah."

19. He said: "Nay, I am only a messenger from thy Lord, (to announce) to thee the gift of a holy son.

20. *She said: "How shall I have a son, seeing that no man has touched me, and I am not unchaste?"*

21. *He said: "So (it will be): Thy Lord saith, 'that is easy for Me: and (We wish) to appoint him as a Sign unto men and a Mercy from Us':It is a matter (so) decreed."*

22. *So she conceived him, and she retired with him to a remote place.*

These verses tells us about the appearance of Angel Jibrael to Maryam in the form of a man. She was very scared.

Some background information on Maryam (AS)

Maryam Bint Imran or Virgin Mary the mother of Jesus (Isa), is considered one of the most righteous women in the Islamic religion. She is mentioned more in the Qur'an than in the entire New Testament and is also the only woman mentioned by name in the Qur'an. According to the Qur'an, Prophet Jesus (Isa) was born miraculously by the will of God without a father. His mother is regarded as a chaste and virtuous woman and is said to have been a virgin. The Qur'an states clearly that Jesus was the result of a virgin birth, but that neither Mary nor her son were divine. In the Qur'an, no other woman is given more attention than Mary and the Qur'an states that Mary was chosen above all women:

Behold! the angels said: "O Mary! Allah hath chosen thee and purified thee – chosen thee above the women of all nations. {Qur'an, surah 3 (Al Imran), ayah 42[4]}

Verses 23-33 Birth of Jesus

23. *And the pains of childbirth drove her to the trunk of a palm-tree: She cried (in her anguish): "Ah! would that I had died before this! would that I had been a thing forgotten and out of sight!"*

24. *But (a voice) cried to her from beneath the (palm-tree): "Grieve not! for thy Lord hath provided a rivulet beneath thee;*

25. *"And shake towards thyself the trunk of the palm-tree: It will let fall fresh ripe dates upon thee.*

26. *"So eat and drink and cool (thine) eye. And if thou dost see any man, say, 'I have vowed a fast to (Allah) Most Gracious, and this day will I enter into not talk with any human being'"*

27. *At length she brought the (babe) to her people, carrying him (in her arms). They said: "O Mary! truly an amazing thing hast thou brought!*

28. *"O sister of Aaron! Thy father was not a man of evil, nor thy mother a woman unchaste!"*

29. *But she pointed to the babe. They said: "How can we talk to one who is a child in the cradle?"*

30. *He said: "I am indeed a servant of Allah. He hath given me revelation and made me a prophet;*

31. *"And He hath made me blessed wheresoever I be, and hath enjoined on me Prayer and Charity as long as I live;*

32. *"(He) hath made me kind to my mother, and not overbearing or miserable;*

33. *"So peace is on me the day I was born, the day that I die, and the day that I shall be raised up to life (again)"!*

Maryam secluded herself from society and gave birth to Isa (AS) under a date palm tree, which served as her source of nourishment during labour. When she returned to her people with a son in hand, she was denounced and condemned for supposedly falling in sin but that did not deter Maryam as her faith in Allah (SWT) was supreme and unrelenting. Allah (SWT) did not leave Maryam (AS) alone, He had granted several miracles to the child, Isa (AS), who was a miracle himself. As the people were doubting Maryam (AS), Isa (AS) spoke from his cradle, thereby astonishing the people and confirming Maryam's (AS) story.

Apart from talking since infancy Prophet Isa (AS) had other gifts from Allah (SWT);

"And [make him] a messenger to the Children of Israel, [who will say], 'Indeed I have come to you with a sign from your Lord in that I design for you from clay [that which is] like the form of a bird, then I breathe into it and it becomes a bird by permission of Allah. And I cure the blind and the leper, and I give life to the dead - by permission of Allah.

Verses 34-37 – Prophet Isa (Jesus)

34. *Such (was) Jesus the son of Mary: (it is) a statement of truth, about which they (vainly) dispute.*

35. *It is not befitting to (the majesty of) Allah that He should beget a son. Glory be to Him! when He determines a matter, He only says to it, "Be", and it is.*

36. *Verily Allah is my Lord and your Lord: Him therefore serve ye: this is a Way that is straight.*

37. *But the sects differ among themselves: and woe to the unbelievers because of the (coming) Judgment of a Momentous Day!*

These verses are discussing the status of Prophet Isa in Islam. Allah is telling us here that he has no need to take a son. Prophet Isa declared that Allah is his lord and only Allah must be worshipped.

This is the whole truth about Prophet Isa. It has nothing of the claims advanced by those who assign to him a divine nature, or those who make false accusations against his mother. What Allah states here is the complete truth, giving details of his origin and birth. There is no room for doubt or argument. It is not for Allah to take for Himself a son. Most sublime is He in His glory. He needs no son, because offspring are only needed by mortals, so that their line of existence is continued.

Offspring are needed by the weak so that they have the support of their children against their enemies. But Allah is immortal, and able to do what He wills, having power over all things. All creatures come into existence when He says to them, 'Be'.

This means that He accomplishes any purpose of His merely by willing it to take place, not by having help from a son or partner.

Verse 37 refers to the conflicting views and beliefs advanced by various groups concerning Jesus, his birth, nature and status. All are highly objectionable as compared with the clear and simple truth.

"Yet are the sects at variance among themselves." (Verse 37) Constantine, the Roman Emperor, held one of three famous synods, attended by 2,170 bishops. They differed a great deal about Jesus. Each group expressed a certain view. Some said that he was God who descended to earth in person, giving life to whomever He willed and caused others to die, before returning to heaven. Some said that he was God's son, while others claimed that he was one of the three entities forming the Godhead: the Father, the Son and the Holy Spirit. A different group claimed that he was one of three deities: God was one, Jesus another and his mother the third. However, another group said that Jesus was God's servant, messenger, spirit and word. Others made yet different claims. All in all, no more than 308 agreed on any one view. The Emperor decided to support that view, expelling all those who did not agree, and persecuting those who opposed it, particularly those who advocated God's oneness.

Verses 38-40

38. How plainly will they see and hear, the Day that they will appear before Us! but the unjust today are in error manifest!

39. But warn them of the Day of Distress, when the matter will be determined: for (behold,) they are negligent and they do not believe!

40. It is We Who will inherit the earth, and all beings thereon: to Us will they all be returned.

Since such deviant beliefs were established by synods composed of large numbers of bishops, the sūrah warns unbelievers about what happens to those who deviate from the faith based on God's oneness. This warning tells them of a scene that will take place on a great and eventful day witnessed by much larger numbers.

They will be made to hear what they dislike and see what they are wont to avoid.

"Hence, warn them of the Day of Distress." (Verse 39) That is a day when distress will be at its most acute, when distress will be a quality of the day itself. They need to be warned, because such distress is of no use to anyone: **"When everything will have been determined while they remain heedless, persisting in unbelief"** (Verse 39) It is as though the day is directly linked to their unbelief and heedlessness. Prophet Muhammad (Pbuh) is commanded to warn people against that day, which will come, no doubt.

Verses 41-47 Story of Abraham and his father

41. (Also mention in the Book (the story of) Abraham: He was a man of Truth, a prophet.

42. Behold, he said to his father: "O my father! why worship that which heareth not and seeth not, and can profit thee nothing?

43. "O my father! to me hath come knowledge which hath not reached thee: so follow me: I will guide thee to a way that is even and straight.

44. "O my father! serve not Satan: for Satan is a rebel against (Allah) Most Gracious.

45. "O my father! I fear lest a Penalty afflict thee from (Allah) Most Gracious, so that thou become to Satan a friend."

46. (The father) replied: "Dost thou hate my gods, O Abraham? If thou forbear not, I will indeed stone thee: Now get away from me for a good long while!"

47. Abraham said: "Peace be on thee: I will pray to my Lord for thy forgiveness: for He is to me Most Gracious.

In verse 41 Allah is telling Prophet Muhammad (AS) to tell us the story of Ibrahim (AS)

He (the father) said:

The father of Prophet Ibrahim (AS) Azar, was a sculpturer who would carve idols.

These idols the people will find themselves in temples with people worshiping them. The prophet saw the stupidity of such practice.

But as a wise son, he did not make his father feel foolish, nor did he openly laugh at his conduct. He told him that he loved him, thereby hoping to generate fatherly love. Then he gently asked him why he worshipped lifeless idols who could not hear, see, or protect him. Before his father could become angry he hastily added: "0 my father! Verily! There has come to me of knowledge that which came not unto you. So follow me. I will guide you to a Straight Path. 0 my father! Worship not Satan. Verily! Satan has been a rebel against the Most Beneficent (Allah). 0 my father! Verily! I fear lest a torment from the Most Beneficent (Allah) overtake you, so that you become a companion of Satan (in the Hell-Fire)."

Verses 48-50

48. "And I will turn away from you (all) and from those whom ye invoke besides Allah. I will call on my Lord: perhaps, by my prayer to my Lord, I shall be not unblest."

49. When he had turned away from them and from those whom they worshipped besides Allah, We bestowed on him Isaac and Jacob, and each one of them We made a prophet.

50. And We bestowed of Our Mercy on them, and We granted them lofty honour on the tongue of truth.

These verses are telling us that Prophet Ibrahim (AS) left his homeland and went further afield to preach Islam.

"We bestowed on them of Our mercy." (Verse 50) This is a reference to Abraham, Isaac and Jacob, as well as to their offspring. They were all recipients of Allah's mercy, which is mentioned here as the most bounteous gift granted by Allah in the general ambience of the sūrah. Furthermore, it was the quality of Allah's bounty that compensated Abraham for the loss of his people and homeland, giving him reassurance in his new solitary environment. **"We granted them the high honour**

of [conveying] the truth." (Verse 50) They were truthful in their mission, enjoying trust and honour among their people. Their word was listened to and received well.

Verses 51-55 Prophet Musa (AS)

51. Also mention in the Book (the story of) Moses: for he was specially chosen, and he was an apostle (and) a prophet.

52. And we called him from the right side of Mount (Sinai), and made him draw near to Us, for mystic (converse).

53. And, out of Our Mercy, We gave him his brother Aaron, (also) a prophet.

The Surah moves on, speaking about the same branch of Abraham's seed and reminding us of Musa and Haroon.

Musa is described here as one who was chosen for the task of dedication to God's call. He is identified as a prophet who is entrusted with a message that he must deliver to people. A prophet is not given the same task. He is an advocate of faith which he receives from Allah directly. Among the Children of Israel there were many prophets who were given the task of advocating the message delivered by Musa and judging among people according to the Torah revealed to him by Allah: **"Indeed, it is We who revealed the Torah, containing guidance and light. By it did the prophets, who had surrendered themselves to God, judge among the Jews, and so did the divines and the rabbis: [they gave judgement] in accordance with what had been entrusted to their care of God's Book and to which they themselves were witnesses."** (5: 44)

The grace granted to Musa is highlighted as he was called out from the right side of Mount Sinai. [That was the right side of Musa as he stood at that moment facing the Mount.] He was drawn so close as to be spoken to in communion. We do not know how this communication took place, or how Musa understood it. Was it a voice heard by Musa through his ears in the normal way, or was it an address received by his whole being. Nor do we know how Allah prepared Musa to receive His own words. But we believe that all this took place.

Verses 54 to 55

54. Also mention in the Book (the story of) Isma'il: He was (strictly) true to what he promised, and he was an apostle (and) a prophet.

55. He used to enjoin on his people Prayer and Charity, and he was most acceptable in the sight of his Lord.

These verses highlight a special quality of Ishmael's, which was his being true to his promise. This is a characteristic common to all prophets and all God-fearing men and women. The fact that it is highlighted here suggests that in Ishmael's case it must have had very special significance. Moreover, Ishmael is given the status of messenger of God, which means that he preached God's message to the Arabs of old. Indeed he was their highest grandfather. We know that even shortly before the advent of the message of the Prophet Muhammad, there were some individual Arabs who believed in one God. Most probably they were the last remnants of Ishmael's followers.

This surah also mentions that the fundamentals of his faith included prayer and zakat, which he ordered his family and his people to observe. Moreover, the surah leaves us in no doubt that Ishmael earned Allah's pleasure, which imparts a sense of contentment and satisfaction to anyone. This contentment is another aspect that permeates the whole surah, in the same way as mercy. In fact, the two aspects of mercy and contentment are mutually related.

Verses 56-57 Prophet Idris

56. Also mention in the Book the case of Idris: He was a man of truth (and sincerity), (and) a prophet:

57. And We raised him to a lofty station.

58. Those were some of the prophets on whom Allah did bestow His Grace,- of the posterity of Adam, and of those who We carried (in the Ark) with Noah, and of the posterity of Abraham and Israel of those whom We guided and chose. Whenever the Signs of (Allah) Most Gracious were rehearsed to them, they would fall down in prostrate adoration and in tears.

The sūrah mentions all these prophets in order to compare them, a group of God-fearing believers, with later generations of pagan Arabs and unbelieving Israelites. The gulf separating the two is vast. There is nothing to bring the newcomers close to their ancestors.

In this scene of the role of prophethood in human history, we see only the main features described: of the seed of Adam,' and of those whom We carried in the ark with Noah,' and also 'of the seed of Abraham and Israel.' Adam's seed includes all, and Noah refers to all who came after him, while Abraham combines the two major branches of prophethood: Jacob as the head of the Israelite tree and Ishmael to whom the Arabs belong and from among whom came the last of all prophets.

Some background information on Prophet Idris

Prophet Idris was born during the lifetime of Prophet Adam. He was from amongst the followers of Sheath (Seth) and ruled the progeny of Adam following the death of Sheath. He was truthful, patient and an extraordinary individual— it is reported in hadith by Abu-Dharr that Idris was the first man to introduce the art of reading and writing to mankind.

Idris was a sincere servant of Allah, hence Allah chose him as a Prophet and Messenger, and elected him as the ruler over the children of Adam.

What began after death of Sheath is the people of Kabeel (Cain) lost guidance and sin and corruption began increasing rapidly and spreading. Idris could not bear to watch his own people falling prey to the influence of shaitan. So Allah instructed Prophet Idris to call for Jihad (holy war) against the corrupt followers of Kabeel (Cain) —Idris was the first Prophet and Messenger in the history of Islam to perform Jihad against corruption.

And as commanded by Allah, Idris gathered an army of men and battled in the name of Allah against the transgressors and emerged victorious.

One day, Prophet Idris was informed by Allah that he would receive the rewards of all the good deeds performed by man each day till his last breath.

Prophet Idris was overjoyed with the news and thanked Allah immensely for all His blessings. But Idris was quite old, and was not quite ready to depart earth as enjoyed spreading good. So, he decided to speak to the Angel of death and plead him to delay his death. The Angel agreed to Idris's plea and decided to meet with the Angel of death together with Idris.

The Angel flew to the fourth heaven with Prophet Idris on his wings and met with the Angel of death. Idris's dear companion said to the Angel of death, *"Prophet Idris wants to know if you could prolong his life"*. The Angel of death was stunned; he replied, *"And where is Idris?"* *"He is upon my back"*, answered the Angel. The Angel of death replied, *"How astonishing! I was sent and told to cease Idris's soul in the fourth heaven. I kept thinking how I could cease it in the fourth heaven when he was on earth. Subhanallah (glory be to God), He made it happen!"* And as the Lord instructed the Angel of death, the soul of Idris was taken in the fourth heaven.

Following the death of Prophet Idris, corruption began to increase rapidly again. Several generations later, with no Prophetic guidance, Satan finally managed to influence the children of Adam to commit their first act of *shirk* (polytheism).

Verse 58

Other prophets from among the descendants of Adam, Noah, Abraham, and Israel, are mentioned.

Allah favoured the prophets listed above and they would fall weeping in prostration before Him.

Verses 59-65

59. But after them there followed a posterity who missed prayers and followed after lusts soon, then, will they face Destruction,-

60. Except those who repent and believe, and work righteousness: for these will enter the Garden and will not be wronged in the least,-

61. Gardens of Eternity, those which (Allah) Most Gracious has promised to His servants in the Unseen: for His promise must (necessarily) come to pass.

62. They will not there hear any vain discourse, but only salutations of Peace: And they will have therein their sustenance, morning and evening.

63. Such is the Garden which We give as an inheritance to those of Our servants who guard against Evil.

64. (The angels say:) "We descend not but by command of thy Lord: to Him belongeth what is before us and what is behind us, and what is between: and thy Lord never doth forget,-

65. "Lord of the heavens and of the earth, and of all that is between them; so worship Him, and be constant and patient in His worship: knowest thou of any who is worthy of the same Name as He?"

The surah makes it clear that the door remains wide open for all who wish to repent and mend their ways. Through that door comes the scent of Allah's mercy and the aura of abounding grace. Repentance that initiates a sincere acceptance of the divine faith and good works, thus making its positive significance a clear reality, ensures escape from that ruinous fate. Those who resort to such repentance will not end up in disillusion, but will rather go to heaven, where they are subjected to no wrong. They go there for permanent abode. Allah has promised entry into this garden to His servants and they believed in it before they could ever see it, because Allah's promise always comes true.

The surah then draws an image of heaven and its dwellers: **"There they will hear no idle talk, but only the voice of peace."** (Verse 62) Their talk is free of idle remarks, loud noise, futile argument. It is a conversation when only one type of voice is heard. It is the type that fits in with this pleasant atmosphere, full of contentment. That is the voice of peace. Provisions are certain to come in this heaven, without the need for hard work, worry or anxiety. They will never be exhausted: **"Their sustenance shall be given them there morning and evening."** (Verse 62) In such a blissful atmosphere, requests, demands and worries are out of place.

"Such is the paradise which We shall give the righteous among Our servants to inherit." (Verse 63) Anyone who wishes to share in this inheritance is aware of the way to ensure it: repentance, firm belief and good works. Descent and ancestry are of no avail. Certain people descended from those God-fearing prophets and the goodly people who followed divine guidance and whom God selected for honour, but their descendants neglected their prayers and followed their own wanton desires. Their descent benefited them nothing. They are certain to end in disillusion.

This passage of the surah ends with a declaration of Allah's total Lordship of the universe. Hence, people are directed to worship Him alone and to bear with patience the hard tasks involved. Furthermore, the possibility of anyone having something in common with Allah is absolutely negated.

Reports are unanimous that the angel Gabriel was ordered to say the first statement to the Prophet: **"We descend only by the command of your Lord."** (Verse 64) This was in reply to the Prophet when he felt that revelation was slow in coming. In fact Gabriel had not come to see him for some time, and he experienced a feeling of loneliness, keenly missing the angel whom he loved. Gabriel was then ordered by Allah to tell him: **"We descend only by the command of your Lord."** He conducts all our affairs: **"To Him belongs all that is before us and all that is hidden from us and all that is in between."** (Verse 64) He forgets nothing. Revelations are bestowed when He in His wisdom wills that they be bestowed.

The previous verse ends with the statement: **"Never does your Lord forget anything."** (Verse 64) It is fitting that this comment should be followed with the injunction to worship God alone and remain steadfast, declaring at the same time His Lordship over all things: **"He is the Lord of the heavens and the earth and all that is between them."** (Verse 65) No one else has any share in this Lordship.

"Worship Him alone, then, and remain steadfast in His worship." (Verse 65)

Worship Him and persevere in shouldering the responsibilities that such worship entails. These include the responsibility of attaining the high standard that allows one to present oneself before Him and of maintaining this high standard. Worship Him alone and mobilize all your abilities and potential for meeting Him and for learning from that sublime source. This is a hard task, requiring one to free oneself of all restrictions and responsibilities, activities and distractions. Yet this task is coupled with a pleasure that cannot be fully appreciated except by those who have experienced it. Yet the pleasure cannot be gained except by those who rise to the task and fulfil it with the determination it deserves. Dedication is the key word here, and without dedication, the pleasure will not be forthcoming, nor the results one hopes for.

"Worship Him alone, then, and remain steadfast in His worship," remembering that worship in Islam does not denote merely the rituals of worship. It includes all activities, feelings, intentions and thoughts. It is hard to direct all these towards heaven and make their aim the winning of God's pleasure. As it is hard, it requires perseverance. It requires that one directs every human activity on earth to pleasing God, ensuring that it remains free of all restrictions, temptations and desires.

Thus we see how Islam is truly a comprehensive system for life. When man implements this system, feeling that whatever he does, large or small, is meant as worship of God, he rises to the pure and enlightened level of worship. Such a system requires, for its proper fulfilment, perseverance and endurance at the time of suffering.

The command is given to us all that we must **"worship Him alone."** He is the only One in the universe who deserves to be the recipient of our worship. The passage concludes with the rhetorical question: **"Do you know any whose name is worthy to be mentioned side by side with His?"** (Verse 65) This question also asks whether we know any equal to God. Supreme is He above all things!

Verses 66-75

66. Man says: "What! When I am dead, shall I then be raised up alive?"

67. But does not man call to mind that We created him before out of nothing?

68. So, by thy Lord, without doubt, We shall gather them together, and (also) the Evil Ones (with them); then shall We bring them forth on their knees round about Hell;

69. Then shall We certainly drag out from every sect all those who were worst in obstinate rebellion against (Allah) Most Gracious.

70. And certainly We know best those who are most worthy of being burned therein.

71. Not one of you but will pass over it: this is, with thy Lord, a Decree which must be accomplished.

72. But We shall save those who guarded against evil, and We shall leave the wrong-doers therein, (humbled) to their knees.

73. When Our Clear Signs are rehearsed to them, the Unbelievers say to those who believe, "Which of the two sides is best in point of position? Which makes the best show in council?"

74. But how many (countless) generations before them have we destroyed, who were even better in equipment and in glitter to the eye?

75. Say: "If any men go astray, (Allah) Most Gracious extends (the rope) to them, until, when they see the warning of Allah (being fulfilled) - either in punishment or in (the approach of) the Hour, - they will at length realise who is worst in position, and (who) weakest in forces!

So far the surah has given us accounts of a number of prophets, including Zachariah and the birth of John, his son, Mary and the birth of Jesus, Abraham and his split from his community and their false deities. We have also heard about the generations that followed them, and whether they lived in accordance with the guidance God gave them or they fell into error. The surah comments on these accounts declaring that Lordship belongs solely to Allah, who alone deserves to be worshipped, without partners. This is the essential truth that these histories of earlier prophets bring out in full relief.

The passage begins with a scene in which man is shown to be astonished about the reality of resurrection. **"What!" says man, 'When I am once dead, shall I be raised up alive?'"** (Verse 66) The first point here is that this surprise is attributed to mankind in general. In fact, this same comment was expressed by many peoples during different periods of history. Hence, it is only normal that it should be attributed to the human kind in general. The surprise, or the objection results from man being oblivious of how he came into being. Where and what was he before entering this life? The fact is that he had no existence and then he began to exist.

This denial of the truth of resurrection is followed by an oath implying a stern warning. Allah, in His glory, swears by Himself, which makes this the most solemn and serious oath, that they will all be resurrected and gathered together. This is, then, a forgone conclusion: **"By your Lord, We shall most certainly bring them forth."** (Verse 68) **But they will not be alone. They will be driven "together with the evil ones."** (Verse 68) This shows them to be one category with the evil ones who always incite them to deny the truth of faith. Thus the two groups are leaders and followers.

At this point, a vivid picture is drawn showing them sitting on their knees around hell, in total misery and humiliation: **"Then We shall most certainly gather them, on their knees, around hell."** (Verse 68) It is a fearsome scene, with multitudes upon multitudes of people brought together to the vicinity of hell and made to sit on their knees around it, suffering its heat and watching its fierce fire burn. They expect to be thrown into it at any time. They, thus, feel their misery to be compounded with humiliation.

This image is followed with one in which we see the most hardened of these evil-doers being pulled and dragged towards it: **"Thereupon We shall drag out from every group those who had been most obstinate in their rebellion against the Most Merciful."** (Verse 69) The sound here is stressed heavily, so that it gives an even more graphic and lifelike picture of how they are dragged out. Although the next image is left to our imagination, we nonetheless see them being thrown into hell.

Allah certainly knows best which people are more deserving of punishment in hell. No one is taken at random, or by chance from that huge multitude. It is Allah who has brought them here and He knows them all, one by one. He knows what each and every one of them deserves: **"For, indeed, We know best who most deserve to be burnt in the fire of hell."** (Verse 70) Those, then, are the ones who will be chosen first for the fire.

The believers witness this fearful scene as they too are brought near to it: **"There is not one among you who shall not pass over it: this is, for your Lord, a decree that must be fulfilled."** (Verse 71) They arrive there, look at hell as it burns fiercely, asking for more feed.

Now the surah leaves with us this scene of the Day of Judgement to paint an image of this world in which the unbelievers are shown behaving arrogantly towards the believers, branding them as poor and weak, and boasting about their own wealth and petty social values.

The first side stands out with its wide variety of temptations: wealth, beauty, power and influence. It uses all these to serve people's interests, and provide them with all manner of pleasures. The second side appears too humble by comparison, yet it looks with disdain at wealth and beauty and it ridicules power and influence. It calls on people to join its ranks, without offering them any personal gain, material interest or favours that rulers and governments can provide. It simply offers them the faith, pure and simple, without adding to it any adornment. It seeks strength through being on God's side, nothing else. In fact, it makes clear to mankind that accepting it will involve hardship, effort and struggle. Also clear is the fact that none will be rewarded for anything in this life. The reward to be expected will be in the form of being close to God, enjoying His pleasure in the life to come.

The elders of the Quraysh at the time of the Prophet used to listen to God's revelations being recited to them, but then they would say to the believers who lacked all riches: **"Which of the two sides has a better position and a superior community?"** (Verse 73) Which side: the elders who denied Muhammad's message, or the humble who responded to him? Al-Naḍr ibn al-Ḥārith, 'Amr ibn Hishām, al-Walīd ibn al-Mughīrah and their powerful clique, or Bilāl, 'Ammār, Khabbāb and their brothers, poor and deprived as they were? Had the message preached by Muhammad been any good, would his followers be those who had no power or influence in the Quraysh society? Would they have met in a humble place like al-Arqam's house? Would his opponents be those who enjoyed all the luxuries and social prominence?

Such is worldly logic, advanced by those who have no aspiration to any truly high horizon. It is divine wisdom that keeps faith free of all adornment and superficial attraction, offering no temptation. Thus, only those who take it for its real value, without hope of immediate gain, will accept it. By contrast, those who are after wealth, worldly interests, pleasures and the like will turn away from it.

Verse 76

76. "And Allah doth advance in guidance those who seek guidance: and the things that endure, Good Deeds, are best in the sight of thy Lord, as rewards, and best in respect of (their) eventual return."

They claim that they follow better and superior guidance to that advocated by Prophet Muhammad (Pbuh) and his followers, and their evidence is their wealth and luxuries. Be that as it may! Prophet Muhammad (Pbuh) will appeal to his Lord to give increase to each side: the one in error and the one following right guidance. Then when what Prophet Muhammad (Pbuh) promises comes to pass, which is the triumph of the believers over those in error, or the final punishment they receive on the Day of Judgement, they will realize which of the two sides is worse in position, weaker in forces. On that day, the believers will rejoice and feel their superiority: **"God advances in guidance those who seek His guidance. Good deeds of lasting merit are, in your Lord's sight, worthy of greater recompense, and yield far better returns."** (Verse 76) This is certainly better than all that in which human beings find pleasure and enjoyment.

Verses 77-95

77. Hast thou then seen the (sort of) man who rejects Our Signs, yet says: "I shall certainly be given wealth and children?"

78. Has he penetrated to the Unseen, or has he taken a contract with (Allah) Most Gracious?

79. Nay! We shall record what he says, and We shall add and add to his punishment.

80. To Us shall return all that he talks of and he shall appear before Us bare and alone.

81. And they have taken (for worship) gods other than Allah, to give them power and glory!

82. Instead, they shall reject their worship, and become adversaries against them.

83. Seest thou not that We have set the Evil Ones on against the unbelievers, to incite them with fury?

84. So make no haste against them, for We but count out to them a (limited) number (of days).

85. The day We shall gather the righteous to (Allah) Most Gracious, like a band presented before a king for honours,

86. And We shall drive the sinners to Hell, like thirsty cattle driven down to water,-

87. None shall have the power of intercession, but such a one as has received permission (or promise) from (Allah) Most Gracious.

88. They say: "(Allah) Most Gracious has begotten a son!"

89. Indeed ye have put forth a thing most monstrous!

90. At it the skies are ready to burst, the earth to split asunder, and the mountains to fall down in utter ruin,

91. That they should invoke a son for (Allah) Most Gracious.

92. For it is not consonant with the majesty of (Allah) Most Gracious that He should beget a son.

93. Not one of the beings in the heavens and the earth but must come to (Allah) Most Gracious as a servant.

94. He does take an account of them (all), and hath numbered them (all) exactly.

95. And everyone of them will come to Him singly on the Day of Judgment.

The surah then picks up on another type of boast and decries it. The immediate cause of the revelation of these verses is reported by Khabbāb ibn al-Aratt who said: "I was an ironmonger, and I had money due to be paid to me by al-`Āṣ ibn Wā'il. I went to him to demand payment. He said, 'By God! I am not going to repay you until you reject Muhammad and his message.' I said, 'I shall not reject Muhammad until you have died and been resurrected.' He said to me, 'Well! Wait then. For, when I have been resurrected after my death, I will have wealth and children. You can come to me then and I will pay you what I owe you.'

A stern warning is, then, very apt here to stop such arrogant claims: **"By no means! We shall record what he says, and We shall long extend his suffering."** (Verse 79) We will write down whatever he says, so that it is not forgotten, admitting no dispute on the Day of Judgement. This is again a merely descriptive image, because no dispute or argument is possible as Allah's knowledge encompasses every little detail. Moreover, the punishment meted out to such sinners will be increased manifold, in time and volume, so as to continue without interruption.

A further image of warning is added: **"and We shall divest him of all that he is now speaking of and he shall appear before Us all alone."** (Verse 80) Thus, everything that he speaks about of his wealth and children will be taken away from him, so that he is left with nothing.

"He shall appear before Us all alone." (Verse 80) He will have nothing of what gave him his standing in society. Thus, he will have no money, property, relatives, followers or supporters as he appears before Allah all alone, a powerless individual.

Have you, then, considered this person who denies God's revelation, yet speaks about his fortunes on a day when he has no position or influence? It is a day when he will be deprived of all that gave him power in this life. This is just one type of unbelief, false claims and ridicule of the truth.

Have you, then, considered this person who denies Allah's revelation, yet speaks about his fortunes on a day when he has no position or influence? It is a day when he will be deprived of all that gave him power in this life. This is just one type of unbelief, false claims and ridicule of the truth.

The surah continues its discussion of different aspects of unbelief. Those who deny Allah's revelations ascribe divinity to beings other than Allah, and they will worship such false deities hoping that they will give them power, victory and glory. Some worshipped angels, while others worshipped jinn. They called on those whom they worshipped, appealing to them for support against their enemies. But the very angels and jinn they worship now denounce their action, disassociate themselves of their worship and condemn their attitude. As the Qur'ān describes their position, those who were worshipped in this present life will on the Day of Judgement "turn against them," and will give a testimony that condemns the unbelievers who worshipped them.

Satanic forces, or devils, will always incite them to commit sinful actions. These forces have been given the chance to tempt and misguide human beings, ever since Satan, or Iblis, requested Allah to allow him such opportunity. The Prophet is instructed not to precipitate matters: **"So, be not in haste."** (Verse 84) He should not be over-grieved about them. They are given a chance, with a definite time limit, during which everything they do or say is counted and recorded. The verse here describes the accuracy of the reckoning: **"We only allow them a fixed number of days."** (Verse 84). This is an awesome image, because when the recording is made by Allah, it does not overlook or miss anything out. Someone who feels that his boss is carefully monitoring his actions so as to identify any mistake will inevitably feel uneasy and worried. So how does the person who knows that God Almighty is watching him feel?

The outcome of all this reckoning is shown in yet another image of the Day of Judgement. The believers will come to God in a procession met with honour and hospitality: **"The day** [will surely come] when We shall gather the God-fearing before [God] the Most Merciful, as honoured guests." (Verse 86) On the other hand, the unbelievers will be driven like cattle until they arrive at their last abode: **"And drive those who are lost in sin to hell as a thirsty herd."** (Verse 86) There will be no intercession on that day, except for one who has done a good deed in this worldly life. Such a deed will be like a promise from God which He will honour. Allah has promised those who do good works to give them an abundant reward, and God does not fail to honour His promises.

The surah then refers to another monstrous claim often made by different unbelievers. The Arab idolaters of the past used to claim that the angels were God's daughters, while the unbelievers among the Jews claimed that Ezra was the son of God, and the unbelievers among the Christians made the same claim for Jesus. The whole universe shudders as such false claims are alleged, because monotheism is inherent in the nature of the whole universe.

The very sound of these verses and their rhythm add to the air of anger at this false claim. In fact the whole universe rejects this claim most vehemently. It shudders and quivers with abhorrence as it hears this falsehood against God Almighty. It is a reaction similar to that of a person who feels that his very integrity is attacked, or that the honesty of someone he loves is assailed. The shudder is common to the heavens, the earth and the mountains. In their beat, the words here show the movement of a violent quake.

The very sound of these verses and their rhythm add to the air of anger at this false claim. In fact the whole universe rejects this claim most vehemently. It shudders and quivers with abhorrence as it hears this falsehood against God Almighty. It is a reaction similar to that of a person who feels that his very integrity is attacked, or that the honesty of someone he loves is assailed. The shudder is common to the heavens, the earth and the mountains. In their beat, the words here show the movement of a violent quake.

As soon as the offensive word is uttered, **"They say: The Most Merciful has taken to Himself a son,"** the expression of horror immediately follows: **"Indeed you have said a most monstrous falsehood."** (Verse 89) Everything that is settled and stable is thus shaken. The whole universe is in anger at this false allegation against God, the Creator. The statement is shocking to everything in nature.

The universe is created and functions on the basis of the basic principle of God's oneness: **"Indeed you have said a most monstrous falsehood, at which the heavens might be rent into fragments, and the earth be split asunder, and the mountains fall down in ruins! "** (Verses 89-90)

In contrast with this loneliness and isolation, the believers are given a comforting, friendly surrounding: **"God will certainly bestow love on those who believe and do righteous deeds."** (Verse 96) The mention of love in this context is bound to comfort and penetrate people's hearts. It is a type of love that spreads in heaven and spills over to fill the earth and comfort people. The whole universe is given a full share of it.

Abū Hurayrah, a companion of the Prophet, reports that Allah's Messenger said: "When God loves a human being, He calls in Gabriel (Jibrael) and says to him:

'Gabriel, I love this person, so you love him too.'

Gabriel then loves that person and calls out to all those living in heaven, saying:

'God loves this person, so you all love him too.' Thus all those who live in heaven start to love that person. He will also be loved on earth. But if Allah dislikes someone, He also calls in Gabriel and says: 'Gabriel, I dislike this person, so you hate him too.' Gabriel then hates that person and calls out to all those living in heaven, saying: 'Allah dislikes this person, so you all hate him too.' Thus all those who live in heaven start to hate that person. He will also be hated on earth." [Related by al-Bukhārī, Muslim and Aḥmad].

Verses 96-98 Conclusion

96. On those who believe and work deeds of righteousness, will (Allah) Most Gracious bestow love.

In contrast with this loneliness and isolation, the believers are given a comforting, friendly surrounding: **"God will certainly bestow love on those who believe and do righteous deeds."** (Verse 96) The mention of love in this context is bound to comfort and penetrate people's hearts. It is a type of love that spreads in heaven and spills over to fill the earth and comfort people. The whole universe is given a full share of it.

This happy news to the believers and this warning to those who deny the truth and argue against it are the message the Qur'ān gives. God has made the Qur'ān easy for the Arabs to read and understand, as He has put it in His Messenger's own language: **"And so have We made [the Qur'ān] easy to understand, in your own tongue, so that you may give good tidings to the God-fearing and give warning to those who are given to futile contention."** (Verse 97)

The sūrah concludes with a scene that we contemplate in our minds for a long time, hardly able to shift our gaze:

How many a generation have We destroyed before their time! Can you find a single one of them now, or hear so much as a whisper of them? (Verse 98)

This scene begins with a violent shock before overwhelming us with a total and deep silence. It is as though it takes us to the valley of death to show us how earlier people met their fate. In that great valley which stretches much further than the eyes can see, our minds imagine the life that used to prosper on earth, the people that moved about everywhere, their feelings, hopes and aspirations. But all that is gone.

Complete silence pervades. For death has overtaken all, leaving only a host of rotting cadavers. Not a single one stirs, not a single sound, not even a breath. **"Can you find a single one of them now?"** (Verse 98) Look around and see. **"Or can you hear so much as a whisper of them?"** (Verse 98) Listen as much as you wish. There is nothing but a deadly silence. None remain except the One who never dies. Eternal He is and limitless in His glory.

Allah loves those who believe and act righteously.

Qur'an is only in the Arabic language, but has been made easy for one to learn and memorise.

Those who oppose the call for Truth err in thinking that, in doing so, they will not come to any harm. There is evidence of the opponents of Truth being wiped out, but they do not take any lesson from it.

Chapter 20

Towards Understanding Surah Taha

Surah Taha has 135 verses and was revealed in Mecca. Revelation happened around the same time as Surah Maryam, almost six to seven years before Prophet Muhammad's SAW migration to Yathrib (Medina).

The subject matter of the Surah is to assure the Prophet and his followers that the message of the Qur'an will eventually succeed. The story of Prophet Moses is mentioned in detail. Then it is mentioned how the enemies of Islam are opposing it and what will be the consequences of this opposition for them.

What was happening at Mecca at this point in time.

Situation for our Prophet and his followers were not good. The oppression of the disbelieving Qureshi in Mecca's was very severe. They turned from verbal accusations and abuse to physical and socio-economic torture and bans. This was the time also when many Muslims migrated to nearby country of Abyssinia.

Surah Taha transformed Umar Al-Khattab RA from an enemy of the Prophet to one of his SAW's strongest and most beloved supporters.

Umar had once been a staunch opponent of the Prophet SAW. On one occasion, he had carried his unsheathed sword in anger, headed directly towards the Prophet. His sole intention was to kill Prophet Muhammad SAW. Along the way, he met a companion of the Prophet SAW who asked him where he was headed.

This companion asked him to rethink his plans, considering that the Prophet's tribe was sure to kill him if he were to proceed. The companion told him to instead focus on fixing the problems in his own home. It was then that Umar RA heard of his own sister and brother-in-law's acceptance of Islam.

Enraged by this news, Umar raced to Fatimah Al-Khattab's home, where Khabbab bin Al-Aratt had been teaching Fatimah and her husband the verses of Surah Taha.

Umar RA heard the verses being recited as he passed by the house. Upon Umar's entrance, Khabbab hid in fear and Fatimah concealed the piece of writing, carrying the verses, under her seat. When questioned about the verses, Fatimah and her husband denied having any knowledge of it. Umar raised his hand to hit her husband and Fatimah rose from her seat to stop him, causing Umar to hit her by accident.

Seeing his sister in a bloodied state, Umar's heart softened. He asked gently about the scripture. Fatimah replied that she would not show it to him in fear that he might destroy them. He vowed not to do so, saying that he only wanted to have a look. Fatimah told him that he was unclean and was not allowed to touch the blessed revelation until he had purified himself.

After he performed a Ghusl, Umar RA was given the scripture. He read it silently, then praised the verses. It was then that Khabbab RA came out of hiding. He mentioned to them the du'a that the Prophet had made the previous day:

"O Allah! Honor Islam through the most dear of these two men to you: Through Abu Jahl or through 'Umar bin Al-Khattab."

Khabbab mentioned that when he heard that du'a, he had hoped that it would be Umar who would accept Islam. Umar requested to be brought to the Prophet SAW, where he accepted Islam.

Since then, Umar RA became one of the strongest supporters of Islam. Abu Jahl, on the other hand, distanced himself further from Islam because he refused to denounce the religion of his forefathers. His honour, intelligence and good character disappeared in the face of the Prophet's message, earning him the name of Abu Jahl, meaning the "father of ignorance".

Why was Surah Taha revealed

To console the prophet and to advise that the Qur'an is not meant to cause distress to him.

The verses in Surah Taha also serve as a reminder to us who think that our life is pained, constrained, inconvenienced and burdened by Islam. These verses are an antidote to such a disease of the heart. They were revealed with the following context.

Because of the rejection of his message, Prophet Muhammad SAW had been going all out in his worship to Allah SWT, to bring the people to accept Islam. He strived to maintain his night prayers, even missing out on sleep. Rasulullah SAW wanted to do his very best in service to Allah, and because he was trying so hard, life became difficult for him.

The rejection of his message by the people of Mecca pressured him even further to try even harder. He was pained in his heart and heavily felt the burden upon him.

Some of the companions of the Prophet SAW had been mocked for choosing to lead a 'life of suffering' by accepting the message of Islam. Some of the first believers had even sacrificed their own lives for this message. The Quraysh made a mockery out of this, asking the companions why they would bring upon themselves such a 'wrath'. They could choose to leave the religion and continue to live a comfortable life. These verses were sent to comfort them.

Verses 1-8

Allah tells us in this verse that the revelation had not been sent to make Rasulullah SAW and his people miserable. In reality, the *syari'at* (code of law) had been sent to ease and facilitate, so that we may not be left in confusion. We know that *ibadah* (worship) have been commanded upon us only to the extent where it is manageable. We are told not to force ourselves to do more than we can afford to. Do the supplementary *ibadah*, but not to the extent that you make life difficult for yourself.

Even in obligatory worship, we are told not to force ourselves beyond what is feasible. If you are sick and it is Ramadhan, you are allowed to postpone your obligatory fasts to outside of Ramadhan, when you are well again. If you are injured and cannot stand, you are allowed to perform your prayers seated. Even for Hajj, our fifth pillar of Islam, we are not allowed to sell all that we own just to be able to afford to go for Hajj. Hajj is not compulsory on those who do not have the means to perform it.

Before the revelation of these verses, Rasulullah SAW had been performing *ibadahs* in extreme amounts such that he started to make his own life difficult. He was wearing himself out because he wanted to do his very best in performing his role as the Messenger of Allah, out of obedience and gratitude to Him. Allah SWT did not want this, He does not expect us to torture ourselves for His sake.

So if the Qur'an had not been sent to make our lives miserable, why had it been sent?

But only as a Reminder to those who fear (Allah). [20:3]

It was sent as a reminder to the people who fear Allah SWT. We need to fear Allah in life, and if we truly fear Allah, we need reminders so that we will not forget and that we remain on the right path.

Verses 9-99 Story of Prophet Moses

The follow- on verses 9 to 99 described the Story of Prophet Musa (AS)

The Qur'an is a source of guidance for all humanity on how to live a perfect and Divinely guided life.

One of the ways to deliver this guidance to us is through giving examples of real people who lived in the past and detailing their life stories from which we can take heed and plan for the future.

So verse 9 to 99 tells the story of Prophet Musa (AS). Musa is the most talked about prophet in the Qur'an. In this surah his life events are narrated from different angles so that his personality emerges in a different perspective every time.

Musa's Journey from Maidan to Egypt.

The prophet and his family were travelling back to his homeland Egypt when he saw a light. He went to investigate it. The location was Mountain Tur, and the light was the fire coming from the burning bush.

As he was approaching he hears the voice of Allah calling him.

MIRACLES GIVEN TO PROPHET MUSA

Prophet Musa (AS) was overwhelmed by the address of his Lord. He felt endless pleasure. Allah continued to address him:

"O Musa! What is that in your right hand?"

Musa answered this address of his Lord in excitement:

"It is my rod. I lean on it when I am tired. I herd my sheep with it and beat down fodder for my flocks. And I find other uses in it."

Prophet Musa (AS) wanted to speak more due to the pleasure of the divine address but he could not find anything else to say about his rod. Upon his answer, Allah Almighty said,

"O Musa! Throw it!" As soon as Musa released the rod, it became a snake, active in motion. The prophet was scared and turned his back. He was getting ready to escape. The snake looked terrible. Meanwhile, the divine voice was heard again:

"O Musa! Turn to it and do not fear. Seize it and pick it up. You are under our safety. We shall return it at once to its former condition." Thus, Allah told him that his fear was groundless. Thereupon, Musa's fear disappeared. He held the snake. As soon as he touched the snake, it returned to its previous state. It became a rod again. Allah Almighty addressed Prophet Musa (AS) again:

"Now put your hand close to your chest; it will come forth white without harm or stain as another miracle."

Musa obeyed this order; he put his hand close to his chest and removed it. He saw that his hand became snow-white and shone in the darkness. This is called the miracle of white hand.

From then on, Prophet Musa (AS) had full belief and reliance. After that, Allah Almighty told him what to do:

O Musa! Both the miracles of the rod and the white hand have shown you some of our signs. Now go to the Pharaoh with these two miracles and call him to the true path. He transgressed all bounds. We will support you with some other miracles if it is necessary."

These talks between Prophet Musa (AS) and Allah Almighty and the miracles given to him were a prophethood contract. He has to go to Firun (Pharaoh) and call him to Islam

However, Prophet Musa (AS) had some concerns.

First of all, the risk of being caught and punished because of his previous crime when he returned to Egypt. This being the case, it was difficult for him to go to the Pharaoh and call him to believe in Allah.

The lisping in his tongue, which occurred when he was a little child, also worried him. He feared that he would not be able to talk fluently and convey his message to the Pharaoh. Suddenly, he remembered his brother Harun (Aaron) in Egypt. Harun was a sweet and fluent talker. It was possible for him to talk to the Pharaoh easily with the help of his brother. Besides, it was possible to encounter the reaction of the Pharaoh more easily as two people. With this thought in mind, he kneeled down and started to beg Allah:

"O my Lord! Expand my breast and give me endurance. O Lord! Ease my task for me. Remove the impediment from my speech so that they may understand what I say. And give me a minister from my family, Harun, my brother because he speaks better than me and will explain our cause better. I fear that they will deny me and that I will not be able to answer them. Besides, I killed one of them by mistake. I fear that they will try to take revenge from me if I go there alone.

O Lord! Send my brother Harun as a prophet, too. Add to my strength through him so that we may celebrate your praise without stint and worship you more. O Lord! You know and protect us better than us."

Prophet Musa (AS) was right in his concern and worry. For, he was going to face someone who claimed to be a deity and call him to the right path. He was going to prove that the Pharaoh's way was wrong. Besides, Haman, who was the minister and consultant of the Pharaoh and who was very intelligent, was going to be against him. He was going to struggle against Haman and overcome him.

Upon these worries of Prophet Musa (AS), Allah Almighty stated that He had saved him from his previous hardships and that He was going to save him from his future troubles.

Allah told him how to treat the Pharaoh with his brother Harun as follows:

"O Musa! Go with your brother with My Signs, which show the trueness of your cause. Do not slacken while conveying my revelation, which includes orders and prohibitions, to the Pharaoh. Go both of you to the Pharaoh for he has indeed transgressed all bounds. His situation should not activate your feelings and make you treat him harshly. Speak to him mildly. Do not make him angry; he may listen to you. Do not lose hope that he will believe in Allah when you mention him your evidence and the wrath of Allah. If you do not have any hope that he will believe, you will not be able to be successful in your duty of conveying My message."

With these words, Allah Almighty attracted the attention of Prophet Musa (AS) and Harun to two important issues in calling people to the right path:

a. One of the most important principles in calling people to the right path and guiding them is not to get angry or furious and not to act in rage. For, a call with fury and anger will incite the obstinacy of the addressee and increase his opposition. Such a call will be harmful rather than useful.

b. Even if the person to whom the message of Allah is conveyed is a very cruel person like the Pharaoh, it is necessary to address him without losing hope. If one

conveys the message to such a person unwillingly just for the sake of getting rid of the responsibility of conveying the message, it will not be of any effect. It is necessary to be sincere and to do it for the sake of Allah. It is necessary to have good thoughts about the addressee and to convey the message hopefully and wisely.

STRUGGLE AGAINST THE PHARAOH

Prophet Musa (AS) enjoyed the most pleasant moments of his life during his talk with Allah Almighty. From then on, he was a prophet appointed by Allah. He had to go to Egypt at once and start his duty. He returned to his family immediately. He set off for Egypt with them without losing any time. Meanwhile, his brother Harun also received revelation and was given the duty of prophethood. He was told what to do with his brother Musa.

When Prophet Musa (AS) arrived in Egypt, he found his brother Harun first. They started to wait for the hard day, when they would encounter the Pharaoh. They could not get rid of the worries they had due to the terrible oppression and mercilessness of the Pharaoh. Therefore, they begged Allah Almighty as follows:

"Our Lord! We fear that the Pharaoh will hasten with insolence against us or he will transgress all bounds by talking insolently about You or kill us before we finish our talk and show our miracles. What shall we do then?"

Allah Almighty answered these two sincere slaves of His as follows:

"O my prophets! Do not Fear at all! For I am with you. Go both of you to him without worrying and say, `Verily we are messengers sent by your Lord. Stop oppressing Children of Israel. Let them go to the holy land, their hometown. We have come from your Lord with a sign. Peace to all who follow guidance. We were told by your Lord that the divine wrath that is bound to come will hit those who deny the prophets and do not accept their call."

Thus, Prophet Musa (AS) and Hz. Harun found out what to do by revelation. Then, they went to the palace into the presence of the Pharaoh.

When the Pharaoh saw Musa and his brother together after so many years, he was surprised. He did not expect such an encounter. He asked them,

"Why did you come here?" Prophet Musa (AS) started to tell the Pharaoh the reason why they came:

"We are the messengers of Allah, who is the Lord of the Realms. Allah sent us to call you to the right path. Stop oppressing Children of Israel. Let them go to the holy land."

The Pharaoh was leaning on his throne and listening to what Prophet Musa (AS) was telling him in astonishment. Was the person who was addressing him like that Musa, who was brought up in his palace? How dare he could say such things? He could not understand it. When the prophet finished his words, the Pharaoh spoke furiously:

"O Musa! What happened to you? Did we not cherish you as a child among us? Did you not stay with us for many years, eat our bread and drink our water? Do you remember you also committed a crime and ran away? Now you deny what we did for you and deny our bounties."

By saying that he brought up Musa in the palace, the Pharaoh wanted to show his ingratitude and make his speech valueless. Thereupon, Musa said,

"O Pharaoh! I did it by mistake. I feared that I would be killed before I could prove my innocence. Therefore, I escaped from Egypt when they started to look for me. Then, my Lord invested me with judgment and wisdom and appointed me as one of the messengers. My duty is only to convey the message of my Lord. It is up to you to accept it or not. As for my bringing up, which you reproach me is because of killing the sons of Children of Israel. Otherwise, I would not have stayed in your palace. My mother and father could have brought

me up. Would they have allowed me to be brought up in your palace by putting me on the Nile if they had not feared your oppression?"

Upon this explanation of Prophet Musa (AS), the Pharaoh could not say anything. Musa was not a person that could be silenced easily.

In order to deepen the argument, the Pharaoh mentioned the phrase "the Lord of the Realms" in the statement of Musa and Harun: "We are the messengers of Allah, who is the Lord of the Realms." The Pharaoh said:

"O Musa! And what is the `Lord of the Worlds?' Who is He?"

With this question, he wanted to put Prophet Musa (AS) into a difficult position. Musa answered this question by changing the direction of the question with the style of wisdom as follows:

"If you seek to be convinced with certainty, you will understand that the Lord of the heavens and the earth and all between."

The Pharaoh could not say anything upon this answer. He wanted to resort to demagogy in order to eliminate the effect of this answer on the people around. He turned to them and said mockingly,

"Do you not listen to what he says? I am asking something but he is giving me a different answer."

Prophet Musa (AS) acted sagaciously and did not allow the Pharaoh to use demagogy any longer. He said,

"Your Lord and the Lord of your fathers from the beginning."

With this sentence, Prophet Musa (AS) stated that the Pharaoh was a human being like everybody else, that he also had a mother and a father, that he ate and drank like them and that he was bound to die. Thus, he wanted to eliminate the idea in the minds of the people that he was an extraordinary being.

When the Pharaoh saw that his preaching was of no use, he started to insult and slander. In fact, all oppressors that are defeated by the truth resort to insult, slander or force. The Pharaoh said to the people around:

"Truly your messenger who has been sent to you is a veritable madman. You see that he does not answer my question and mentions something else."

Thus, he aimed to confuse their minds.

Actually, his question was answered in the best way. The existence, power and will of Allah Almighty were mentioned; it was stated that man was His creature and that he had to obey His laws. That was what was necessary for man. It was impossible for man to perceive more. How could man, whose understanding, knowledge, learning, etc is limited and who is weak, perceive the personality of Allah, who is free from all kinds of material conditions and who is free from time and space? It would be something like expecting the whole ocean to be included in a coffee cup.

When Prophet Musa (AS) saw that the Pharaoh was in a difficult position, he expanded the issue. He said:

"Oh Pharaoh! Yes, He is the Lord of the east and the west, and all between."

Thus, he stated that the whole universe and everything in it belonged to Allah Almighty, showing that the Pharaoh was only a weak creature. Thereupon, the Pharaoh got furious. He said,

"I swear that if you put forward any god other than me, I will certainly put you in prison."

Prophet Musa (AS) continued to speak without heeding the threats of the Pharaoh:

"Would you put me in prison even if I showed you something clear and convincing?"

If the Pharaoh had rejected this offer, he would have been in a situation like accepting defeat beforehand. Therefore, he spoke as follows since he did not believe that Musa could do what he said:

"Show it then if you tell the truth."

Thereupon, Prophet Musa (AS) threw his rod on the ground. The rod suddenly turned into a horrible snake.

Then, it started to move. The Pharaoh and the people around him were terrified.

They were speechless. After that, Prophet Musa (AS) put his hand close to his chest and drew out his hand as another miracle.

His hand became snow-white and started to shine and shed light.

In order to save the Pharaoh from this frustrating position, his men said, "My God! He became a great magician. He studied magic for years abroad in order to grab our sultanate. He learnt it well. Shall we kill these two magicians or shall we give them a different punishment?"

At that time, Egypt was a center of magic.

The Pharaoh did not know what to do. He asked his men, "What is your opinion about the issue?" They said,

"Killing them or any other punishment will be of no use. If we do so, people will think that we are defeated and that we are weak. Therefore, it is necessary to organize a competition and humiliate them. We must despise them in the eye of the public. Dispatch to the cities heralds to collect our best magicians. They will show their talents. We will see whether Musa and Harun can resist them. If we act differently, it will be against us."

Then, the Pharaoh felt relieved. He liked this idea.

He had the best magicians and sorcerers in the world. It could be easy for them to overcome Musa. With this thought in mind, he said to Prophet Musa (AS) :

"Do you want to replace us and overthrow us with your sorcery? We have talented sorcerers. This cause will not be over and you will not be regarded to have defeated us until my sorcerers show their magic. Decide an appropriate place and time so that we will come together. Everybody will show their skills there."

Musa accepted this offer gladly.

Moses thanked and praised Allah Almighty, who gave him the opportunity to talk and compete. They decided the late morning of the day of festival as the time of competition and the square where everybody gathered as the venue

THE SORCERERS BELIEVE

The Pharaoh summoned the most skilled sorcerers all over his country to the palace. He was sure that they would overcome Prophet Musa (AS); therefore, he invited the people to come to the place of the competition at the determined time in order to recover his prestige and to strengthen the belief of his people in him. The sorcerers of the Pharaoh made the Pharaoh promise that he would give them great rewards if they overcame Musa.

On the day of festival, a large number of people gathered in the determined place. The sorcerers declared proudly that they felt confident and that they would win.

Finally, the time for the competition came.

The sorcerers turned to Prophet Musa (AS) and asked, "Are you going to start? Or shall we start?" Hz. Musa said, "You start."

Thereupon, the sorcerers threw their ropes and their rods; they showed all of their skills. The square became full of snakes and centipedes all of a sudden.

The equipment of magic thrown on the ground seemed like snakes moving to the right and left to Musa and everybody in the square. Everybody was in fear and excitement. When the sorcerers saw this scene, they started to utter cries of victory and said,

"We swear by the magnificence of the Pharaoh that we will overcome Musa. Prophet Musa (AS) felt worried when he saw what they did.

However, Allah Almighty consoled and strengthened him by revelation:

"O Musa! Do not fear! You are superior to them. You are going to overcome them. They are sorcerers but you are My prophet. What you have in right hand is a miracle granted to you by Me. Throw the rod in your right hand bravely. It will quickly swallow up the magic of the sorcerers. What they have faked is but a magician's trick. There is no salvation for the magicians and their magic. Their tricks will be revealed and the will be embarrassed soon."

This divine consolation increased Musa's courage; he threw his rod. As soon as it fell to the ground, it became a large snake acting very fast; it swallowed all of the tricks and magic of the sorcerers.

When Musa's snake swallowed all of them and nothing was left, Prophet Musa (AS) held this large snake with his hand. Suddenly, it was transformed into his rod.

The sorcerers were astonished. They used all of their tricks and magic but they were overcome by Prophet Musa (AS). Then, Musa could not have been a magician but a prophet. And what he did was really a miracle. The sorcerers definitely believed

They kneeled down and prostrated in adoration. They declared that they believed in the Lord of the Worlds, the Lord of Musa and Harun.

They all took place in front of the people. When the sorcerers believed in Allah, it became clear that Musa was right and superior. The Pharaoh became disgraced. Therefore, this declaration of the sorcerers' infuriated him. He started to threaten them:

"How can you believe in him before I give you permission? Surely he is your leader, who has taught you sorcery! I will show you soon. I will cut off your hands and your feet on opposite sides, and I will cause you all to die on the cross. I will show you what it means to be against me and to support Musa."

As it is seen, the Pharaoh interpreted the sorcerers' accepting the truth of what Musa said and their believing in him as follows:

Prophet Musa (AS) was actually the leader of the sorcerers. This competition had been planned before. This was nothing but an excuse made up by his soul and Satan so as not to accept the truth.

The sorcerers who believed in Allah ignored these threats of the Pharaoh's and said,

"O Pharaoh! We definitely believed in the honesty of Musa and the existence of our Lord, who created us out of nothing. Now it has become clear that you are a liar. Do whatever you want. You can only take our life in this world. The eternal life and bliss in the hereafter is enough for us. We hope that our Lord will forgive us our faults. We are proud of becoming foremost among the believers.

This answer infuriated the Pharaoh more. He ordered his men to hang the magicians upside down in the market square and cut off their hands and feet. They died a slow death.

When Prophet Musa overcame the Pharaoh, Children of Israel believed in him altogether. They adopted him as the "saviour", whom they had been waiting for years and who would take them to the holy land.

The Pharaoh panicked when they believed.

He increased his cruelty and torture inflicted upon Children of Israel.

Then Allah commanded Prophet Musa (AS) to take the people of "Bani Israel" out of the slavery of Pharaoh.

Prophet Musa (AS) led the Bani Israel to the other side of the Red Sea. They settled there Allah called Prophet Musa (AS) went to Mount Tur to receive the Torah.

In his absence his people started worshipping the statue of a calf, being led astray by Samiri. Musa banished him and burnt the idol.

The purpose of all these stories from the past is that we may learn from it.

Verses 100-114

In these verses Allah is telling us of the punishment of those who turn away from the Qur'an and some spectacles from the Day of Resurrection.

We are told that whoever turns away from the Qur'an will bear a terrible heavy burden on the Day of Resurrection. When the trumpet is sounded and Allah gathers the sinful, they will murmur to one another that they stayed only ten days on earth, but the more perceptive of them will say that their stay on earth was only a single day.

On that Day Allah will blast the mountains into dust and leave a flat plain and people will follow the caller from whom there is no escape. Every voice will be hushed for the Lord of Mercy. Only whispers will be heard. On the Day of Judgement, intercession will be useless except from those to whom the Lord grants permission and whose words He approves. All faces will be humbled before the Living, Ever Watchful One. Those burdened with evil deeds will despair, but whoever has done righteous deeds and believed need have no fear of injustice or deprivation.

Verses 115-127

The story of the angels bowing down to the ground before Aadam (AS) and warning him against Iblis (Satan)

Allah commanded the angels to bow down before Aadam (AS) and they did, but Satan refused, so Allah told Aadam that Satan is an enemy to him and his wife and to not let him drive them out of Paradise. And as long as he stays in Paradise, he will not go hungry, feel naked, be thirsty, or suffer from the heat of the sun.

But Satan whispered to Aadam, tempting to lead Aadam to "the tree of immortality and an everlasting kingdom." Adam disobeyed his Lord; both he and Eve fell for Satan's whispers and ate from the tree. They became conscious of their nakedness and began to cover themselves with leaves.

Later his Lord brought him close, accepted his repentance, and guided him. Allah expelled them from Paradise. Allah told them that whoever follows His guidance when it comes, will not go astray nor fall into misery, but whoever turns away from it will have a life of great hardship. Allah promises to raise the one who turns away as a blind person on the Day of Resurrection. He will ask Allah why was He raised blind when he had sight before! Allah's response will be that since he ignored his revelations when they came to him, it is only fitting that he is ignored on this Day. This is how Allah rewards those who go too far and who do not believe in His revelations. Allah says that the greatest and most enduring punishment is in the Hereafter.

Verses 128- 129

Taking lessons from previous nations

Do they not draw a lesson from the many generations Allah destroyed before them, through whose dwelling places they now walk? There truly are signs in this for anyone with understanding! If it were not for a preordained Word from the Lord, they would already have been destroyed. Their time has been set.

Verses 130-132 Directions to the Prophet

Thus do We relate to you some of the history of past events; and thus have We given you, out of Our grace, a reminder. **All who shall turn away from it will certainly bear a heavy burden on the Day of Resurrection. For ever shall they bear it; and grievous for them will be its weight on the Day of Resurrection, the day when the Trumpet is blown. For on that day We shall assemble all the guilty ones, their eyes dimmed [by terror], whispering to one another, 'You have spent but ten days on earth.' We know best what they will be saying when the most perceptive of them shall say: 'You have spent there but one day!'** (Verses 99-104)

Just as Prophet Musa' history is related in the Qur'an, so do We also relate other past events. The Qur'an is described here as 'a reminder', because it reminds us of Allah, His signs and messages, as well as other signs given to people of old.

It is an encouragement to hold on to true and lasting values, to maintain one's ties with Allah and be contented. This is the best way to resist the temptation of the splendour and attractions of this life. When we maintain such values, we are free to rise above the lure of false temptations, splendid as they may appear. **"Enjoin prayer on your people."** (Verse 132) The first duty of a Muslim is to make his home a Muslim home, enjoining his family to attend to their prayers so that they all maintain their ties with Allah. Thus, they are united in their approach to life. Life in a home where all members turn to Allah for worship is certainly a happy one. **"And be diligent in its observance."** (Verse 132) Be diligent so that you offer your prayers complete and its effect becomes a reality. Prayer restrains man from loathsome deeds and indecency. This is its true effect. To attain the level where prayer provides such restraint requires diligence in its observance. Unless we reach the stage that our prayer yields this fruit, it remains a mere sequence of phrases and movements. Prayer and worship generally are duties assigned to the Prophet and believers. Allah does not gain anything by them. He is in need of no one: **"We do not ask you for any provisions. It is We who provide for you."** (Verse 132) Worship nurtures God-consciousness within the worshipper. Hence, **"the future belongs to the God-fearing."** (Verse 132) It is man who benefits by prayer, both in this life and in the life to come. He offers his worship to Allah and he enjoys, as a result, a state of contentment. He is comfortable, reassured. Furthermore, he ultimately receives a much greater reward in the hereafter. As for Allah, He needs nothing from anyone.

Verses 133-135

As the surah draws to its close, it refers again to those people who, enjoying position and power, reject Allah's revelations and demand that the Prophet deliver a miracle. They make such demands even after the Prophet has given them the Qur'ān which explains in all clarity what previous messages from Allah were like. **"They say:**

'Why does he not bring us a sign from his Lord?' Has there not come to them a clear evidence of the truth in the earlier scriptures?" (Verse 133) They need no physical miracle. Hence, their demands betray their arrogance. The Qur'an is more than sufficient as proof. It links the new message with Allah's previous messages, uniting them all and clarifying what was left in general terms in previous messages.

Allah has given those who deny the truth everything they need to recognize the truth and believe in it when He sent them His last Messenger: **"Had We destroyed them with a calamity before his coming, they would have said, 'Our Lord, if only You had sent us a Messenger, we would have followed Your revelations rather than be humiliated and disgraced.'" (Verse 134)** At the time when this verse was recited, they had been neither humiliated nor disgraced. The verse describes their inevitable end which will bring them humiliation and disgrace. It may be that they will then say: 'Our Lord, if only You had sent us a Messenger.' Now a Messenger is sent to them and they have no excuse to justify their rejection.

As the surah describes their end, the Prophet is commanded to leave them alone, without grieving for them. He should announce to them that he will await the end, and let them await it as they wish: **"Say: Everyone is hopefully waiting; so wait, if you will. You will certainly come to know who has followed the even path, and who has been rightly guided." (Verse 135)** Thus the surah ends. It started with assuring the Prophet that the Qur'ān was not revealed to him to cause him any distress. It defined the role of the Qur'an as **'an admonition to the God-fearing.'** (Verse 3) The end is in full harmony with the beginning. It provides a reminder and an admonition for those who may benefit thereby. As the Prophet conveyed his message complete, the only thing that remains is to await the end, which is determined by Allah.

About the Author

Serena Hussain-Yates has been living in the United Kingdom for the last 37 years, having migrated from her native country Guyana.

A mother to four adult children and fourteen grandchildren, the author is the founder of BURTON SISTERS CIRCLE, a dawah giving organisation.

Contact details:

serenabibi@aol.com

www.ingramcontent.com/pod-product-compliance
Lightning Source LLC
Chambersburg PA
CBHW061123070526
44584CB00033B/4202